soul
picnic

THOMAS DUNNE BOOKS   ST. MARTIN'S PRESS   ♨   NEW YORK

THE MUSIC

soul

AND PASSION

picnic

OF LAURA NYRO

Michele Kort

THOMAS DUNNE BOOKS.
An imprint of St. Martin's Press.

www.stmartins.com

Title spread: Laura and Beautybelle on Nyro's West Seventy-ninth Street apartment
terrace, 1969. This image was the original cover of New York Tendaberry. (Photo by
Stephen Paley, courtesy of Michael Ochs Archives)

Design by Susan Walsh

Library of Congress Cataloging-in-Publication Data
Kort, Michele.
    Soul picnic : the music and passion of Laura Nyro / Michele Kort.—1st ed.
        p. cm.
    Includes bibliographical references (p. 277), discography (p. 315), and index.
    ISBN 0-312-20941-X
    1. Nyro, Laura. 2. Singers—United States—Biography. I. Title.

ML420.N97 K67 2002
782.42164'092—dc21
[B]
                                                                2001054779

First Edition: May 2002

10   9   8   7   6   5   4   3   2   1

FOR MY MOTHER SPIRITUAL, SHIRLEY J. KORT

CONTENTS

FOREWORD AND
ACKNOWLEDGMENTS

I first heard Laura Nyro sing "Wedding Bell Blues" in the fall of 1966, on KHJ "Boss Radio" in Los Angeles. I was awakened by my clock radio, and the song drifted into my head while I was still woozy with sleep. Songs heard that way have an eerie, lasting resonance. But this song would have insinuated itself no matter what hour I first heard it, with its descending, syncopated piano intro and pleading first word: "Biiillllllllll." I was sixteen years old, raised on the Beatles and Motown and sixties soul, and "Wedding Bell Blues" had in it all I loved: a rich melody, a catchy rhythm, an engaging spirit.

I thought the singer was black and I thought the lyric was "I look at you and see the passion I *demand*." I was wrong on both counts, but wrong in the right ways. Black music was the soil in which the Russian Jewish/Italian Catholic Laura Nyro's songs and harmonies grew. And if she actually sang about the "passion *eyes of May*," the woman still demanded passion—in life and in music. Along with many others of my late-sixties generation, I identified with her imperious need.

Ever since, my life has been both informed and transformed by Laura Nyro's music. I saw her onstage each time she appeared in Los Angeles, except for one tour when I caught her in San Francisco instead. For my college graduation present to myself in 1971, I flew to New York City for the winter holiday—primarily because I wanted to hear her sing at Carnegie Hall that Christmas Eve. I collected each of her albums the moment they were released and nearly wore out the grooves (remember records?) by playing them incessantly. Although Nyro let out very little personal information, I noted how she married and divorced, gave birth to a son, moved from the city to the country. In 1989 I learned that she now lived with a woman. As I listened to her grow and change, burn and mellow over the decades, I sometimes missed the high-intensity romanticism of her youthful music, but I also came to appreciate the healing, nurturing quality of her later work. In any case, I had gladly signed up for the entire ride with her.

After I heard the shocking news that she had died, I recalled the last time I had seen her perform, sitting just a few feet from her, at McCabe's Guitar Shop in Santa Monica, California. That night I noticed the warm vibration of her voice moving the air around me. Now that she was gone, I would never feel that sensation again, never again be graced by her sensual and giving presence. I cried every time I thought of that. Researching and writing this book has been my way of keeping Laura Nyro alive for myself, for the generation of those who loved her and for those still to discover her music.

Considering that Nyro was extremely private made me wonder if I was violating her desires, even posthumously, by writing this book. I came to the conclusion that in death, the privacy she so fiercely maintained could no longer be disturbed, as long as I respected her family's right to privacy about deeply personal matters. But her role in cultural history needed to be reclaimed. Today's singer-songwriters, especially the women, owe her a huge debt, even if they only felt her stunning impact second- or third-hand. It seems not just proper but essential to carve her name deeply into the story of popular music in the last half of the twentieth century.

■ ■ ■

I have a parade of people to thank for helping me realize this project, beginning with Sherry Barnett, who gave me the idea, and then to my agent, Ellen Geiger, who believed in the book (and me) and guided me through a proposal and to St. Martin's Press. Thanks to Anne Savarese at St. Martin's for signing me, to Melissa Jacobs for taking over as my editor and maintaining the patience of a saint, and finally, to Carin Siegfried for kindly and smartly shepherding the book through to publication.

This book could not exist without the cooperation of the more than one hundred people I interviewed. First thanks (for the first interview) to Jimmie Haskell, and extra special thanks to Louis Nigro, Danny Nigro, Anne Johnson, and Geoffrey Blumenauer. Further thanks for the memories, wisdom, and generosity: Lou Adler, Carol Amoruso, Brian Auger, David Bendett, Cheryl Bentyne, Herb Bernstein, Sid Bernstein, Jim Bessman, David Bianchini, Gil Bianchini, Scott Billington (Rounder

Records), Hal Blaine, Alan Bomser, Esq., Karla Bonoff, Donald Boudreau, John Bristow, Charlie Calello, Felix Cavaliere, Richard Chiaro, Desmond Child, Deanna (Nigro) Chirillo, Barbara Cobb, Wanda Coleman, Bobby Columby, Kay Crow, Richard Davis, Keith Decker, Michael Decker, Lupe De Leon, Richard Denaro, Don De Vito, Patty Di Lauria, Marc Eliot, Mark Feldman, Jean Fineberg, Peter Gallway, Diane Garisto, David Geffen, Gail Gellman, Sharon Glassman, Barbara Greenstein, Roy Halee, Roscoe Harring, Lee Housekeeper, Bones Howe, Janis Ian, Che Johnson, Gary Katz, Al Kooper, Patti LaBelle, David Lasley, Will Lee, Harriet Leider, Mark Linett, Michael Maineri, Marsha Malamet, Melissa Manchester, Esther Marcus, Steven Marcus, Arif Mardin, Steve Martin, Misha Masud, Nydia Mata, Alan Merrill, Helen Merrill, Estelle (Nigro) Meyer, Artie Mogull, Essra Mohawk, Carman Moore, Andy Newmark, Jan Nigro, Janice Nigro, Michael Nigro, Beth O'Brien, Michael Ochs, Milt Okun, Maggie Paley, Stephen Paley, D. A. Pennebaker, Alan Pepper, Richard Perry, Pamela Polland, Joel Pope, Kaye Pope, Bernard Purdie, Chuck Rainey, Elliott Randall, Vicki Randle, Laverne Reed, Annie Roboff, Edith Roth, Ellen Sander, Swami Satchidananda (special thanks to Prem Anjali), Carol Schmidt, Jerry Schoenbaum, Stewart Schreiber, Ellen Seeling, Joel Selvin, Willette (Nigro) Smythe, Phoebe Snow, Lew Soloff, Guy Spiller, Elysa Sunshine, John Tropea, Andy Uryevick, Jimmy Vivino, Wendy Waldman, Lynn Weiss, Cory Wells, Vicki Wickham, Allee Willis, Toni Wine, Joe Wissert, Wayne Yurgelun, Ed Ziegman, and Paul Zollo.

Aesthetic thanks to photographers Stephen Paley, Linda Johnson, Mark Hanauer, David Gahr, Henry Diltz, Sherry Barnett, Alan Bingham, Pat Johnson, and to Prem Anjali and the Integral Yoga Institute. Particular thanks to Louis Nigro, Jan and Janice Nigro, Danny Nigro, David Bianchini, the Michael Ochs Archives, Barbara Greenstein, and to Howard Frank at Lou Adler's office. Thanks also to Carol Amoruso, Charlie Calello, and Michael Decker for providing photos.

I've made good friends and acquaintances among the "tribe" of Laura's fans. First, thanks go to Glen Stegner for his extraordinary website in tribute to Laura (lauranyro.net) and for hooking me up with the right folks. Extra special kudos to Patricia Spence Rudden (keep an eye out for her long-aborning academic book on Nyro's songwriting), and to Charles Carlino for his sleuthing and Internet companionship. Early thanks to Susanne Engel for her bibliography and tapes, and to Jodie Serkes for contacts and friendship. For articles, tapes, research, and general support, much gratitude to Michael Proft, Steve (Supersleuth)

Gorski, Richard Knight, Kenna Broadbent, Norio Kuronuma, Harold Gaugler, Martin from London, Frank Dalrymple, Philip Healy, Gary Joseph, Gary Levine, Zuri Lieno, John Stix (Cherry Lane Music), Dennis Weston, and Stephen Paley (you make *every* list here!).

Along the way, a number of other people have helped out with contacts: Thank you to Susan Bouthillier (and for your keen thoughts on poetry and Laura's lyrics!), Rudy Calvo, Jo Duffy at the June Mazer Collection, Maria Florio, David Lasley, Carol Lipnik, Marsha Malamet, Kevin Perrier, Evie Sands, Judy Scheer, Brendan Okrent, Yolanda Retter, Roz Winter, and Wendy Werris.

Since this is my first book, I'd also like to thank my high school English composition teacher, Mrs. Walker (wherever you may be on heaven or earth), for teaching me how to organize my thoughts; my journalism mentors Timothy Saasta and Rich Wiseman; my touchstone editors, Susan Brenneman and Mary Ellen Strote (the latter gave a wonderful first read to a few chapters), and my other longtime editor-friends who have plied me with work and support over the years, especially Martha Nelson and Peg Moline and, more recently, Judy Wieder, Anne Stockwell, Suzanne Gerber, Sharon Cohen, Mary Jane Horton, and Susanne Stoeckeler. Thanks to Gloria Steinem for her inspiration both as a journalist and a feminist. God bless the Internet (how did people write books without it?). And much love to Linda Garnets for eighteen years of faith and guidance, and to my other healers for all their ministrations.

Finally, deep gratitude to my family and friends for their love and endless encouragement, especially to my dad, Norman Kort, sister Melissa Kort, and Miriam Cutler (who also lent her fine eye to the manuscript). Thanks also to my newest angel, Aunt Eva, who left us last year at age ninety-four, and to my beloved nephew Isaac for the wonderful distraction.

I told my mother I'd dedicate this book to her simply because she tracked down several important sources for me, let alone having always been my biggest cheerleader. Cruelly, the dedication is posthumous, as she passed away on July 25, 1999. This is for you, dearest Mom.

From the dark edges of the sensual ground
This song of soul I struggle to outbear
Through portals of the sense, sublime and whole,
And utter all myself into the air.
   —"THE SOUL'S EXPRESSION,"
      ELIZABETH BARRETT BROWNING, 1844

PRELUDE

The Troubadour, Los Angeles, May 1969

The pulse of the popular music scene is taken at this small West Hollywood nightclub, and tonight the heartbeat will be supplied by a mysterious newcomer. She has been heard, on two astonishing albums that have gained a cult following, but hardly seen.

The smoky room, a-jangle with waitresses delivering gelati and double espressos, is filled to capacity with unabashed fans and coolly reserved record execs. Everyone feels the buzz, and as the lights dim, a hum of anticipation rises with the smoke. The spotlight illuminates a grand piano, adorned by a vase holding a single red rose.

"Ladies and gentlemen," a voice intones, "Laura Nyro."

A long-dark-haired twenty-one-year-old—a girl, really, but with the hauteur of an experienced woman—is led down a narrow path between tables to the tiny stage. The crowd applauds fervently, Nyro responding with a shy Mona Lisa smile on her full red lips. She sits, smoothing her long gown around the piano stool, and begins a syncopated melody, pounding the keys with surprising force. Then she joins her own accompaniment with a sometimes caressing, sometimes wailing voice. Her listeners, reverently silent, feel alternately chilled and warmed by her irresistible melodies and cutting revelations.

For the next hour, they will be captive to her spell. Some will be puzzled by her unbridled emotionality. Some will calculate a financial boon for re-recording her catchiest compositions. Some will simply worship at Laura Nyro's secular altar tonight, and for many nights over the next twenty-five years. Some will feel *saved* by her music.

None will forget her.

soul
picnic

1
ONE CHILD BORN

She was named after a song.

Her father, Louis, loved the complex melody of "Laura," the title theme from the 1944 Otto Preminger film. A professional trumpeter, Lou may have been playing at the very moment his Laura was born, since he had a band date that mild, windy autumn night. On breaks, he would telephone Lebanon Hospital in the Bronx to learn whether his wife, Gilda, had delivered. Finally, after one such call, in the early hours of October 18, 1947, he returned to announce, "Fellows, I have a daughter."

Her surname was Nigro. The proper Italian pronounciation would be NEE-gro, but Lou's family pronounced it NIGH-gro to avoid a racial tease. After high school, Laura would choose Nyro as her last name, but pronounce it NEAR-oh rather than the predictable NIGH-ro. That wasn't surprising. Her trademark would be an obstinate insistence on treading a path less taken.

The dark-haired, chubby-cheeked Laura wasn't a particularly remarkable baby. "She slept through the night," is what her father remembers. By age three, however, she began showing some precocious talent and spunk, quickly absorbing the lyrics and melodies of songs she heard on the radio. Lou recalls a Catskills resort's talent night at which the three-year-old sang a song that went, "If I knew you were coming I would bake a cake," and followed it up with a little dance. "The applause was tremendous," he says.

Her aunt Esther Marcus, Gilda's sister, pictures her niece at that age offering a lispy rendition of a very grown-up tune from *Showboat*: "Fish gotta swim / Birds gotta fly / I'm gonna love / dat man til I die." Esther also recollects her niece's early willful streak. When Laura came with her grandmother to visit Gilda and newborn baby brother Jan at the hospital, she insisted on wearing a long dress rather than something more appropriately casual. "At three years old!" Esther says. "My mother [Laura's grandmother] said, 'That's what she wants to wear, I do not argue with her.'

"Laura was very quietly stubborn," says Esther. "She very much did what she wanted to do."

Laura's parents first met in 1938, when Louis Nigro was a nattily dressed twenty-three-year-old. Gilda Mirsky, a Nigro family friend, was only thirteen. Lou remembers her looking at him with adoring adolescent eyes, but he didn't take much notice of her until six years later, when they met again at a family New Year's Eve party. By then, Lou was a trumpeter in a U.S. Army band, while the high-cheekboned, darkly attractive Gilda had shed her baby fat. Lou was smitten.

The two began dating and quickly became serious about each other. After just a few months, Gilda suggested they tie the knot. "Lou, we're grown people," she said, although she was only nineteen. "I know what I want, and I think you know what you want. Let's go over to Borough Hall and get a license." Even as he imagined his carefree life slipping away, Lou found himself taking the half-mile walk to the Bronx's civic center. "You know what saved me?" he says. "It was closed."

Nonetheless, they married scarcely a year after they started going out, in January 1946. To avoid a three-day wait in New York City, they opted for a small civil ceremony in Yonkers. "The judge looked like the typical judge in a small-town movie, with glasses perched on the tip of his nose," says Lou. "It was a real quickie marriage." So quick that when Lou's older brother Mike went downstairs to add a nickel to the parking meter, he missed the ceremony entirely.

A civil wedding at least circumvented the need to choose a secular venue. Theirs was a mixed marriage: Gilda was Russian Jewish, Lou half Russian Jewish and half Italian Catholic. Neither, however, had been raised in formally religious households.

Lou's father, Joseph Nigro, a tailor from a small town near Naples, and his mother, Esther Passov, from Kiev in the Ukraine, didn't pressure Louis, Michael, or younger sister Kaye to choose one creed over another. Their primary religion was work, and Joseph and Esther literally spoke each other's languages: He learned Yiddish and Russian; she learned Italian. Their skill in foreign tongues came in handy with their polyglot clientele in lower Manhattan, where they variously sold boys' pants, dry goods, and groceries.

After Joseph became ill with a kidney disorder, the family moved to the Bronx, an area still considered "country" in the 1930s, but quickly becoming a suburb for young couples and their broods. The Nigro children remember a household filled with music—Esther Nigro sang Russian folk songs, and the brothers taught themselves piano on a huge upright someone had given them. When Lou was about ten, the brothers also played ukuleles, strumming their instruments in Crotona Park, across the street from their Fulton Avenue apartment.

"We'd start to play and everybody would sing," says Lou. "Anyone who played an instrument was very, very popular." The first horn Lou took up was the saxophone, but he "never got anywhere with it" and switched to trumpet instead. Fortunately he didn't need his right pinkie to play it, because he had lost the tip of that finger after catching his ring on a nail while vaulting a schoolyard fence.

The arts also permeated Gilda's side of the family. Her mother, Sophie Meyerowitz, from Gezelitz, Ukraine, was the daughter of a cantor, and her older brother William occasionally took on cantorial duties as well, also showcasing his fine baritone for a time in the Metropolitan Opera's chorus. As a career, William Meyerowitz pursued art, not music, and became fairly well known as a painter, printmaker, and art teacher in Manhattan and in Gloucester, Massachusetts. His work and that of his wife, fellow artist Theresa Bernstein Meyerowitz, provide a unique visual history of Laura's maternal family, since both depicted Laura's mother, grandmother, great-grandmother, and great-aunts. In one painting by William, Sophie has her arm tenderly around her mother, and with her long dark hair, heavy-lidded eyes, and full red lips, she is a dead ringer for her granddaughter Laura.

Laura and her brother Jan would see their artist relatives at family holidays, and would occasionally visit their West Side studio or their Gloucester home, leaving Laura with strong early impressions of visual art integrated with music. The two strains combined in William and Theresa, as well: Her work included many paintings of musicians and their listeners, while critic Stanley Olmstead wrote of William that he captured "pulses in our national instinct which are aural, yet heard with infinite rareness—translating them to color." Great-niece Laura would later "hear" colors, thus translating those "pulses in our national instinct" into melody.

Given the fertile cultural heritage on Gilda's maternal side, it's not surprising that her mother, Sophie, met future husband Isidore Mirsky in the standing room section at the Metropolitan Opera House. Mirsky, who had come to the United States from Vilna, Lithuania, was an artist, too, but on houses rather than canvas.

"He was used by decorators because he could mix colors better than anybody," says his daughter Esther. "He once painted a staircase for me, and the way he stained the wood it was like the best piece of furniture."

Like Joseph and Esther Nigro, the Mirskys were secular first-generation immigrants. The real faith in their home was progressivism: Isidore and Sophie were Communists. That political philosophy was particularly popular among Russian Jews, who had fled a world where they had been restricted to certain jobs, confined to the narrow western edge of the country (known as the Pale of Settlement) and terrorized by the anti-Semitic riots known as pogroms. Laura's grandparents translated their political beliefs into action, working for the rights of the impoverished in their New York community.

Gilda, her sister, Esther, and younger brother Gary grew up as classic "red diaper" babies, marching in annual workers' May Day parades and attending antiwar, pro-union, and pro-tenant rallies. New York–born historian Amy Swerdlow, who also had a red-diapered childhood, has written that the legacy of such an upbringing is "commitment to a world of justice, peace, and joy." It was a commitment that would be felt by third-generation Laura as well, expressed over and over in the songs she grew up to write.

When Isidore and Sophie moved from Harlem to the East Bronx in the early 1920s, Sophie made sure they chose a neighborhood with a settlement house—that late nineteenth-century social invention which served as a community center for immigrants and poor families. Esther remembers the siblings taking classes there from WPA-funded artists, and Gilda—who was bright and creative, with a fine singing voice— earned a starring role as the mother in Dead End, Sidney Kingsley's 1935 drama about a gang of East River tenement toughs. She was only twelve, but her acting ability drew interest from a Broadway agent, Esther says. Isidore, however, whose charm and revolutionary zest were counter-balanced by weekend drinking and gambling binges, would have none of it.

"You would think that Communists would be progressive as far as women's rights and so forth, but in my father's case it didn't work that way," says Esther. "I think he was caught between the culture he was brought up in and a new sense of economy."

Gilda would later strongly support her daughter's desire to perform, thus perhaps fulfilling some of her early dreams. And Isidore Mirsky, although he always enjoyed his whiskey ("painters have to drink," he'd say), mellowed with age. Laura adored the long-white-haired gentleman, considering him a parental figure and even a soul-mate, while fully embracing his progressive legacy. She would stay close to Mirsky, the longest-lived of her grandparents, throughout his life, he becoming her greatest fan and she doting on him.

Indeed, Laura connected more strongly to her ancestral past than to her immediate inheritance. "I feel the genes of previous generations in me," she would tell a journalist in 1969. "There's not much of my father's and mother's generation in me."

■ ■ ■

Shortly after Gilda and Lou married, they moved to a tiny one-bedroom apartment at 1374 College Avenue, just a few blocks east of the Grand Concourse. The Concourse, a wide tree-lined avenue along the crest of a hill, was at one time the Champs Elysées of the Bronx. If you lived in its handsome five- or six-story brick apartment buildings, you were *somebody*. And you were probably Jewish if you lived in the Grand Concourse neighborhood at that time, although the area also boasted a large population of Italians.

By the time Laura was eight, her family had moved into a much larger apartment a block off the Concourse, at 1504 Sheridan Avenue. Despite its proximity to the boulevard, Laura would remember the neighborhood as "kind of dirty. Down. Slummy," populated with a rainbow coalition of Puerto Ricans, Irish people, Jews, and Italians. In the mix, though, she found a sense of closeness and community. "Right within two blocks, there was poverty and harmony," she said in an-other 1969 interview—"poverty" and "harmony" being two words that would often appear in her lyrics.

Postwar opportunities for musicians were plentiful, so Lou regularly played weddings, bar mitzvahs, and club dates. Gilda worked as a book-keeper, including stints with a costume jeweler in Manhattan and for the American Psychoanalytic Association (which expanded her duties to include conference arrangements). The numbers that she dealt with in bookkeeping, Gilda would tell Laura, kept her mind calm amid the stresses of life.

Just as they had been raised, Lou and Gilda didn't stress religion at home. "But my mother, being the person she was, provided a model of compassionate and ethical behavior in everyday life," says Laura's brother Jan. "She was what you might call a spiritual atheist—someone who didn't believe in God or religion, but who led a deeply spiritual life."

The closest Laura and Jan came to a religious education were the Sunday school classes they attended when Laura was around eight years old at Manhattan's Ethical Culture school—perhaps the only formal education Laura ever admitted enjoying. The Ethical Culture Society, founded in 1876 by social critic and educator Felix Adler as a sort of Jewish-originated version of Unitarianism, espoused humanistic values such as the need to decrease suffering and increase creativity. One of its main tenets reads: "The mystery of life itself, and the need to belong, are the primary factors motivating human religious response."

A spiritual searcher throughout her life, Laura would never subscribe to organized religion, finding it boring and corrupt. "To me God is earth—an earthly thing," she told British journalist Penny Valentine in 1971. But she did credit Ethical Culture with giving her a strong educational base. "We learned about people and about life," is how she described it.

Laura's musical training began, quite richly, at home. She heard a lot of big band jazz because Lou, rather than using a trumpet exercise book, would practice by playing along with a Woody Herman or Count Basie record. Gilda's record collection included Broadway musicals, but she also loved symphonies, concert piano pieces, and opera (as did Grandpa). Laura particularly remembered the voice of soprano Leontyne Price, and she loved hearing the impressionist composers Ravel and Debussy, whose chordings deeply influenced jazz artists.

Laura also knew and appreciated folk music, especially dark songs of love and loss such as "All My Trials," "Hey Nelly Nelly," and "Two Brothers." And like any youngster of the 1950s, she adored rock and roll. "Laura and I had our collection of rock and roll 45s, which we played endlessly," says Jan Nigro. "We had a little box record player in our room, with 45s scattered all over."

Laura sang from the time she could make noises and wrote poetry as soon as she could string words together. She loved reading poetry from an early age, too, exploring books by poets from different countries. By age six or seven, she had written her first musical composition, an "Indian song" with fourths in it (a harmonic interval that evokes the clichéd Hollywood version of Native American music). Enamored with her accomplishment, she played it day and night.

Writing songs just came naturally: "I saw music as my first language," she would later tell an interviewer. Her singing ability, too, came as a gift. By the time she was about seven or eight, her aunt Esther said to Gilda, "Laura has an unusual voice. She is special."

■ ■ ■

When the Nigros moved to the larger apartment on Sheridan Avenue, Laura no longer had to share a room with Jan, and the living room now had enough space to hold a magnificent seventy-year-old Steinway grand piano. Lou had been tuning the Steinway for an elderly woman—he had used his GI benefits to become a piano tuner, planning for a more stable job than being a musician—and when the woman became frail, she sold it to him for the token amount of $25.

Around the time Lou acquired the Steinway, Laura took piano lessons—briefly. "I came home one day and Laura's hysterical," Lou says. "My wife said, 'She doesn't want to go for the piano lesson because the teacher hollers at her.' Laura was extremely sensitive. So we stopped the lessons."

Without formal training, Laura thus learned piano primarily on her own, developing an individual style and sense of harmony. "She didn't even have a knowledge of chords; she'd figure out her own and memorize them," says her father of her later musical development. "It was amazing; her chords were so different."

At one point, Lou grew concerned that Laura, who tended to sit on the grand piano's bench with one foot tucked under her, would scratch the finish on his pride and joy. That's when he got his daughter a seventy-three-key upright for her room. "Then she could plunk away as much as she wanted," he says. "I closed the door. But I never discouraged her." Lou and Gilda supported both their children's interest in music—Jan would develop into a pianist, singer, and guitarist as well. Laura also took guitar lessons for a time, when she was about ten years old. She even wrote "Laura and Elvis" on her lesson book, obviously identifying with the idol of the day.

Besides playing music and listening to it in the house, the Nigro children were exposed to the New York cultural scene by their mother. Among other excursions, Gilda would take them to the New York Philharmonic's Young People's Concerts, put on by conductor-composer Leonard Bernstein, a figure revered in the Nigro household. "Gilda was a real go-getter where art was concerned," says Alan Merrill, a Bronx neighbor whose mother, jazz singer Helen Merrill, was Gilda's close friend, and whose aunt married Gilda's brother, Gary. "Gilda also made the best tuna fish sandwiches," adds Merrill. It was a talent her daughter would inherit, and would inspire the name of Laura's first music publishing company.

Gilda was, in fact, the central figure in Laura's life, as mothers were for most children in the fifties. "My mother was a great woman of depth, heart, and mind," says Jan. "Her wisdom and love were influential in the human being and artist Laura became."

Laura and Gilda had an almost sisterly connection, says Carol Amoruso, who became one of Laura's best friends at Joseph H. Wade Junior High School. "I remember she could tell her mother—and I could tell her mother—things that I would never tell my mother. Like when we would cut school, she would tell her mother!" But when Laura revealed a little too much about herself, Gilda would respond, "Laurie, I'm your mother—don't tell me any more!"

Gilda had a certain naivete about her—jokes tended to go over her head—but she had an unmistakable intelligence and warmth. "Gilda was a very supportive human being," says Laura's cousin Dan, one of Mike Nigro's children. "It didn't matter if you were her child. She was so in tune to making everyone feel comfortable."

Laura was less intimate with her father, a traditional, emotionally restrained man of his era. "My father was very protective," Laura once told an interviewer. "He comes from a certain school. He and I come from such different schools." It wouldn't be until later in her life that they would draw closer.

Laura and Jan had a typical big sister/little brother relationship, "alternating between being co-conspirators and antagonists," he says. "She knew how to push my buttons, but I had ways of getting back. As I hit my teenage years, I also knew I had someone I could confide in."

When Laura hit her teenage years, she entered a typical rebellious stage. During the summer when she was fourteen, she spent a couple of weeks with Aunt Esther on Long Island when it became clear that she and her family needed a breather from each other. It may have been during that visit that Laura heard her cousin Jeffrey Marcus practicing piano pieces by Philadelphia composer and teacher Vincent Persichetti. Much later, Laura would identify a "mystery modern" element in her songwriting as being inspired by Persichetti's music.

"Jeffrey played a lot of Persichetti in the beginning," confirms Esther

Marcus. "I remember listening to it and thinking, What the hell is that? because it was so modern. It took me about three months to begin to hear it and appreciate it."

Esther describes the teenage Laura as being quite pretty—and still wearing long dresses. Her hair was short at the time, though, and she dreamed of growing it. To speed the process, Esther bought her an artificial hairpiece known as a fall. But Laura wanted even more to change in her life.

"You know Aunt Esther, I'm fourteen years old, and nothing has happened to me yet!" she said pleadingly. Her aunt promised to do something. "I called my girlfriend's son, who was sixteen, and I called my neighbor's son, who was sixteen, and I called one of my neighbor's daughters, and I made a little party in the house," says Esther. Both boys seemed to like Laura, and she liked one in particular. They scheduled another date, with Esther as chaperone, and Laura read him poetry she had written—a familiar outlet for the brooding young adolescent.

Laura herself remembered her younger days darkly. "I was a very sad little girl. Sometimes I had good times," she said in an early record company bio. She could close herself into her room and tune into her own private world, where her most painful feelings could be transformed into verse. "I had friends, but I started an internal journey at such a young age," she told journalist Harry Clein. "I was always kind of alone."

A "Creative Writing" notebook from when she was thirteen—probably put together as a school project—shows both her precocious talent for poetic musings and an often gloomy imagination. "You have served / you have hurt / And now you create / For it is only death herself that endures life," reads a section of her poem "The Plan," dated December 3, 1960. In other poems, she wrote of the ocean depositing "human scraps" along its banks ("The Ocean"), of a person journeying through the fires of hell ("Pitch Nothing"), and of a mother dying ("My Mother"). Only in a few instances, most notably her poem "Hot (warmth)," dated November 22, 1960, did young Laura focus on the more optimistic, sensuous images that would later appear in her song lyrics: "Midnight blue is the ocean / High and silky are its waves / so impatient, as they tide / the shore in champagne foam . . ."

Fortunately, Laura's teacher realized the young teen's obvious abilities. "These are excellent! You have a genuine gift for poetic language," the teacher wrote on the book's title page, and sprinkled the praises "excellent," "very good," and "Your images are unique and exciting" at the bottom of other poems. One can only imagine what sort of boost such an imprimatur must have given to Laura's creative aspirations.

Laura's cousins remember her as a sweet, soft-spoken, affectionate, and markedly different young girl. "Laura had an aura about herself," says cousin Steve Marcus. "She was really very deep and thoughtful. It was always there. Laura explored the emotional and sensual sides of everything."

"Whenever we were with Laura, it was always sitting down talking," adds her cousin Deanna Chirillo, one of Mike Nigro's seven children. "It was never about doing any activity, unless she was playing the piano and we were singing." All the Nigro cousins grew up close to one another, both geographically and personally. In one unplanned show of family unity, Laura, Kaye's son Joel Pope and Mike's daughter Willette were born within a month of each other. Aunt Kaye ended up caring for all three infants while they were crying one afternoon.

"So I breast-fed Joel," she says, "and then I breast-fed Willette, and then I breast-fed Laura." Considering they all nursed from the same well, so to speak, it's perhaps not surprising that Laura's generation of first cousins includes an inordinate number of musicians.

In the summers, the cousins—including those from Gilda's side— spent much of their time together at bungalow colonies in the Catskill Mountains in upstate New York, the preeminent summer resort for American Jews from the 1920s to the 1960s. The Sullivan County area provided a cool escape, since Bronx summers could be brutal in stifling hot, airless apartments. "If you were from the Bronx, the Catskills were like your second bedroom, right up the thruway about an hour and a half away," says rock music biographer Marc Eliot, who lived a few blocks from the Nigros.

Laura's father would typically take a trumpet job with a resort hotel band, and then the families would rent bungalows nearby. A typical bungalow colony, as The New York Times described it, was "an oval cluster of cottages bordering a green sward at the opposite ends of which, more often than not, are a day camp for children and a social hall for mothers and the transient fathers."

It was in that verdant New York countryside where Laura Nigro would gain much of her musical confidence and flair. Cousin Willette recalls Laura being glued to the piano in the bungalow colony's play-house, making up songs. Uncle Mike Nigro remembers her getting up to perform the folk chestnut "Michael Row the Boat Ashore" at age ten, accompanying herself on guitar.

Marc Eliot met Laura around 1960 at the Far-Site bungalows near White Lake, where Gilda worked as the summer bookkeeper. He was about thirteen, she eleven or twelve—a cute, plump, shy girl in tomboyish jeans and a T-shirt. They would join with other kids' from the bungalows and sing current radio hits by artists such as Neil Sedaka. One night, Marc and Laura performed together in a kids' talent show.

"We worked out a routine of the song 'Never on Sunday,' " he says. "After we did it we had this discussion about how we were never going to perform for anybody again unless we got paid, because we didn't think this place appreciated what we did!" (When Eliot saw Laura five years later at a camp where he and Jan were campers, she had indeed become a professional, having come only to visit and give an informal guitar-accompanied performance. "It was amazing to see the same girl again, now all hip and bohemian," says Eliot.)

By 1963 or 1964, Laura was instigating group sing-alongs at the small, informal Camp Eva in Mountaindale, New York—a "wonderful community of people," says Jan—where Gilda also kept the books. Misha Masud (then known as Maxine Schreiber) remembers Laura gathering a dozen or so girls together and teaching them a medley of African American spirituals and freedom songs, such as "Pick a Bale of Cotton" and "Amen," for which Laura had arranged harmonies.

"She had us singing our hearts out and performing for the camp, and none of us knew we could do any of that," says Masud, who would remain friends with Laura throughout her life. "When I was with her, I felt that she brought out the best in me in every way. And her voice was special even then—the power, the depth of feeling."

Masud's brother, Stewart Schreiber, also developed a long-term friendship with Laura out of their Camp Eva experience. His first impression was of a reticent person who was nonetheless easy to talk with. "A one-to-one kind of person," he says. But then he heard her belt out a song at a camp talent show. "Such a clear talent," he says. "I couldn't imagine that this was the same girl who was so reserved and soft-spoken."

Laura also met Barbara Greenstein, who would remain a close friend, at Camp Eva. The first time she saw Laura, says Greenstein. "She was draped across the cot with her long black hair down to her tush, blowing smoke rings, like the Alice in Wonderland caterpillar. No one else smoked then—and smoking in the bunk! She was a nonconformist, but not out of rebellion. She was just born different. There was no arrogance, no aggression around her. No one was offended by it. They were just thrown off by it, but she was very sweet and a lot of fun."

In the summer of 1964 at Camp Eva, Laura experienced the first of what would be many triumphs as a composer, and it happened at Sing Night, part of the traditional end-of-summer competition known as Color War. That was when the camp would divide into two teams and eagerly compete in various contests. "Color War was such a big event in the lives of the campers," says Jan Nigro, who was on the green team that year along with his sister.

The music for Sing Night usually included a march for the team's entrance, comic songs poking fun at counselors and campers, and a farewell song expressing love for each other and sorrow over their imminent departure. Usually the team would simply make up new words to popular tunes—but Laura wrote original tunes and arranged complex harmonies.

As general of the green team, Laura chose the name Green Utopians. "It was so typical Laura. She decided that we stood for humanity and our songs could never put down the other team but only praise ourselves," says Barbara Greenstein, the co-general of the team that year. "The songs were so extraordinary that the judges gave us a standing ovation."

"People who were there will tell you they were her first masterpieces," says Jan Nigro. "The inspirational ones were so powerful, so exquisite. She had worked out these soaring harmonies that left the audience stunned. Her songs had such *passion* extolling the virtues of the green team; I still remember many of those songs thirty-five years later.

"We lost Color War because we couldn't play ball [Jan was the best athlete on the otherwise-sorry squad], but we *killed* on Sing Night. It was the first clue to all of us that there was something great happening. And that might be the first time Laura realized more fully the scope of what she could do, what she was *born* to do."

2
TEENAGE PRIMAL
HEARTBEAT

If summer idylls in the green hills of Sullivan County encouraged her to create harmonies, it was the grittiness of everyday life in New York City that most strongly fueled Laura Nigro's early lyrics and melodies.

For New York kids of the late 1950s and early 1960s, the streets became outdoor amphitheaters filled with the sound of doo-wop—the harmony-rich, falsetto-heavy, urban-based music named for the preponderance of nonsense syllable lyrics. Laura recalled that the first rock and roll song she heard was the haunting 1954 doo-wop classic "The Wind" by the Detroit group Nolan Strong and the Diablos. "It was," she said, "earthy, romantic music that inspired more leaps of faith and less cynicism." She also loved doo-wop ballads such as "Oh, What a Night" by the Dells and "Happy, Happy Birthday Baby" by the Tune Weavers, yet the first two 45s she bought were heavier on rock than romance: "Bye Bye Love" by the Everly Brothers, and "Mr. Lee" by the Bobbettes.

After 1958, a sort of neo doo-wop, performed a cappella, was all the rage in New York City, with groups of young black, white, and Hispanic singers vying for street corner supremacy. "The New York a cappella sound . . . was rarely heard outside [the city]," wrote pop musicologist Barry Hansen, "but immortalized itself with hundreds of 45s." A cappella stylings were later applied to the gospel-injected Motown and soul sounds that would push doo-wop aside. Music seemed to leap out of the radio and into the neighborhood, where harmonizing was a daily practice. Although a cappella was mainly boys' territory, Laura insisted on being part of it. She teamed up with a group of young Puerto Ricans in the subway station—"about four guys and me doing rock 'n' roll."

"I was sitting at the top of the steps and they were down in the train station singing. I mean, it was beautiful," she told interviewer Paul Zollo. "And then I just . . . started hearing this other harmony . . . and I just started singing. And they didn't ask me to leave."

Her junior high friend Carol Amoruso remembers Laura being the ringleader of nightly subway songfests, which Amoruso joined as well. "Laura was really the inspiration," she says. "She just loved it so much, and loved arranging so that everybody had their harmony parts."

Laura, Carol, and the Puerto Ricans, who were primarily apartment building supers, says Amoruso, liked to sing both in the echo-heavy subway station at the Grand Concourse and 170th Street and in a building on a nearby corner. "There was a fabulous old gothic building where the resonance was really wonderful," Amoruso recalls. "So we'd sing under the staircase, and of course the super there would come out brandishing his flashlight, ready to bang us on the head, and we'd have to run. I guess that's when we made for the subway station."

Their repertoire included popular doo-wop songs of the day, such as "Gloria" by the Channels, songs by Frankie Lymon and the Teenagers, and cuts from the 1959 album *The Paragons Meet the Jesters*—a New York battle of the doo-wop bands, on which the Jesters recorded their version of "The Wind." Laura and her friends also harmonized to classic "girl group" material by the Chantels and the Shirelles. The Chantels, led by the Bronx's own Arlene Smith—whose keening soprano undoubtedly influenced Laura—was one of the first popular girl groups, known for their 1958 song "Maybe." The Shirelles scored the first-ever girl group No. 1 record, in December 1960, with the Gerry Goffin/ Carole King classic "Will You Love Me Tomorrow?," a song Laura would record nearly forty years later.

As media critic Susan J. Douglas has pointed out, girl-group music marked a radical departure from the sedate moon-June fantasies of the fifties. In the Shirelles' hit, for example, "these girls were not singing about doggies in windows or old Cape Cod. They were singing about whether or not to go all the way." Girl groups, wrote Douglas, gave voice to a young teenager's real concerns about finding her own identity, whether as a conformist or a rebel. It certainly gave voice to an angst-filled, hungry-for-experience girl like Laura.

Amoruso turned her friend on to another up-and-coming girl group of the time, Patti LaBelle and the Blue Belles, whose hit "I Sold My Heart to the Junkman" Amoruso had heard on a Harlem-based radio station. In a synthesis of several of her early influences, Laura would later record an album with Patti and the group that became known as

Labelle—and one of the songs on it would be "The Wind." Nyro must have appreciated another Philadelphia-based girl group as well, the Orlons ("The Wah Watusi," "Don't Hang Up," "South Street"). The syncopated riff and opening melody of their 1964 B-side "Envy (In My Eyes)" sounds astonishingly similar to one of Nyro's early compositions.

Laura also loved Motown groups such as Martha and the Vandellas and Smokey Robinson and the Miracles; she later covered several of their songs. Her other soul music favorites included "Sally, Go 'Round the Roses" by the Jaynetts, and the songs of balladeering boy groups, such as the L.A.-based Vibrations and Chicago's Curtis Mayfield and the Impressions. She told a journalist that she had listened to Mayfield's records on her little record player "for hours and days and weeks and months and years," finding great comfort in his music. Nyro's singing voice was, in fact, informed as much by the male falsetto as by female voices.

But she certainly loved female singers as well, such as folk goddess Joan Baez, whose music she first heard when she was fifteen. She also learned from the great female jazz singers of the era: the painfully intimate Billie Holiday ("the great mother-musician-teacher of the art of phrasing," Laura called her), the lush-voiced Sarah Vaughan, and the fierce Nina Simone. Her mother, Laura said, had turned her on to Holiday, explaining to her at a young age about "Strange Fruit," Holiday's quietly horrific song about lynching.

Not surprisingly, Laura's musical heroes and heroines were predominately African American. She would later describe herself as a "dark woman," even though her skin was white. "As a woman, as an artist and in my sensuality I always knew the beauty of darkness, shadow, and color," she wrote.

Among her black instrumental role models, jazz maestros John Coltrane and Miles Davis reigned supreme. Of Davis, she told one writer, "I knew that he wasn't kidding me, or jiving me, because he was playing about life, yet what he was playing was so warm to me, and I took him all in at that age. I feel that somehow he got lost in my blood, he got mixed in somewhere inside." After the trumpeter died in 1991, Laura was among those who paid tribute to him in *Rolling Stone*, crediting his early records with teaching her about space and phrasing. "What he did reminds me so much of what the Impressionists did in art," she said.

From Davis's and saxophonist Coltrane's bands, she learned chord structures and progressions that were "off the beaten track," as she put it. McCoy Tyner, who played chunky "extended" chords behind Coltrane's improvisations on songs such as "My Favorite Things," may have been the pianist who most influenced Laura's early stylings.

But it was all the music all together—classical, rock, girl group, Broadway, soul, folk, jazz—that became, for Nyro, "the real language of life," as she would later say in a radio interview. "That's what I heard as a kid," she added. "It felt like a joyful communication."

She heightened the experience of listening to music, especially Davis and Coltrane records, by taking some of her earliest forays into mood-altering drugs. "We had a routine every Friday night [when Laura's parents would go out] where we would drink a bottle of Robitussin," admits Amoruso. An over-the-counter cough medicine, someone nonetheless had to sign for it because it contained codeine, so Laura and Carol's older male friends would buy it using silly aliases such as "Chuck Wagon." The girls and their friends would then get together at the Nigro apartment to swig the sickly-sweet cherry syrup, lie on the floor in a numb, mellow haze, and soak in the sounds of their jazz heroes.

Amoruso found Laura to be "so deep, so intense. People didn't super-super gravitate toward her. But she had a wonderful sense of humor, and loved to laugh a lot, so that brought people to her."

Another Bronx acquaintance, Ed Ziegman, shyly admired her. "She was different [from] anyone I ever met," he says. "She always had this deep, contemplative look on her face. She and Carole seemed independent-minded earlier than most girls."

Amoruso remembers her friend showing a sensitivity that was preternaturally mature for a fifteen-year-old. She treasures a note written in beautiful script and encased in a gold-foil-lined envelope, that captures Laura's caring spirit:

> At our age, true friendship is precious and goes much further [than] borrowing clothes and giving a daily report of 170th St.'s [the neighborhood shopping street] gossip coverage, which some of our other friends can't seem to realize. I don't believe in a person having too many best friends, and in fact I don't think there is any such thing. But you and I have been together through thick and thin, and right now you are at your thickest—that means Barry, of course—and I am very happy for you, since he

is the closest thing to being good enough for you. In time, I may find my own Barry, and then together we will be the two most perfect couples. Carol, do you remember last Saturday night when I called you about 12 o'clock midnight and I told you my time-old problem, which by now is getting quite repetitious? [The problem was either her weight or boy trouble.] Well, I know I could never speak to anyone else like that and find so much comfort and faith as you gave to me that night. And you being only 15 years old have passed your years incredibly. A letter like this could only be sent to you, because only you will understand it as you have understood everything else over the past year, and I truly hope you will be there to understand for many years to come. Happy birthday, and have many many many more. Love always, Laura

"Isn't that sweet?" says Amoruso. "Barry, who was this very sweet boyfriend of mine, loved Laura. We were, like, joined at the hip at that point, so he had no choice."

Barry also had noticed, with affectionate humor, that Laura was turning into a voluptuous young woman. "Our bodies were budding at that point, and he would call me 'Corn Muffins' because I had small breasts, and he would call Laura 'Separate Bathtubs,' " recalls Amoruso with a laugh. "He would say that she couldn't get them both in the bathtub with her at the same time."

Laura may have been comfortable with her budding sexuality, but often felt uncomfortable with her weight, says Amoruso. During one period, she wore a black poplin raincoat with white stitching everywhere she went. "We'd go to these parties and she wouldn't take the raincoat off," says Amoruso. "It was really sad." Boys like Ed Ziegman didn't hold a few extra pounds against her, though.

"She was zaftig, not fat," he insists. That Yiddish expression connotes a pleasant, sensuous plumpness; its literal translation is "juicy."

Ziegman liked the fact that Laura wore dark makeup and an all-black wardrobe, finding that it made her attractive and older-looking. But to her parents, the look was a little too slutty, according to her brother. "I remember some closed-door sessions between Laura and my parents about her wearing Ronettes-like hair and makeup," says Jan Nigro, referring to the teased-up 'dos and thick black eyeliner favored by the famous girl group. "It was just not the wholesome look my parents wanted for her." They also weren't happy with the fact that Laura was smoking, but since Gilda smoked as well, it was probably hard to make a strong case against it.

■ ■ ■

As she had demonstrated at Camp Eva's Sing Night, Laura Nigro had begun to blossom as a songwriter. Amoruso remembers Laura's early compositions to be "little stupid stuff about the boys that we were hanging out with," and on the liner notes for her first album Laura herself would say that she had enjoyed rewriting pop songs of the day with racy lyrics. In any case, she had come to realize that music was, as she put it, the language she now wanted to speak.

So it made perfect sense that instead of going to William Howard Taft High School, right across the street from where she lived, Laura would apply to the High School of Music and Art. Located at 135th Street and Convent Avenue in Harlem, it was a five-mile ride southwest on the subway. Founded in 1936 by New York City mayor Fiorello LaGuardia, Music and Art offered the nation's first publicly funded program for students gifted in visual arts and music. This was not the Fame school, however. That was the High School of Performing Arts, made famous by the movie and television series Fame.

Laura, who also loved to paint, applied to Music and Art as an art major, submitting a portfolio. But she was accepted, more appropriately, into the voice major. Even as she began studying classical music, operatic singing, and theory, though, her heart remained in the streets. She wasn't practicing her scales while riding the subway to Music and Art with neighborhood friend Ziegman, who played the bassoon; instead, they were harmonizing in a corner of the subway car to "What's Your Name" by Don and Juan, "Diamonds and Pearls" by the Paradons, "Chapel of Love" by the Dixie Cups or "The Bells of Rosa Rita" by the Admirations.

A classmate of Laura's, Sharon Glassman, remembers a quiet, worldly girl who was heavyset and beautiful. "Her eyes were amazingly big and brown and very soulful-looking," says Glassman. "She looked very much like a beatnik, which was befitting of that time. I remember being in awe of her, because here I was this girl from the Bronx, totally unsophisticated, and there was Laura, who seemed very sophisticated and hung out with sophisticated girls who all smoked cigarettes."

Though she had little personal contact with Laura, despite sitting in front of her in class, Glassman remembers a particular incident that illustrated her classmate's devilish streak. "One day I decided to wear a straw hat to school," she says. "It wasn't very big or wide-brimmed, but our teacher, Mrs. Dolgow—who looked like Peter Pan—asked me several times to please remove it because it would be disruptive. I kept saying no, but I was very close to just removing it when Laura said in a loud whisper, 'Oh, don't take it off, she's wrong.' All I needed was ever so little encouragement." The next thing Glassman knew, she was removing her hat in the principal's office.

"When I went back upstairs, Laura never said anything," says Glassman, "but in her eyes there was 'I'm sorry.' "

Although an art major, Glassman was well aware of Laura's musical prowess from hearing her sing in the school's resonant, marble-walled bathroom with her friends Helen and Phyllis Stokes, who were twins. "What voices!" says Glassman. At lunch breaks and after school, schoolmate Elliott Randall, who would become a well-known rock guitarist, would also join the trio to sing a cappella. "We all had our various ranges and would fall into doing the parts," he says. "Laura would take the high parts and do a lot of falsetto stuff, because the Stokes sisters had medium-range voices. I'd do baritone."

"I didn't know Laura very well—our one point of contact, really, was making vocal music together—but I do remember that she was as intense as she was all the way through her life," continues Randall, who played guitar on one of her albums nearly thirty years later. "She was always very focused on music. Even when we sang at school, she would say, 'We want to get this right, we want to get this right right now.' "

Along with the other musical flavors Laura had been tasting, an additional ingredient was thrown into the stew while she attended Music and Art: the joyful, brilliant melodies of the Beatles. She even remembered the lovely spring day on campus when she saw a newspaper photo of the Beatles arriving in America. "They were waving and we were listening to 'I Want to Hold Your Hand' on the radio and I felt this thunderbolt in my heart," she told an interviewer in 1984.

Aside from those musical discoveries and the friendships she was making, Laura hated school. "There was a lot of striving for good grades," says Ed Ziegman, "and I think Laura was not academically motivated as much as she was motivated by her own talent."

"It's a great school and they offer some great things, but when you're really into what you're doing, you don't want to go through that," adds Laura's classmate Toni Wine, another precocious pop music talent who was hired as a professional staff songwriter at age fourteen. "I mean, who wants to go to P.E. classes?"

Although talented fellow students such as composer Michael Kamen loved the school—he was class president in Laura's senior year, and would go on to meld classical and pop music in his New York Rock and Roll Ensemble and in later work with David Bowie and Metallica— Laura's dissatisfaction was shared by other budding pop musicians. "Music and Art was very classically oriented; its attitude was 'If you don't play classical music, then you're not playing music," remembers Randall. "Whatever sort of adventurous things that people like me or Laura were trying to do weren't really being supported by the faculty at Music and Art."

Singer-songwriter Janis Ian, who spent a year at the school just after Laura graduated, also rued her decision to go there. "I had a lot of teachers who were very annoyed that I had a hit record [her poignant tale of interracial romance, "Society's Child"], so they took it out on me," she says.

Laura tried to solve her school problem by simply not going. At one point, she even went to the school dean and told her she was taking a three-week leave of absence. "I was the type of hooky player who played hooky without guilt," Laura said.

After three years at Music and Art, Laura was just short of qualifying for her diploma. Gilda went to plead her case with Laura's English teacher: "Do you realize what half a point may do to my daughter's life, psychologically, knowing that she did not graduate?" Replied the teacher, unmoved, "She'll never get anywhere if she doesn't finish this writing composition."

Undaunted, Gilda went to the principal's office and cried. It worked. Laura graduated on time and attended the June 29, 1965, ceremony at Carnegie Hall—a place where, just four years later, the officious English teacher would have had to pay to see her student perform. Laura didn't forget the grading incident, though. In June 1970, after she had become a certified pop music sensation, the school's alumni association voted her its LaGuardia Memorial Award "in recognition of outstanding achievement in the field of music." Laura refused to accept it herself; Gilda went in her stead.

■ ■ ■

Unsurprisingly, Laura didn't go on to college. Instead, to earn money in the year after high school, she took occasional jobs as a domestic—diapering babies, taking children to the park, helping make suppers. She loved babies, she told an interviewer, but the jobs didn't last because she "couldn't keep the children very clean." What she *could* do was sing for them. It wasn't what the parents bargained for, she said, but was of value nonetheless.

Her real profession had become songwriting and she seems to have been rather prolific, her early lyrics showing an economy of style, an attraction to clever rhymes, and a melancholy about love. In "Blindman's Bluff," for instance, she compares her life to the children's game, ending with "I think that I shall quit the game / forget your face, erase your name / And let the game of solitaire begin / At least I know in solitaire / sooner or later I'll win." Laura could also write a nursery rhyme-ish, amusing lyric like "Hi," which sounds like it's about being hi(gh): ". . . blue is red / My cat is dead / But I don't have a cat—is that / the sun the moon or some balloon / Up in the sky, where children Fly / Forget it Kid—You're just plain high / My my mouth is feelin' dry."

On the same page of lined notebook paper that Laura wrote out the lyrics of "Blindman's Bluff," she also listed two groups of what obviously are song titles. The first group contains "In and Out," "Struck Gold," "Hands," "In Time," and "Enough of You," while the second includes "Where Does Love Go," "Never Meant to Hurt You," "Blindman's Bluff," "The Rain," and "Come Love's Way." Considering that many albums of the time contained five songs on each side, could she already have been imagining her own recording? Of the songs on the list, though, only the similarly titled "I Never Meant to Hurt You" ever made it to vinyl.

As she started pitching her songs to publishers, Laura seems to have thought of herself more as a songwriter than as a performer, but she did make her own demos. Alan Merrill, a budding rock and roller himself (he cowrote the classic Joan Jett hit "I Love Rock 'n Roll"), played blues harp on her first studio demo, while Laura played piano. "She rehearsed me after school for a couple of weeks," he says. The three songs they cut were "He's a Runner" (which would appear on her first album) and two more never-released titles, "Freewheelin' " and "Stand Straight, Die Right." Merrill still remembers the chorus of the latter, Shirelles-sounding tune:

Stand straight die right
Tonight's the night
For our fighting to end
and to make up again

In "Freewheelin' " Merrill says that Laura made reference to being a kindred spirit of Bob Dylan, which explains the title. Dylan's 1963 album *The Freewheelin' Bob Dylan* contained some of his best-loved songs, including "Blowin' in the Wind," "Don't Think Twice, It's All Right," and "A Hard Rain's a-Gonna Fall." Nyro must have been paying careful attention both to Dylan's songcraft and to his evocative, stream-of-consciousness lyrics.

Once Laura started meeting publishers, she didn't find them very daring. They asked her, "Can't you write simple melodies?" She felt that they were trying to categorize her, and she refused to be pigeon-holed. One of the pigeonholers was Bobby Darin, the famed singer who had become a music publisher of note, having purchased Trinity Music in 1963. Laura had thought Darin was cute, but he must have been flummoxed by her. He suggested she go home and write some-thing along the lines of "What Kind of Fool Am I" referring to the overblown Anthony Newley/Leslie Bricusse ballad from the musical *Stop the World, I Want to Get Off!* When she returned to see Darin a second time, Laura sat down at the piano and defiantly played, "What Kind of Fool Are You."

Laura hadn't yet found someone who recognized talent that didn't fit into the neat boxes of the time. Was she a girl singer? Cabaret chanteuse? Pop songwriter? Her idiosyncratic style was ahead of its time, and certainly ahead of those she was trying to sell herself to. But she wouldn't to suit others' tastes.

She did change something about herself for her own reasons. As she took her first tentative steps toward a music career, she decided to take a new last name. She once told an interviewer that she had tried out different names and personalities when she was young, and the one she landed on at age eighteen was the one that stuck. Moreover, she might have wanted a new persona in order to separate herself from her prosaic life as a Bronx teenager. And despite her own lack of prej-udice, she certainly didn't want to risk snickers from people mispro-nouncing "Nigro" as "Negro," especially at a time of intense national preoccupation with race and civil rights.

Jan Nigro remembers seeing Laura's list of possible name changes, all variations on Nigro. Her father recalls that she seriously considered "Niagra," a name she had used on her creative writing book in 1960. But Lou had pointed out to her that it would not lessen the wisecracks. "Laura," he said, "if you trip, someone will say, 'Niagra falls.' "

She settled instead on Nyro—pronounced, coincidentally, the same as the surname of a well-known earlier Music and Art alum, pianist Peter Nero. Spelled with a y, though, it would almost always be mispronounced as Nigh-ro—just as her father also warned.

Perhaps the Ny represented New York (NY); perhaps it had a resonance to kindred spirit Bob Dylan's name (which was often similarly mispronounced as Die-lan). "I think it was just an unusual name that she liked the sound of," says Jan Nigro. Whatever it stood for to her, Nyro was certainly unique: There was not another in any New York City phone book.

3
MORE THAN A NEW DISCOVERY

It's not surprising that Laura Nyro initially saw herself more as a song-writer than a performer.

The great pop divas of the era (Aretha Franklin, Dionne Warwick, Barbra Streisand, Dusty Springfield), the most popular folksingers (Joan Baez, Judy Collins), and the girl singers and groups (Lesley Gore, the Supremes, the Shangri-Las, the Ronettes) rarely wrote their own songs. Many of the girl groups had been more like chattel, the artistic power residing with male writers, producers, and label heads, such as Phil Spector, George "Shadow" Morton, Bob Crewe, Berry Gordy Jr., Holland-Dozier-Holland, Smokey Robinson, and Quincy Jones.

On a separate, rarely intersecting track were the notable female song-writers of the era, most famously Carole King, Ellie Greenwich, and Cynthia Weil, who emerged from the environs of the Brill Building at 1619 Broadway in Manhattan. There and in a building across the street, a number of music publishers were housed, and teams of songwriters churned out classic pop that mixed Tin Pan Alley's melodic and lyrical sophistication with rock and R&B. The Brill Building's female song-writers only occasionally recorded their own compositions, except as demos.

But a few exceptional females of the time managed to both write (for themselves and others) *and* sing, most notably Jackie DeShannon on the West Coast. R&B singers such as Barbara Lewis ("Hello Stranger") and Baby Washington also wrote their own material in the early 1960s, as did artists in the folk tradition such as Buffy Sainte-Marie and Judy Mayhan. Janis Ian, who emerged out of the Greenwich Village folk scene, the lesser-known Essra Mohawk from Philadelphia, and the Canadian Joni Mitchell—who would become Nyro's preeminent singer-songwriting peer—also rose from the traditional soil of folk music, but would cross-fertilize it with rock, pop, and jazz.

Then there was the brilliant iconoclast Nina Simone, who created a unique jazz-folk-classical-R&B amalgam. Her piano-based music, dramatic presentation, and whisper-to-a-shout vocal dynamics certainly helped shape Nyro's style. As writer Kathy Dobie described Simone, "She chose homeliness over elegance; the sound of emotions made plain, rather than restrained." Nyro listened to Simone growing up, and late in her career would perform and record "He Was Too Good to Me" a Rodgers and Hart song she'd heard on a Simone record when she was fifteen.

Despite having the idea that she would be just a songwriter, Nyro ended up being "discovered" for her singing as well. Her first champion, Artie Mogull, literally found her in the Yellow Pages: He needed the secondhand piano in his office tuned, and came across Lou Nigro's name in the phone book. While adjusting the piano's pitch, Lou did some pitching himself.

"The guy comes up to my office and starts tuning the piano and tells me his daughter writes songs," Mogull says in his trademark gruff tone. "I said, 'Listen, do me a favor, just tune the goddamn piano!' The guy wouldn't let up, so just to get rid of him I said, 'Jesus Christ, tell her she can come tomorrow and play me some songs.'

"The next day," he continues, "this rather unattractive girl comes up to my office and the first three songs she played me were 'Stoney End,' 'And When I Die,' and 'Wedding Bell Blues' "—all future chart hits for other singers, though Mogull may be exaggerating which three Nyro songs he first heard. Nonetheless, he flipped over both her voice and her material, and signed her to a management contract, recording contract, and publishing contract.

Mogull's tale contains the key elements of the short, conflicted relationship he would have with Laura Nyro: a disdain for her looks and style uneasily coexisting with a recognition of her talent and commercial potential. "I thought she could be the female Dylan," he says. Since he had recently formed the publishing company Dwarf Music with Bob Dylan, he knew of what and whom he was speaking.

One can only imagine how Mogull impressed the naive eighteen-year-old, who usually brought Gilda along with her to meetings with publishers. On one hand, Mogull was associated with someone she admired, Dylan; on the other, Nyro must have soon realized that she had dived into waters whose depths had been measured for business-men, not artists. "He probably had contempt for her, and she didn't get him at all," says Milt Okun, whom Mogull would bring in to produce Nyro. "He was a wild kind of guy, with wonderful ideas for her, but I think she saw him as something from outer space."

In his own defense, Mogull, who later held executive positions at several major record companies, says, "I'm famous for being the artist's man in the record company. She's the only artist I ever had that I didn't get along with." He also had never been an artist's manager before—and never would be again.

Shortly after that first meeting, Mogull took Nyro with him to the studio of arranger-producer Okun in order to make demos of several songs. A tape of that session has survived, and it reveals just what different planets Nyro and Mogull came from.

The tape begins and ends with Laura playing two songs that would appear on her first album—"And When I Die" and "Lazy Susan." In between, she sings several of her own compositions that would never appear on her albums, including two from her aforementioned list of ten songs. There's the torchy "Enough of You" ("I've had a time / I've had it rough / Now haven't I had enough of you"), the word-playing "In and Out" ("In / One day I'm in up to my chin / But all in doubt / I look about / And all within / I'm down and out"), the Gershwin-esque "The Moon Song" ("I'm a feather in tar / don't you smile/ or I'll pocket a star / fresh from June") and an upbeat, return-from-the-dumps song in which she professes "No more aching head / no more wishing I was dead / Trouble's taken out / And Lucky's taking over."

The demo displays Nyro's mature vocal talent and knack for charming, rangy melodies, evocative imagery, and intricate internal rhymes. Her style seems almost fully formed, if less lyrically personal than it would later be. She was writing songs with the idea that they might be recorded by other artists, so they're a bit generic and nonspecific, but they're polished compositions within the popular song tradition.

Yet after her first few tunes, Mogull says to her from the engineer's booth, "Laura, I never asked you this: Do you do any songs other than those that you've written?"

"No," she replies.

"You don't know any pop songs?" he asks again. " 'Stardust'? 'Moon River?' "

Laura answers, with barely concealed disappointment, "Yeah, I know some of it. I know . . . of course I know there are other songs, and I know a few lines from each one. A few, maybe."

"There is Irving Berlin," says the auditioner.

Laura laughs. "And there's Bob Dylan," she answers back slyly. Mogull, knowing he's been bested in the exchange, replies, "Yeah, I know him."

Others in the studio laugh, but Mogull remains relentless, asking again if Nyro knows *any* pop standards. "Misty!" Laura suddenly remembers. "Oh, I mean, 'When Sunny Gets Blue.' " Gamely, she strikes a few chords of the Johnny Mathis hit and sings a few bars, searches for another key, then launches into a completely different song—the Leiber-Stoller classic "Kansas City." Frustrated that she doesn't know the piano accompaniment to that one either, she stops again. Finally, she makes one last stab at a popular song, singing a cappella, "I don't know what it is that makes me love you so," the first line of Dusty Springfield's pop classic "I Only Want to Be with You."

"I would do it if I could," she tells Mogull. At last he relents: "Okay, do one more of yours."

Upon hearing the tape more than three decades later, Artie Mogull says, "Can you imagine me being stupid enough to ask her if she could do Irving Berlin? I was dumbstruck by her talent, but we didn't get along so well."

Mogull involved his business partner, Paul Barry, in his dealings with Nyro, but also needed musical advice. Enter Okun, to whom Mogull gave a 20 percent cut of Nyro's contract. Okun was then working with three popular folk acts, the Brothers Four, the Chad Mitchell Trio, and Peter, Paul and Mary, the last being a group that Mogull had signed to Warner Bros. Records.

An opera buff, Okun says that when he met Nyro he felt like the kindly cobbler Hans Sachs in Richard Wagner's opera *Die Meistersinger von Nürnberg*, who teaches the rigorous rules of songwriting to young knight Walther von Stolzing. Like von Stolzing, Nyro had plenty of talent, in Okun's opinion—melodic tunes, poetic lyrics, and a voice with the enticing "ping" he heard in those of great opera singers. But Okun also felt that Nyro's songs meandered. "Laura needed someone to tell her what the rules were," he says.

Okun, who had been a pianist for Harry Belafonte, made it a condition of their working relationship that Nyro's compositions be restructured into more AM-radio-friendly forms. "Laura was not at first interested in my comments," he remembers. "Luckily, her mother was with her almost every time she came to see me and sort of forced her into accepting it. One day they were coming up the stairs—I was on the fourth floor—and I heard them arguing about a certain song. Her mother was saying something like 'But it goes on for ten minutes!' And Laura was saying, 'Yeah, but that's what it is!' " Nyro would maintain that sort of creative argument with producers and arrangers throughout her songwriting life.

Nyro and Okun's relationship improved with time, he says. In his favor, besides Gilda Nigro's influence, was the fact that famous folk artists such as Peter (Yarrow) and Paul (Stookey) tended to drop by his East 34th Street studio when Nyro was there, and she could see the esteem in which they held him.

While Okun worked on her song structures, Mogull went looking for a recording deal. He first tried Warner, where he had previously run the music division. "Mike Maitland, who was at that time the president, didn't think she had it," says Mogull. "All the people who now say they flipped over her, none of them thought she had it."

Other New York music business people would kick themselves for passing on Nyro. Songwriter Marsha Malamet, whose compositions have been recorded by artists such as Barbra Streisand, Luther Vandross, and Patti LaBelle, says that she got her first publishing deal, in a way, because of Nyro. New York publisher Bob Lissauer, still chiding himself for having turned Nyro down, belatedly decided that "If another woman comes in here and hits that piano like she's making love to it, I'm going to sign her." Fortunately for Malamet that woman was her.

Mogull found a more open ear for Nyro at Verve/Folkways Records. Verve had been founded as a jazz label in 1949, was purchased by MGM in 1958, and in 1964 merged with the Folkways label. Charged with infusing the lineup of pure folk artists with more pop-edged ones was Jerry Schoenbaum, who had run MGM's classical division, Deutsche Grammaphone. Schoenbaum would soon form the Verve/Forecast label to carry the underground music emerging out of the nightclubs in Greenwich Village.

"There was the Gaslight, Café à Go Go, the Bitter End—what they called basket clubs, where the artist sang and passed the basket around," recalls Schoenbaum of the Village scene. (Nyro herself played at least once at the Bitter End, an engagement Gilda invited the relatives to attend.) "Over a period of months, I signed the Blues Project, Richie Havens, Tim Hardin, and Janis Ian."

"Jerry Schoenbaum was great—he had a vision of what Verve should be and stayed pretty true to it," says Ian, who played the basket clubs as a young teen. "He was intensely loyal. In my case, he rereleased 'Society's Child' three times until it became a hit. That was unheard of. I think MGM's vision was actually that the label was going to be a tax loss for them, and they were kind of surprised when he started making money with it."

Nyro auditioned for Schoenbaum on his office upright, and he was impressed if not bowled over. "Her tunes were so strange and different from what was going on—the chord structure was different, the amount of bars in a tune were different, and the lyrics were rather interesting," says Schoenbaum. "She wasn't the greatest singer I had ever heard, but she handled her tunes very well. I said, 'Yeah, I'll take a bop at her.'

"Remember, in those days you weren't spending millions of dollars on every artist," he continues. "You could put out an artist with an investment of maybe $50,000 or $60,000. None of my artists were very expensive—yet. I would imagine she got something like a $5,000 or $10,000 advance." *Variety* announced on August 3, 1966, that Nyro—who the trade paper called a "songstress-writer"—had signed with Mogull and would be recording for Verve/Folkways.

Since Okun arranged for folk artists, he felt he wasn't the right person to handle Nyro's pop- and jazz-style material. His first choice to do her arrangements was Charlie Calello, known for his work with producer Bob Crewe and the Four Seasons, but Calello was busy. So Okun turned to Herb Bernstein—"a personable, sweet, bright, funny guy"—who had replaced Calello on Crewe's staff when Calello took a job at Columbia Records. "Herb really had a sense of how to package it all," says Okun.

A former high school basketball coach, Bernstein had scored a hit in 1966 with his first production for Crewe—Greenwich Village folksinger Norma Tanega's whimsical "Walkin' My Cat Named Dog"—and the hits kept coming for him with groups such as the Happenings. Nyro's music "blew me away," says Bernstein, but like Okun, he also found her songs too unconventional to be hits.

"She was very artsy-fartsy," he says, the same opinion he'd held of Tanega. "If you heard 'Wedding Bell Blues' [the song that would be the first single from the album] the way she first played it for me, you wouldn't believe it was the same song. She had that little riff—*dah bah buh DOO buh DOO*—that she used a lot, but she'd stop every sixteen measures and go into another tempo. I said, 'Look, I'm as artistic as the next person, but you have to think of the commerciality of these things. If you're gonna change tempo every thirty seconds, you're gonna lose the average listener.' "

Yet Bernstein respected Nyro's artistic spirit even as he tried to tame it. "She was very concerned with the integrity of her music," he says. "Each song to her was another baby. Every song had to be just right. She had great ideas, and I would sit with her at the piano. What I wanted to do was incorporate all her thoughts into my arrangements. She would give me the feel and I would try to capture it."

Nyro initially wanted to accompany herself on piano, but Okun says she wasn't sold on playing. "She didn't think she was a great musician and she felt she'd get nervous," he claims. Because her sense of rhythm was idiosyncratic, he felt it would be hard for her to lead other musicians through Bernstein's arrangements, so Okun hired pianist Stan Free instead. Jerry Schoenbaum then suggested that Nyro accompany herself on guitar and vary the chord progressions by using a capo, a movable bar across the fingerboard that uniformly raises the pitch of all the strings, but that didn't go over well. "I don't remember what she said," says Schoenbaum, "something to do with her nails or that she wasn't happy with that suggestion, and that took care of that."

The attitude Nyro faced about her piano playing was par for the course in those days, says Janis Ian, especially for women musicians such as Nyro and her: "Quite often you weren't allowed to play on your own records. It was a lot more difficult to be treated seriously as a woman player. And you weren't expected to be a songwriter, or to lead a band. Those were things the boys did."

Nyro would never again make a record without playing keyboards. Her next two albums announced right under her name that Laura Nyro was "Accompanying Herself on Piano," a statement that strongly suggests she may have been more sold on the idea of playing piano than her first set of mentors were.

During the recording of that first Nyro album, done mostly at Bell Sound on West 54th Street and mixed at MGM, Nyro would sing along with a rhythm section, later overdubbing some of the vocal tracks. Bernstein remembers that at one of the sessions, Nyro brought along a few of her former high school classmates.

"I couldn't believe it, everyone had an opinion!" says Bernstein. " 'That's too fast, that's too slow, why is there hand-clapping, Mr. Bernstein?' I said, 'Listen, aren't you late for class?' "

On harmony vocals, Bernstein used a three-woman group he'd discovered and been working with, the Hi Fashions, and later added the voices of some of the best studio singers in the business, including Linda November ("she did every commercial in the world"), Leslie Miller (the voice in the advertising classic "Like a good neighbor, State Farm is there"), and Laura's high school friend Toni Wine. Besides Stan Free, the other backing musicians were also top New York players: Bill La Vorgna on drums, Lou Mauro on bass, and Al Gorgoni, Jay Berliner, and Bucky Pizzarelli on guitars.

For additional color, Bernstein used two harmonica players—the bluesy Buddy Lucas (who also provided the memorable opening and closing figures for Tanega's "Walkin' My Cat Named Dog") on "Wedding Bell Blues," "And When I Die," and "California Shoeshine Boys," and the chromatic harmonica jazz virtuoso Toots Thielmann for the haunting sounds on "Lazy Susan," "Billy's Blues," and "He's a Runner." "No one in this world played harmonica like Toots," says Bernstein. "With him, I wrote a little bit and then let him improvise."

Employing an uncommon pop instrument such as the harmonica was part of the creativity necessitated by a low budget and primitive four-track recording technology. The lack of tracks limited Bernstein's ability to record instruments and voices separately, so he had to weave together instrumentation as he recorded.

"They said I could use strings on only four or six sides [album tracks]," he remembers. "On the other sides I had to use only three, four, or five instruments. Unless it's a jazz album, I don't want to use piano, bass, drums, and guitar—then it's just another album. So I'd use piano, an acoustic bass, maybe a jazz harmonica, maybe a bass flute, a cello. Maybe forget the piano and use a harpsichord. And I could only use six strings; I didn't even have enough tracks to double them.

"You didn't have flexibility—you had to make instant decisions, boom," he continues. "On 'Wedding Bell Blues,' we couldn't decide whether to use a regular piano or a tack piano [they settled on the regular]. Nowadays if I had the same problem, I'd say, 'Let's do it both ways and put them on different tracks and we'll decide later.' If it were done today, that album would have had a much fatter string sound, sounded much more alive. But the budget was nothing—I'll bet it wasn't more than about $15,000. You can't cut two sides today with that."

Bernstein was pleased with the album's outcome, except for an unforeseen edit on the song "Billy's Blues." "I ended it with two chimes [as it had begun]," he says. "When they put the album together, some genius cut off the two chimes. No one ever knows it, but that's one of my artistic tantrums. Two lovely, meaningful chimes were cut off."

Bernstein thought Nyro was satisfied, too. On the album's liner notes, she was quoted by interviewer Bob Shelton, a New York Times writer, as calling him "a genius and a pussycat." "She adored me and I adored her," says Bernstein. When he saw her years later, backstage at the Bottom Line nightclub in New York, he says she kissed his fingers.

In her interview with Shelton, Nyro had described her sound as "polished soul," but after the fact she felt her music had been over-polished. When she spoke to Down Beat writer Chris Albertson in 1969, she sounded bitter about her first recording experience, complaining that Bernstein had written half the arrangements in just a few hours, chopping out difficult changes.

"I mean, I work months and hours and years and a lifetime on my songs," said Nyro. The producers had brought down her music, she said, leaving her no joy, understanding, or sensitivity. "Just incredible fights, and I was always crying—I mean, that's the way all those old people really knew me."

Comparing the Verve album with the earlier demo tape, one indeed can hear a difference. On the demo, Nyro changed moods and tempos with ease and confidence, the compositions sounding fully realized rather than meandering. If anything, they breathe with her as she sings them.

Toni Wine, who hung out in the studio listening to playbacks and harmonizing with Nyro, doesn't recall her being unhappy during the recording, however. "I know that she was thrilled to hear her music coming back at her live, loud and clear, and she had smiles from ear to ear when we'd all be listening to the playbacks," says Wine. "But I think she would have loved to hear her records on the radio the way she played them in her living room. That was unrealistic back then, and that might have been hard for her. Later on down the line, going into the studio with just a piano in a very artistic mode would and did happen for many artists. But in the mid-sixties, the tracks on records were just in a more commercial mode."

"She wasn't completely happy with it, but she didn't complain a lot," adds rock journalist Ellen Sander, who became Nyro's friend shortly after the album was recorded. "She was already, in her mind, doing the second album as soon as the first one came out."

By the time she did record that second album, the pop music industry would be willing to let Nyro and others have unprecedented creative freedom. But that precedent had not yet been set when her first album, More Than a New Discovery, was released in February of 1967. If it hadn't come out exactly as Nyro wanted, the album still holds up as a remarkable introduction to her talent, displaying sophistication that belied her youth and a remarkable ability to synthesize pop, soul, jazz, gospel, folk, and Broadway into a new hybrid entirely.

The album's ten songs are evenly divided between rollicking shuffle-beat numbers and downbeat jazz-flavored laments, although even the upbeat songs deal mainly with disappointment in love. Only "Blowing Away" portrays full-out joy, a celebration of being high on a drug and/or the sexual energy of a new beau.

The songs are full of named characters, including Bill (the man she's eager to marry in "Wedding Bell Blues"), "Lazy Susan" (both a flower and a seductive friend who snatches her boyfriend Johnny), the playful "California Shoeshine Boys," and the slippery Flim Flam Man ("Hands off the Man"). Like pop tunesmiths of a just-past era, who had written songs such as "Tell Laura I Love Her" and "Johnny Get Angry," Nyro offered a cast that was easy to identify and to identify with. The name "Bill" alone would later help her earn substantial songwriting royalties, as girls who wanted their Bill to marry them would call radio stations requesting "Wedding Bell Blues."

One of the most memorable characters in More Than a New Discovery was not a person but a place—a street called "Buy and Sell." With a miniaturist's skill, Nyro sketched out an avenue where "cocaine and quiet beers" help "pass the time and dry the tears." Torchily sung, the song is both sad and stylish, with a mood-lifting bridge that offers a momentary respite from the singer's tale of what may be a prostitute's life. This and the other ballads on the album (including "He's a Runner" and "I Never Meant to Hurt You") carry the weight of jazz standards.

As grown-up as the jazzy songs are, the album's most astonishing lyric belongs to "And When I Die," a hand-clapping gospel holler that recalls Nyro's camp days. Few sixteen-year-olds—Nyro's age when she wrote the song—could have speculated so artfully about their own death: "And when I die / and when I'm gone / there'll be one child born / and a world to carry on." The song posits faith in the future, spoken with, as Laura told an interviewer many years later, the "folk wisdom that teenagers have."

When Laura was in her late twenties and a friend's four-year-old son asked her what the song meant, she told him, "You know, everything is in cycles, and everyone is going to die. I'm going to die." Then she added presciently, several years before she would indeed become a mother, "And I'm going to bring new life into this world."

■ ■ ■

Considering that Nyro was so young and romantically inexperienced at the time she was writing songs for her first album, she culled many of her song ideas simply from observation and fantasy. "She had a couple of boyfriends," says Carol Amoruso, "but they were on-again, off-again. A lot of what she wrote was her imagination, but also came from a sense of longing." Adds Barbara Greenstein, "The songs were so intensely sophisticated, but Laura was naive about life at that time."

She had, however, what her brother calls "a precocious understanding" of human struggles. "It's compassion," says Jan Nigro. "Somebody can be a great musician but not have that part of themselves developed. Laura had fully developed parts of herself that all came together to form great songs."

Nyro also had a writer's knack for observing events around her and transforming them into lyrics. Alan Merrill claims that several songs from that first album drew inspiration from events and people in his and his family's life.

"Lazy Susan," Merrill believes, was about his crush on Susan Shapiro, the large-breasted valedictorian of Julia Richman High School. "I was always talking about Susan to Laura, obsessively," he says. "Laura craved a close, loving relationship with that sort of intensity for herself. She felt that Susan just had things come to her so easily, and envied her."

The model for the Flim Flam Man (which "Hands off the Man" would later be retitled), Merrill guesses, was a man related to both him and Laura—her uncle Gary, who was married for a time to Alan's aunt Dorothy. "He was an actor/artist/dreamer/ladies' man," explains Merrill. "A good-looking charmer. A fun guy to be around. His plans to succeed always seemed to fall through, though, and that sometimes got him in serious trouble." Barbara Greenstein, however—who thinks others attribute more specificity to her songs than Nyro intended—says that Nyro wrote the song for a 1967 movie, The Flim-Flam Man, which starred George C. Scott. Perhaps a publisher had suggested she submit a composition; in any case, it wasn't used.

Finally, "Wedding Bell Blues," Merrill claims, was written about his mother Helen's affair with a handsome—and, unfortunately, married—B-movie actor of the 1940s named Bill. "My mother was frustrated at not being able to marry him," says Merrill. "Laura was paying close attention to the family gossip regarding the affair."

Helen Merrill confirms the story. "Boy, she really nailed that one," she says. "What she wrote was very amazing—it was about anybody. That's what a great artist can do—she made it into a universal love affair, not just mine."

Given the ripeness of Nyro's voice, and lyrics, listeners assumed the singer was much older than nineteen at the time of the album's release. That's what Ellen Sander thought when she first heard one of Laura's songs filtering out of Artie Mogull's office, across the hall from the magazine where she worked as an editor.

"I think Milt Okun was there and they were playing this record and someone said, 'This is the next big singer,' " says Sander. "I thought, Really? She sounded kind of pop, kind of operatic—she didn't really fit my idea of what was coming along. But she was extremely compelling. And when I listened to the lyrics, they were so personal! The writing was so good. I mean, I was awed. I assumed that this was some mature older woman, statuesque, an operatic background or at least a legitimate show background. Then one day I was asked to come over and meet Laura Nyro—and I saw what appeared to be a teenager."

What quickly struck Sander was Nyro's creation of a dramatic persona. "I think Laura knew how to construct a mystique from the very beginning, probably from the time she was a little girl," she says. "She already had this incredible, fascinating veil of mystique around her. It wasn't phony. It was just a part of her personality that she relied on. As far as she was concerned, she already was a huge star. The rest of it was just the details." In 1969, Nyro told writer Michael Thomas exactly that.

"People say, 'You're going to be a big star,' " said Nyro. "Well, I really feel that I always have been a big star."

"Laura kind of broke the mold," Sander goes on. "She was very different from a lot of the personalities in rock and roll that I was to meet in the next several years. You couldn't help but be fond of her, because she was so vulnerable in such an endearing way."

Even though Verve knew it had a special artist on its hands—Schoenbaum himself takes credit for adding *More Than* to the initial album title *A New Discovery*—the company promoted Nyro in ways that ignored her sensibilities. The ad for the first single, "Wedding Bell Blues," featured a waist-up photo of a glum Nyro in a wedding dress and veil, carrying a bouquet of flowers. "I Don't," read the large caption, followed by the copy "Not every girl gets her man to say I do."

Nyro remembered stuffing herself into the wedding dress on a week when she felt particularly fat ("I weighed 180 pounds at that time," she said, perhaps exaggerating how much she was carrying on her 5 foot 3 inch frame). "I looked so uptight—the most uptight bride you've ever seen." The effect of the ad was to cheapen the poignancy of the song, making it seem like a novelty record.

Verve's ad for a later single off the album, "Goodbye Joe," showed a marked visual improvement, illustrated by two chiarascuro views of Nyro's face. But the accompanying copy was even worse: "That 'Wedding Bell Blues' gal has lost another man and found another hit!" The record company didn't know what to say about her, Nyro figured, so they could only make inane jokes that enraged her.

Nyro also told of being saddled with an "image maker" with a name out of a British farce—Terry Cloth. "He had a huge gap between his teeth and, like, he looked at me like he wanted to devour me," she complained to Michael Thomas.

Her promotional appearances felt hellish as well. The local *Clay Cole* television show may have come off without a hitch, but according to an interview she gave the short-lived *Eye* magazine, when she was lip-synching her song at a teenage hop in Miami, the record got stuck. She also was booked on an aircraft carrier with "six million trillion zillion" shaven-headed, drunken, screaming sailors, she noted disdainfully. Her opening act seemed right off a circus midway: "two huge black cross-eyed roller skaters in orange costumes."

(Before the album had been recorded, as a favor to Artie Mogull, Nyro also performed at a high school dance in the New York City suburb of Ardsley, where Mogull's best friend's son went to school. "I think I probably talked her into it," says Mogull. "She was at the stage when she didn't want to do anything to displease me—a stage she got out of quickly.")

More Than a New Discovery didn't make the *Billboard* charts, but Verve did manage to get radio airplay for "Wedding Bell Blues," which had been released in September of 1966. Listed in *Billboard*'s "pop spotlights" on September 17, 1966, the single was described as the "debut of a big talent (composer-performer) with a compelling folk-rock sound, loaded with sales potential." But "Wedding Bell Blues" only "bubbled under" the Top 100 for twelve weeks, beginning on October 22, 1966, eventually reaching No. 103. That's not surprising, considering that women were quite the minority on the charts in those days: On the *Billboard* Hot 100 of December 17, 1966, there were 84 male vocalists listed compared to only 7 females.

In certain regional markets, however—including Miami, and along the Pacific Coast—"Wedding Bell Blues" was quite a hit. In Los Angeles and San Diego it reached No. 3 on AM "Boss Radio" stations KHJ and KGB respectively. Hugely popular KHJ morning "Boss Jock" Robert W. Morgan gave Nyro extra play by turning her surname into a running gag over the course of a week. He made phone calls to various people asking them to pronounce N-Y-R-O, finally hearing the correct pronunciation from Laura herself.

Ironically, the single was hardly played at all in Nyro's own hometown. "I can't give you an answer why it didn't start on the East Coast, but broke pretty wide open on the West Coast . . . up to Washington, Oregon," says Jerry Schoenbaum. "At that time there were a lot of independent distributors, and it's quite possible that one of them liked the record, got it played on a secondary station, and it moved into major markets. I didn't control the promotion of my artists—which was an argument that led me to leave that company."

On the flip side of "Wedding Bell Blues" was another song for which Nyro would later gain songwriting acclaim, "Stoney End." The single version, however, is different from the one on the album. On the former, the lyric goes: "I was born from love / and I was raised on golden rules / till the love of a winsome Johnny / taught me love was meant for fools." On the album, she sang: "I was born from love / and my poor mother worked the mines / I was raised on the good book Jesus / till I read between the lines."

Herb Bernstein has no recollection of the single version, but one can speculate that Verve was nervous about including "good book Jesus" on an AM-radio-friendly 45. Indeed, when the female vocal trio the Blossoms recorded the song in 1967, lead singer Darlene Love cut off the lyric at, "I was raised on the good book . . . / till I read between the lines."

Neither "Wedding Bell Blues" nor "Stoney End" was the first Nyro composition to draw interest from another recording artist. That honor went to "And When I Die," which Milt Okun had spotted as "a major potential hit" even before he began production on Nyro's album. He thus arranged and produced a version for Peter, Paul and Mary, which appears on *The Peter, Paul and Mary Album*, released in August 1966. "She was over-the-moon happy about that, because she loved them," says Alan Merrill. The Peter, Paul and Mary rendition matches that on Nyro's demo tape (although the folk trio powered their fervent folk-gospel arrangement with guitar rather than piano). The giveaway is their use of the additional phrase Nyro used on the demo but not on the album version: "There'll be one child born / coming as I go / and a world to carry on . . ."

The Peter, Paul and Mary Album stayed on the *Billboard* charts for a year, peaking at No. 22, but their version of "And When I Die" remained little known. In just three years, though, the Blood, Sweat and Tears version would make it all the way to the *Billboard* Top 10. By then, Nyro was well on her way in the music business, and Okun, Bernstein, and Mogull were all out of her artistic life.

4
MONTEREY AND GEFFEN

After recording *More Than a New Discovery*, Laura moved into Manhattan from the Bronx. "She wanted her own place," says Louis Nigro. But the first apartment she moved to, a "dumpy-looking place," according to her father, was unacceptable to her parents. "We said, 'Laura, you are not going to stay there,' and we pulled her out."

Lou and Gilda were more satisfied with 888 Eighth Avenue, where Laura rented a small cramped studio with just enough room for an upright piano, a bed, and a few chairs. It was in a building and a neighborhood popular with people in the music business. Most important to parents, the building had a doorman. "We were right in the middle of hooker haven," laughs Toni Wine, who lived across the street on Eighth Avenue and 55th Street, "but it had a doorman, so it was okay!"

"Friends often hung out with Laura there," says Barbara Greenstein, "because we all still lived at home and she had her own apartment." Around then, Nyro also had her first real boyfriend—a guy named Tom—but Greenstein never met him. "Her relationships with her boyfriends were kind of private. We didn't go double-dating," she says. Nyro would later immortalize the brief but intense relationship in the song "Tom Cat Goodbye," suggesting that Tom was just about as reliable as a tomcat.

Alan Merrill remembers that Laura was proud to be on her own, but a bit scared at the same time. "I went there a lot," he says. "Tommy James [of the Shondells] lived down the hall, and we once ran into Bobby Darin outside of her building. Bobby knew who Laura was and said hi. Laura looked at me like, 'I'm getting somewhere, aren't I?' I was impressed and knew that things were changing for her in a big way."

Nyro was also nervous about being out on her own when she was booked for her first notable performing engagement, which was across the country in San Francisco. So Gilda accompanied her there, joined at times by brother Jan and cousins Joel Pope and Steve Marcus. It seems odd that a New York singer would make her debut on the West Coast, but given that "Wedding Bell Blues" had been a hit on that side of America, it made sense.

The venue—the hungry i on Jackson Street in San Francisco's North Beach area—seemed odd, too. The landmark basement nightclub (founded in 1950) primarily showcased top comedians, such as Mort Sahl, Shelley Berman, and Woody Allen (who opened there for Barbra Streisand in 1963). In 1966, though, it began engaging low-key rock artists such as the Lovin' Spoonful. Not long after that, Nyro signed to open for Berman, from mid-January through mid-February of 1967.

When Nyro and her mother arrived at the club on the Saturday prior to her Monday night opening, they were astonished to learn that club owner Enrico Banducci was unaware of the booking, which had been made by an agent friend of Mogull's. "So I called Shelley Berman at a hotel in Florida, introduced myself and told him the story," says Mogull. "He was very gracious—he called the owner and said, 'Put her on the bill.' " Nyro's name, however, never appeared in the San Francisco Chronicle's ads for the club or in its calendar notices. When renowned Chronicle columnist Herb Caen reported that Berman's opening took place before an "overflow crowd that hasn't been seen around the old cellar for many a midnight," he didn't mention an opening act at all.

The unpublicized Nyro felt she was a shock to the comedian's audience which she characterized as "truck salesmen and car salesmen and drinkers and coughers" who came there only to laugh. Her sly retort was to sing "And When I Die" with a smile—as if to describe her onstage experience rather than her worldview. She later told Down Beat she could no longer play in clubs where people drink, because they would then talk and "clunk things." She wanted to do only concerts, she said.

Her cousin Joel, though, remembers Laura sounding "superb" and being well received by Berman's fans. He also recalls Nyro having a great time in the city, trying out different shops and eateries by day and strolling along nearby Fisherman's Wharf each night after her performance. In addition, her San Francisco stay included a meeting with jazzman Dizzy Gillespie, her father's favorite trumpeter, who was staying at the same small hotel as Nyro while playing at Basin Street West. "She came back [from their encounter] and was really thrilled," says Steve Marcus.

Nyro's appearance at the hungry i coincided with the burgeoning of the Haight-Ashbury acid-rock music scene. The week that Nyro opened, Janis Joplin and Big Brother and the Holding Company played the hippie Matrix nightclub and the Jefferson Airplane played Basin Street West (on a strange double bill with Gillespie). Nyro's style and sound were a far cry from that of the hippie bands, but much to her amusement she heard her music described on a local radio station as "the San Francisco Sound." Nyro didn't share the hippie's tie-dye, free-form aesthetic either: In a caricature done by an artist while she was in San Francisco, she's wearing a busty purple gown with matching purple lipstick, her hair cut in bangs.

While in San Francisco, Nyro shot a video of the song "Wedding Bell Blues" for Dick Clark's teen music TV show, *Where the Action Is.* Dressed in a black knee-length dress and overcoat and a large knit cloche, Nyro looks as if she's about to burst out laughing as she lip-synchs the song while standing at the bottom of a stairway in San Francisco's Aquatic Park, a cable car in the background. The only action in the video is when she walks up the stairway as the song ends.

Where the Action Is was broadcast nationally, and some of her earliest fans became enamored of her after seeing that video. "I went screaming to the record store," says singer-songwriter David Lasley, who lived in Detroit at the time. "They didn't have the record, but they knew about it. 'It's by someone named Laura Nigh-ro,' they said."

■ ■ ■

Nyro's next big engagement was also in northern California, but it was far more attention-getting than opening for Shelley Berman. The Monterey Pop Festival, held June 16 through 18 at the seaside town's fairgrounds, proved to be a seminal event in rock history. Considering the hoopla it generated, especially after the release of filmmaker D. A. Pennebaker's marvelous documentary, it should have boosted Nyro to celebrity status. It certainly did so for Jefferson Airplane, Big Brother and the Holding Company, and Jimi Hendrix. But instead, not only was Nyro absent from the film *Monterey Pop*—at her own request, according to Pennebaker—but the festival proved more a setback than a launch.

Monterey's thirty-two acts ranged from Indian sitar master Ravi Shankar (validated in the rock world by his association with Beatle George Harrison) to folkie Scott McKenzie, who was known for the saccharine ballad "San Francisco (Be Sure to Wear Flowers in Your

Hair)," to the aforementioned cusp-of-stardom rock bands. Festival co-producers Lou Adler, a record producer, and John Phillips of the Mamas and the Papas also wanted to book a few little-known artists, and Adler's personal pick was Nyro, who'd impressed him both with her singing and songwriting. In fact, he had produced The Blossoms' cover version of "Stoney End" for his Ode Records label.

Nyro would later say that she loved Monterey Pop and sensed its historic impact while she was there. But even before she took the stage, there were inauspicious signs about the reception she would receive. Strolling the festival grounds with Ellen Sander, she encountered Paul Simon, one of the festival's governors. "I'm Laura Nyro," she said. "I really love your album." As Sander recalled, "Simon looked at this large grandmotherly girl with masses of dark hair falling around her black-shawled shoulders and paled. 'Well, it's okay,' he said and abruptly walked away."

Nyro, a Bronx street girl worth her salt, wouldn't let the perceived snub stand. She chased Simon down and, according to Sander, told him, "When people tell me they like my album, I thank them." Then she "flounced away."

At her Saturday night performance, Nyro had to capture the attention of 7,000 marijuana-smoking fans rather than just one celebrity, and she was not what the audience had come to expect from the psychedelic-heavy roster. In a tip of the hat to girl-group R&B, Nyro brought along two of the Hi Fashions as her backup singers. The black women wore blue cocktail dresses, while Nyro dressed in a long black off-one-shoulder creation. Its single sleeve unfolded into a wing when she raised her left arm, an effect Nyro probably thought would be dramatic but instead seemed merely kooky. Thirty years later, her goth outfit and long red fingernails would have been the height of rock style, but surrounded by Summer of Love bell-bottoms, Indian ponchos, and bedspread prints, she looked out of step.

The house band, for which Nyro provided charts, didn't help matters, even though it included top L.A. session players who frequently worked for Lou Adler as the Wrecking Crew: drummer Hal Blaine (the "ghost" drummer on numerous pop albums), bass player Joe Osborne, pianist Don Randi, organist/pianist/bass player Larry Knechtel, and horn players Jim Horn and Tommy Tedesco. The Crew could learn charts in seconds or else fake it, says bandleader Blaine, but had only one rehearsal with Nyro. For the rest of her career, Nyro would perform at the piano, controlling tempo and mood; that night at Monterey she sang standing at the microphone, leaving her at the mercy of both the band and the crowd.

Nyro's performance also wasn't helped by the haze of drugs that surrounded the event. Lighting crew chief Chip Monck, for example, was on his first acid trip. "I looked at Laura Nyro and she was going, 'Black . . . out,'" he recalled. Monck just stared at her, thinking how *wonderful* everything was at that moment, but he didn't make a move to dim the lights. In 1997, Laura herself admitted to journalist Johnny Black that she had been high (probably on marijuana) while performing, and that she and the musicians had been fooling around as they hit the stage.

Nyro hadn't captured Monterey Pop's zeitgeist, says Lou Adler, and she knew it. "Her approach—a big band doing the arrangements—was unlike what became the theme of the festival," he says. "Even though we were trying to show, and did show, everything that was happening in pop at that time, the psychedelic style of the Airplane, Jimi Hendrix, and the Who overshadowed all of the other music."

Right after the festival, *Teenset* magazine wrote simply that "Laura Nyro staged one of the more unusual acts." But as one concertgoer harshly characterized her performance thirty years later, Nyro was "a dreadfully pretentious woman offering up exactly the sort of formulaic pop-music piffle we had expected to avoid by gathering in Monterey." Of course one man's piffle is another's artistry. *Rolling Stone* magazine's historians were much kinder when they concluded that Nyro simply "seemed to try too hard for the laid-back audience."

"I think a lot of the audience came there to stomp and cheer and smoke drugs, and she didn't really fit in with that," says producer Dayton "Bones" Howe, who had worked as Lou Adler's engineer for much of the sixties and was then producing another of the festival's acts, the Association. "She was kind of esoteric for that crowd." Filmmaker D. A. Pennebaker, however, sided entirely with Nyro: "She was really *ahead* of everyone else," he says.

Most damningly, in one review—perhaps by someone who wasn't even there—Nyro's performance was coined "the disaster that was the unknown Laura Nyro's short set." Through the years, that "disaster" took on epic proportions. Most frequently, it was reported that she was booed off the stage. Jerry Schoenbaum, who was backstage to see Nyro as well as some of his other Verve acts, said, "If they didn't boo, they were pursing their lips as if they were ready to."

Nyro characterized her experience at Monterey Pop as the storm that preceded her breakup with Verve—a storm that just happened to take place onstage with thousands watching. Protected only by an imaginary cloud inside her head, she felt like she was walking to her death, and in her black gown she felt dressed for the part. The audience, she said, was left flabbergasted by her.

It certainly didn't soothe her to hear Artie Mogull's backstage response when she asked how he liked her set. Mogul said, "I'll tell you how I liked it: When I was a kid my father took me to the circus, and at one point, three elephants came out and danced to music. That's what you looked like out there."

"I don't for one moment defend what I said to her when she walked off the stage at Monterey; I was wrong to have said that," he now admits. "I was more worried about my reputation than hers." Still, he can't resist a parting shot: "But she pissed me off!"

At least Michelle Phillips of the Mamas and the Papas showed some compassion. As Nyro came offstage, Phillips "put her in a limo and lit her a huge joint and opened a beer and drove around for about thirty minutes comforting her," she wrote in her 1986 autobiography. While doing this good deed, Phillips missed much of the evening's most exciting set, by soul singer Otis Redding.

Nyro's exaggerated Monterey disaster made good copy, and Nyro herself embraced the mythology of a cataclysmic disappointment. It was like "a crucifixion," she said in 1969. "It was like the essence of failure. And I believe in great failure and great success. I don't like anything in the middle."

No one actually went back to the original evidence until 1997, when Pennebaker began to archive his Monterey footage on digital tape as he and Adler prepared the "Lost Monterey Tapes" for the cable television network VH1. Pennebaker found footage of Nyro singing "Poverty Train" and the tail end of "Wedding Bell Blues." Combined with Adler's audiotape of Nyro's complete four-song set, the two sources document a far different story than that of abysmal failure.

On the first two songs of her short set, "Eli's Comin' " and "Stoned Soul Picnic," Nyro and the Hi Fashions sound sharp and tuneful. The band, however, appears poorly mixed and uninspired. At the beginning of the third song, "Poverty Train" (which, along with the first two, would appear on Nyro's next album), the young and innocent-looking Nyro swivels back toward the pianist and motions him to slow down. Then, although shy about making eye contact with the audience, she proceeds to give a confident and poised performance of a song full of foreboding about hard drugs—an ironic message at a festival whose subtext was the liberation of the soft drug culture of marijuana and LSD.

As seen on the video, the audience was polite, but gave her nowhere near the rapt attention she would later receive as a performer. "There wasn't a tremendous amount of acceptance and applause for her, but I'm sure that's because the audience felt what *she* was feeling—this insecurity and uncertainty of how she was being presented or how she was presenting herself," says Adler.

Unfortunately, Nyro compounded the discomfort with some awkward stage patter as she introduced the Hi Fashions before her final number. Then, closing with the only song the audience might have been familiar with, "Wedding Bell Blues," she peppered her rendition with lounge-singer inflections—hardly a winning strategy in that setting.

Looking back on Monterey thirty years later, Nyro told a journalist, "I learned from Monterey that I was a formidable musician, but I had to get my shit together." However, the film and the audiotapes clearly disprove one false notion about her performance: Even if she was not ready for prime time, she certainly wasn't *booed.* A careful listening to the end of "Poverty Train" reveals a sound similar to "boo," but with a far different meaning: It's the first syllable of someone shouting, "Beautiful! Beautiful!"

A few days after the festival, Nyro gave the performance she *should* have given, only this time in a San Francisco hotel room. She had invited Ellen Sander over for takeout dinner with the High Fashions, and they were joined by the Fifth Dimension—the black vocal quintet currently on the Top 10 charts with the Jimmy Webb song "Up-Up and Away"—who were staying in the same hotel. During the meal, Sander recalls, Nyro started to mope about how poorly her set had gone, but then announced to the Hi Fashions, "Girls, let's sing the new album!"

"I remember we opened the balcony doors of the hotel room, and she walked in and out of the balcony between songs," says Sander. "I think it was the best performance they ever gave."

■ ■ ■

David Geffen had not been at Monterey. He first heard of Laura Nyro when TV director-producer Steve Binder mentioned her as a potential guest on *The Steve Allen Show*, a summer variety series packaged by the William Morris Agency, where Geffen was an agent. At Binder's urging, Geffen listened to *More Than a New Discovery*; after one spin, he was "mesmerized."

The shortish, feisty Geffen was twenty-four years old at the time, the son of a scholarly but chronically unemployed father and an entrepreneurial mother who ran a corset and bra business out of their Borough Park, Brooklyn, home. He'd already dropped out of two colleges, but fudged a UCLA degree to get a job in the William Morris mailroom, where he worked his way up to secretary and then agent.

When Bones Howe met Geffen, it was in a tiny office at the end of a long William Morris hallway. "His office was just big enough for a desk and his chair on one side and my chair on the other side," says Howe, who had just produced the No. 1 hit "Windy" for the Association, a group Geffen wanted to represent. "He was at the very end of the train. This was obscurity."

If the office was small, the personality was already writ large. "When David walked into the room, it was like he had this sign: 'I'm huge!' " says arranger Charlie Calello, who would soon be working with him. "In a matter of two minutes, he had the room, he had control of the conversation, and he could intimidate anybody."

He was a networker extraordinaire, gaining information while exchanging gossip with a multitude of friends. "The human Rolodex" is what Jac Holtzman, the former president of Elektra Records, calls him. Adds Ellen Sander, "There are three ways to get a story around: telephone, telegraph, and tell David Geffen."

"If he liked you and wanted you to be his friend, you had no choice," adds Stephen Paley, who became both Geffen's and Nyro's friend and one of Nyro's most trusted photographers. "There was once this science fiction movie about a spaceship that would just suck things up into it. David was like that mother ship; if he wanted you, there was no fighting it. He's very charismatic and likable and very enthusiastic."

Geffen wanted Laura Nyro. He contacted Artie Mogull, whom he knew, but was met with disdain. "Oh, forget her, she's insane, she's crazy," Geffen recalls Mogull saying. Geffen reported an even harsher exchange with Mogull in music executive Joe Smith's 1988 book *Off the Record: An Oral History of Popular Music*: "You don't want to represent her. She's a dog," he claimed Mogull said (which Mogull denies). In any case, Geffen insisted on being introduced.

Their first encounter was either at Geffen's office (that's what he told *Life* magazine in 1969) or, as he said more recently, at 888 Eighth Avenue—"a dark, crummy little apartment with a lot of cats." He found Nyro to be a "very strange girl," with hair down to her thighs, purple lipstick, odd clothes, and Christmas ornament earrings. But he was smitten.

"It was a very strong connection from the very first second," he says. Geffen seemed to get Nyro when no one else did. "She felt misunderstood by everyone involved with her at the time," he says. "Artie was insensitive—*charming*, by the way, but a charming rogue. Laura was despondent when I met her. And I was just crazy about her."

It wasn't a romantic relationship, although later it would be falsely rumored that Geffen wanted to marry her. ("It would be like marrying your daughter," says Stephen Paley. "He was more of a father-brother-protector-Svengali.") Rather, they were perfect soulmates as artist and agent: Nyro gained a devotee to her music, and Geffen discovered the first figurehead for his titanic ambition.

"I wanted her to be the biggest star in the world," he was once quoted as saying. "That was my dream for her. I don't know whether that was *her* ambition, but it was *my* ambition." In fact, her friend Barbara Greenstein can't recall Nyro ever talking about having huge career aspirations. "I don't remember once having a conversation about 'Oh, I want to be a star,' or 'I want to be famous,' or even 'I want people to hear my music.' She was very pure as an artist. She was not a business-minded person."

Although business was the essence of what David Geffen was, Nyro became more to him than just a meal ticket. "David was always very ambitious for himself, but there was one interesting, unprotected place in him—he really loved Laura Nyro," said singer David Crosby (who Geffen managed in the group Crosby, Stills, Nash and Young), in a 1998 interview. "That was a window into something in him that was not primarily about money."

For Nyro, Geffen was more than just a business functionary, too. On her subsequent record albums, she would refer to him as "agent and friend" or "manager and friend." "They would talk for two, three, four hours at a time on the telephone," says Lee Housekeeper, who would work for Geffen as Nyro's aide-de-camp and road manager. "They'd talk about everything—business, life. I think she was like an alter ego to him. The Beatles went to the Maharishi; David went to Laura. She gave him a very soulful side, a way to relate to artistic people, from which he benefited immensely. And she benefited immensely from his business acumen."

On the other hand, Nyro came to expect Geffen's ministrations, says Ellen Sander: "She enjoyed him and socialized with him, and she knew he was doing good stuff for her, but I think emotionally she took him for granted."

Geffen began the resuscitation of Nyro's professional life by helping her escape her management-publishing-recording contract with Mogull, Barry, and Okun. The law firm of Barovick, Konecky & Bomser found a loophole through which Nyro could squeeze: Contracts signed by minors under twenty-one had to be court-approved in New York. Nyro had been only eighteen when she signed, and the papers had not been run past a judge (Mogull admits that he had ignored his lawyer's advice to do so). Therefore, Nyro sued.

"It was very distasteful—I was a little embarrassed and upset," says Okun of the suit. "The two guys I was associated with didn't mistreat her, but they didn't like her particularly. I wasn't used to that— managers are usually in love with their artists, unreasonably often! But this kind of cold-blooded attitude . . . And Barry was much worse than Artie. Artie admired her and thought her stuff was great; Barry was a straight businessman."

The court disaffirmed the management and recording contracts, but Mogull and his partners did get to keep Nyro's publishing on More Than a New Discovery. Explains Mogull, "In the songwriter's contract with a music publisher, the phrase is used, 'I hereby sell, assign, and transfer,' and in the state of New York, a minor under twenty-one but over eighteen is held liable for a sale." Eventually, after various court appeals, Geffen offered to settle with Mogull, buying back the songs for $470,000. Strangely enough, Bob Dylan was entitled to a share of that payday, since he was Mogull's publishing partner. "But he wouldn't take it," Mogull says. "He didn't want to make money on another writer."

Nyro now needed a new recording label, and Geffen steered her toward Columbia Records. "I thought that Columbia was the classiest record company at the time," he says. "Barbra Streisand was on it, Bob Dylan, Miles Davis. I thought it was the right place for her." The time was right as well. Longtime Columbia A&R man Mitch Miller, whose "Sing Along" albums had been huge successes, had left the label, and the label's new president, Clive Davis, had decided to move away from

MOR (middle of the road) music and into the cutting-edge rock that he had heard at Monterey Pop.

Although Nyro had left a poor impression at Monterey, Davis nonetheless agreed to meet with her and Geffen in a small eleventh-floor room at Columbia's Black Rock headquarters at 51 West 52nd Street. According to Davis in his 1975 autobiography, Nyro complained that the room was too bright, so they turned off all the lights and she played the cycle of songs that would become her next album in the blue glow of a television screen. "The strength of her writing," wrote Davis, "was so obvious that I decided to sign her immediately."

When asked in 1994 about the incident, Nyro only laughed and said she didn't remember the TV lighting. Geffen claims Davis didn't sign her nearly that fast, either. "When I originally went to Clive Davis, he said, 'She's got a commercial voice but she doesn't write commercial songs,' " says Geffen. But in early 1968, Nyro was signed to a Columbia contract, which Geffen negotiated and attorney Alan Bomser of Barovick, Konecky & Bomser drew up.

"She wanted a lot of control over all the artistic stuff, and they gave it to her," says Bomser. The music lawyer also helped Nyro form her own publishing company, along with Geffen, working out the details during many hours of meetings with the two of them. "He was tireless," says Bomser of Geffen. "He was tremendously devoted to Laura."

Bomser particularly remembers a dinner meeting at Nyro's new apartment, a seventeenth-floor "penthouse" at 145 West 79th Street, in an area of town Nyro called "uptown downtown." A step up in class from her Eighth Avenue place, the apartment was still quite small, essentially one room with a foldout bed, a tiny kitchen, and a piano facing a wall on which she'd placed a heart-shaped mirror. However, it opened onto a huge terrace, with a large black water tower to one side. Nyro's parents had insisted she needed protection when she moved there, and that's why Bomser was greeted by Nyro's fierce guardian Beautybelle, a large German shepherd.

"Then Laura cooked us this horrible dinner of raw roast chicken," says the lawyer. "She apologized and said that that always happened when she did roast chicken—she could never get it cooked. But she said she would make us some tuna fish salad, because that she knew how to do superbly."

"Laura didn't really cook," explains Geffen. "Tuna fish—you opened a can and put mayonnaise in it." Tuna fish had also been Gilda Nigro's specialty, so perhaps her daughter had a genetic predisposition. When it came time to name Nyro's publishing company, Bomser says it was he who suggested the name Tuna Fish Music. "She loved the idea," he says. "I mean, that's the only thing she knew how to make."

"I wouldn't call it anything else," Nyro said of her company's name. As for the tuna itself, she insisted it be Bumble Bee brand, white meat, with Hellman's mayonnaise, a teaspoon of cream cheese, some diced red onion, and a pinch of lemon and pepper. From there, she said, you could branch out.

Tuna Fish Music would prove to be a most lucrative asset for both Laura Nyro and David Geffen, making the $470,000 they had to pay Artie Mogull look like a bargain. For Nyro, having her own publishing company and a Columbia contract that gave her full artistic control meant that she could pursue her muse with complete freedom. It's not surprising that the first line of her next album would be, "Yes I'm ready / so come on, Luckie."

5
ELI'S COMIN'

Laura Nyro had been ready to record a second album almost as soon as she finished the first. "She didn't use up her songs on the first album; she had more," says Milt Okun. Besides, it was common record business practice in those years for artists to put out albums as quickly as nine months after the previous one.

Before the lawsuit, Bernstein fully expected that he would be arranging and Okun expected to produce. Okun had already worked about six months with Nyro on her new compositions. "This time it was much more collegial," he says. "She really got the point. We would play records of artists she liked—Dionne Warwick and I forget who else—and I played her tapes of commercial albums. I showed her that very rarely was there a song that didn't have a shape to it."

Bernstein actually recorded several new songs with Nyro, including "Time and Love" (which wouldn't appear until her third album), "Sweet Blindness," and "Stoned Soul Picnic." Verve had even come up with a name for the new album—*Soul Picnic*—and given it a product number, FT/FTS-3029. The company advertised both Nyro's and Janis Ian's forthcoming albums under the headline "The Loners."

But when Nyro dissolved her relationship with her managers, producer, and record company, the recording process began anew. "Geffen didn't like my work and pushed her to go elsewhere," says Bernstein with some bitterness. "He said I bastardized her songs, that I made them too commercial. Maybe I should count my blessings—I got all her best tunes."

Geffen turned instead to Charlie Calello, the arranger who had been unavailable the first time he was asked to work with Nyro. Only twenty-nine years old, Calello had already packed in more than ten years of experience in the recording industry as a performer (bass and accordion), arranger, and producer. Working with Bob Crewe and his company, Genius, Inc., Calello had arranged Four Seasons classics such as "Dawn (Go Away)" and "Rag Doll," as well as peppy Top 40 hits for Shirley Ellis ("The Name Game"), Lou Christie ("Lightnin' Strikes"), and the Toys ("A Lover's Concerto"). Now a staffer at Columbia, he had asked Davis for a chance to work with one of the label's hot new artists, and Davis mentioned Nyro. Responded Calello, "I know Laura—she asked me to do her first record!"

He first met with Geffen and Nyro at her apartment, on a night he remembers vividly. "I went up there around eight o'clock, and Laura dimmed all the lights, lit candles, sat down at the piano, and played me the entire new album from start to finish," says Calello. "At the end, when she turned the lights on, I was in tears. I was totally, totally, totally blown away. I said to David, 'I must make this record.' "

At that point, about half a dozen arrangers had been interviewed, but Calello's enthusiasm clinched the deal. Calello and Nyro also shared something in common: Both their fathers were trumpeters. Plus, Nyro had a thing for a certain type of Italian guy. "Laura thought that Sonny Bono was very sexy," Geffen reveals. "Charlie Calello was very connected to her music, and he was the kind of guy she liked—sort of uncool and . . . Sonny Bono–ish."

Calello seemed more in tune with Nyro's independent spirit than her previous producers had been. He began by taping her singing at the piano, and from those demo performances wrote relatively spare arrangements. "After she wrote a song on the piano, the song was complete," he says. "If you added a bass, that was the finished arrangement. If you added a drum, it was already overarranged."

When Nyro listened to the initial piano-vocal tracks, she began adding such excellent harmonies that Calello realized he didn't need backup singers. Having an artist sing with herself was an innovative recording strategy that would become a hallmark of Nyro's recording style and a key influence on other artists. Nyro had sung with herself on her first album's "Blowing Away," but Calello could more easily multitrack Nyro's voice than could Herb Bernstein just a year and a half earlier. Although four-track recording was still the standard, Columbia had purchased two eight-track machines, which gave Calello the luxury of recording six tracks of background vocals. He then mixed them down to only a pair of tracks, thus freeing multiple tracks for his orchestrations.

Working in the studio in January and February of 1968, Calello cut the rhythm tracks live, with Nyro accompanying herself on piano. However, on two of the harder-driving songs, "Farmer Joe" and "Eli's Comin,' " Calello wrote down Nyro's piano parts for Paul Griffin, whom he considered the best R&B piano player in New York City. "When Paul played the part," says Calello, "he played all the *grease* that made it sound really cool."

Calello remembers a certain electricity in the studio during Nyro's recording sessions. "Of course we redid her vocals later, but I'll never forget how the musicians were so blown away by the music that you could see them hanging around after the sessions. It was an experience."

The initial drum tracks didn't please Calello, though, and he decided to remove them and hire another drummer. "Laura was totally freaked that I was taking the drums off; she almost had a nervous breakdown," he laughs. The new drummer was a high school buddy of Calello's, Artie Schroeck, who was known more as a piano and vibraphone player and hadn't played drums in a while. Calello offered to rent him a drum set and Schroeck proved an excellent replacement, "fitting into the overall comfort level," Calello says.

Also in Calello's comfort zone were guitarists Ralph Casale, who had handled the guitar solos on "Lightnin' Strikes" and other Lou Christie songs that Calello had arranged, and Hugh McCracken. The latter told Calello at the end of the sessions, "Man, there were two records this year: *Sgt. Pepper's* [*Lonely Hearts Club Band*, the Beatles tour de force, released the past June] and the Laura Nyro record. That was history."

Just as Bernstein had used Toots Thielmann and other top New York players, Calello also spotlighted well-known jazz musicians. Joe Farrell provided feathery flutes for "Poverty Train," turning it into a sort of "Alice in Wonderland," said Nyro. Famed tenor saxophonist Zoot Sims, who had played in big bands and led his own combos, did snaky, cocktail-lounge-at-closing-time riffs for the bluesy "Lonely Women."

"When I brought him into the studio, he had not played on a record in two years," says Calello of Sims. "His career was floundering, but as a jazz player he was known all over the world. Laura had no idea who he was."

But she was quite moved by the playing of the man who entered Columbia's huge studio on a gray, rainy afternoon, head down. "Then he did a thing with his sax where you just hear the air coming out and, like, it's all scratchy and broken and he communicates his lone-liness into the song," she told Down Beat. "Charlie and I sat there cry-ing . . . It was so beautiful."

Lou Nigro attended some of the recording sessions because he wanted to hear the great trumpeters Calello had hired, including Bernie Glow (who had played with everyone from Tommy Dorsey to Miles Davis) and Mel Davis. Laura even asked her dad if he'd like to play a session—Calello's dad Pat played on the record—but Nigro demurred.

Calello calls the making of the album "just a lot of fun," but also remembers Laura causing the occasional commotion. One day, for ex-ample, Geffen had to remove a tearful Nyro from the studio because she was worried that Calello's sweetening session for "Poverty Train" would ruin her music. When she came back and heard the atmospheric flute and sound effects, she gushed to him, " 'Oh, Charlie, oh, I love it, oh, Charlie,' " he says, imitating a girlish voice. "She was like a little child."

Another time Nyro disrupted a night session with some illegal mer-riment. "She had gone into the studio and rolled a double joint about six inches long, and she smoked it with the band in the foyer between the studio and the control room," says Calello. "She got everybody stoned. We were making this great take, and all of a sudden Laura would stop and start to giggle, 'Oh, Charlie, I feel the keys on the piano, oh, the black notes, I love the way they feel.' So the band stopped playing! In the middle of the take she's running her hands across the piano, feeling the keys. I'm laughing about it now, but back then, I went into the studio and said, 'Laura, how could you do this—this is CBS, and Arthur Godfrey [the network's famed radio and TV host] is in the next room!' "

Like many young people of the late 1960s, Nyro frequently indulged in recreational drugs, especially marijuana, and like her peers Nyro often smoked pot to enhance cultural experiences. Bobby Columby, drummer for the band Blood, Sweat and Tears, remembers going with Nyro on a Christmas Eve around 1968 to see the film Fantasia at the Little Carnegie Theater on 57th Street in Manhattan.

"She had smoked I don't know how many joints," says Columby. "She was definitely ready to see Fantasia, let's put it that way. In the opening sequence, [conductor Leopold] Stokowski holds up his baton and colors spring out as he moves his arm. Well, Laura moaned loudly when she saw this, and people turned around, thinking we were having sex! I put my hands up like, 'No, I'm not doing anything!' "

On her new album, Nyro celebrated the joys of getting high (whether on pot or alcohol) in the songs "Stoned Soul Picnic" and "Sweet Blindness." But in the cautionary "Poverty Train," she wrote, "You can see the walls roar / see your brains on the floor." Although the song specifically mentions cocaine, Calello says she told him it was about heroin. As one former Bronx drug user remembers, he and his friends knew all the words to that song, since the lyrics resonated quite accurately with their lives. "You get on a train," he says, "and find there are no stops to get off."

Nyro had tried the other famed hippie drug of the era, LSD, she told *The New York Times* in 1968, although by then she said she had given it up because of its possible genetic damage. When she was eighteen, though, the drug had seemed useful to her, even when she'd gone on a frightening, life-altering "trip" during which she hallucinated half man/half rat monsters. She resisted the metaphorical monsters during nine acid-hazed hours, she said, until they finally withdrew. "I won the struggle for myself," she concluded. "I stopped being a loser and became a winner instead." That day, she said, she became a woman.

David Geffen, who dropped acid with Nyro, sees her drug usage as part of the times and of her emotional needs. "In those days people self-medicated, and Laura self-medicated a lot because of depression, anxiety, all kinds of stuff," he says. "I'm not a doctor, but I was a witness, so to speak, for all of this. She went into enormous depressions, very much connected to men in her life and other disappointments."

If Geffen sometimes used drugs with Nyro, he still couldn't condone her wasting studio time. Calello remembers Nyro smoking pot during a recording session and Geffen chastising her with, "You're so irresponsible!"

Geffen also acted parentally toward Nyro when it came to her taste in couture. Says Calello, "David would walk into the studio and say, 'Laura, come over here—that dress is hideous, get that dress off! How could you wear a dress like that, it's four sizes too small for you!' " Nyro would softly reply that she *loved* the dress, and Geffen would grumble, "Don't ever wear it again! I'm going to bring people in here who will see you in that hideous dress!"

"These are the kind of conversations they had," says Calello. "They had this love-hate relationship, but it was really funny. David watched over every step she made."

Geffen affirms that Nyro's uncommon style drove him batty. "Laura had these dresses made—she had horrible taste—and one of them was like a ball gown with plaster of paris fruits sewn on, like bananas," he says. "It was unbelievably heavy, and it was like a joke." When Geffen arrived one day at her apartment to take her to an important business meeting, she was wearing that dress. "She looked, what can I tell you— yikes!" he says, laughing. "I said to her, 'Laura, you look terrible, put on a different dress.' And she said to me, 'Listen, I'm going to tell you something and I want you to get this: When I looked in the mirror, just like when you looked in the mirror this morning, I thought I looked great or I wouldn't have come out.'

"Which was a very important lesson for me," says Geffen. "I didn't realize that Laura looked in the mirror with that ridiculous dress on and thought she looked beautiful! She was a wild girl."

"Laura was like a flower," offers Calello. "She was delicate. She'd walk into the studio one day and be totally bubbly, and then she'd be depressed for four days . . . She wasn't into money. She wasn't into extravagance. She just wanted to write her songs and sing."

Nyro was already developing a reputation as a perfectionist in the studio. As someone who worked on the sessions told Ellen Sander, "You either love her or hate her, most times both at once. She's brilliant, stubborn, and strong willed. She never feels that something is finished. She keeps changing, perfecting, defining. We've got a brilliant album here, we all know it. But we almost died trying, Laura included."

"I do need a lot of help and direction but I don't want anyone telling me what to do," Nyro told Sander. Sander concluded that her friend got what she wanted in the studio *despite* the fact that she didn't always know exactly what that was.

As the recording and mixing sessions drew to a close, Calello felt certain that Nyro's album, now entitled *Eli and the Thirteenth Confession*— a sly fusion of the song titles "Eli's Comin' " and "The Confession" and the fact that the album contained thirteen songs—would be "huge." He suggested to Geffen that they organize a finishing party, inviting trade magazine journalists and Columbia's sales, publicity, marketing, and promotion staffers to a premiere of the album. Geffen, no slouch in the promotion department, thought it was a great idea and helped Calello set it up.

The final mix wasn't done until one morning at 5 A.M., and five hours later the party began. Nyro and Calello walked in together, and the producer addressed the crowd: "Ladies and gentlemen, this morning you're in for a rare treat: You're going to hear the continuation of the career of Laura Nyro." In a Nyro-esque touch, the lights were dimmed, and the people who could help make or break the album nursed their coffees and Danish while the album played.

"Most of them couldn't hear 'Come to Jesus' in the key of C," Calello says, "but because all these people were together, they assumed it was an event. Her career was off and running."

Calello's career at Columbia, however, would soon end. "Laura's album got me fired, because I spent too much money on it," he explains. "We used to make records for about $15,000 an album back then, and I had spent $36,000. I got a call from Walter Dean, who was in charge of business affairs, and he said that this was outrageous, that I was spending all the company's money, and how could I do this for an artist that no one knows of?"

Eli and the Thirteenth Confession was released on March 13, 1968. On the front cover, in a photo taken by Columbia's art director Bob Cato, Nyro appears as a dark Madonna with luxuriant red lips. On the back cover, in black-and-white silhouette, she bends over to bestow a kiss on the head of what appears to be a younger long-haired girl. Few realized that this photo was actually a multiple exposure, and that the "younger" figure is Nyro as well, shot in three-quarter profile. As one writer put it, the second image represented "the parting chrysalis of Nyro's own life." Nyro herself said that she was kissing seventeen years of her life— her childhood—goodbye.

Inside the album was a lyric sheet, a rare addition at that time in pop music. This sheet was even more rare: In response to Nyro's wishes to scent the album, art director Cato used a perfumed ink for printing the lyrics. Decades later, the textured paper still maintains a pleasant aroma.

But Eli and the Thirteenth Confession left an even stronger musical impression than an olfactory one: It sounded like almost nothing else in pop music at the time. From the dramatic opening chords of "Luckie" to the wailing coda of "The Confession"—in which the music crescendos while Nyro repeatedly sings, "Love my lovething / love is surely gospel"—Nyro created her own sort of musical, full of shifting moods within an overall story structure. Calello had kept her idiosyncratic tempo changes intact, but while the rhythms veer wildly from Nyro's signature shuffle to bluesy interludes to hard-rocking climaxes, her flexible vocal dynamics made the shifts sound organic, just as they would on Broadway or in an opera recitative. In some songs, one can hear echoes of great female jazz stylists such as Billie Holiday or

Nina Simone, while in others, Nyro employed her doo-wop falsetto to stunning effect.

Calello's arrangements were as eclectic and clever as Nyro's melodies. Songs like "The Confession" start with acoustic guitar strumming, for example, while in "Eli's Comin' " Calello uses a polyrhythmic horn arrangement similar to the one in Shirley Ellis's novelty hit "The Name Game." "I had the trombones play one rhythm, the trumpets play another rhythm, the baritone sax play another rhythm, and the rhythm section play another," Calello explains. "That was totally unusual back then. I really didn't write arrangements—I wrote *records*."

Janis Ian, who later hired Calello to work with her based on her admiration for *Eli*, praises his and Nyro's distinctive use of instruments as voices. "They weren't the backdrop anymore; they were an integral part of the song," says Ian. "Most people use classical instruments just because they can't think of anything else to do. What Laura and Charlie were doing was building everything around the song's framework, and it all worked as one piece. It was staggering for that time."

Calello is quick to credit the record's artistic success to Nyro. "The secret behind the sound of the record," he stresses, "started with the songs. The songs were brilliant." Lyrically, Nyro had developed an evocative and elusive vocabulary—perhaps under the spell of Bob Dylan's stream-of-consciousness wordplay, as well as the influence of the poetry she'd been reading since childhood. She obviously loved words for their own sake, making up her own compound words such as "lovespell" or "lovething." The pure sounds of the words engendered emotion, and that became more important than literal meaning. As reviewer Pete Johnson suggested, the significance of certain Nyro lines could hover just beyond comprehension until he *stopped* thinking about them—and then the meaning would dart into his mind.

For example, no one knew exactly what "Surry down to a stoned soul picnic" meant, but a picture emerged nonetheless. Surry—which isn't in the dictionary with that spelling—sounds like a type of locomotion, such as *sashay*. If one identifies it with Rodgers and Hammerstein's "Surrey with the Fringe on Top," the word may summon an image of an old-fashioned vehicle taking a group of marijuana-mellowed friends to a "stoned soul picnic." Then again, asked by Calello what *surry* meant, Nyro would only say, "Oh, it's just a nice word."

Musically, Nyro again showed a knack for irresistible melodies that danced all over the scale, and thus were tailor-made for showing off her multioctave range. Her chords, Calello observes, were more typical of jazz than pop. "She used rock and roll chord progressions, but with a unique way of playing harmonies," he says. "For example, she'd play a G chord with a C bass [normally, the bottom note would be a G, and C is not part of the standard G chord]. She was one of the first people that I ever knew who played that style, and although people have used it since, no one has ever used it the way she did. Laura would come up with these alternate, substitute chords. She was very instrumental in changing, harmonically, the structure of music. You look at a great painting and say, 'Ah, this is Monet, this is Renoir.' Well, when you heard a Laura Nyro song, you knew it was Laura Nyro."

On her first album, Nyro had sounded supper-club smooth; on Eli, she raised the intensity of her performance, displaying a nakedness that perhaps Bernstein and Okun had wanted to clothe. Certain critics throughout her career would accuse her of being shrill in her high range, but Nyro used her upper register for emotional emphasis, as many a hard rocker has done. In comparison to Eli, her first album sounds restrained, while the all-stops-out vocals on her second effort makes the lyrics feel lived rather than merely imagined.

That vocal intensity set a perfect tone for Nyro's coming-of-age memoir: the tale of a resilient young woman bowed but not broken by life and love. Eli begins with three cheery songs: "Luckie," "Lu," and "Sweet Blindness." In the first, the Devil is pushed aside as "Luckie's taking over and his clover shows." In "Lu," Nyro's "walking on God's good side" with a new boyfriend (whose name is not to be confused with her father's). And in the third song, she delightedly ventures "down by the grapevine / drink my daddy's wine / get happy."

"Luckie" is reminiscent of one of the songs at her Mercury audition in 1966, in which she mentioned "clover" and suggested that luck, or Lucky, was taking over. However, the tune is completely different, and in the earlier version Lucky had battled "Trouble," rather than his new foe, the Devil. That satanic character would haunt a number of Nyro songs, both on this and her subsequent album.

The next two Eli songs take a somber turn, with "Poverty Train" and the gloomy "Lonely Women," in which "a gal could die without her man." The first side of the album then closes with the rousing "Eli's Comin'," a hard-driving ode to an irresistible but menacing man from whom a woman had "better hide your heart."

Side Two opens with "Timer," which Nyro was heard to say in

concert that she had written about her cat. (She loved cats from child-hood, says her dad, taking in strays and even mail-ordering a Maine coon cat.) But Calello says she told him that the song, which begins "Uptown / goin' down / ole lifeline," was really about a person's race against time. She wondered, he says, where time goes and how it eventually runs out. In a sense, the song was her follow-up to "And When I Die," as she again squarely faced the inevitability of life's end. As Nyro would conclude in the new composition, "God is a jigsaw / a jigsaw Timer."

She follows that cut with the irresistible "Stoned Soul Picnic," a song of which Broadway composer extraordinaire Stephen Sondheim said that, in its complexity, economy, and spontaneity, it summed up for him what music is all about. Then comes one of Nyro's most treasured songs, the provocative "Emmie." It's a slow-paced reverie about a girl who is "the natural snow / the unstudied sea . . . you ornament the earth for me."

Is Emmie's admirer Nyro herself? Or is Nyro imagining a man sing-ing the song to his lover, whose name he has "carved in a heart on a berry tree"? Could it be about a poet she probably admired, Emily Dickinson, who professed her own loves in such perfumed sentiments?

Nyro would describe "Emmie" as being about "the eternal femi-nine," but over the years many listeners took it to be directed toward a female lover. When she rerecorded the song in the late 1980s for a live album, Nyro changed the ending in a way that may have more closely revealed at least what it had come to mean: Originally, she had sung a repeating coda of "She got the way to move me, Emmie" (sounding like former Brill Building writer Neil Diamond's "She got the way to move me, Cherry," from his 1966 hit "Cherry, Cherry"). In the remake, Nyro offered a litany of Emilys: "Mother (my friend) / Daughter (my friend) / Sister (my friend) / Lover . . ." The last word she sang was as close to coming out as Nyro would ever do onstage, but by naming all the possible Emilys she also proved that the song wasn't simply about a singular romance.

There may have been a particular woman who at least partially in-spired "Emmie." "David Geffen told me she wrote it for me," says Nyro's journalist friend Ellen Sander. "When I asked Laura if that was true, she kind of looked down and said, 'Yeah. . . . Well, it's sort of a combination of you and someone else.' But I think she added the 'someone else' to take me off the hook." Over the years, Sander told few people that the song might have been written for her, because she felt that would wrongly imply that the two had been lovers.

"She was very physically affectionate with me—hugs and kisses and caresses and things like that—but it never felt sexual," says Sander. "I kept looking at those lyrics, which were so sensual, and I always wondered, 'How did she know that?' There was just a certain way things were phrased that were so revealing, as if someone had been there with me. I actually meant to talk to her about how intimate that song was, but I never did. I was immensely flattered and I thanked her, but at the time I felt a little, um, *exposed*."

Following "Emmie" on the album, "Woman's Blues" starts off sultrily, but quickly turns into an angry tirade against a man who runs off and, strangely, "leave me motherless." The song uses three different tempos, while the next song, "Once It Was Alright Now (Farmer Joe)" is even more rhythmically complex and lyrically perplexing (sample: "Got a date / with the town shoe maker you know / she said I can't wait for your cornfields / baby to grow"). As critic Janet Maslin put it, that song "makes inexplicable rhythm changes half a dozen times, never repeating itself or returning to its original melody." But, Maslin noted, "Even at her most erratic and obscure, Nyro had a desperate intensity that made her as awesome as she was bewildering."

In the album's final cut, "The Confession," Nyro daringly asks someone to tell her "winsome" lover that she's had "others at my breast." Then she softens, adding, "But tell him he has held my heart / and only now am I a virgin / I confess." Explaining the song to an interviewer with the Los Angeles Herald-Examiner she said, "I had just finished with a man and I knew I had to write this song about it. It had to be, you know, joyful. I didn't know what the notes would be, but I knew what they'd sound like." Assuming that what she had "finished" was a sexual experience, Nyro's postcoital exuberance was stunningly bold.

Nyro had, in fact, displayed female sexuality on Eli and the Thirteenth Confession in a way rarely heard in pop music. Blues and R&B singers had long been unabashed about sexual content, and blues-based rockers such as Janis Joplin were bringing that permissiveness to rock, but Nyro displayed a sexual attitude more akin to a classic jazz singer: languorous, provocative, and knowing. As writer Patricia Romanowski put it, "She brought to the late-sixties false utopia of guilt-free fucking a scalding dose of scintillating shame and delicious submission."

In her lyrical explorations of the dichotomy between virgin and

whore, God and the Devil, Nyro was exploring a personal urban the-
ology, unmediated by any church's or temple's teachings. "The struggle
in the city is between health and sickness—God and the Devil," is how
she once described it. As *Ms.* writer Sheila Weller saw it, Nyro was "less
a woman yielding to the Whore Madonna typecast than one speaking
rather eloquently of the reverence toward love that is most fully possible only after innocence is long lost." Nyro appeared very soft and
feminine, yet at the same time remained an empowered woman. Her
heart could be torn asunder, but she wouldn't die. And her frequent
scuffles with the Devil, Weller suggested, were just a way to be tested,
the reward for survival being a renewed purity.

What made Nyro's album particularly revelatory was that she was
singing of her own life, not the inventions of an anonymous songwriter. Even if she couched her sexual adventures in poetics and allusion, Laura Nyro was confessing about herself. As she told a friend
during the recording of *Eli*, "When this album is finished, my mother
is going to know exactly where I've been."

"The songs always had some underlying meaning about her own
life," says Calello. "*Eli* was one of her boyfriends—I don't know if his
name was Eli, but she wrote it using the name Eli. It wasn't that she
would write a song, she would write *experiences*. And she could not
conclude the experiences into one song. When she put the tunes together, the whole story of *Eli and the Thirteenth Confession* played in her
brain. It wasn't thirteen songs—it was a complete work."

Other than the music trade magazines, the press didn't immediately
respond to the album's release. *Rolling Stone*, the leader of the rock press
pack, ran Columbia's portentous advertisement for the album in April
of 1968—"She Doesn't Explain Anything. She Fills You With Experience"—but otherwise ignored it for six months.

The magazine finally reviewed the album on September 28, 1968.
Critic Jon Landau, who would go on to fame and fortune as Bruce
Springsteen's manager, generally gave the work a favorable notice, writing that Nyro "has a lot going for her: a fine voice, a great melodic and
lyrical sense, and plenty of style." He especially liked her simpler, beat-
driven songs, such as "Lu," but felt she overused her falsetto and made
too many tempo changes. Landau concluded that Nyro needed a little
more self-restraint and control. "It will come," he wrote. Little did
he know that she was just beginning to unleash herself, not rein herself in.

The album peaked at only No. 181 on *Billboard*'s album chart, but

gradually sold more than 125,000 copies. Even if it wasn't an immediate blockbuster at the cash register and wasn't played much on the
radio, it defnitely was a hit among music cognoscenti. As critic Digby
Diehl wrote in July 1968, "The most played album in L.A., everywhere
except on the airwaves, it seems, is Laura Nyro's *Eli and the Thirteenth
Confession*."

6
NEW YORK TENDABERRY

By the time *Rolling Stone* finally reviewed *Eli*, Nyro's music had already made the *Billboard* charts—but not in her own voice. It was the Fifth Dimension, the group she had once serenaded in her San Francisco hotel room, who made the songs palatable to the record-buying masses.

Originally known as the Versatiles, the Fifth Dimension had been signed by pop star Johnny Rivers to his Soul City Records, then renamed and molded into a black version of the Mamas and the Papas. After their first album, the Fifth were produced by Bones Howe, who had engineered the Mamas and the Papas' first album. Although the Fifth Dimension had made Nyro's acquaintance, it was Howe's connection to David Geffen that led them to record her music.

Before *Eli and the Thirteenth Confession* was released, Geffen, who by then had unofficially dubbed himself Howe's manager, loaned the producer an acetate copy of Nyro singing the songs to her own piano accompaniment. When Howe heard it, he felt sure he'd discovered "dead smashes" for the Fifth Dimension in "Stoned Soul Picnic" and "Sweet Blindness." But Geffen told him he'd have to wait until Clive Davis chose Nyro's first single from the album.

Meanwhile, Howe surreptitiously made a tape copy of the acetate and took it to a meeting with the Fifth Dimension. "I've got a No. 1 R&B record for you guys," he told them, and played "Stoned Soul Picnic." "They were kind of white soul," says Howe of the black group. " 'Stoned Soul Picnic' was exactly right for their image, because they had this uplifting, happy, fresh sound." The group loved the song and wanted to cut it right away, so Howe decided to go ahead. Even if Columbia released Nyro's version as a single, he'd put his version on the Fifth Dimension's next album.

The gamble paid off. When Columbia released "Eli's Comin' " as

Nyro's first single off the Eli album, Soul City released "Stoned Soul Picnic." The Fifth Dimension had smoothed out Nyro's intensity while emphasizing the song's lilting quality, and the public loved it. "Stoned Soul Picnic" climbed to No. 1 on Billboard's R&B chart, as Howe had promised, to No. 3 on its pop chart and it was eventually certified gold (a million copies sold). It would be the start of a string of Nyro-penned hits for other artists. Meanwhile, Nyro's own single of "Eli's Comin' " flopped.

Someone at CBS, Howe says, later told him that Clive Davis had played the Fifth's single at an A&R meeting—supposedly the only time Davis had brought a competitor's work to the table in that manner—and demanded of his staff, "How could you people let somebody on the outside get a song like this away from us?" Nonetheless, the single was a boon to Columbia as well, boosting sales of Nyro's album, which reportedly increased from 8,000 units in Eli's first three months of release to 17,000 in the two months after "Stoned Soul Picnic" became a hit.

At the same time as the Fifth Dimension were beginning to find success with a Bones Howe arrangement of a Nyro song, Clive Davis and David Geffen somehow convinced Nyro to let Howe produce a single for one of her newest compositions, "Save the Country." Nyro had written the overtly political song in a flush of inspiration after the June 5, 1968, assassination of Robert Kennedy, which had followed on the heels of Martin Luther King Jr.'s murder on April 4. Perhaps because its message of peace, love, and tolerance was so important to Nyro—in the chorus, she pleaded "Save the people / save the children / save the country / now"—she was willing to accept a more mainstream pop arrangement if that would ensure that the song reached a large audience.

Only a week after Kennedy died in Los Angeles, Nyro cut the track in that city, at the CBS studios on Sunset Boulevard. At Davis's suggestion, Howe produced it exactly as he would a Fifth Dimension record, using the same musicians and the group's contagious sing-along sound. Released on June 26, 1968, the single sounds bouncy and bright, propelled by insistent hand claps and Nyro's urgent soprano. Howe thinks the arrangement actually softened the song's commentary, however. "Pop music at that particular time wasn't willing to accept something that politically concerned," he asserts. "It was 'Smoke dope and have a great time.' "

Even with its sparkly veneer, the single didn't make Billboard's Hot 100, although it did well on certain local stations such as Detroit's

WKNR, where it reached No. 17. Its biggest impact may have come when it was played once an hour by L.A. radio station KRLA during the riots at the Democratic convention in Chicago that August.

The lack of chart success may not have hurt Nyro's feelings, because it didn't feel like her record anyway, but it certainly strengthened her resolve never to compromise her artistry in the future. One of her friends told journalist Robert Windeler that Nyro was "really mad" about the trade-off she had made. "She compromised with them once and she never will again," the person said.

Nyro told Howe, "Look, you sock it to the people; I don't want to sock it to the people. I just want to put my music out there, and if they like it they'll come to me." "She didn't want to be a produced artist," Howe says, "and that was my role—I was *supposed* to sock it to the people. I was supposed to get their attention." Years later, he looked back on his production of "Save the Country" through the prism of his experience with another iconoclastic singer-songwriter, Tom Waits (who also had been brought to him by David Geffen). Howe found that he needed only to create a suitable studio climate for Waits rather than to mold the artist's work into a rigid pop structure.

"If I had known that back then, I would have treated Laura completely differently," says Howe. "I probably would have said to Clive, 'Don't do this, it's a mistake.' But there wasn't yet a market for albums on their own. People would go out and buy the album only because they loved the single and wanted everything else that went along with it. The whole marketing of music was completely different in those days."

■ ■ ■

Even if she couldn't score a Top 100 chart hit, by the fall of 1968 Nyro had begun to spark a loud public buzz. In *The New York Times* on Sunday, October 6, William Kloman wrote, "Laura Nyro is now the hippest thing in music. By the end of the year she may be the hottest as well."

To illustrate how she was both hip and hot, even Frank Sinatra was singing her song. He never released a recording of a Nyro composition (as has been often and erroneously reported), but did perform "Sweet Blindness" with the Fifth Dimension on his November 25, 1968, TV special, *Francis Albert Sinatra Does His Thing*. Trying a bit desperately to connect with the huge audience of baby boomers that had become the nation's primary music consumers, Sinatra announced, "The title of our show is in the patois of the youth of today. The young people are doing wonderful things today. . . . They're becoming a force in politics, they're protesting poverty, they're demonstrating for civil rights—but most important, they are buying records!"

After the Fifth Dimension enacted an arm-waving version of "Stoned Soul Picnic," Sinatra came on as the "Sixth" Dimension, wearing a glittery pastel blue and white pants outfit to match the group's garb. Unfortunately, he sang his lines flatly, missing the cocktail-party irony with which he could have imbued, "Please don't tell my mother / I'm a saloon and a moonshine lover." At least he admitted to his audience, "Don't look now, Francis Albert, your generation gap is showing."

In a similarly awkward grab for credibility with late-sixties teens, Bobby Darin hosted Nyro, along with Stevie Wonder, Judy Collins, and Buddy Rich, on the January 15, 1969, NBC-TV special, *Kraft Music Hall Presents the Sound of the Sixties*. Sporting a mustache and long sideburns, Darin solemnly introduced Nyro by reading the lyrics to "And When I Die" from an oversized book. "Those words were written by a lady who writes some pretty good songs," he said in his best hipsterese (certainly not mentioning how he'd once asked her to write "What Kind of Fool Am I").

Nyro, her lips wine-red, wore a long black dress with a ruffled collar and filmy sleeves, à la Morticia Addams. Sitting on the edge of a white piano bench, facing the camera but too shy to look directly at it, she sang "He's a Runner" from *More Than a New Discovery*, backed by a taped arrangement. She then slid in front of the keyboard and performed an impassioned "Save the Country," ending with an almost screaming "Now!!!!!" Nyro didn't have an easy rapport with TV cameras, but her unusual presence and vocal power were riveting.

The special would be Nyro's only major TV network appearance. The one other significant telecast she graced in America was *Critique*, a public television series moderated by *What's My Line?* host John Daly. The show was devoted to the work of a single artist, and on January 1, 1969, that artist was Nyro. She performed six songs at a grand piano and gave a whispery interview to journalist William Kloman. The show also included Daly's interview with David Geffen and a panel discussion about Nyro's music with critics Michael Thomas and Patrick O'Connor.

The program was almost laughingly serious in trying to bestow a high-art label on a popular musician. Just as Bobby Darin had, Daly portentously declaimed lyrics from "And When I Die," then argued with the critics whether Nyro should be considered a poet. For Nyro's fans, though, the show remained a unique opportunity to hear her perform, and even hear her *talk*, in her soft, charming Bronx accent.

The program illustrated why Nyro would never spend much time on the tube. She seemed both too timid and too uncontrolled. Television was too public a medium for such a private person and for her unadorned playing and singing.

■ ■ ■

Nyro's cloak of privacy extended to her love life as much as everything else about her. Even with her closest friends, she operated on a lifelong "don't ask, don't tell" policy. "If I saw Laura with a guy, I never asked anything about it," says Ellen Sander. "It was unsaid. She was very sweet and kind to me, and I felt like the price for that was that I didn't ask too many personal things. I know she was very vulnerable to the men in her life, but I also know it was intentional—that [the relationships] were a great source of inspiration to her."

In fact, Nyro had told Kloman on *Critique* that she had occasionally sought out romantic experience in order to create from it. "I suppose it's a little bit of that," she admitted. " 'Cause like sometimes, if I meet a man or something that's very groovy, I say, 'Oh, good material!' " With that, she let out a loud, embarrassed laugh.

Nyro was more circumspect about her relationships than Joni Mitchell, whose well-publicized liaisons with David Crosby, Graham Nash, Jackson Browne, and James Taylor would earn her the moniker "Old Lady of the Year" from *Rolling Stone*, along with a diagram of Mitchell's trail of broken hearts. Unbeknownst to the public, Nyro had only slightly less luck than Mitchell in scoring handsome boyfriends from rock's ranks.

Her most serious rock and roll man was Jim Fielder, the lanky, mustached, well-respected bass player for jazz-rock band Blood, Sweat and Tears, which also recorded for Columbia Records. Though born in Texas (he was just fourteen days older than Nyro), Fielder attended high school in Anaheim, California, where his best friend and garage-band mate was Tim Buckley, another influential singer-songwriter who, like Nyro, melded jazz influences into his work. Over the course of Fielder's career, the formally trained musician has recorded not only with Buckley and

Blood, Sweat and Tears but also with such disparate artists as Frank Zappa, Buffalo Springfield, Al Kooper, and Neil Sedaka.

Nyro may have first met Fielder, or at least cemented their budding connection, at a surprising "tryout" she had with Blood, Sweat and Tears. "I thought *Eli and the Thirteenth Confession* was fantastic—one of the best pop records I'd ever heard," says the band's drummer Bobby Columby. "Somehow I got to meet Laura, and when we were looking for a lead singer after [original member] Al Kooper got fired, she was our first choice. She loved the idea. We even had a rehearsal together, at the Café à Go Go. We played 'Eli's Comin' ' and maybe one other song, and it was fantastic. I remember some workmen coming in carrying wood over their heads, and they just stood there with all this wood and listened to the whole song. Her songwriting fit exactly into what we did. I thought this was what we needed, and it would work because she was on the same label."

Sander thinks it was never more than a lark for Nyro. "No one took it too seriously that she would sing lead for Blood, Sweat and Tears, but she thought at least it would be fun to hang out and sing with them," she says. In any case, Geffen nixed the collaboration. "Laura thought it was an exciting idea, because she always wanted horns," says Geffen. "I did not think it was a good idea."

"I was shocked," says Columby, "because David Geffen had made me believe he thought it was a great idea. But according to Laura, Geffen told her it was pointless—that we were never going to make it and she was going to be an enormous star, so why be a part of our band? At that point, we hadn't had hits yet."

Even if Geffen was right about Nyro's potential involvement with the band—it would have taken her in a direction that would hardly have showcased the quieter, more mysterious elements of her appeal—he was rarely so wrong about a band's potential. After David Clayton-Thomas was installed as the lead vocalist, Blood, Sweat and Tears' next album was a huge success. And Nyro remained a fan of the band, insisting one time that Sander come with her to see them rehearse. When the band kicked into full gear and Clayton-Thomas cut loose with his bluesy wail, "Laura put her hands to her head and screamed," Sander wrote in *Hit Parader*. "Just screamed and screamed. They couldn't hear her, the music was too loud. But there was this wild expression in her eyes and she was screaming for joy."

Nyro maintained a comfortable relationship with Fielder for perhaps a year. "The world may have been 45 rpm, but they were decidedly 33," says Columby. "We used to joke about how long it must have taken them to get out of bed in the morning—open their eyes, smoke a joint, have some tuna fish, and lay there for the rest of the day. Jimmy didn't have Laura's genius, but he had her temperament. He was really laid-back, almost a cowboy style."

"He was a real gentleman," remembers Sander. "He was a sweet, gentle soul, bright and quiet. An aw-shucks kind of guy. Have you ever known a guy who was one of the girls? That was Jimmy. He just could fit in, he was affable."

When Geffen took acid for the first time, at Nyro's apartment, he got to spend an extended time with Fielder, who was there along with Nyro and Sander. "Jim Fielder didn't talk during the entire acid trip," Geffen recalls. "He just played bass. I said to Laura, 'I wish I understood bass.' "

"They appeared to be happy and intensely in love with one another," says Donald Boudreau of Nyro's relationship with Fielder. (A high-school-aged fan who had gotten to know Nyro, Boudreau was hired by her to walk Beautybelle while Nyro was in the studio.) He particularly remembers a hot summer afternoon during which Fielder barbecued hamburgers on a hibachi grill on Nyro's terrace. "They both found it difficult to keep their hands off one another," he says.

In the songbook Nyro would publish in 1971, she included a sexy, uncaptioned photo by Stephen Paley in which she stands looking out from that terrace while a cowboy-booted man, his face obscured, hugs her fishnet-stockinged legs. The man is Fielder, as is the figure Nyro is kissing in one of her own paintings on the facing page—a painting Boudreau saw displayed in Nyro's apartment at the time. Nyro did not paint the work from imagination, however: She copied another Paley photo taken at the same terrace session.

■ ■ ■

Nyro began to record her second album for Columbia at the beginning of October 1968. That's what she told William Kloman when he interviewed her at her apartment for The New York Times, during which she served him an oddball feast of cheese, artichoke hearts, tuna fish, Diet Pepsi, Sara Lee blueberry cheesecake, and chocolate ice cream cones. She had already chosen a name for the album—New York Tenda-berry—and she pictured the cover as a stylized drawing of the Manhattan skyline at night, with fake diamonds shining from the windows of buildings. Inside she wanted a photo of herself surrounded by ducks.

She elaborated on the latter concept for Los Angeles critic Pete Johnson, imagining herself kissing a duck, with baby ducklings at her feet. Like Kloman, Johnson couldn't resist describing the setting and Nyro's culinary spread during their interview: She had festooned a room at a Hollywood motel where Blood, Sweat and Tears was staying with bunches of purple flowers and burning incense, and set out pinkish ice cream, green-tinted pear halves, and, of course, tuna. Nyro told Johnson that she planned to assemble her own band to tour with, and that she expected her new album to be different and stranger than anything she had done so far.

The strangeness of the album wouldn't be out of tune with the times. The Beatles had released their more despairing *White Album* in late November, and Nyro, too, was obviously hooked into a universal angst sparked by the Vietnam War. If *Eli* was Nyro's *Sgt. Pepper's*—a sophisticated transcendence of pop stereotypes—then *New York Tendaberry* would be her *White Album*. More accurately, considering its darkness, it would be her black album. Nyro would later say that the music for *Tendaberry* came out of "my very wild time of exploration," and that a lot of it related to abstract art. She was eager to be experimental—"with everything," she added knowingly.

Charlie Calello was initially expected to produce the album, but felt that Nyro's new songs needed work and that she was no longer willing to listen to his advice. Besides, he was concerned about how much he would earn for what promised to be a long and arduous task, since he hadn't earned any royalties as a producer on *Eli*. In those days, he says, "it was really not identified what production fees were to be, what arranging fees were going to be." Calello did cut basic tracks for two or three new songs, then walked off the project, deciding it was less stressful and more lucrative to work solely as an arranger.

So Geffen, who had left William Morris to help start a rock booking division at the Ashley Famous Agency, went looking for someone to coproduce the album with Nyro. One of the candidates was Joe Wissert, then in his early twenties, who had been cutting hits for the Lovin' Spoonful and the Turtles ("Happy Together") and would later produce Boz Scaggs's commercial breakthrough, *Silk Degrees*. He had struck up a friendship with Nyro soon after her single "Wedding Bell Blues" came out, and had wanted the Turtles to cut "Stoned Soul Picnic," but they preferred to do only original compositions. Before recording *Tendaberry*,

Nyro invited Wissert to hear her play the album's songs at Geffen's Central Park South sublet.

"I remember so well. It was a winter afternoon and it had just started to snow," says Wissert. "I could look across Central Park and see the snow coming through the barren trees, and it just got heavier and heavier. It was such a magical time, and to hear Laura sit down and play the songs in that environment—it was awesome, just awesome."

Much as he admired her work, though, he had grown attached to the looser studio atmosphere in Los Angeles, where he lived then. An album titled New York Tendaberry, which sounded perfect on a snowy Manhattan afternoon, couldn't be set to vinyl in a land of endless sunshine. So Nyro eventually settled on another friend of Geffen's to produce: the esteemed recording engineer Roy Halee, who had worked with Blood, Sweat and Tears, Simon and Garfunkel, and Bob Dylan. "I think she loved Simon and Garfunkel and she heard that this guy Halee did Dylan's first album, and she wanted to try me out," says Halee. "And certainly David did."

Halee hadn't seen Nyro perform for an audience, but after she played for him he decided that her vocals and piano should be captured live, with everything else overdubbed. "The songs were so intense that I thought we should at least try to get the best possible vocal-piano combination we could," he says. "The only problem with that was that her time was not great, so it was hard for musicians to follow along, particularly rhythm sections. It was rolling the dice to record it that way, and if the album has flaws, it's in that area. But I just wanted to take the chance of getting her and the piano the way it really was."

Halee didn't bargain on how long the project would take. Nyro's perfectionism, backed by Columbia's indulgence, caused the recording of piano and vocals to stretch on for months. "We'd spend three or four nights on one song," says Halee, who was working on Simon and Garfunkel's Bridge Over Troubled Water album at the same time. "I don't think there was a budget, because we just went in and went in and went in and kept doing it."

Nyro multitracked her own voice even more elaborately than she had on Eli, aided by recording technology that had again leaped forward, from eight tracks to sixteen. But the opportunity for recording more tracks increased the studio time Nyro felt she needed to get things right. "Frankly, to give her carte blanche was a mistake, in my opinion," says Halee. "Laura and I got along well in the beginning, but as the project progressed we didn't get along too well because I thought it was taking too long. I wanted to get on with it."

So did Columbia. "She was under enormous pressure," says Nyro's road manager Lee Housekeeper. The record company wasn't that far removed from the days when Mitch Miller was head of A&R and entire albums would be recorded in a day or two—with full orchestras. "Laura was a good target in those days because she dared to be creative," says Housekeeper. "And on top of that, she was a woman. Everyone called her overindulgent, even though Simon and Garfunkel were also taking that kind of time. But they were selling zillions of records, and they were men."

Indeed, Nyro's plodding craftsmanship wasn't out of step with that of her most sophisticated male peers, including the Beatles, who were tackling projects that were long both in nature and time of execution. The Beatles set the standard for such experimentation with *Sgt. Pepper's Lonely Hearts Club Band*—considered by many to be the first concept album—which reportedly took hundreds of studio hours to produce.

Even if Nyro couldn't sell records at the same pace as Columbia's other premier artists, she gave the label credibility and clout. "Clive was able to sign quite a few artists based on 'Look what kind of care and feeding I give to artists like Laura,' " says Housekeeper. "David had fermented this in Clive. He said, 'Look, you may not be selling a lot of records [with Laura], but you're going to be able to sign big artists.' " Geffen used the proximity-to-Nyro strategy himself to sign Crosby, Stills and Nash, says Housekeeper. When he brought the three to his apartment, they were taken aback by the old-fashioned record collection on the shelves—which belonged not to Geffen but to the woman he had sublet from, well-known artists' manager Helen Noga, whose clients included Johnny Mathis. To recover an edge, Geffen asked Housekeeper to bring Nyro over as a sort of live exhibit of his *real* taste.

"She was a very well respected *artist*," says Housekeeper, "and David Crosby envisioned himself in the same way. She was very important to David Geffen's ability to get the respect of other artists."

Geffen used every weapon in the arsenal when it came to gaining position for himself and Nyro. At one point during the lengthy recording of her new album, Clive Davis tried to postpone her sessions until Simon and Garfunkel finished their album. In response, Geffen asked Housekeeper to lie to Davis, telling him that Nyro had complained about the postponement to *Life* magazine, which was then doing a story on her. It worked. "Within fifteen minutes, Clive called back and said, 'Well, we found some more time,' " says Housekeeper.

Nyro may have racked up enormous charges against royalties while making New York Tendaberry, but there was a method to her supposed madness. "As much time as Laura spent in the recording studio she spent in preparation," says Housekeeper. "She had extensive notebooks and knew exactly what she was going to do. But that didn't mean that if she didn't like what she heard she wouldn't go try something else, so there *was* experimentation done in the studio."

"People were always frightened to let me try things," Nyro told Life. "With this album, at the beginning nobody knew what I was doing. Nobody. I knew what I was doing. . . . To have something really good, you have to pay dues for it." And she single-mindedly paid those dues. "When I record, that's all I do," she said to another reporter. "I'm not a human being, I'm not a woman. I don't have to take Benzedrine or anything, I'm on natural 'speed.' I can't sleep at night. I don't like to talk to anyone."

She did agree to talk with Life's Maggie Paley, who was a friend of, but no relation to, photographer Stephen Paley. (It was Stephen who had urged Maggie to do the story so that he could take the photographs, most stunningly a shot of a pensive Nyro seated on a fire escape in a sleeveless black flowered gown with a plunging scoop neckline.) Maggie Paley found that the key to Nyro's trust was to get involved in her everyday life—shopping, talking about men, even smoking marijuana with her. "It's like we were friends, which was very nice," she says. "Most people one does stories on don't *want* to make it personal that way, but it seemed to be the only way Laura could do it—to kind of bring you into her world."

Especially amusing in Life was Paley's account of Nyro's visit to a Los Angeles clothing boutique, where she spent four hours putting together clothing combinations for herself, and then to a shoe store where the singer bought sleazy silver platform shoes to go with her new dresses. When Nyro tried adding a variety of rhinestone clips to the shoes, the saleslady remarked tartly, "She can wear them when she goes into her dance."

"Laura sort of behaved toward herself the way I behaved with my dolls as a child," says Maggie Paley. "She dressed herself up."

■ ■ ■

Nyro finally finished her vocal tracks for New York Tendaberry in the summer of 1969, but then needed someone to realize her ideas for orchestrating the album. Her first choice had been Gil Evans, the distinguished arranger for Miles Davis, but Evans never replied to her letter.

Halee suggested L.A.-based Jimmie Haskell, who had arranged Simon and Garfunkel's "Old Friends" on the Halee-engineered Bookends album and had orchestrated Bobbie Gentry's recent storytelling hit, "Ode to Billie Joe." So Haskell was flown to New York for an interview with Nyro in an undisturbed corner of the reception area in Columbia's huge Studio B, on the second floor of the company's 49 E. 52nd Street complex. In his early thirties at the time (as was Halee), the bearded, soft-spoken arranger brought a cassette recorder to capture Nyro's even quieter voice on tape. Their meeting remained whispery, very polite, until Nyro caught Haskell looking down at his recorder to see if it was still taping. "Are you listening to me?" she said sharply. It was the only time he would ever hear her raise her voice.

The meeting proved convincing. Nyro appreciated how Haskell had created a syrupy delta sound for Bobbie Gentry. "You can almost hear the crickets and bugs," she told Down Beat. "I'm not going to ask him to give me a Gil Evans sound or anything like that," she went on. "All I want him to give me is this tendaberry"—the word she had invented to describe the juicy, tender core under New York City's rough concrete skin (which was also, perhaps, her pronunciation of "tender berry").

Haskell would give Nyro anything she wanted. At her suggestion, he went so far as to wear a silly propeller beanie while conducting recording sessions. Nyro may have just gotten a laugh out of it, but Haskell found it practical. "With the beanie on, I never seemed angry," he says. Years later, when he spoke to Nyro on the phone for the first time since he'd finished the album, she couldn't immediately place his name. Then she remembered: "Oh, the arranger with the beanie!"

Haskell quickly understood Nyro's unique vernacular, especially how she'd describe instrumentation without ever mentioning an instrument. "She preferred talking in colors, rather than saying, 'Give me some brass here,' " says Haskell. Instead, she might ask for "blue."

"So maybe a blue instrument would be a viola?" he'd ask her. "Yeah, that would work," she'd say. "A brown instrument would be something like a bass clarinet?" "Yeah, that would work." "A loud brown instrument would be a trombone? And white would be brass?" She might also ask string players to give her a grating sound, like pebbles, over sand, or ask horn players to sound "like Indians on the warpath." As Nyro told Associated Press writer Mary Campbell about one of her new songs, "I would describe the instrumentation on 'You Don't Love Me When I Cry' as a warm pale blue with a few whitecaps on it. When you hear it, you'll see."

Nyro obviously "saw" music in colors, shapes, and textures—perhaps having a mild form of synesthesia, a sensation deriving from a sense other than the one being stimulated. Joni Mitchell has said that both she and Nyro could speak of music only in such terms. "It used to be embarrassing to myself and to Laura Nyro in particular to play with technical musicians in the early days," explained Mitchell. "It would embarrass us that we were lacking in a knowledgeable way, and that we would give instructions to players in terms of metaphors—either color descriptions or painterly descriptions."

But if Nyro was technically naive, her creativity still impressed the most astute musicians. In a mostly true 1989 short story, "Nyro Fiddles," about his visit to a *New York Tendaberry* recording session, author F. Paul Wilson wrote: "I go over and hang with one of the trumpets I know who with a couple more years could be old enough to be Laura's father and he tells me it's anarchy, pure and simply anarchy, but wait and see . . . they'll start to play and she'll point things out and say do this and try that and before you know it everything falls into place and it's beautiful, man. The girl's crazy, but she sure as hell knows her music."

Like Calello, Haskell marveled at Nyro's unusual chords. "She came up with these chord progressions that were really wonderful," he says. "She played piano fantastically—great arranger's piano. All the basic chords and notes that anyone would ever need, but no frills. Her songs and her singing came first, and the piano playing was there so she would have a basis to play her songs."

In consultation with Nyro, Haskell first wrote arrangements for the rhythm section, led by drummer Gary Chester (who also hired the other musicians for the sessions). Chester, ironically, introduced himself to Haskell as "the Hal Blaine of the East Coast," in deference to the famed L.A. session drummer with whom Haskell often worked—and who had led Nyro's Monterey backup band.

To complete the instrumentation, Haskell met nightly with Nyro at her 79th Street apartment, a setting he remembers as dark and full of tapestry and overstuffed furniture. There she would serve him cheese and crackers as they worked for a couple more hours, after which he'd return to his midtown hotel to spend the wee hours writing charts.

Nyro herself traveled regally to the recording sessions in a horse-drawn carriage through Central Park. "She thought it would put her in a really nice mood when she came to the studio," says Lee House-keeper. "Columbia figured it was cheaper than a limousine, so why not?"

Nyro also set a dramatic scene inside the studio. "She'd sashay in in a magnificent gown," recalls Halee. "She would set up candles and lamps in the studio, and then every night she would have a beautiful dinner catered, with tablecloths and wine. This was, like, *every* night."

Again, the recording sessions included a visit from an extraordinary jazz artist—this time Nyro's hero Miles Davis. He was asked to play a trumpet solo on one track, but after listening to it demurred. "I can't play on this," he said. "You did it already." Nyro wasn't hurt by the refusal. "She was very excited that he had been there," says Maggie Paley. "There was not any kind of feeling of rejection. She felt he had given her high praise." Stephen Paley's camera captured Davis at the session, wearing huge sunglasses as he sat on a stool beside Nyro and she looked at him shyly and adoringly.

Other famous musicians dropped by the studio, usually because they were Nyro's acquaintances or fellow Columbia artists, such as Simon and Garfunkel. Haskell remembers a studio scene that was half séance, half circus, as Nyro sat in the engineering booth with the lights out, surrounded by candles and friends. Halee and Haskell usually accepted her studio whims as part and parcel of any artist's creative flow. "If it captured the performance and made her at ease, who cares," says Halee. On one occasion, though, Haskell politely shooed Nyro's visitors from the studio, having noticed that they were spoiling her concentration just when a large, expensive brass section was scheduled to play.

But on another night, a friend of Nyro's proved to be a session saver. Nyro had dramatically rearranged the song "Save the Country" from the single version, slowing it down and making it less a "sock it to the people" production. The new arrangement included an accelerating brass ending that required the trumpeters to hit some very high notes. As Haskell had predicted, the players' lips weakened during the long, late-night rehearsal, and they began blowing sour notes (known as clams). With the session approaching disaster, Nyro calmly announced, "We have a trumpet player in the booth who can do it."

Haskell, not surprisingly, was skeptical—but the player turned out to be Lew Soloff, the outstanding trumpeter for Blood, Sweat and Tears. "She had a bunch of really good trumpet players there, great trumpet players who were friends of mine, but it was near the end of a long date," says Soloff. "I don't remember if the part was hard or not, but I was fresh. I remember the trumpet players saying, 'Come on, man, we're tired, help us out!' And I probably had my horn with me—I always had my horn with me, basically—and if I didn't, I only lived three blocks away from the studio."

Soloff aced the difficult high notes in one clam-free take, helping to make the song's ending a miracle of runaway intensity as the horns strain to keep up with Nyro's speeding piano. "Laura was a very natural musician," says Haskell. "She must have envisioned the entire arrangement in her head—the brass taking over, the exciting feeling—while she was playing it on the piano. She must have been feeling something of that white color in her head."

By the time *Tendaberry* was finally completed, it had cost Columbia about $50,000 to $60,000, according to Housekeeper's estimate—double the ordinary cost for albums in those days. But David Geffen tried to save a few dollars on, of all things, Jimmie Haskell's salary. After his ten twenty-hour days in New York with Nyro, Haskell had sent a bill for money he was owed. Geffen, however, felt that Haskell had already been paid enough on his contract as an orchestrator. "I'll sue!" said an astonished Haskell. "You can't sue me," Geffen responded. "You've got to sue the artist—that's Laura. Ha-ha."

Haskell immediately called a well-known recording industry lawyer, who advised a conservative resolution: Under union rules, the arranger could ask for additional compensation for having worked out of town and having worked without eight hours of sleep and without meal breaks. Coincidentally, the extra fee turned out to be exactly the amount Haskell felt he deserved.

■ ■ ■

Artistically, *New York Tendaberry* proved well worth the expense and the long wait. Roy Halee, even though he had grown impatient with Nyro, has only the highest praise for her accomplishment. "I'm prejudiced, but I think it's one of the greatest albums ever made in pop music," he says. "She was an original, and the music reeked of George

Gershwin. It was like American classical pop, it really was. It's more *her* than the other albums. The other albums were Charlie Calello or people like that, but this album was really her, you know what I'm saying?"

"We just captured the sound," adds Haskell. "The right sound." That sound was a remarkable marriage of elements: Nyro's voice at the peak of its range and power; her fiery piano playing (she sported a callus on her left pinkie from pounding out bass notes); Haskell's taut orchestrations and wisps of instrumental color (Nyro *did* compose in colors); a dusky, haunting ambience; and an amazing amount of soundlessness. Halee may have engineered "The Sounds of Silence" for Simon and Garfunkel, but he brilliantly captured that paradoxical sound on Nyro's record.

As she had on *Eli and the Thirteenth Confession*, Nyro once again told enigmatic tales of pain and love, but as writer Jim Bessman points out, this album was "more mature in tone, minus the girlish giddiness and pure pop" of *Eli*. *New York Tendaberry* romanticizes the city more than a man. As one fan wrote, "When I listen to it, I feel transported through the city, momentarily dropping down on characters and the passion plays that occur every day, finishing with the haunting love song [the title tune] to one of the great cities of all time." Nyro's work brings to mind George Gershwin's quote about his own New York–inspired music: "I tried to express our manner of living, the tempo of our modern life with its speed and chaos and vitality."

Nyro opens *Tendaberry* with the melancholy line "Two mainstream die / you don't love me when I cry," quite an about-face from the rapturous opening of "Luckie" on *Eli*. Her journey in *Tendaberry* is fraught with even more emotional peril than her passage from a child to a woman in *Eli*: Here she faces New York in all its suffering and pleasure, her vision no longer softened by youth's innocence.

She maps out the city in songs such as "Gibsom Street" and "Mercy on Broadway," and stares down lovers in the upbeat "Captain St. Lucifer" and "Tom Cat Goodbye," echoing the start-and-stop pacing and elusive characterizations of *Eli* but with edgier undertones. In comparison, her previous battles with the devil now seem almost cheery. At the end of "Tom Cat," for example, she whispers and screams, "Gonna find him / gonna kill my lover man."

Nyro also interweaves *Tendaberry* with jazzy tone poems that are variously tender and embittered: "You Don't Love Me When I Cry,"

"The Man Who Sends Me Home," "Sweet Lovin' Baby," and the title song. Any of them would have sounded perfect sung in a smoky Manhattan boîte.

Only the optimistic "Time and Love" and the clarion "Save the Country" could be classified as songs with traditional pop structures on *Tendaberry*. Several critics at the time praised those two—which would be covered by a number of artists—above the others, perhaps comforted by their gospel chordings, sing-along choruses, and Nyro's familiar syncopated piano rhythm. But still, Nyro's versions maintain a jaggedness that the covers couldn't or wouldn't emulate. "Save the Country," as one listener put it, would sound like "jingoistic pabulum" when later done by the Fifth Dimension, but out of Laura's mouth it held "a wonderful dark irony that dissolves into a kind of manic ecstasy."

Ask college women of the time what their favorite cut on the album was, and the dorm choice would probably have been the most provocative, erotic song on the album, "Captain for Dark Mornings." The singer is "soft and silly" Lillianaloo, a woman who is "sold by sailors / worn by tailors / soldiers wound me." The song ventures over ever-shifting vocal moods as the singer submissively offers to "lay me down and die / for my captain"—the captain being Nyro's recurrent image in *Tendaberry* for her lover. The ending, as Nyro's voice trails off repeating, "captain say yes," drawing out the final "s" in a long whisper, is as sexually suggestive as Molly Bloom's final "yes I said yes I will Yes," in James Joyce's novel *Ulysses*.

"She was always looking for her captain," says Bones Howe. "The captain was the man of her dreams. It's all there in her lyrics. Like all good writers, it's been changed and disguised to some degree. But she saw him in a lot of different guys. She was a woman who had great longings for a perfect love."

If the notion of a captain could be easily sussed out, most of Nyro's other lyrics on *Tendaberry* remained more opaque than ever. In "Captain St. Lucifer," for example (a song Barbara Greenstein remembers her writing while vacationing on the island of St. Thomas), Nyro sings of "buckles off shingles / and a cockleshell on Norway basin"—whatever *that* meant. "She was so deliberately ambiguous back then," says Patricia Spence Rudden, an English professor at New York City College of Technology who has studied Nyro's compositions since the outset of Nyro's career. "That's what made it so fascinating. Young songwriters write cryptic lyrics because they're young and *need* to be misunderstood."

Like any writer, Nyro would pick up lyrical ideas wherever they could be found. Donald Boudreau recalls how she even included something *he* had written—the title of his poem "Grace and the Preacher." It had referred to a girl he was attracted to (Grace) and her very religious boyfriend (the Preacher), but with his permission Nyro transplanted the phrase into "Sweet Lovin' Baby" with a wholly different and mysterious resonance: "Grace / and the Preacher / blown fleets of sweet-eyed dreams / tonight." One can only imagine what personal meaning she had attached to the phrase, or whether she just enjoyed the harmonious juxtaposition and multiple connotations of the words.

Nyro was almost certainly influenced by the abundance of other poetry that she had read. Could, for example, her troubling tale of "Gibsom Street"—about a woman going to get an abortion, some have suggested—have been partly inspired, even if subconsciously, by Christina Rossetti's "Goblin Market"? In that long Victorian-era poem, a girl named Laura is seduced by fruit sold by evil "goblin men" near the river. She's then rescued by her sister, who cries to her, "Did you miss me? / Come and kiss me / never mind my bruises / Hug me, kiss me, suck my juices." In comparison, Nyro wrote of going to "Gibsom cross the river," where "the devil is hungry / the devil is sweet." At the song's end, a man gives the singer a strawberry, and she "sucked its juices never knowing / that I would sleep that night on Gibsom Street." For Nyro, overheated Victorian passion could just as easily be experienced on a New York side street as in the rural English countryside.

■ ■ ■

New York Tendaberry was released on September 24, 1969, its packaging even more elaborate—though less aromatic—than that of *Eli and the Thirteenth Confession*. On the cover, in a photo taken by another Nyro lensman favored, David Gahr, Nyro is shown head back, eyes closed, her thick, dark hair blowing in the wind. Inside, a black-and-blue-colored booklet contains the lyrics, on the back of which is Stephen Paley's twilight-in-the-rain photo of Nyro's 79th Street terrace. An earlier design of the cover had featured a Paley photo of Nyro and Beautybelle together on the terrace, and Columbia had manufactured several thousand copies before Nyro changed her mind. The rejected covers should have then been destroyed but weren't, so when Columbia ran out of the first printing, some copies with the Paley cover were accidentally sold (and remain a collector's item).

Unlike the slow response to *Eli*, critical response to *New York Tendaberry* was immediate and effusive. Its release was "an event of major importance in contemporary music," wrote the UCLA *Daily Bruin* music critic Jim Bickhart.

In Rex Reed's words, Nyro was "the singer who has done the most to raise pop music to the level of serious art." "*New York Tendaberry* is her best album yet," crowed Pete Johnson in *Coast FM and Fine Arts*. "She has carefully eliminated every element extraneous to her art. . . . The time devoted to this album has resulted in absolutely incredible performances of a number of songs whose irregular structures would pose insurmountable to nearly any other vocalist."

"At 22, Miss Nyro has an incredible potential," added Robert Hilburn in the *Los Angeles Times*. "She seems to be racing more against the giants of the past (including Gershwin) than the rivals of the present." Hilburn also pointed out that Nyro's urban concerns were at odds with a prevailing American trend toward more rural themes, as in Dylan's *Nashville Skyline* and the popular Delta-infused work of Creedence Clearwater Revival. Critic John Gabree, author of *The Age of Rock*, proclaimed that her lyrical battles pitting God versus the Devil and religiosity versus sensuality coincided with the "moral fervor" of her generation. "Raw convulsive music of shifting meters, mated with ambiguous, searing lyrics, it is contemporary-urban, personal and grand," he wrote.

Some critics were more circumspect, tempering their praise with a disdain for the cultlike devotion Nyro had begun to evoke. *New York Times* reviewer Don Heckman suggested that the obscurity of her work nourished such a response: "The elusive poetess, the real-life projection of man's hidden fantasies, has been with us a long time, from Sappho to Edith Piaf," he wrote. "Laura Nyro is the latest." Odd that he spoke of man's fantasies and yet mentioned the woman-oriented Sappho, a perhaps unconscious choice of role model considering how female-heavy Nyro's audience was.

New York Tendaberry sold faster than any Nyro album ever would, spending seventeen weeks on *Billboard*'s album chart and peaking at No. 32. As a source of cover songs, however, only "Save the Country" and "Time and Love" would prove particularly popular, and neither became a Top 10 hit. The rest of the material on *New York Tendaberry* must have seemed a puzzlement to mainstream pop artists. Until the punk and metal eras, who would want to cover "Gibsom Street," with its implications of illicit sex and a street so vile (yet seductive) that "they hang the alley cats"?

There were few hooks or catchy choruses among the gems that made up *New York Tendaberry*. Laura Nyro was moving deeper and deeper into her own world of art and emotion, where she would be the only one brave enough to sing her songs.

7

TOP TEN

Nearly two years after the disappointment of the Monterey Pop Festival, Nyro finally began a tentative return to performing. Geffen had kept her away from the stage because he wanted to wait until an audience was ready to receive her. He also had to convince her to perform alone rather than with a band.

"She wanted to have horns—she was very ambitious about the kind of band she wanted to put together—but we couldn't afford it," he says. "I talked her into doing it just at the piano."

The two had flown down to St. Thomas in the Virgin Islands, a place Nyro also went to several times with Barbara Greenstein, and rented a piano for Nyro's hotel room. There she worked out the type of presentation that would mark her work for the next several years. She would perform at a grand piano turned sideways to the stage apron: a style perfectly suited to her quiet but charismatic demeanor and her dramatic songs. In concert, Geffen says, "She was spellbinding."

Despite being in the midst of recording *New York Tendaberry*, Nyro hit the road on weekends in March and April of 1969. Her first gigs were at eastern universities, including Tufts in Medford, Massachusetts; Bucknell in Lewisburg, Pennsylvania; Wesleyan in Middletown, Connecticut; and Princeton in New Jersey. On one of the bills was R&B sax great King Curtis, and at Princeton it was the budding superstar James Taylor.

Lee Housekeeper served as both road manager and lighting man. " 'Steel blue' was one of the cues, right over her head on certain songs, and she used magenta a lot," he remembers. Their no-frills tour consisted of Laura, Housekeeper, and an adjustable piano stool (a regular bench wasn't high enough for her taste). Nyro and Housekeeper would either drive to the shows or take a flight from Newark Airport, where they sometimes encountered other weekend-touring artists such as Harry Nilsson, Richie Havens, and Taj Mahal. Barbara Greenstein remembers coming along on some dates as well. For certain gigs, Housekeeper hired a private plane, and he recalls Nyro enjoying the pilots' company. "One night in her room, she had the pilot and copilot and myself—all real dedicated nonsingers—singing these rounds, these parts she was working on," says Housekeeper. "We were awful."

Housekeeper reserved rooms for Nyro at local inns that had four-poster canopy beds, fresh flowers, and fireplaces. "Laura did not like a Holiday Inn thing," he says. The lodgings were a restful oasis after a week of six- or seven-hour recording sessions that required "a lot of pre-work, a lot of after-work, and a lot of emotion," says Housekeeper. "There was one show when I didn't think she could get out of the car and go onstage, but she did. She never missed a concert."

At the time, college students on the East Coast were financing outside entertainment with student activity fees, and their naivete in dealing with agents led to generous rates for artists. "You could work one college, then go fifty miles to another, and you would do well," says Housekeeper. Colleges were also fertile ground for "breaking" an unusual, highly personal performer such as Nyro. Students would talk up and pass around an album such as Eli and spread Nyro's music by endless spins on portable dorm stereos.

Nyro also benefited in some measure from a radical change in radio formats and listening habits. Top 40 AM radio—with its tinny sound, short playlists, two-and-a-half-minute songs, and loud deejays—was being overtaken by "underground" stereo FM radio. Although FM radio had been in existence for thirty years, and had been available in stereo for a decade, it had long been considered a format strictly for classical music buffs. In the mid-sixties, however, the FCC ruled that companies owning AM-FM combination stations had to program each one separately. Since FM wasn't yet a money-making endeavor, companies could afford to experiment with programming their FM stations, and one of the first experiments was progressive rock. The word underground was applied to the free-form style of radio, to the music itself—grass-roots in origin, askew of the mainstream, chance-taking, rule-breaking—as well as to the type of local publications (the underground press) that initially supported the music.

The years 1967 to 1969, the period during which Nyro released her first three albums, marked the height of underground radio, which provided a soundtrack for the hippie counterculture and its antiwar, pro-pot, free-love messages. Considered to have started in the spring of 1967 under the auspices of KMPX-FM disc jockey Tom Donahue in San Francisco, underground FM allowed deejays to talk more slowly, play lengthier songs, and challenge listeners with more sophisticated album cuts rather than just singles. By the end of 1968 there were more than sixty commercial underground, or "flower power," stations in the country.

Then, just as new wave rock in the 1980s and alternative or grunge rock in the 1990s quickly became co-opted by major record companies, "underground" became a corporate mantra as well. As Columbia Records advertised itself in 1969, "Columbia Is Underground *and* Deep," listing an eclectic roster of artists that included Nyro. Even Clive Davis admitted that another Columbia ad line from the period—"The Man Can't Bust Our Music"—probably deserved the ridicule heaped upon it by the rock press.

Yet as early as February 1969, *Teen Set* writer Mike Gershman was complaining that underground radio "blew a golden opportunity." At first, he said, it had provided a welcome relief from bubblegum artists like the Monkees by giving exposure to hard-rock and blues bands. "But what of the singer-songwriters?" he asked. "Have you heard Laura Nyro, Nilsson, David Ackles, Gordon Alexander, Gordon Lightfoot, Randy Newman, or a dozen others on your underground station? Not very often. . . . Underground radio has become Top 40 for hippies. New artists are rarely exposed anymore. All I hear is Stones, Doors, Beatles, Airplane, and other stuff I can get on the AM dial, plus a smattering of blues artists."

■ ■ ■

The audiences for Nyro's first college shows were respectful, though somewhat unfamiliar with her work, says Housekeeper, but as the tour continued the enthusiasm grew. "I remember how amazed she was when people started responding to her," he says. "She loved it when she got that response."

Nyro's first hometown concert was a little-publicized show on March 22, 1969, at Memorial Hall of Pratt Institute, the art and design college in Brooklyn. Her dressing area was the girls' locker room off the gymnasium. Eager fans hardly noticed the less than classy surroundings, presenting her with flowers and roaring with delight when she came onstage in a red velvet gown with a lace mantilla around her shoulders.

"She smiled silently, sipping a plum-colored liqueur from a tall glass," wrote journalist Rex Reed. "Then she slashed her long black mane across the stage light, threw her fingers at the keyboard with reckless passion, and gave us what we had been waiting for."

The East Coast college tour was just a warmup, though. After she finished recording *Tendaberry*, Laura Nyro's *real* introduction to pop music society would take place, once again, on the West Coast. This time it would be in Southern California, at the small nightclub that had become the ultimate showcase for singer-songwriters: the Troubadour in West Hollywood.

Established in 1957 by Doug Weston, the Troubadour provided an intimate setting for serious popular music. "You could hear people *breathe* at the Troubadour," says producer Joe Wissert. By the time Nyro appeared there, on Memorial Day weekend of 1969, the club had also taken on a unique role in the record industry: It bestowed on up-and-coming artists prestige and a commercial kick-start. Artists began to require Weston's imprimatur, so they would agree to his rather brutal contract, which mandated at least one return visit to the Troubadour and first rights to produce their next Los Angeles concert.

"It was basically the only game in town," explains Michael Ochs, brother of the late singer-songwriter Phil Ochs and founder of the renowned archive of music photos that bears his name. "In New York there were a number of clubs, but in L.A. the Troubadour was the only showcase of that magnitude at that time."

Ochs was doing West Coast publicity for Columbia Records when Nyro was booked at the Troubadour, and he helped start a buzz about her by papering the opening-night house with journalists and record executives. "I thought it would be great if Mo Ostin [head of Warner Bros. Records] or Jerry Moss [head of A&M Records] would talk to people and say, 'Oh, I saw this woman Laura Nyro, and thought she was incredible.' Then the word would *really* get around." A similar buzz-generating strategy would be used a few years later to launch Elton John from his first American appearance at the Troubadour.

Ochs nearly got fired for overspending his $500 publicity budget by tenfold, but his scheme worked: Nyro's opening came off as a major event. She got rave reviews in the *Los Angeles Times* and *Los Angeles Herald Examiner* and made the cover of *Coast FM & Fine Arts* magazine. Wrote Pete Johnson in the *Times*, "Her writing, her singing, and her piano playing radiate originality and make her an indescribably powerful performer."

It would be another six months before Nyro made a similarly hyped East Coast debut. In the meantime, she was briefly listed on the lineup for the Woodstock Festival in Bethel, New York, held that August 16 and 17 not far from where she had spent her teen summers. It's not surprising that she didn't go to the festival, though; the Monterey Pop Festival certainly remained too fresh in her memory.

Instead, Nyro waited until Thanksgiving weekend for her formal presentation to New York, and it would be at the classiest possible venue: Carnegie Hall. Both her performances on Saturday night, November 29, sold out in a day, and much of her family attended the first show. Grandpa Mirsky was one of the oldest members of the audience. "I will never forget him there," says Laura's aunt Kaye. "He stood up to applaud and was beaming from ear to ear." Laura, too, would remember hearing her grandfather yell out, "Bravissima, Lauriska!"

Nyro entered to a standing ovation, wearing a V-necked sleeveless white chiffon gown—an "Elizabeth Taylor dress," *Rolling Stone* writer Vince Aletti called it, further describing Nyro a bit unkindly as looking "like an Italian housewife-whore." (In fact, it was a Russian seamstress who made many of Nyro's fancy performance gowns.) Later in the show, Nyro slowly and sensuously draped a diaphanous black shawl over her shoulders, Aletti reported, making the simple gesture an event that heightened the drama of her singing.

She opened her hour-and-a-half set (for which Roy Halee did the sound) with "New York Tendaberry," then performed songs from all three of her albums. She also covered the 1961 Ben E. King classic, "Spanish Harlem," which Aletti thought garnered the biggest response of the evening. Nyro's voice, *Billboard*'s Nancy Erlich decided, was "gentle as a razor."

Throughout her career Nyro rarely spoke in concert, besides a few whispered thank-yous. She was basically shy, preferring soulful one-on-one interactions. But on that late November night, comfortably wrapped in the warmth of her home crowd, she was almost chatty as she introduced "Buy and Sell" from *More Than a New Discovery*. "Where I live," she told the audience in a rehearsed but spontaneous-sounding rap, "the houses are tied together by clotheslines, and the women hang up things like little socks and their husband's muscle shirts. You know, in this town, when you open your windows it doesn't smell like flowers . . . [long pause], it smells like . . . [another long pause] . . . *pizza.*"

The audience listened with "breathless attention" both to her words and to her set, then insisted on three encores, although, as Aletti put it, *every* song after the first seemed like an encore. Critics weren't as enamored as her fans, though. *The New York Times*'s John S. Wilson complained that Nyro's gospel-style shouting and the "rugged support" of her piano accompaniment made it hard for him to distinguish her words. Don Heckman in *The Village Voice* praised her "bloody good songs" but derided her vocal style and her worshipful following.

"I would get a great deal more pleasure from her performances if they were not so unremittingly intense," wrote Heckman. "Her voice becomes shrill and overbearing when it is continually kept in its upper register, her piano sounds dullingly impressionistic with its continued emphasis on open fourths and fifths, and occasional spurts of gospel-like rhythms aren't enough to compensate for long stretches of static, hanging sound."

None of those quibbles, he crabbily acknowledged, would deter the "Nyro freaks" who loved the singer for who she was as much as what she did. And nothing would deter a certain chorus of critics from continuing to make that sort of cranky assessment of Nyro's "shrillness" over the next few years of her career.

■ ■ ■

Nyro had indeed begun to develop an awed cadre of "freaks." Songwriter Julie Gold, who later wrote the Bette Midler hit "From a Distance," remembers seeing Nyro as a "mystical Madonna" from her teenage vantage point at the Troubadour. "She'd have no verbal interaction with the audience, except invariably someone would shout out, 'We love you, Laura!' and she would sensually whisper, "I love you, too,' " said Gold. "Otherwise, she'd sit at the piano and play her guts out, and all of humanity gathered into that circle between her hands and the piano keys."

Although only a year or two older than many in her audience, Nyro seemed to have emotional wisdom far beyond her years. She thus became a guidepost for soul-searching young women, especially high school and college students, and her songs became a soundtrack for their lives. "I felt like I found a soulmate, a voice for my own *tumel* [Yiddish for inner turmoil]," says New York psychoanalyst Ellen Steingart, who discovered Nyro's music at age fifteen. "It's a thrill you only have when you're a teenager. She made suffering seem like a beautiful thing—something regal."

Nyro had a "primordial sense of the whole range of female emotions, and a vision rich in mercy, wisdom and joy," wrote journalist Sheila Weller. As a romantic young post-collegiate woman, Weller, too, wanted desperately to be "earthy and wise and spiritual" and found that desire mirrored in Nyro's music.

"I wanted to quit school and follow her around," adds Brendan Okrent, a senior director of repertory at ASCAP, the songwriter's performing rights organization, who was then a student at Ohio State University. "Her music was the first racy, offbeat thing I ever heard. It was a life-altering experience."

"I think people knew she was being very truthful onstage, and that's a rare thing," says singer-songwriter Janis Ian. "Not confessional—just trying to hit a universal in a way that made sense to everyone."

While women made up a huge portion of her audience, Nyro's music spoke to men as well. "She mesmerized me," says music critic David Nathan, author of *The Soulful Divas*. "She was one of the only performers who could be alone at the piano and completely enrapture an entire audience."

"Laura Nyro was as much a part of my growing process as were college mixers, failed romances, a manic fear of being drafted, and English Romantic poetry," wrote *Newsday*'s Stephen Williams in 1988. The power of her songs, he explained, helped him maneuver through his own anxieties. "She was twenty, and I was twenty, and she didn't know it, but we were pals."

Nyro became a code of sorts for certain sensitive young straight men: If they could crack it, they could perhaps gain entrée to the women who attracted them. Wrote one fan, "Laura Nyro was the first secret of girl music. The girls who listened to Laura Nyro usually didn't listen to the Beach Boys. They didn't curl or iron or dye their hair. They were the smartest, but not pleasers. They were obsessed with thought and feeling. They had older boyfriends, longer hair, black boots, old velvet dresses, even shawls. . . . Some of us boys stumbled upon the bizarre notion of trying to learn something from these girls by listening to this music. Not out of nobility, but because we wanted to understand these mysterious beings who drove us crazy with desire."

Or more simply, as another man put it, "Nothing beat Laura in setting up a romantic evening with a date."

Then, of course, there were straight men who just plain found her sexy. "True, she can be awfully morose," wrote journalist Allan Ripp, "but that's when I like her most: alone at the piano, her head tilted in lament, her raven hair falling backward and her voice rising to meet the pain. She is a possessed woman, and so I would like to possess her in turn."

For some gay men, Nyro became a successor in their affections to the female cultural icon of the previous decade, Judy Garland. As Charles Kaiser wrote in *The Gay Metropolis 1940–1996*, Nyro's songs celebrated "everything that was different and original about the new decade." He also asserted, perhaps a little strongly, that her songs "explicitly celebrated the joys of cocaine and bisexuality—the guilty pleasures that performers from Garland's generation had only been able to enjoy [in] secret."

Gay audiences have long gravitated toward divas who can wring out emotion with the drama of their voices and their extravagantly emotional stage presentations, and Nyro fit the profile of a diva perfectly. As gay *Village Voice* entertainment columnist Michael Musto put it, she "could make you cry without knowing why." Wrote another gay male Nyro fan, "in my queer life it was Laura Nyro who taught me to scream and wail. And it was Laura Nyro who molded my image and concept of what is feminine."

For singer-songwriter Desmond Child (who has written hits for Bon Jovi, Aerosmith, and Ricky Martin, as well as performing in the 1970s with his group Desmond Child and Rouge), Nyro's music opened up feelings that were homoerotic and religious in equal measure. "I grew up Catholic, and when I first saw her picture on the cover of *Eli*, she looked like the Virgin Mary," he says. "It was like a religious experience. And at that time I didn't know what was gay, straight, or bi, but when Laura sang songs like 'Emily,' it evoked this sexual revolution inside of me. Even 'Black-Eyed Susan' seemed very sexual, the way she described a woman in the song. Laura hit home for gay people because she dared to be singing about these intimate relationships with women."

■ ■ ■

On the Thanksgiving weekend that Nyro sold out Carnegie Hall, she also achieved unprecedented success as a songwriter: Three of her compositions—"Wedding Bell Blues," "And When I Die" and "Eli's Comin' "—were all on the *Billboard* magazine Top 10.

The artists who covered Nyro were a genre-bending mix: a whitish-sounding black group (the Fifth Dimension), a jazz-rock ensemble (Blood, Sweat and Tears), and a straight-ahead rock band with three strong male leads (Three Dog Night). Popular music in general was quite eclectic at the time. In the week of Nyro's achievement, *Billboard's* Hot 100 ran the gamut from the Beatles ("Come Together" and "Something") to Elvis Presley ("Suspicious Minds") to Peggy Lee ("Is That All There Is") to Sly and the Family Stone ("Hot Fun in the Summertime") to the Archies ("Sugar, Sugar") to piano duo Ferrante and Teicher ("Midnight Cowboy") to James Brown ("Let a Man Come In and Do the Popcorn Part One"). Nyro's stylistic mélange *within* each of her songs was, in a sense, a microcosm of a pop music landscape that easily integrated British and American rock and roll, soul music, bubblegum, and old-fashioned pop standards.

"Eli's Comin' " had been brought to Three Dog Night by Chuck Negron, one of the group's three vocalists (along with Danny Hutton and Cory Wells). "I had seen Laura perform in clubs around New York," he wrote in his autobiography, *Three Dog Nightmare.* "I liked her sound."

Unlike most rock groups at the time, Three Dog Night relied on outside writers. Considering that the band was just starting its run of twenty-one hit singles, getting one's composition picked for a slot on their second album was like winning a lottery. "We were going against the grain, because bands at that time were trying to emulate the Beatles and write their own songs," explains Wells. "We got submitted hundreds, thousands of pieces of material from every publisher, every songwriter, every manager out there. Here were all these other songwriters who had no avenue to shop their wares, so we were a commodity they could zero in on."

Negron suggested Wells sing lead on "Eli," feeling that Cory's rough-hewn voice was more appropriate than his own sweeter, higher sound. The group slowed down the tempo slightly, but made the song more steely by changing the singer's gender. Nyro may have been reminding *herself* to "hide your heart, girl," but the men of Three Dog Night turned the song around: They were the ones issuing a stern warning to a female friend about the forbidding (and rival?) Eli. "That was our forte, basically—we would take songs that were either not palatable to the public, like Randy Newman stuff, and change it and make it commercial, or we'd do it in a completely different direction to sort of give it another character," says Wells.

Negron pushed for "Eli" to be the second single off their album, *Suitable for Framing*, following their No. 4-charting "Easy to Be Hard." "It was "a great, upbeat, 'come-and-see-me' record, a number that people would turn out to see at a concert," he thought. He was on the mark about its appeal, since it shot to No. 10 on the *Billboard* chart.

Taking even more liberty with Nyro's music were Blood, Sweat and Tears, who transformed "And When I Die" from a folk spiritual into a giddy, tempo-shifting, jazz-rock adventure. If it seemed drawn from the same stream as Aaron Copland's *Appalachian Spring*, that's exactly what the band intended. "Dick Halligan did the arrangement [and the piano solo], and he wanted to do an Aaron Copland–esque suite kind of thing, a light-comedy version of the tune," says drummer Bobby Columby.

"And When I Die" was the third hit single off the album *Blood, Sweat and Tears*, a rare trifecta for bands in those days (but one that Three Dog Night would match). BS&T's success with "Spinning Wheel" and "You've Made Me So Very Happy" had already surprised Clive Davis, who earlier told the players, "Great album; no hits."

"I felt that 'And When I Die' was a hit," says Columby. "I thought that if I did a little edit [from the album version] and made the spaces between the verses a little shorter, it would feel a little more tied together. Clive was terrific—he said, 'I'm with you, let's do it.' And it went to No. 2 and helped sell the album." It also effectively remade Nyro's song. Sammy Davis Jr.'s later cover of the song, for instance, would mimic the Blood, Sweat and Tears version to a T.

In concert, Blood, Sweat and Tears gave the song an even longer and more baroque arrangement. They began playing "And When I Die," then segued to a long tuba solo by Dave Bargeron, segued again to John Lee Hooker's "One Room Country Shack," and finally returned to Nyro's original.

On their third album, *Blood Sweat and Tears 3*, the group would record another Nyro composition, "He's a Runner." Once again, they used Nyro's basic tune as a jumping-off point for a jazz interpretation. "I had an idea of doing it pretty much with a Bill Evans Trio kind of feel, with some warm horns playing," says Columby. "The song has beautiful chords. And I thought it would be interesting for a man to sing it—he's warning a woman that the guy she's with ain't no good." (In other words, Eli's comin' *again*.)

The most successful of the three Nyro songs in the Top 10 of November 1969 was "Wedding Bell Blues," recorded by the Fifth Dimension. "Stoned Soul Picnic" had been just the first of what would be eight Nyro covers for the group, and they had already followed it with the No. 13-charting single "Sweet Blindness," both songs appearing on their *Stoned Soul Picnic* LP. "Her melodies opened up to where she put real music in there—beyond the three-chord songs of the time," said Billy Davis Jr., the group's lead male vocalist, to *Billboard*'s Jim Bessman. "And she had such a special way of coming from the heart in her lyrics."

Having already landed two hits with Nyro compositions, it was a no-brainer for the Fifth Dimension to bet on her again. Bones Howe chose "Wedding Bell Blues" because he thought it would have personal resonance: Davis and groupmate Marilyn McCoo had become an item, and McCoo had expressed concern to Howe about whether the once-married Davis had a long-term commitment in mind.

"I've got a great idea," Howe said to her. "You should sing 'Wedding Bell Blues'—'Bill, I love you so, I always will'—as a surprise." Howe would record the musical track, sneak McCoo into the studio for her vocal, and not play it for the unsuspecting Bill(y) until it was time to record background harmonies.

This was McCoo's first lead assignment for the group, and it didn't come easily; Howe says it took twenty-two edits to get her pining vocal down. Nonetheless, not only did McCoo nab a husband, but the single hit the top of the charts on November 8, 1969.

"It just exploded," says Howe. "What none of us had ever thought about was that there are thousands, *millions* of men named Bill across the country. Girls with boyfriends named Bill started calling up requesting the song. So we had this huge requested record."

As they did in all their Nyro covers, the Fifth Dimension smoothed out the edges of Nyro's original. McCoo may be pleading to her Bill, but she does so with a lilt in her voice. Nyro, in contrast, sang from a deeper well of sadness and anger. Says producer Joe Wissert, who thought Laura's version should have topped the charts back in 1966, "The song is so good that it transcended even a bad interpretation."

The Fifth Dimension weren't the only ones covering the song in 1969. Singer Lesley Gore of "It's My Party" fame had brought several Nyro songs to the attention of her Mercury Records producer Quincy Jones, but he only agreed to cut "Wedding Bell Blues," the "most benign of all her songs" to Gore's mind. Despite a favorable review in

Billboard, her chipper rendition came out the same week as the Fifth Dimension's and was buried by theirs, stymying her bid for a commercial comeback.

Earlier that year, on May 2, Gore's birthday, she and her songwriter brother Michael had produced their own unabashed Nyro pastiche-homage, "Ride a Tall White Horse." It includes lyrics familiar to Nyro songs (picnic, wine, mama), a variety of tempos, syncopated piano accompaniment, and the melody of Nyro's song "Timer" in its chorus line. "It's basically a demo," said Gore in 1996 liner notes. "We were major fans." The song was never released but has appeared on Gore anthologies.

In the next few years, it seemed as if *everyone* was covering Nyro: jazz artists Maynard Ferguson, Roy Ayers, Chet Baker, and Carmen McRae; R&B artists Melba Moore, Thelma Houston, the Supremes, the Friends of Distinction, the Staple Singers, and Diana Ross; and pop singers Mama Cass Elliott, Petula Clark, and Bobbie Gentry. It was an era in which pop and jazz artists tended to fill out their albums with current hits, and Nyro was one of those stamped a hitmaker.

Most cover versions of her songs were forgettable, and some were even annoying, as when she became Muzak at the hands of the Longines Symphonette Society or badly conceived big band jazz on New York arranger Ron Frangipane's *The Music of Laura Nyro*. On the other hand, a few artists spun her songs into artistic (if not financial) gold: The Staple Singers did a little-known, gorgeous soul-gospel rendition of "Stoned Soul Picnic" with Booker T. Jones (of the MG's) playing organ; *Hair* star Ronnie Dyson turned "Emmie" into a gender-confusing male-to-female love song sung in his androgynous tenor, and another *Hair* alum, Melba Moore, brought out Nyro's Broadway elements in her covers of "Time and Love" and "Captain St. Lucifer."

Artists across the Atlantic picked up on Nyro's music as well. British jazz-rock keyboardist Brian Auger and vocalist Julie Driscoll, cornerstones of the band Brian Auger and the Trinity, recorded "Save the Country" in an intriguing slowed-down version. They had both been bowled over by *Eli*, which to Auger captured not just the urban landscape but the consciously western flavor of Copland or Rodgers and Hammerstein. "To me, it's a piece of Americana, that record," he says. When Auger and Driscoll came to the United States to promote their album *Street Noise*, on which "Save the Country" appears, Nyro showed up at their press conference to meet them. "She was very gracious and thanked us for doing a version," says Auger. "We were a little bit in awe."

Nyro never spoke unkindly of others' covers of her songs, feeling flattered rather than critical or jealous that her versions didn't become hits. "If anyone does a song of mine I have no critical taste at all. I just love it," she told British TV producer/artists' manager/journalist Vicki Wickham in 1971. In one of her last interviews, Nyro insisted that hearing a male voice sing "Eli's Comin' " had been one of the great thrills of her life.

Privately, Nyro confided to Ellen Sander that at times she was nervous about others doing her songs, concerned that they would be misconstrued. But she also realized that there would always be room for different interpretations, and as a songwriter she had to let go. Of her most frequent interpreters, the Fifth Dimension, she said, "To me, [they] were like an ice cream soda. It was sweet pop. I thought that they brought good vibes to my music."

By the end of 1970, Tuna Fish Music was listed at No. 23 among Billboard's Hot 100 publishers. Columbia trumpeted Nyro's success as a songwriter, hoping it would encourage her own record sales—"Attention Fifth Dimension, Blood, Sweat & Tears and Three Dog Night: Laura Nyro has a new album, but you'll have to wait your turn," read one of the company's ads. That wasn't really true, however. Nyro would never have a big hit single in her own voice, so no one would have to wait their turn.

But if her no-interference contract with Columbia had won her creative freedom, her clout as a songwriter forever unlocked the shackles. Since she wasn't dependent on record sales for her biggest financial reward—which came from songwriting royalties—she could continue to follow her muse wherever it led her.

8
SINGER-SONGWRITER

At the end of 1969, Laura was "one of the hottest songwriters and performers in the music industry," in the words of music trade magazine *Cash Box*, which featured her on its cover. Her rise, the magazine pointed out, had been "so gentle and so quiet that it seemed that all of a sudden she just burst out of nowhere to the top of the charts."

In fact, Nyro was becoming one of the standard-bearers for the entire singer-songwriter movement. As author Iain Chambers described it, singer-songwriters emerged from the folk music tradition of troubadours with guitars, yet "still fully participated in the cultural aura and 'unity' of rock music." They were characterized by their highly personal lyrics, as opposed to the more generalized sentiments of pop writers from the immediate past. "The essence of the best singer-songwriters' work has been change under pressure, a growth toward self-knowledge," wrote rock critic Janet Maslin.

The singer-songwriting men of note had been led by Bob Dylan, the first to span the divide between folk and rock, and those that followed included Leonard Cohen, Harry Nilsson, and James Taylor. But women artists no longer had to remain second fiddles: Formerly relegated to being singers or songwriters, they had quickly become accepted in this new form of pop music. The authors of *Rock of Ages: The Rolling Stone History of Rock and Roll* went so far as to say that "the arrival of the singer-songwriter boomlet moved women into the pop forefront for the first time since the Beatles precipitated the decline of girl groups."

The phenomenon of women singer-songwriters became so commonly recognized that *Newsweek* ran a feature story about it in July of 1969, featuring Nyro, Joni Mitchell (best known at the time for having written the Judy Collins's hit "Both Sides Now"), the single-monikered Melanie (known for the childlike "Brand New Key" and the Woodstock anthem "Lay Down [Candles in the Rain]"), Lottie Golden, and Elyse Weinberg (the latter two quickly faded from view). Writer Hubert Saal suggested, with a slight paternalism, that the male world of rock music had lacked the personal touch, which these women provided with "voyages of self-discovery, brimming with keen observation and startling in the impact of their poetry."

Mitchell and Nyro, the primary goddesses of the singer-songwriter pantheon, became beacons of permission for other women musicians. These two women weren't just allowed to be confessional, but *encouraged* to be so by their listeners, who yearned to identify their own feelings in the songs. Mitchell's and Nyro's work thus became part and parcel of second-wave feminism, which craved personal expression as a tool to break down decades of the feminine mystique. Rock music critic Robert Christgau said of Mitchell, but it's equally applicable to Nyro, that, "In a male performer such intense self-concern would be an egotistic cop-out. In a woman it is an act of defiance."

Nyro broke from the gate as a singer-songwriter slightly before Mitchell, and her impact on other female musicians was profound. "Laura inspired any woman who ever sang a note, especially in the sixties and seventies," says Marsha Malamet, who recorded the Nyro-influenced album *Coney Island Winter* for Decca in 1969. "She was it. Everyone took things from her, because you go to the best."

"There was her, Joni Mitchell and a little bit later Carole King," says Karla Bonoff, known both for her own recordings and for having written "Someone to Lay Down Beside Me" and "Lose Again" (both sung by Linda Ronstadt) and "Home" (sung by Bonnie Raitt). Bonoff, who was signed by Columbia in 1977, nearly ten years after Nyro, says she listened to *New York Tendaberry* countless times, absorbing Nyro's piano chordings into her own songs, such as "Someone to Lay Down Beside Me."

"Laura didn't stick to pop songwriting style," says Bonoff. "She just had a wild, free style that up until then I really hadn't seen anyone doing."

Wendy Waldman, a close friend of Bonoff's from the San Fernando Valley and later her bandmate in the group Bryndle, also wore out *New York Tendaberry*. "Nyro's music was so liberated, so self-realized, so fearless," says Waldman, whose first solo album came out on Warner in 1974. " 'Mad Mad Me' [a Waldman song popularized by Maria Muldaur] would never have happened without Laura. I grew up in a classical and film-music family and heard these sounds in my head that I could never quite put together—from the Rolling Stones to Vivaldi to Gershwin to Cole Porter. Then came Laura Nyro, and anything she liked was fair game in her writing. All the great songwriters have combined certain elements, maybe three at a time, but she would combine ten of them. It was so ahead of its time that it's still ahead of its time."

Phoebe Snow, the New Jersey–raised singer-songwriter who first became popular for her folk-blues song "Poetry Man" in 1974, agrees. "I think she was one of the first proponents of really boldly displaying all her musical influences and making them into an amalgam that was a style that defined her," says Snow, who would get to know Nyro years later. "Nyro's work is so towering—so stellar and important to twentieth-century music."

Nyro herself would explain that she was "liberated" as a songwriter because she was influenced not just by various styles of music, but by poetry and the visual arts as well ("If I could, I'd live inside a Gauguin," she said in one of her press kits). "I didn't work within limitations," she told an interviewer in 1994. "When you come from a background of being in the arts, you tend to believe in the notion that anything goes."

Even Carole King, whose classic tunes Nyro had loved and been shaped by, was somewhat influenced by her acolyte. King and Toni Stern's song "I Don't Believe It," which appears on the 1968 Ode Records album *Now That Everything's Been Said* by the King-fronted group the City (produced by Nyro admirer Lou Adler), sounds positively Nyroesque in its syncopated piano rhythms. More significantly, the public acceptance of both Nyro and Mitchell must have strengthened King's own resolve to be taken seriously as more than a songwriter. Her hugely successful solo album, *Tapestry*, released in March of 1971, is inconceivable without predecessors like *Eli and the Thirteenth Confession* and *New York Tendaberry*. Nyro had cracked open the door, but *Tapestry* broke it down, unleashing a flood of new female artists into the music world.

Nyro's impact was so pervasive that some songwriters wrote about her in their songs. Rickie Lee Jones began a song on her 1979 debut album with the lyric "Sal was working at Nyro's Nook in downtown." Nyro had first made a strong impression on Jones when, as a fifteen-year-old in Elma, Washington, Jones came across her name in an article at her high school library. "To be honest, the moment I saw the name I knew I had to find out who she was," says Jones. Not long afterwards, she caught the *Critique* television show. "She was flawed, strange vocally, but un-deniably full of the spirit, bold, with strange new musical ideas. . . . Her long black hair and dramatic performance mesmerized me.

"It was always my road to have high drama onstage," Jones goes on. "She gave me a map."

Melissa Manchester even more directly sang about Laura's influence in one of her songs, "Funny That Way," a cut on her 1973 debut al-bum *Home to Myself*: "No I don't have the soul of Joni / And I cannot see myself as Miss Laura." Critic William Ruhlmann guessed that she was "thus marking out the competition," but Manchester says she meant only that Nyro had experienced a more raw upbringing in the Bronx than she had. If anything, Manchester wanted to *be* Laura Nyro.

"There was never a voice that has sung or written so eloquently about the basic fundamental component of femaleness," says Man-chester, three years Nyro's junior and also the daughter of a musician (her father played bassoon). "I just never heard anybody running down the hallways of their soul, just running and running and running and running, trying to outdistance some devil. I *worshipped* her music, I didn't just like it. She was the muse. Even before I made albums, when I was just making demos, you can hear all of the shuffle stuff that was just so gorgeous and infectious and contagious—that came directly out of Laura."

In fact, when Manchester was eighteen and auditioning for a song-writing class at New York University taught by Paul Simon, he asked her, "Have you been listening to Laura Nyro?"

"Yes," she replied.

Said Simon, "You need to stop now."

■ ■ ■

Although Nyro's appeal to other women artists would have been obvious, she inspired male musicians as well. For one, Broadway com-poser Stephen Schwartz, in his hit pop musical *Godspell*, added the in-struction "à la Laura Nyro" to his song "Bless the Lord." Jazzy singer-songwriter-guitarist Kenny Rankin, who became friends with Nyro after she came to see him perform at Manhattan's Bitter End in Greenwich Village in 1967, has said, "She had, and still has, a great influence on my music and the way I write and play. To me, her first recording, *More Than a New Discovery*, is a masterpiece that . . . will stand the test of time."

Rock's Todd Rundgren, who copped Nyro's piano chordings and "shuffle stuff" in some of his early recordings, was yet another artist to include Nyro in a song he wrote. His "Baby Let's Swing," from his 1970 solo debut album *Runt*, begins, "Laura, I saw you open in L.A." and ends, "Now I love to shuffle / Ever since I heard you sing." Rundgren has said that he was "obsessed" with the *Eli* album, and that Nyro once asked him if he'd lead a band for her—a request he had to pass up because at the time he was still part of the band the Nazz.

Desmond Child emulated Nyro's harmonies in his group Desmond Child and Rouge, and captured her melodic and lyrical spirit in the Top 40 hits he wrote for acts such as Bon Jovi ("Livin' on a Prayer") and Ricky Martin ("Livin' La Vida Loca"). "Listen to the storyline of 'La Vida Loca,' " says Child: " 'Woke up in New York City / In a funky cheap hotel / She took my heart / And she took my money.' It's like Laura's 'Gibsom Street' or 'Buy and Sell.' To this day, Laura's had an enormous influence on me and other songwriters writing for top artists."

Nyro's piano playing, unstudied as it was, left an impression on jazz cognoscenti as well as pop musicians. "Laura Nyro was a big influence on my approach, the triads and stuff like that," jazz pianist and composer Billy Childs has said, calling her his all-time favorite songwriter. The African American Childs first listened to his older sister's Nyro records at age fifteen and tried to duplicate the chords. Nyro's records weren't particularly popular in the black community (unlike the Fifth Dimension's cover versions), but Childs explained that his sister had a number of white girlfriends.

Just the fact that Nyro accompanied herself on piano rather than guitar helped change pop music performance and songwriting. After she appeared on the scene, a number of artists returned to the keyboard, which hadn't taken center stage in rock music since the days of Jerry Lee Lewis and Little Richard.

"There's no doubt that she opened the piano door for me," says Wendy Waldman. "I started writing songs when I was fourteen, and that was a real guitar era. I had studied piano like all good children of artistic families, but I didn't like the discipline of it, and I became a blues hound. But Laura was, too! She just translated it to piano."

Nyro opened the "piano door" for Joni Mitchell as well. "On account of her I started playing piano again," she told the British music magazine *Mojo*. Her 1971 piano-based album *Blue*, a strong departure from her previous folk-tinged work, also shows Nyro's imprint in its moodiness and rangy melodies.

"There's a certain freedom in *Blue* that was literally Laura's trademark," says Pamela Polland, a talented but overlooked West Coast singer-songwriter who recorded for Epic and Columbia in the late sixties and early seventies. "If Joni was paying attention to Laura, then I'm sure there would have been this thought: 'Oh my God, there's so much more I could be doing.' "

Stephen Paley remembers that Mitchell, who would eventually surpass Nyro in popularity, was deferential to her at this early point in their careers. "Laura was the queen," says Paley. But Mitchell was only one of many popular artists of the day who showed a reverence toward Nyro. "I was always amazed watching other artists go over to Laura and just be completely mesmerized by her," says Paley. "She was really an artist's artist."

Even one of her great heroes, Bob Dylan, wanted to meet Nyro. Making a rare social appearance at a fancy industry party that Clive Davis threw at his luxe Central Park West apartment for Janis Joplin in late 1969, Dylan asked to be introduced to Nyro.

"I love what you do, I love your chords," he said to her. "Would you teach me to play the piano like you?"

To which Laura, giggly and awestruck, replied that she'd teach him piano if he taught her guitar. "They just nudged each other over and over with their elbows, hardly speaking but grinning like mad," says Alan Merrill, Nyro's escort for the evening.

Nyro became friends with a number of music celebrities of the time. "She had a lot of artist friends for a while," says Richard Chiaro, who worked as Nyro's booking agent and road manager after Geffen moved to California in 1969. "She was generally comfortable with artists. Stevie Wonder came down and sang with her at a piano once. In L.A., I think Joni Mitchell came over to the Chateau Marmont [the West Hollywood hotel famous for celebrity guests] for Laura and me to teach her yoga."

Nyro also was friendly with Buffy Sainte-Marie, the Cree Indian singer-songwriter whose "Now That the Buffalo's Gone" had become a folk protest classic. Nyro recounted to Donald Boudreau a winter visit at Sainte-Marie's Maine house when the pipes froze, forcing them to wash the dinner dishes in the snow.

"She and Buffy apparently had to put on many layers of winter clothes, and there they were, these two legendary divas, dressed like roly-poly Eskimoes in the frigid windy cold, washing dishes. Laura laughed so hard retelling it that tears rolled down her face," says Boudreau.

Nyro also visited Sainte-Marie's house with Stephen Paley on a week-long writing retreat (Sainte-Marie wasn't there), during which Paley photographed Nyro and her dog Beautybelle in the wintry Maine setting. "Beautybelle was a human dog," says Nyro's friend Barbara Greenstein. "She was one of the girls—she understood everything. We used to say that one day Beautybelle was going to pick up the phone and call me." Like a human, though, Beautybelle could get carsick—and Paley remembers her throwing up in the rental car on the way back to the airport.

Another time, back in Manhattan, Paley arranged for Nyro to meet soul-gospel singer Lorraine Ellison, whom Nyro admired for the tear-wrenching, cult-classic 1966 single "Stay With Me Baby." Nyro came with Paley while he photographed Ellison for a Warner Bros. album cover in the Manhattan brownstone garden of another Paley pal: Stephen Sondheim. The famed Broadway composer had praised Nyro's "Stoned Soul Picnic," and Paley remembered that he particularly liked the "surry on down" part. It was "a big love fest" when the eclectic trio of icons met that afternoon, Paley says, and he preserved it for posterity in photos.

Nyro impressed the pop culture elite in general, not just musicians. Lee Housekeeper remembers actor Peter Sellers showing up at the Troubadour before one of Nyro's performances there and asking her out to dinner. Nyro offered only to dine with him at the music club, so Housekeeper, disguised in a red busboy uniform, brought food over from the next-door restaurant. Mid-meal, he realized that Nyro didn't even know who she was breaking bread with, so he blurted out, "Laura, this is Peter Sellers, he was in Dr. *Strangelove!*" Sellers proceeded to perform scenes from some of his movies, and Nyro was delighted.

A couple of years later, when Nyro was performing in Santa Monica, California, her friend Barbara Greenstein remembers Jane Fonda calling their hotel and asking if she and Nyro could hang out. "And we decided we didn't want to!" Greenstein laughs. "Laura wasn't starstruck ever, except around Bob Dylan or Miles Davis."

One person who did not fall under Nyro's spell was Janis Joplin, the most popular female rock singer of the era. When David Geffen brought Joplin to Laura's apartment for a typical Nyro luncheon of tuna fish finger sandwiches and pink champagne, "Janis thought she was making fun of her," says Geffen. "They did not hit it off. Janis was a heavy drinker and a very, very different kind of woman."

Clive Davis also noticed discomfort between Nyro and Joplin, stemming perhaps from Joplin's insecurities. During one of the bluesy belter's first New York gigs, Davis took Nyro backstage to meet her, but Joplin acted cold. "Laura wanted to tell her how much she'd loved the performance, but Janis barely nodded a greeting as she drank straight from a Southern Comfort bottle and talked to a new boy she was eyeing," wrote Davis. After cover versions of Nyro's songs became hits, Joplin directly expressed her competitive jealousy to Davis: "I can see I'm not the number one female in your eyes anymore," she told him. "You're turned on to Laura now."

The Nyro-Joplin rift even made it to Rolling Stone's gossip pages in September of 1968. Noting that Joplin was leaving her band Big Brother and the Holding Company and might feel pressured to change her style, the writer opined, "Janis is neither Billie Holiday nor Aretha Franklin, and . . . trying to get her to be like that might make her end up like Laura Nyro." In the next issue, Joplin responded bizarrely to the already confusing comparison by saying, "I understand I'm not Aretha Franklin, but Laura Nyro is the best cook in the world." Could she have been referring to the tuna fish and champagne feast?

Nyro may have been sensitive to Joplin's feelings, though. At the Clive Davis party where she met Dylan, Davis reported that Nyro camped out in the back bedroom with the guests' coats, saying she was afraid to step into Janis's spotlight. Then again, perhaps the back bedroom was just a convenient place to hang out undisturbed with Bob Dylan. "It was just me, Dylan, and Laura in Clive's coatroom for about an hour," says Alan Merrill. "Laura and I were later sitting on Clive's sofa in the middle of the party, people watching. Every star on the Columbia label was there. At one point, Laura got up from the couch to go to the bathroom and I was sitting on her white wedding dress by accident, and we both heard it rip. She just laughed, told me not to worry about it."

Even as Nyro was becoming the toast of the town, she couldn't always mask the pain of being labeled different in her younger days. Both Lee Housekeeper and Stephen Paley remember her taking them on late-night limousine rides to a White Castle hamburger joint in the Bronx, known for its tiny hamburgers, or sliders.

"She said she'd promised herself that when she had a hit record she was going to take a limousine to this particular White Castle and get some sliders," says Housekeeper. "She was telling me how her class-mates had made fun of her. I said, 'Don't you want to get out of the car and thumb your nose at someone?' She said no. It was just a private little experience she wanted to have."

∎ ∎ ∎

As a performer of "rare magnetism," in *Cash Box*'s words, Nyro had wowed Los Angeles and New York. But to complete her ascension, she needed to conquer at least one more region that had disappointed her in the past: the San Francisco Bay area. The venue chosen for her Northern California comeback was the Berkeley Community Theater, at which she was booked on Saturday, January 24, 1970, as part of a college-based tour. (Given its proximity to the University of California, the theater may as well have been on campus.)

Dispelling any bad memories, Nyro packed the hall to overflowing, with extra seats set up in the orchestra pit, standing room along the walls, and squatters in the aisles. "Even her detractors would have had to admit that Laura Nyro's return to the West Coast was a triumph," wrote one of those detractors, Ralph J. Gleason of *Rolling Stone*. Gleason belonged to the fraternity who criticized Nyro's "shrill" upper register, her appearance ("she looks like the girl down the block dressed up in a long white gown for her First Communion," Gleason suggested), and her die-hard fans, but he nonetheless liked some of her songs—as long as *she* wasn't singing them. "As a singer of her own songs," he wrote, "she does not turn me on."

In Southern California, at the opposite end of the critical spectrum, *Los Angeles Times* pop music critic Robert Hilburn had lavished kudos on Nyro a week earlier. Her January 17 appearance at UCLA's Royce Hall, wrote Hilburn, "was an exercise in excellence that more than made up for any disappointment caused by its brevity [the show lasted less than an hour]." The power of Nyro's live performance made her recordings pale, he said, and unlike the unaroused Gleason he found that Nyro's version of songs such as "Wedding Bell Blues" made the covers "almost unbearable by comparison."

Even the jazz press appreciated Nyro. Michael Cuscuna of *Down Beat* went so far as to call her one of the finest jazz singers of the past several years. He compared her dramatic flair to Kurt Weill's theater songs, her shifts in rhythm and unorthodox harmonies to Burt Bacharach, and her voice—though higher and less breathy—to jazz vocalist Morgana King's (a singer whom Nyro adored and called "a goddess").

But it was with college students, not jazz fans, that Nyro would find her most faithful audience. Billboard's March 28, 1970, list of top campus attractions listed Nyro No. 1, with Joplin No. 2. Also that year, UCLA students voted Nyro the most popular female singer in rock, again outscoring Joplin (who had won the previous year). Grace Slick of Jefferson Airplane came in a close third, and Dusty Springfield a distant fourth. "Miss Nyro's reputation and popularity have grown considerably over the last year," wrote UCLA's Daily Bruin, the student newspaper that sponsored the poll.

Nyro's hard-core fans, as critics like Gleason had noticed, were rabidly appreciative. "They were mainly young girls and gay guys, and they were all nuts," says Lee Housekeeper with some overemphasis. "The letters Laura got! Overwhelming letters—you saved me from suicide, things like that. We screened her letters."

"Her fans would gobble her up if you let them," adds Chiaro. "They wanted autographs, they wanted to hug her, ask her questions." Nyro received her fans graciously, if shyly, occasionally rewarding them with that hug or a friendly kiss.

Her managers always tried to stay close to Nyro for fear that some fans would be too invasive, though. At Royce Hall, Chiaro remembers youths in white-face knocking on her dressing room door and saying something strange when Nyro opened it to greet them. "She got real freaked out by it," he says. Stephen Paley recalls another time, in New York, when Nyro let a fan on the street kiss her and he instead bit her lip, making it bleed and bringing her to tears.

"She would do things like that," says Paley of her willingness to allow the kiss in the first place. "She was very accessible if she was in the mood to be, or she could be very aloof and mysterious."

"Most people were just adoring her, and it's not hard to accept adoration," says Chiaro. "She had a really great heart, she was a very loving person. And she was a very simple person. If it was simple and loving, it was easy for her."

9
BEADS OF SWEAT

With money coming in from performing, record sales, and especially her publishing, Nyro could afford a larger and more glamorous apartment than the one-room penthouse on West 79th Street. She passed that apartment along to Grandpa, suggesting that he pay the rent to her. She could then secretly charge him much less than the actual rate. "He was a very proud man," says Louis Nigro.

Housekeeper remembers many outings Nyro took with Grandpa, including frequent dining excursions to the Triple Inn on Upper Broadway for chili. As much as Nyro looked after the older man, he took care of her as well. "He loved to clean—he was always cleaning, he always had a rag over his shoulder," says Laura's cousin Steve Marcus. "He did the dishes and went around and cleaned the house, cleaned the ashtrays. He'd always be there to serve her in some way. He thought she was the greatest thing. The greatest *peacemaker* in the world, that's what he'd say to me."

The fact that Grandpa moved to Laura's former apartment led, in a strange confluence of circumstances, to his finding a bride for Laura's brother. In 1972, Janice Reed, then an eighteen-year-old Nyro fan, had gone looking for Laura's apartment on a visit to New York City, having been told it was on West 79th between Columbus and Amsterdam Avenues. "Does Laura Nyro live here?" she asked a number of doormen to no avail, but as she was about to give up one of three older men conversing in front of a building said to her in a husky voice, "I'm Laura's grandpa."

Long story short, Grandpa and Janice hit it off (he reminded her of her own Russian Jewish grandfather), and although they chatted for only ten minutes, Grandpa silently decided he wanted her to marry Jan—and later told Jan so. "I met a girl—she carries the femininity like nobody's business!" he said to his grandson in his Russian-accented English, hitting his wrist on a table for emphasis. A few weeks later, when Janice returned to the city, she went back to West 79th to see Mr. Mirsky, and this time he insisted on taking her to meet Jan, then living uptown with his parents. When they got there and Jan and Janice first realized the similarity of their names, Grandpa said, "Yes, one of you will have to change your name." Then he said, "I've got to go," and suddenly left them to get acquainted.

Although the match didn't click immediately, a year later they finally made the connection Grandpa had hoped for. They've been together ever since, and neither has changed names.

Meanwhile, Laura had moved to a much snazzier address—the Beresford on 7 West Eighty-first Street, just across the street from the pocket park behind the Museum of Natural History. According to Stephen Paley, she paid under $100,000 for her spacious seventeenth-floor coop, quite a steal considering a one-bedroom apartment in the prestigious building cost nearly $2 million in 2000. Designed by architect Emery Roth and completed the month before the stock market crash of 1929, the Beresford has three ornate towers, making it look dramatically taller than its twenty-two stories.

Although only a short distance from Nyro's previous dwelling, the Beresford was quite a step up. The building had a uniformed doorman and plush red carpet leading into the lobby, and her apartment included an expansive terrace with a breathtaking vista of Central Park and Manhattan's downtown skyline. It certainly was more befitting of her new pop star status, but her professional success did not guarantee approval from the conservative coop board.

"She came in [to a board meeting] wearing her long dress in the middle of the day, and she looked like a witch," says Stephen Paley. "So Judy Prince [theater director Hal Prince's wife] and I called up Isaac Stern [the famed violinist], Phyllis Newman [the actress/producer, married to lyricist Adolph Green], Leonard Lyons [a well-known gossip columnist for the New York Post]—all the people we knew who lived in the building—and asked them to tell the board that she's a great artist and that they should overlook her eccentricities. They got her in."

Nyro, being Nyro, didn't change her style to fit her luxe new environment, sending the Beresford doorman out to get her such non-gourmet treats as Drake's Devil Dogs and Häagen-Dazs rum raisin ice cream. And she redecorated the apartment according to her own iconoclastic taste. Her large living room was only sparsely furnished, with a piano alongside a wall and a beautiful large harp. She had her bedroom painted lavender, a color her young friend Donald Boudreau says connoted spirituality to her. Most stunningly, on the wall of the long hallway that led from the living room to the den and her bedroom, she installed bamboo, then lit the path with bare red lightbulbs.

"It was like you were in Tahiti," says musician Felix Cavaliere, who would produce Nyro's next album, "and you were walking down one of those aisles where the drummers go. In the winter, the bamboo would heat up and pop, because bamboo is not made for an apartment in New York City. What can I tell you? This was so out. I would have loved to have seen the people who came in to purchase this place after Laura."

Outside, on the brick terrace, Nyro stationed a bed to use for summer reading, naps, or romantic trysts. But the terrace held dangers, too: One day she called her father with the question "Dad, do you have a shovel?" Her cat had fallen off the balcony, and she wanted to bury him in the park that night.

Nyro always seemed to plan her environments to attract her muse, choosing particular objects for that purpose, says Boudreau. He recalls that during the writing of New York Tendaberry, a lamp shaped like a bunch of berries hung over the terrace doorway in her 79th Street apartment. For her next album, which would have an autumnal or wintry feel, she purchased an expensive mobile of colored autumn leaves. But when she got it home, she snipped off the leaves and scattered them across the top of her piano. Since the album would include a song about Christmas, she also put up a fully decorated artificial Christmas tree inside the apartment, despite the fact that it was springtime.

Nyro would follow the initial inspiration for her songs with extensive rewriting, sometimes over a period of years. Since she didn't know music notation, she generally wrote down only her lyrics, while holding the music in her head. She then worked at "resculpturing and resculpturing" a composition until it was just the way she wanted it. Each album became a "lifeline" of the songs that came together after this concentrated period of writing and resculpturing.

Commercial calculations didn't figure into the process at all. "I know that there are a lot of people who write for a market. I cannot do that . . . that's out," she said. Yet to produce her fourth album, Nyro and Geffen settled on someone with excellent commercial instincts—Cavaliere—whose group the Rascals had scored a string of Top 20 blue-eyed soul hits from 1965 through 1968, including "Groovin' " and "People Got to Be Free."

"David Geffen called me up and said, 'I'm going to introduce you to the most difficult person you've ever met in your life,' " says Cavaliere. " 'There is no one who really wants to produce her because of her attitude—it's extremely difficult to work with her. I know that she likes your music very much and I know that you would probably get along. Would you be interested?' "

Even with that less-than-enticing introduction, Cavaliere said yes, and he immediately clicked with Nyro. "To know her was to love her," he says. "She was a very sensual . . . she was just so attractive to many of us. We became friends, we became really close friends. For a while, I don't know, I thought there'd be a romance involved there, but it didn't go in that direction."

Nyro and Cavaliere shared a common love of soul music. "There's a special thing about the New York/Philadelphia/East Coast kind of oldies thing," he says. "You loved that stuff, you grew up on that stuff, and Laura definitely had that. She knew all the songs, all the words." Cavaliere also remembers taking Nyro to see Nina Simone perform. "She basically liked everybody in the feminine realm," he says of Nyro's musical tastes. "It was innate in her."

Cavaliere and Nyro soon began to share something else besides music: He introduced her to his spiritual teacher, Swami Satchidananda, an Indian-born yogi, then in his mid-fifties, who had opened an Integral Yoga ashram in the United States. Satchidananda's oft-expressed goal for yoga practice was to develop "an easeful body, a peaceful mind, and a useful life"—attributes that must have matched Nyro's desires for herself.

When Nyro first met Satchidananda, in Harriman, New York, she "burst into tears," says Cavaliere. "I left, because I felt it was one of those moments that was special for the two of them. She told me later she had never seen anything so clean, so pure, in her life, and it just kind of hit her. Her emotions, she wore them on her hands, you know."

Satchidananda remembers the meeting, too. "It was early on in my days in the USA, and when I first saw Laura I mistook her for an Indian girl," he says. "She didn't look or seem like an American to me. She looked Asian, and so I felt she must have had past lives in the East— particularly because she had a depth and spiritual awareness that was very profound. When she met me she immediately felt an affinity and I think she was drawn to Yoga and the mysticism of India because she was sincerely searching to deeply understand the meaning of life and her purpose here."

"What Swami told me," says Cavaliere, "was that Laura was born a century too late. That she really was from the nineteenth century. That's the kind of mind-set she had."

Over the next few years, Nyro would practice daily meditation as prescribed by the Swami's teachings. Boudreau remembers meditating with her in the hallway of her Beresford apartment, sitting lotus style on the hardwood floor. Nyro also travelled to Sri Lanka with Richard Chiaro for a two-week yoga and meditation retreat with the Swami, a visit at which Cavaliere and jazz harpist/keyboardist Alice Coltrane— the widow of Nyro's jazz hero John Coltrane—were also in attendance.

Nyro was never a fundamentalist about yoga, however. She tried to be "righteous," as her friend Kay Crow (then Kay Zar) put it, but she always cheated. "Laura wouldn't go along with no meat, fish, eggs, or sex," says Crow, who met Nyro through mutual friend Cavaliere. "Let's not forget cigarettes. And then she sneaked a little pot, too. She couldn't follow the rules, but she liked the philosophy."

■ ■ ■

On the recording front, Cavaliere decided to bring in a coproducer for Nyro's album: Arif Mardin, the respected arranger who had worked with the likes of the Rascals, Aretha Franklin, and Dusty Springfield (on her 1968 classic, Dusty in Memphis). "I knew I couldn't handle her by myself," says Cavaliere.

Nyro was well prepared for the recording sessions, but as promised by Geffen, she still proved a challenge to her producers. "We had a very interesting but very difficult time with her," says Cavaliere. "She was real tough."

He and Mardin surrounded her with musicians that they knew she would admire. Side One of the album would feature the Muscle Shoals (Alabama) rhythm section of drummer Roger Hawkins, guitarist Eddie Hinton, bass player Dave Hood, and vibraphonist Barry Beckett, who provided tasty backup on such great albums of the time as Aretha Franklin's 1970 Spirit in the Dark. On Side Two, Cavaliere and Mardin used a top-notch New York rhythm section, featuring Rascals drummer Dino Danelli, bassist Chuck Rainey, guitarist Cornell Dupree, and percussionist Ralph MacDonald. They also added Eastern instruments like the oud (a Southwest Asian/North African stringed instrument) and employed two extraordinary soloists, Alice Coltrane on harp and Duane Allman (also a Muscle Shoals regular) on electric guitar.

"It wasn't done on purpose like that," says Cavaliere of the separate bands for each side. "I think that's just what happened. We tried things and threw some ideas out to Laura—like, she always thought Dino was a great drummer, and wouldn't it be nice to try a little rock thing?"

Cavaliere wanted to create a good-time atmosphere around the production, but felt that Nyro treated it as more emotionally complex. "As traumatic as giving birth," says Cavaliere. "Every note, everything on that album, was her private property. We would literally have to bargain with her for our ideas, because she would not change a thing. Like a tempo change, for example—when you have a song you're trying to get played commercially on the radio, you can't all of a sudden stop the rhythm, go have a sandwich, and come back. You can to some degree play around with melody, but the rhythm seduces people into listening. But she would stop and get real slow and dreamy, then pick it up again! However she felt it, that's where it went. Well, goodbye radio." In other words, Nyro took the same attitude toward this album as she had toward every other project she'd done since she'd been handed the creative reins by Columbia.

The Muscle Shoals "boys," although unaccustomed to such eccentric rhythm changes, acted like southern gentlemen, Cavaliere remembers: "They said, 'Yes, ma'am, if that's what you want, that's what we'll do.' They just tuned right into her and followed her."

In order to get Nyro to make certain changes, Cavaliere and Mardin would craftily ask for two changes, making a bigger deal about the less important one. Sometimes it worked. "She'd think, Well, I can't turn them down twice," says Cavaliere. "Arif and I would actually shake hands after we got one of these changes, because she was impossible."

The strategy failed, however, with Nyro's vocal on the Carole King/ Gerry Goffin classic "Up on the Roof," the first cover song Nyro had recorded. "We had done a few takes, and somebody must have said the word *commercial* about one of them—God forbid!" says Cavaliere. "And she didn't like that vocal, for whatever reason. We went in the following morning and she had just erased it. She said, 'Now which one do you like?' She was like a brat. We knew each other well enough so she could turn around and punch me. She was a Bronx kid; she knew how to hit."

Even though Nyro's artistic honesty took precedence over commercial considerations, the 45 rpm version of "Up on the Roof" would still prove to be the most successful single in her recording career, reaching No. 92 on the *Billboard* Hot 100. It would do even better on the "Easy Listening" chart, reaching as high as No. 30.

Cavaliere found Nyro irresistible, even as she drove him crazy. "I mean, she used to listen to mixes on a Panasonic radio," he says. "The thing cost about five-fifty. 'How dare you criticize our mix listening to it on mono?' I said. 'That's how I want to hear it,' she'd say. We will never see her like again. I just loved her."

The courtly Mardin remembers Nyro as a "wonderful lady" whose harmonic concepts sometimes reminded him of Aaron Copland. "Quite modern, the way she was playing piano," he says. But formally, she was still a naif. "You'd have to try to penetrate into her thinking, into her brain, because she would have this imagery," says Mardin. "We succeeded, but it was difficult."

To do the instrumental arrangements, Mardin would listen to Nyro accompany herself on a song, then have the chord sequence transcribed for the bass player. "Sort of a head arrangement, but very organized," he says. "She would have definite ideas—'I don't want the bass to be too loud here, have the guitar player strum here.' She was very precise, and we made sure that her music was recorded the way she envisioned it."

"Laura was in total control," says Kay Crow, who was at one of the sessions. If she wanted to do something different, she'd try to sweet-talk Cavaliere: "Oh, but Fe, I think we should do it this way—don't you think if we do it this way we could make a fuller sound? And bring in some *blue* horns?"

"And Felix would say, 'Well, I don't know, let's do it both ways,' " says Crow. "But when it was the way Laura wanted to do it, she would make her own performance better!"

"Laura was passive-aggressive; if she didn't like something, she would just shut down," says road manager Richard Chiaro. "There was no conversation, no argument, no negotiation. She was really afraid to give up control of her songs. Other writers became that intransigent later on, but she was one of the first. Arif Mardin had a real hard time with her, but he was a sweetheart."

Despite being "bold, sassy, feisty, stubborn," as Chiaro puts it, Nyro also was extremely insightful. "She had such a bottom line of knowing what was important emotionally," he says. "She taught everybody a lesson. She brought the best out of a lot of people. She was such a talent that people really wanted to be part of it."

"People call it perfectionism, but it's the only way it can be for an artist," says Nyro's longtime friend Patty Di Lauria. "She could only let it go when it felt right to her, and she couldn't pretend otherwise. People who respected her respected that. It's not about wanting to be difficult. Business-type people and managers and fathers don't always understand that."

Nyro still talked in colors and textures, relying on others to translate. During the string session for "Up on the Roof," for example, the players were old-timers—"guys who would chomp on cigars and read the Racing Form," says Mardin—so one can imagine the blank stares they gave Nyro when she asked them to play a section as if it shimmered. Finally, one violinist growled in a patois straight out of Guys and Dolls, "All right, she wants ponticello, give her ponticello." Short for sul ponticello—Italian for "on the little bridge"—it means that one should bow very close to the violin's bridge. And it shimmered.

As she had on New York Tendaberry, Nyro acted the hostess as well as the producer, which could wreak havoc on the recording budget. "She'd take food breaks all the time and order these delicious spreads and just stop everything," says Cavaliere. "After you ate, you couldn't record any more. I mean, the budget went through the roof when you did these stops—double-scale, triple-scale musicians, you have them eat for an hour, two hours?" Nonetheless, it took only about four months to finish the album, a much quicker turnaround than New York Tendaberry.

For the cover of the album, Kay Crow had commissioned an artist to do a pointillist reproduction of one of Crow's photos of Laura. But Nyro changed her mind about that concept, just as she had with New York Tendaberry. She instead picked a drawing done by one of her fans.

Art student Beth O'Brien had left a portrait at the stage door, done with felt-tip pen on watercolor paper, when Nyro performed in Boston. Using a "a few photos and imagination," O'Brien's drawing of a pensive, unsmiling Nyro looking straight out at the viewer obviously impressed the subject. To O'Brien's surprise, someone announced over the P.A. before the concert began, "Could the person who left the artwork for Ms. Nyro come to the stage?"

The thrilled young artist was introduced to the singer and left her phone number; a few days later, Nyro called. "I thought it was someone goofing on me, so I hung up," says O'Brien. "She called back and said, 'No, Beth, this is Laura.' She said she liked the drawing and, oops, she made the earring red with her lipstick, and could she use it for an album cover?" The answer was affirmative, of course, and O'Brien received $300 from Columbia and two tickets to Nyro's upcoming concerts in New York. Laura's dab of lipstick, as it turned out, would be the only color on the album cover's snowy-white background.

■ ■ ■

The title of the new work, *Christmas and the Beads of Sweat* (like *Eli and the Thirteenth Confession*, it had been derived from a fusion of song titles, "Christmas in My Soul" and "Beads of Sweat"), gave little clue to the contents of Nyro's latest suite of songs. The opening song, "Brown Earth," does indicate a return to the optimism of *Eli*, as Nyro sets a painterly scene of a neighborhood awakening to the sight of kittens, shooflies, ragamuffin boys, and a "merry boat on the river." She sings, "God's standing on the brown earth / lovelight in the morning . . . white dove's gonna come today," linking the theme of personal happiness to a larger dream of brotherhood, peace, and freedom.

The upbeat second song, oddly and lengthily named "When I Was a Freeport and You Were the Main Drag," deals with the singer's blues over a lover who treats her badly. It contains one of the most amusing lyric lines Nyro ever wrote: "Well I got a lot of patience baby / That's a lot of patience to lose."

"Freeport" may play on the fact that the Long Island town of Freeport was the site of drag races, but Nyro refers to herself as the freeport and her lover as the "drag." Some of her friends believe that the drag was Dallas Taylor, the rugged yet boyish drummer for Crosby, Stills, Nash and Young. He had recently separated from his wife, with whom he had two children. Nyro then went out with him for about six months, perhaps beginning while she was recording *New York Tendaberry*. At the time, Taylor's bandmate Stephen Stills was involved with singer Judy Collins, who also lived on the Upper West Side of Manhattan, and Taylor remembered he and Stills taking the same limo to drop them off at their girlfriends' apartments.

In Taylor's autobiography, a familiar rock-star exegesis of his near death and subsequent recovery from drug addiction and liver damage, Taylor affirmed that Nyro had written a song about him—insisting that David Geffen became jealous of him because of it. ("That's a complete fantasy," says Geffen of his supposed reaction.) Taylor remembered Nyro fondly, describing her as a strong woman whose voice he loved.

He also, rather bluntly, pointed out that she was overweight, large-nosed, and at first glance "plain," but that "she had dark silky hair down to her ass, exquisitely feminine hands, and was quite sexy in the way she carried herself."

Nyro's confident carriage taught a lesson to her friend Kay Crow: "This is what I learned from the woman—it wasn't your size or what you looked like, it's how you felt about yourself," says Crow. "She dressed sexy, she felt sexy, and she came across sexy."

Taylor claimed that he and Nyro broke up over his purchasing his first ounce of cocaine, but that sounds more like a last straw: Alan Merrill, who later hired Taylor to play drums on one of his albums, remembers someone with a heroin problem. When Nyro once described Taylor to Merrill, she had said, "He's a mountain of trouble."

"Nothing ever seemed right with Dallas—she always seemed rattled, and he never seemed comfortable," says Ellen Sander. "I remember seeing her perform at the Fillmore and she announced that song ["Freeport"] with 'I wrote this song when I was waking up every day . . . angry.' She said it with so much feeling that the whole audience seemed to go unh in empathy." Years later, when a fan asked Nyro what the song meant, she answered, "It's all kind of abstract. It's kind of, just, general sarcasm."

The song after "Freeport" on *Christmas and the Beads of Sweat* also has a bouncy groove and an ingratiating melody, but this time without such a painful subtext. In "Blackpatch," Nyro limns a portrait of New York City with "clothespins on wash ropes / window to window tie." In the final verse, she pictures a woman with "lipstick on her reefer / waiting for a match." It's a delightful snapshot of a day in someone's New York life—perhaps Nyro's.

The album takes a very dark turn with Nyro's second "train" song about hard drugs, "Been on a Train." It may have been at least partially inspired by the untimely death of her own twenty-year-old cousin Jimmy Nigro, Mike's son, from an accidental heroin overdose on October 21, 1969. Nyro literally screams, "No No / damn you mister" at one point in the song, hoping to drag the person away from his untimely fate.

Side One ends on a hopeful note, with Nyro's slow, jangly version of "Up on the Roof." She sings it with great sweetness, though her harmonies sometimes have a jarring, dissonant tone, perhaps bringing out the incongruity of finding a "paradise that's troubleproof" in the midst of "all that rat race noise down in the street."

Nyro begins Side Two in a Far Eastern mood with "Upstairs by a Chinese Lamp." According to Boudreau, Nyro owned a "Chinese" lamp with a built-in ashtray, so it's reasonable to assume that she herself is the "sleepy woman by the window" who's dreaming of a man who "takes her sweetness" by a Chinese lamp. The song is sexy and exotic, its orientalism evoked by the use of oud, bells, and soprano sax.

With hardly a pause, Nyro segues into "Map to the Treasure," another erotically charged, Eastern-accented song. Nyro's piano accompaniment is elaborate and insistent, enhanced by Alice Coltrane's magical-sounding harp arpeggios. (Both Coltrane and saxophonist Pharoah Sanders had been exploring Asian sounds in their work at that time, and Nyro may have taken some inspiration from them, along with her own growing interest in yoga and all things Eastern.) "For you I bear down / soft and burning," Nyro sings, offering herself up in much the same way as she did in "The Confession" on Eli. Indeed, the way "Treasure" soars up and down in both tempo and intensity simulates the excitement, and then exhaustion, of a sexual experience.

The next song on Christmas, "Beads of Sweat," hews to a hard-rock groove fueled by Danelli's drumming and Allman's burning guitar licks, albeit spiced with some of Nyro's famed tempo stops. "Listen to the wailing / of the rain in the river," Nyro herself wails. As in "Eli's Comin'," Nyro seems to be running away from an unspecified evil, thus making stormy weather seem both real and metaphorical.

Nyro ends the album with a political protest song, "Christmas in My Soul," which she had previously read as a poem in concert. The season has turned to a darkening late autumn (it's springtime in "Upstairs," and Indian summer in "Map") as Nyro decries "the sins of politics / the politics of sin." She lists specific grievances—the imprisoned Black Panthers and Chicago Seven, the homeless Native Americans—and puts out a call to "fight." The song is almost too earnest, including a militaristic drum roll crescendo near the end. But Nyro comes from such an impassioned place, and her vocal is so tender, that she battles the sentimentality and overspecificity ("it's difficult to see how the verse about the Panthers and the Chicago Seven is going to ride out time and indifference," wrote one critic) to at least a draw.

Columbia released the single of "Up on the Roof" on September 1, 1970; the entire album came out two months later, on November 25. Record World accurately described the critical and popular ambivalence about Nyro in its notice about the new album: "Laura Nyro sings her songs the way the gull flies—now high, now low, now fast, now slow. No seeming logic. Some can't stand this; others can't get enough of it. The latter will buy this album; former will wait for other versions of the unique, beautiful, silver songs."

Predictably, the reviews of Nyro's new work were mixed. In *Rolling Stone*, two different record critics gave their imprimatur to the single, but otherwise slammed Nyro. Reviewing "Up on the Roof," Ed Ward began, "I hate Laura Nyro and her blackboard-and-fingernails voice and daintily soulful pretensions." He then acknowledged ("dammit") that her version of the song, with what he considered flawless production by Cavaliere and Mardin, was an unbeatable reading. He promised to take back the nasty things he'd said about the artist if she continued along a similar musical path in the future.

Two months later, *Rolling Stone*'s assessment of the entire album ran second in the reviews section to that of Janis Joplin's posthumous *Pearl*. Alec Dubro also found "Up on the Roof" beautiful and praised Nyro for reflecting the moods and colors of New York with more artistry than anyone since John Coltrane. But then he complained that her technique had become static, and that many of the cuts sounded to him like her earlier material. He speculated that perhaps she had been turned off by the commercial success of her songs, many of which had become "TV Prime Time staples, performed and misinterpreted by every no-talent with show-biz connections." Moreover, he found her music "too bloody serious": "[It] can be appreciated for its virtuosity, but it's hard to just sit back and dig on it," he wrote.

Britain's *Melody Maker*, on the other hand, loved the album unreservedly, complimenting the musicianship, Mardin's arrangements, and the "descriptive quality" of Nyro's songwriting. *Rock* newspaper, too, gave the album unstinting praise. To reviewer Robb Baker, the title of the album perfectly denoted the strained attempt to reconcile the notion of "peace on earth" at Christmas with America's painful political struggles ("beads of sweat"). "You want to proselytize about it," wrote Baker of Nyro's work, "but quietly, for it doesn't really matter if there are other believers: It's an album that's yours alone, a special country into which others are welcome but cannot be led."

Christmas would spend fourteen weeks on *Billboard*'s album chart, peaking at No. 51. But it was a problematic album for record sellers: To this day, certain stores still list it as a "Christmas" album and stock it only from October through December.

Cavaliere had warned Nyro of that likelihood. "Columbia came to us and said, 'Look, if you put the word Christmas on this, as soon as the holidays are over they're going to pull it out of the rack,' " he remembers. "I said, 'Laura, take the name off, what's the big deal?' But to her it was like, 'You've insulted me, you have insulted me down to my very root, and I will not speak to you the rest of the day.' " To counteract the title, Columbia's ads for the album used the phrase "Songs for every day of the year."

Christmas is a memorable addition to Nyro's oeuvre, but didn't advance her art as dramatically as Eli and New York Tendaberry. Her tempo changes, syncopation, and lyrical concerns had become familiar, and given the stylistic divide between the album's two sides, the album didn't feel as unified as its predecessors. But taken in the context of the previous two albums, Christmas seems like the completion of an important trilogy: Eli took her from girlhood to the first stirrings of womanhood, New York Tendaberry plunged her into the torrent of the city, and now Christmas celebrated a certain settling-in, along with a growing eye to universal concerns.

"At a certain age you become aware of your country," she told British journalist Penny Valentine in early 1971. "With my first album all I thought about was my songs, not much else at all."

It was her growing maturity, Nyro indicated, that allowed her to speak out on political and moral issues—a stance common among popular artists at the time. "I believe there is a world inside and outside each person," she told Valentine. "The more together you are inside the more you can reach out with wisdom."

■ ■ ■

Christmas and the Beads of Sweat marked the end of four remarkably fertile years of creation for Nyro, during which she'd recorded four albums and forty-four songs, only one of which she didn't write. As if to mark it for reference, let alone market her very popular compositions, in mid-1971 Warner Bros. Publications put out The Music of Laura Nyro, a thick songbook of the forty-three Nyro originals. Like many songbooks, it doesn't reproduce her unique piano accompaniments, but its twenty-two pages of photos, drawings, and collages do provide a revealing, if veiled, look at Nyro's private life.

One photo shows a smiling Nyro walking with a tall, mustached man who holds a travel bag: He's jack-of-all-trades Peter Dallas, a friend of "every great female diva in New York," according to former Manhattan cabaret performer Harriet Leider, who came to know Nyro through Dallas. He also worked for some of those divas, including doing lighting for Bette Midler. For Nyro, Dallas acted as a guardian angel, says Leider, not just handling her lighting and sound but advising her on what to wear and standing guard at her dressing room door.

"If someone smiled at her during a show and she liked the color of his eyes, Dallas would not let him backstage," says Leider. "I remember a discussion in the dressing room once about some guy who had sent her flowers. She said, 'Dallas, but they're *gardenias!*' He said, 'I don't care if it was Billie Holiday, he's not coming backstage.' "

In the songbook picture, Nyro and Dallas, who was also a filmmaker, may have been embarking on the trip they took together to India. On the following pages are more travel shots, including Nyro in Japan and Nyro being hugged by Swami Satchidananda (perhaps on her Sri Lanka visit). Those images are followed by the two-page spread of Nyro and Jim Fielder hugging and kissing.

At the back of the songbook is a full-page shot of Nyro behind a glass door at 157 West Seventy-ninth Street, just down the street from her Seventy-ninth Street apartment. Sitting outside the door to Nyro's right is Richard Chiaro, her road manager. Leaning against the door to her left, a cigarette dangling from his mouth, is David Bianchini, the man Laura Nyro would marry. But that's getting ahead of the story.

10
GONNA TAKE A MIRACLE

While still recording *Christmas and the Beads of Sweat* in April of 1970, Nyro went to see Miles Davis perform at the Fillmore East. Nyro even sent Davis a box of red roses backstage, *Rolling Stone* reported. Miles, having released the groundbreaking jazz-fusion album *Bitches Brew* on Columbia Records in 1969, was looking to capture a more youthful audience, which made promoter Bill Graham's Fillmore—a former East Village movie theater that had been transformed into a rock palace of tattered elegance—an attractive venue. Two months later, Nyro made her own first appearance at the Fillmore on a bill with the artist she so admired. The four-day engagement, from June 17 through 20, featured Nyro as the headliner and the Miles Davis Quintet as "Special Guest."

According to Miles in his 1989 autobiography, their connection didn't expand much beyond the professional. "Laura Nyro was a very quiet person offstage and I think I frightened her," he wrote. David Geffen disputes that characterization. "Laura loved Miles, *loved* Miles, thought he was the greatest," he says. "He used to flirt with her all the time. No, she wasn't scared of him, that's not true. She thought he was sexy. And she thought he was the greatest musician. She was a giant, *giant* Miles Davis fan."

Lou Nigro was curious to see the famed trumpeter open for his daughter, but found the Fillmore to be "practically empty" during Miles's set. "Everybody came to see Laura and they didn't want to see him—they were sitting around the lobby, on the steps," remembers Nigro. Davis nonetheless received a warm response (though nothing like Nyro's standing ovation and three encores), and that convinced him that *he* was the main attraction. So he accosted Geffen backstage and accused Geffen of cheating him, since Nyro was earning more money.

"Miles was a *huge* egomaniac," laughs Geffen, who had to explain to Davis that Nyro was the headliner. "He was a crazy guy—he was extremely hostile and violent and crazy. But it was a very difficult time between blacks and whites. He was very conscious of not being ripped off by whitey."

After the *Christmas* album was released in late November, Nyro began another short tour, this time at a Los Angeles venue much ritzier than the Fillmore: the Dorothy Chandler Pavillion of the Music Center. The chandeliered 3,000-seat theater had rarely showcased anything other than symphony and opera, and *Los Angeles Times* critic Robert Hilburn figured that the pop music audience "must have marveled . . . at the acoustics, comfort, and setting." Hilburn marveled over the red-gowned Nyro's performance: "As usual, [it] was a blend of totally impressive writing and vocal ability," he wrote.

Laura's opening act that December 16 and 17, as well as for the rest of the tour, wasn't about to argue over billing: Jackson Browne, a folkish singer-songwriter from Orange County, California, was just getting started in the business, although his songs had already been recorded by the Nitty Gritty Dirt Band and German chanteuse Nico. Browne had sent a letter to David Geffen earlier in the year along with an acetate of his song "Jamaica Say You Will," but Geffen tossed it, unheard, into the trash. His secretary, however, noticing a photo of the angel-faced Browne, fished it out and played it. She brought it back to her boss, who soon signed on as Browne's manager.

Geffen also introduced Browne to Nyro, who was just a year older. Browne would become not only her opening act but—according to several of Laura's close friends—her lover.

"It was never a great big relationship, frankly," says Geffen. "Maybe it was for her. I don't remember it being a cause of tremendous pain. Jackson was very pretty, not at all the kind of guy she was usually interested in. She liked Sonny Bono! Jackson Browne is classically good looking, matinee-idol good looking."

Alan Merrill didn't realize the nature of Nyro's involvement with Browne when she visited Merrill in Japan on one of many trips she took to that country in the 1970s. She brought out a Martin guitar Browne had given her as a present and underneath it was Browne's picture. "I love him," Nyro said, but Merrill thought she just meant that she loved his music or loved him as a friend. "It was the sixties," Merrill explains. "The word *love* was bandied about freely."

Nyro, as always, kept her romances under wraps. "She always asked me about my love life, but didn't give much away about her own affairs, now that I think of it," says Merrill. "I always just assumed she was not in any really close personal love relationships, because she didn't talk about them much. That sly fox."

Stephen Paley, who photographed Nyro and Browne together, remembers Laura staying with Jackson at his small yellow bungalow in Los Angeles, and Jackson staying with Laura in her New York apartment. At one point, Browne ended up on Paley's sofa in New York for a week, Nyro having kicked him out after a fight.

Laura's friend Kay Crow recalls the relationship as being very stormy, even though both were soft in demeanor. "I know she was absolutely nuts about him," says Crow. "But she wasn't easy. Whatever she wanted to do, she wanted to do it now." Crow believes that Browne wrote the song "Nightingale" (recorded by the Eagles on their 1972 debut album) for Nyro. Some of its lyrics: "There goes my baby / singing like a nightingale . . . Tell the Lord above / I've got a brand new love / that cannot fail." Coincidentally, a song that Nyro was performing in concert in 1970 but never recorded, "Mother Earth," contains the line "I've gone where nightingales sing."

Nyro never went public about her relationship with Browne, who was from Orange County in Southern California, just like her former boyfriend Jim Fielder. But Donald Boudreau remembers an intimate moment between them a week after their Music Center shows, when they played the Fillmore East. As Nyro left the stage, says Boudreau, she was met by Browne and they kissed on the lips—a gesture he claims made the audience loudly swoon.

Still an unknown quantity, Browne was hardly noticed at the Fillmore. Down Beat's reviewer praised Nyro by pointing out that only she, the Grateful Dead, and Crosby, Stills, Nash and Young could sell out the hall's 3,000 seats without a strong second act. Nyro also received a worshipful review in the trade magazine Record World, whose Dave Finkle wrote that there was a moment during "Christmas in My Soul," "so moving . . . it lifted what could be called broadly a rock concert into some new realm of excitement."

The relationship between Nyro and Browne doesn't seem to have lasted much beyond the last date of their tour at London's Royal Festival Hall on February 6, 1971. Again Nyro, in an off-the-shoulder Spanish dress, received all the critical attention. Richard Williams of Melody Maker described how she "leaned back ecstatically at the end of each number while the spotlights dimmed to a pinpoint and died." One never felt any sense of falseness in her theatricality, said Williams, "because the music is true and the trappings somehow enhance that honesty rather than give the lie to it."

It seems that Browne was the last of Nyro's rock-star boyfriends, and happily so. She had told Donald Boudreau that it was hard to meet men in professions other than her own, lamenting that affairs with other musicians seemed almost preordained to be transient and short-lived. Nyro instead wanted an unwavering long-term relationship. As she had told an interviewer early in 1970, "Love is the whole thing. It's what makes a woman feel like a woman and a man feel like a man." She added, in a hippie-style sentiment of the times, "Men are beautiful, you know." Her own love life, she asserted, was focused more on settling down than running around: "I like when there is one man, when I can say, 'He's my man.' "

■ ■ ■

By 1971, Nyro's work life had become the typical whirlwind of a successful recording artist: She made an album, toured, wrote new songs, made another album, and toured again, all the while solidifying her reputation as one of the most charismatic performers in pop music. Never relying on her "hits" or a standard set of tunes, she was always experimenting with her repertoire, adding new compositions while still working on them and throwing in favorite oldies as the mood struck her.

In May of 1971, for example, Nyro returned to London to do a televised concert for the BBC, produced by Stanley Dorfmann. Her set opened with covers of two well-known soul ballads—Carole King's "Natural Woman," made famous by Aretha Franklin, and "Ain't Nothing Like the Real Thing," a Marvin Gaye/Tammi Terrell favorite. She also did a medley of three seemingly unrelated songs—her own "Timer," the Five Stairsteps' hit "O-o-h Child," and her now-signature version of "Up on the Roof"—thus beginning a career-long habit of recombining original material with favorite oldies. Nyro sang two new compositions at that concert, the aforementioned "Mother Earth" (a sort of ecological love ballad) and the soaring "I Am the Blues," a song she would later rework and record in 1975.

Nyro would perform again at the Fillmore East that May, on a bill with Spencer Davis and Peter Jameson. In a publication celebrating the club's demise (it would close a month after Nyro's May 30 engage-ment), it was suggested that she'd become "an institution unto herself" at the theater—someone who never used a light show and whose au-dience brought only "adulation and flowers" rather than overdoses and bad trips. "Whenever Laura played the F.E.," wrote Amalie Rothschild in her photographic memoir of the theater, "there was a special atmo-sphere—a real lovefest between her, the audience, and her eerily emo-tional music. Hovering over her piano, with her long black hair flowing, she was a haunted, and haunting, presence."

Despite the excitement she engendered, Nyro was conflicted about performing. On one hand, she battled fear and self-doubt; on the other, she was willing and quite able to create an hypnotic musical séance. She even admitted once to an interviewer that since she had "a dramatic flair, a little, not too much," she harbored a fantasy of doing something *really* remarkable at the piano during a concert. "I want to stop in the middle sometime," she said, "and pick up one of the piano keys—have it made out of sugar or something—and eat it."

Laura would sometimes come offstage and say, "That was really ter-rible, the audience got ripped off," says her road manager Richard Chiaro. He finally told her that she was so good that what was bad to her was still top-notch to the audience. "Bottom line, it was always a really good show," says Chiaro. "She got to believe that after a while."

Her audience was filled with true believers, as the devotional nature of Nyro's concerts had grown along with her status as a pop cult icon. In a review of another 1971 performance, at the Westbury Music Fair on Long Island, critic Ian Dove wrote: "She maintained the religious feeling right to the end and it was a surprise to see her walk off the stage rather than levitate."

Ironically, when Nyro tried to inject a bit of religiosity—albeit of the Eastern persuasion—into one performance, she met with some re-sistance. At yet another New York performance, on February 21, 1971—this a benefit for Swami Satchidananda's Integral Yoga Institute at Carnegie Hall, which also featured the Rascals and Alice Coltrane—she gave a surprisingly long rap about the guru. She said that the first time she had spoken to Satchidananda, she asked him how she could get a certain man to fall in love with her. His answer, she reported, was "You have to be his woman and his lover. You have to be his best friend, you have to be his sister, you have to be his mother. You have to be his maid . . . And then he wouldn't need any other woman."

At this point, someone in the audience yelled out, "Bullshit." These were, after all, the heady early days of the women's movement, when feminists believed that a woman's rediscovered needs took precedence over a man's. Nyro played a few notes on the piano, then stopped and said, "You may think it's bullshit, but I think it's true." The audience heartily applauded, probably more for Nyro's feistiness than for the politically incorrect sentiment.

It was quite rare for Nyro to be so self-revealing onstage. "All Laura wanted to do was show you her art; she never wanted to show you herself," says Chiaro.

■ ■ ■

As Nyro won raves as a performer, other artists continued to steal her thunder on the record charts. The next big hit of a Nyro tune wouldn't be sung by a pop group, but by über-diva Barbra Streisand.

Although Streisand had been the bestselling female vocalist of the 1960s, her show tunes and standards had lost favor by the end of the decade and her individual album sales dropped from about a million copies to 350,000. So Clive Davis approached L.A.-based producer Richard Perry, whose projects had ranged from Ella Fitzgerald and Fats Domino to Tiny Tim, to help reinvent her as a pop singer. "Naturally, he was dying to produce her," wrote Davis.

Perry was also a "huge" Nyro fan, so among the contemporary material he brought to the project were three Nyro tunes: "Stoney End," "Flim Flam Man" (originally "Hands off the Man"), and "Time and Love." "I've always felt that Laura's music could be the basis of a Broadway musical," says Perry, adding a familiar refrain: "She was kind of like the Gershwin of her generation."

Geffen had a hand in the Nyro-Streisand connection as well, having set up a meeting between the two in Los Angeles. According to Ellen Sander, he even told Streisand that Laura had written a song just for her—which she hadn't. When he asked Nyro to confirm this for Streisand she refused, much to his dismay.

Streisand was more than happy to sing Nyro's songs, though, and since Nyro's writing had such a strong theatrical flavor, it provided her the perfect crossover bridge. Released in early 1971 with the title Stoney End, Streisand's album became a platinum seller, and all three Nyro covers would eventually be released as singles. (Streisand also recorded

Nyro's "I Never Meant to Hurt You" on a second Perry-produced album, *Barbra Joan Streisand*, released in August of 1971.)

"Stoney End" proved the most popular Nyro song for Streisand. She hadn't been the first to cover it: Linda Ronstadt had included it on an early album, *Stone Poneys Vol. III*, while Lou Adler had produced two versions of it, the first by the Blossoms and the second—using the same backing track, which featured the Wrecking Crew (of Monterey Pop infamy)—by Peggy Lipton, star of TV's *Mod Squad* and Adler's girlfriend at the time. Streisand finally made it a hit, as *Billboard* had predicted in their Top 60 Pop Spotlight: "The Laura Nyro rhythm number serves as potent, commercial 'today' material for the stylist." Released in mid-December of 1970, the single spent twelve weeks on the charts, peaking at No. 6.

As Bones Howe had accomplished with the Fifth Dimension, Perry's smoothed-out arrangement, along with Streisand's inherent dramatics, proved just the ticket to reach the mainstream. "Laura tended to lean toward the esoteric side in terms of her records," explains Perry. "It was almost as if she didn't want to have a consistent groove that would be the vehicle to appeal to the masses."

Yet Nyro's songs had enough groove to appeal to modern dancers, with two prestigious dance companies appropriating her music as a backdrop for their works. Choreographer Ann Ditchburn of the National Ballet of Canada created the ballet *Brown Earth* for its 1970–71 season, using Nyro's "Brown Earth," "Emmie," "Upstairs by a Chinese Lamp," "Map to the Treasure," and "Beads of Sweat," plus the Goffin/King song Nyro had become identified with, "Up on the Roof."

On May 4, 1971, New York's Alvin Ailey Dance Theater premiered *Cry*, choreographed by Ailey and featuring Nyro's "Been on a Train." Originally performed by Judith Jameson, the company's principal female dancer (and now its artistic director), the sixteen-minute solo depicts a woman's journey from the agonies of slavery to an ecstatic state of grace. Besides "Train," the accompaniment for the dance includes Alice Coltrane's instrumental "Something About John Coltrane" and the Voices of East Harlem's rendition of Chuck Griffin's "Right On, Be Free." Nyro must have been thrilled to keep company with both Coltranes and with a noted gospel choir, let alone having her music dance to by the premier African American company in the nation. Thirty years later, *Cry* remains a mainstay in the Ailey repertoire.

■ ■ ■

With the success of others recording her material, it may have seemed only fair for Nyro to become a "cover girl" herself, doing an entire album of tunes she did not write. The year before, Harry Nilsson had put out a whole album of Randy Newman covers, Nilsson Sings Newman, so the notion had a precedent.

It also must have been a creative relief for Nyro to let others provide material for a change. She had been performing some new songs during her 1970 concerts, including "Mother Earth" and the peace anthem "American Dove," and she would read a poem, "Coal Truck," that could have become a song, but she probably didn't have enough material for a full album.

Moreover, Nyro was an extraordinary song interpreter. Audiences loved when she performed oldies in concert, sometimes spontaneously singing along to "Up on the Roof," "O-o-h Child," or "Natural Woman." She was also known to perform the Kingston Trio's folk chestnut "Tom Dooley," Dionne Warwick's Bacharach–David classic, "Walk On By," and the Crystals' "He's Sure the Boy I Love," all to great response. At her London concert, at which she sang the latter song and Ben E. King's 1961 hit "Spanish Harlem," reviewer Richard Williams noted that she bent them to her will, "making them sound as though she'd written both." In fact, Nyro always used her own chords and start-and-stop tempos on others' tunes, fully "Nyro-izing" them.

Although her recording of "Up on the Roof" had proved the closest thing to a hit single in her career, it's doubtful that commercial considerations drove her to record others' material. Rather, she adored the songs she'd grown up singing and swooning over, from Bronx street corner doo-wop to the soulful sounds of Detroit, Chicago, Philadelphia, and New York's Brill Building. As Lenny Kaye put it in his Rolling Stone review, her new album at the very least would bear "witness to the fact that Laura Nyro has the best record collection on Central Park West."

Gonna Take a Miracle, as it would be titled, may thus be seen as one of the first rock tribute albums, paying homage to an era rather than to a single artist or writer. It was also, British journalist Ian MacDonald suggested, a logical pause from original work after Nyro completed the trilogy that began with Eli and the Thirteenth Confession. The Christmas album had to be the end of that particular string of work, he wrote, because "Laura Nyro had won her personal struggle with the creative gift that had set her apart as a girl. Only one thing left to do: revisit the place it had all begun."

Nyro had been planning an oldies collection since at least the end of 1970, and Stephen Paley claims to have originally given her the idea (his fetching portrait of a wistful-looking Nyro would grace the album cover). But it was Britisher Vicki Wickham who helped ignite the collaboration between Nyro and the women who would add genuine street soul to the album—the female trio Labelle.

Wickham, who had been a producer on the seminal British rock and roll TV show *Ready Steady Go* and would later manage Dusty Springfield, was then settled in New York and managing the Philadelphia girl group formerly known as Patti LaBelle and the Blue Belles. Renamed Labelle (like Patti's name, but with a lowercase *b*) the trio combined Patti's piercing lead with the super-tight, sometimes eerie harmonies of Nona Hendryx and Sarah Dash. The Blue Belles had been best known for fever-pitched versions of "Danny Boy" and "You'll Never Walk Alone," as well as for their 1962 hit, "I Sold My Heart to the Junkman"—the song Laura's friend Carol Amoruso had introduced to her. As Labelle, the trio began to reinvent the whole notion of a girl group, modernizing their look and even writing some of their own songs, the latter being a revolutionary act for a female ensemble.

Besides managing, Wickham was also New York correspondent for the British pop music paper *Melody Maker*. That's why she arranged an interview with Nyro (they had a mutual friend, Peter Dallas). Serendipitously, she brought along Patti LaBelle, who was rehearsing in New York. LaBelle certainly knew of Nyro's songwriting, as her group had included a gospel-tinged version of "Time and Love" on their debut album, *Labelle*, released by Warner Bros. earlier in the year. "It won't take that long, and then we'll go get something to eat," Wickham told Patti.

When Nyro saw the singer at her apartment door, however, she gushed, "Ooh, you're Patti LaBelle!" and the pair spent twenty minutes talking about the Blue Belles before Wickham could get a question in edgewise. Wickham and LaBelle ended up staying for dinner, with Laura and Patti singing at the piano. "Once we met, we became like soul sisters," says LaBelle. "It was instant bond."

Nyro soon asked Patti, Nona, and Sarah to harmonize with her on *Gonna Take a Miracle*. They were ideal geographically as well as musically, since Nyro had already decided to record in Philadelphia with writer-producers Kenneth Gamble and Leon Huff. "I think Laura felt she needed somebody from that era who really understood it," says Wickham. "Philadelphia was Pat's hometown, so I'm quite sure it struck Laura that if she went to Philly, Pat was just up the road."

Gamble and Huff were to Philly what Berry Gordy Jr. was to Detroit: They had created a trademark city-soul sound crafted by a gifted stable of musicians, writers, and arrangers. The first Gamble/Huff hit had been the Soul Survivors' "Expressway to Your Heart," followed by songs such as Madeline Bell's "I'm Gonna Make You Love Me," the Intruders' "Cowboys to Girls," and Jerry Butler's "Moody Woman" and "What's the Use of Breaking Up." Later, the producers became known for the slick sound of the O'Jays, Billy Paul, MFSB, and Harold Melvin and the Blue Notes.

"I think we really found ourselves about 1970," says Gamble, who was the main lyricist and vocal arranger, while keyboardist Huff focused more on the melodies and instrumental arrangements. "The [house] band had really come into its own." That year, Gamble and Huff had also produced Dusty Springfield's Philly-soul album on Atlantic Records, A Brand New Me, but Wickham says that Nyro's interest in the producers wasn't connected to their work with the British singer.

Percussionist Nydia Mata, a longtime fan of Nyro's who also met her through Peter Dallas, a former schoolmate, was at Laura's apartment the day she first got together with the Labelle trio. Nyro had invited Nydia to go see the film Black Orpheus, but then Vicki Wickham called to say she was bringing Patti, Nona, and Sarah over. With Nyro at the piano, "the girls started wailing," says Mata. "Boy, did they sing. And I picked up Laura's little red Chinese drum and started playing along—I couldn't help myself. Talk about being at the right place at the right time! When they left, Laura was freaking out, she was so excited."

Nyro already had several songs in mind for the album, but she took the opportunity of a trip to Japan with Barbara Greenstein to choose more. They carried along with them a stack of Greenstein's 45s and a portable record player. "Many of them made it to the album," says Greenstein proudly.

Despite Gamble and Huff's presence on the project, Nyro remained fully in charge. Gamble remembers that she not only chose the material but had the instrumental arrangements structured around her piano playing and worked out the vocal harmonies with Labelle. "They were so well rehearsed—they knew those songs backwards and forwards," he says. Besides practicing at Nyro's apartment, they harmonized together at the Bellvue Stratford Hotel in downtown Philly, where Laura stayed during the week while recording that July. "We're singing so naturally, really emotionally, like animals," she told Alan Merrill on a phone call to him in Tokyo.

Nyro also insisted that Mata, then just an inexperienced nineteen-year-old, be part of the recording, probably because she had been present when Nyro first sang with Labelle in her apartment. Laura liked to bring "home" along with her. "Laura had decided I was going to play congas, because I told her I played congas," says Mata. "Actually, I had only played congas at parties—I'm Cuban, so it's natural—but I had never taken a conga lesson and I didn't own one. I went into the studio with no idea what I was going to play."

Gamble and Huff had hired their regular percussionist Larry Washington for the gig, but because Nyro wanted Mata on congas they switched Washington to bongos. "This is embarrassing," says Mata, who can laugh at the memory now, "but before every song I'd ask Larry, 'Can you just give me an idea of what you might play on this?' "

The recording sessions at Gamble and Huff's home base, Sigma Sound Studios, took about a month. Gamble remembers that a tired Nyro sometimes begged off the daily session after a couple of hours. "We tried to push her as hard as we could, but I'd always be on her side," he says. "I remember Laura Nyro as the girl with the flower in her hair. Always smiling and soft and very sensitive."

Labelle wasn't quite as patient with Nyro's slow progress on the album's vocals. After spending a week waiting to lay down their parts, Patti and Vicki grew antsy. They finally told Gamble and Huff that the singers needed to finish their vocals in a single day, and Patti bet Leon Huff a thousand dollars that they could do it.

Less than five hours later, LaBelle was a thousand dollars richer and Nyro had obtained wonderful raw-sounding harmonies. "It was a very natural album," says LaBelle. "Whenever we made a mistake that sounded cool, we left it in, even if it sounded flat. If it wasn't too broke, we weren't going to fix it."

"The hardness of the Blue Belles and the softness of Laura Nyro— that's a great combination," says Gamble. "Laura's stuff is so soft and breathy; Patti and the Blue Belles had sort of a hard harmony with a sweet edge to it. It was a great, great collaboration."

Not everything they recorded, or considered recording, made it onto the album: *Rolling Stone* reported that the lineup would also include Gamble/Huff's "Cowboys to Girls," "Ain't Nothing Like the Real Thing" (in a medley with "It's Gonna Take a Miracle"), and the Crystals' hit "Da Doo Ron Ron (When He Walked Me Home)." Nyro may also have intended to record Goffin/King's "No Easy Way Down," a song she had performed live. At Carole King's June 18, 1971, concert at Carnegie Hall, King told the audience that the song had been recorded by "such notables as Dusty Springfield, Barbra Streisand, and Laura Nyro," but only the first two actually put the song to vinyl.

It's hard now to imagine any other songs on the album, because the triumphant melding of celebration and nostalgia seems complete as it is. *Miracle* didn't simply transport the listener back to a more innocent time: With knowingness and sophistication, Nyro drew the music of the past decade into the present, as if she had climbed into the grooves of the beloved old records and resculpted them. One could dance to the album—the upbeat songs are typically faster and more propulsive than the originals—or dreamily linger over the slowed-down romantic ballads. Patti, Nona, and Sarah's background harmonies seal the record's magic, although it's unfair to call them background since they're so upfront in the mix. One can easily picture all four women as teenagers, singing in a subway station in the Bronx.

The album begins with a hand-clapping, finger-snapping, a cappella (until the chorus) version of the Shirelles' early-sixties song "I Met Him on a Sunday," each singer offering a lead line. Nyro, a Shirelle, at last! Before the last "oo-oo-oo-oo" fades away, Nyro and Labelle glide into "The Bells," a 1970 Motown release by the Originals that was cowritten and produced by Marvin Gaye. One of the album's highlights, and a song that Patti LaBelle still performs in concert, "The Bells" is infused with a desperate longing that's in stark contrast to the macho swagger of the male group that first sang it.

Then it's dance time, with the infectious Curtis Mayfield–penned Major Lance hit from 1963, "Monkey Time," which segues into Martha Reeves and the Vandellas' hugely popular "Dancing in the Street" from 1964. Nyro reinvented this and three other sixties Motown favorites—the Vandellas' "Nowhere to Run" ('65) and "Jimmie Mack" ('67), and Smokey Robinson and the Miracles' "You've Really Got a Hold on Me" ('62)—by adding extended vocal finales, much as she had done on some of her own songs. The result arouses a revivalistic spirit, heightened by Labelle's impassioned harmonies and Patti's improvised soaring. On "You've Really Got a Hold on Me," for example, Nyro dramatically speeds up the song for a percussion-driven coda in which the singers keep repeating a line Nyro added: "Hold me baby and don't turn me loose,'cause I love love love . . . ooooh." The sexual charge is unmistakable as the last line slowly fades out with a luxuriant "oooooooooooh."

The rest of the album leans toward lovesick doo-wop and lush R&B balladry. The classic doo-wops are "Desiree" (originally "Deserie," done in 1957 by the Harlem male quintet the Charts) and "The Wind" (Nyro's early favorite recorded by Nolan Strong and the Diablos, and then by the Jesters). Nyro smoothly harmonized with herself only on these songs, and Gamble and Huff wisely stripped down the instrumentation to just voice and piano (plus vibes on "Desiree"). Both feel ethereal, with "The Wind" literally evoking the meteorological phenomenon.

Nyro gives the R&B ballads—"Spanish Harlem" and the Royalettes' minor 1965 classic, "It's Gonna Take a Miracle"—a polish similar to that on her version of "Up on the Roof." "Spanish Harlem" neatly gender-shifts Ben E. King's original "red rose up in Spanish Harlem" to a man "with eyes as black as coal." That prompted critic Vince Aletti to remark, "I like that; men can be roses too."

Gonna Take a Miracle was released on November 17, 1971, and drew mostly favorable reviews. Despite reservations he had about the arrangement of certain cuts, Aletti called it "as good as anything I've heard this year," and rated it the seventh-best album on his annual list—ahead of Joni Mitchell's acclaimed Blue (No. 8) and Carole King's wildly popular Tapestry (No. 10). In the British magazine Sounds, Penny Valentine opined that the songs took on a fresh sheen without losing their original feel, "even though [Nyro] has bent them round her voice and restructured them to her own ideas."

Somewhat less enthusiastic was Rolling Stone's Lenny Kaye, who admitted that the album "succeeds even through its disappointments" but chided Nyro for not deciding whether to be slick or pared down. Critic Robert Christgau graded the album with only a B−, suggesting that "I Met Him on a Sunday" and "Monkey Time/Dancing in the Street" were "ear-openers," but that the rest was Nyro ("the Bronx tearjerker") wrongly trying to turn girl-group rock and roll into "untrammeled lyricism."

Listeners, however, were unreservedly taken with Miracle. "When I first heard the album," says singer-songwriter Melissa Manchester, "I just collapsed. I could not believe the perfection of that vision."

According to a Columbia ad, the album was selling "faster than any album Laura has ever made." The reason, Vince Aletti suggested, was that it was different enough from Nyro's past material to attract listeners who had previously found her "too mannered." It would eventually reach No. 46 on the *Billboard* album chart, and a little higher (No. 41) on *Billboard*'s chart of Best-Selling Soul LPs, where Nyro found herself sandwiched between Stevie Wonder and the Isley Brothers. Her first single from the album, "It's Gonna Take a Miracle," reached No. 103 on *Billboard*'s rankings.

In another music trade magazine, *Record World*, the album was an utter smash: No. 3 on that publication's R&B Album Chart of March 11, 1972. The album also helped launch Labelle's career. "I think it gave them real credibility with the white singer-songwriter crowd," says Wickham. Three years later, they would score a huge hit single with "Lady Marmalade"—cowritten by Bob Crewe, the former employer of Nyro's arranger-producers Charlie Calello and Herb Bernstein—and the trio transformed themselves into space-age divas in platform boots, metallic breastplates, and feathered headgear.

As frosting to the musical collaboration, *Miracle* solidified a personal friendship between Patti and Laura. "Laura became a Labelle groupie," says Wickham. "She literally went on the road with them." Laura would also come visit Patti for a week or more at her Philadelphia apartment, harmonizing with her at the piano to "corny stuff like 'It's My Party' or Marvin Gaye songs," says LaBelle. They cooked together, as Nyro—whose culinary repertoire began and ended with tuna fish—learned to whip up tasty fried chicken under LaBelle's tutelage. Laura also appreciated the easygoing family life LaBelle shared with her husband, Armstead Edwards. "I want a husband like Armstead and a place like this," she told Patti.

Nyro would get married the next year, in fact, and when she planned her honeymoon trip to Japan she invited LaBelle and Edwards to come along for a week as her guest. LaBelle remembers staying one night at a low-class hotel and the next in luxury digs.

"Laura said, 'We're going to live like peasants tonight, and then the next night we're gonna live high on the hog,' " LaBelle remembers. "She respected the lower-class people who didn't have as much money as she did. All the money and stuff that she had, she didn't need it. Without it, she would have still been the wonderful person that she was."

LaBelle and Edwards gained an added benefit from the trip—nine months later, their son Zuri was born. "He was, like, 'Made in Japan' the first night we were there, in Kyoto," says LaBelle. "I told Laura a month later, 'I'm pregnant, and you're the reason, because you got us there and we got drunk on sake!' "

After Zuri was born, LaBelle suffered a serious bout of postpartum depression, and it was Nyro who came to her rescue as "Zuri's nanny and my psychiatrist," she said. She especially recalls Nyro sitting with the infant under the shade of a large oak tree in the yard, rocking him to sleep. When LaBelle's gloom lifted in a few weeks and Nyro was about to leave, LaBelle professed an inability to repay her kindness.

"That's what friends are for," Nyro simply replied.

But the friendship did not survive Nyro's subsequent retreat from the music business and Patti's eventual stardom as a solo artist. When LaBelle would sing "The Bells" in concert in the mid-1980s, she introduced it by mentioning her "good friend Laura Nyro." But in 1986, asked by Interview what had happened to Nyro, who had been out of the public eye for a number of years, LaBelle's answer was "To be honest, I don't know where she is."

11
MARRIAGE—AND A DIVORCE

Nyro closed out 1971 with another unforgettable Carnegie Hall appearance, this time on Christmas Eve. Before the concert, Richard Chiaro and Nyro spent several hours at the nearby Steinway piano showroom choosing an instrument for her to play. As Steinway salesmen rolled their eyes, she tried every piano in the house, judging one to be "too bold," another "too stiff." Finally, like Goldilocks, she found one that was just right.

Nyro opened the show with "It's Gonna Take a Miracle" and performed an entire set, and an encore, in her familiar solo style. For her second encore, though, she called on her "three lovely girlfriends," and Patti LaBelle, Nona Hendryx, and Sarah Dash came onstage to sing "The Wind," "Monkey Time/Dancing in the Street," and "The Bells." Imagine Nyro's confidence that she would be called back that second time, withholding the treat she had planned with an unerring sense of drama.

"The temperature rose many a degree and everyone started dancing and leaping," wrote Vicki Wickham of the audience's fervid response. Given the setting, the holiday night, and the rare combination of a pop innovator and a classic source of her inspiration, it was an enchanting convergence. "It was simply the most beautiful, perfectly paced concert of the year," wrote Mitchell Fink in *Record World*.

The musical celebration didn't stop when the performance ended, either. Wickham reported that Chiaro gave Nyro a party afterwards, and everyone sat around listening to Laura and Patti sing oldies.

Nyro had first performed with Labelle (and Mata on conga) at the outdoor Ravinia Music Festival in Chicago that past July, while still recording *Miracle*. There, they had to compete for the audience's attention with a thunderstorm that suddenly hit the area. The Carnegie performance, however, marked the beginning of a tour for the "quartet" at medium-sized venues, including the Santa Monica Civic Auditorium in Los Angeles, Ford Auditorium in Detroit, the Music Hall in Boston, and Auditorium Theater in Chicago. Labelle still performed only during a prolonged encore segment, although they came out as the first encore, with Laura doing a second encore solo.

In Chicago, Sun-Times reviewer Dick Saunders noted Nyro's increasingly powerful stage presence. Two years earlier, she had reminded him of a more fragile Laura: Laura Wingfield, a woman "too delicate to survive St. Louis," in Tennessee Williams's The Glass Menagerie. This time, her confidence had grown, and Nyro herself suggested to the audience one reason why: "I just got married, you know," she announced.

Laura had met David Bianchini in Gloucester, Massachusetts, in 1971, while visiting her great-uncle and great-aunt, the artists William and Theresa Bernstein Meyerowitz. A tall, lanky blond with a bushy mustache, Bianchini had stopped over with a friend who was delivering something to Nyro's relatives, and soon he and Laura began talking. Then he offered to drive her around Gloucester, a seaport town in which his family ran a construction business, but his Jaguar seated only two—so the friend drove while Nyro sat on Bianchini's lap.

"Later we dropped my friend off and went to get something to eat," he laughs. "That's how it all started." Their connection was instantaneous. After Nyro returned to New York, she and Bianchini corresponded, and he soon came to visit her in Manhattan.

"We had a mental affinity," says Bianchini, who was Nyro's age. "I think she was really looking for someone who was honest and could protect her, because she didn't trust anyone in the business she was in."

For a woman as antiwar as Nyro, Bianchini may not have been an obvious love match. Just a year and a half earlier, he had been an Army soldier in Vietnam, involved in extremely dangerous missions as a LuRP (the acronym for long-range reconnaissance patrol). Five- or six-man teams of LuRPs would be deployed behind enemy lines by helicopter, gather intelligence during a nerve-racking week of stealth, and then sneak back to safer territory. In the course of more than sixty missions, Bianchini was shot and bayoneted, and twice was the only member of his team to survive. He left Vietnam with over a dozen medals.

Despite his heroics, he was far from a gung-ho military man. "I wasn't defending anything," says Bianchini, who got drafted after he dropped out of his last semester of college. "I was basically a hippie.

But since I knew they were going to send me to Vietnam, I took a lot of training. I wanted to be prepared. It was so far out there, so crazy. Facing life-or-death situations at age twenty-three—it was very heavy."

As a self-sufficient war hero with a counterculture sensibility, he certainly cut a romantic figure and was Italian, to boot. "He was a real guy," says Roscoe Harring, Nyro's friend and road manager for many years, who had first met her while doing her sound at the Fillmore East. "He was a man's man," adds Lee Housekeeper. "Sort of Robert Mitchum or John Wayne, but a hip version. I was surprised that he was Laura's type, but she liked a manly man."

Not all the males in Nyro's life were as fond of Bianchini. Lou Nigro, whom Bianchini remembers getting along with, says he had an uneasy feeling about his daughter's suitor. It didn't help that Bianchini called his future father-in-law Dad when they first met in the Nigros' Manhattan apartment. "Somehow I was not impressed with him," says Lou. "I went into my bedroom, and Laura came in and said, 'Dad, I want to talk to you'—which I felt so good about—and just told me that she cared for him so much. I said, 'But what does he do? What will your future be like? If you get married, he'll be living off your money.'" Later, when Bianchini used Nyro's credit card to buy a Mercedes—which he considered the family car—Nigro believed his fears had been realized.

Felix Cavaliere felt equally protective, especially after Bianchini paid a visit to Cavaliere's house in Danbury, Connecticut. "I had a pool table, and this man beat me at my own pool table with one hand behind his back!" he says. "I don't think I ever took a shot." Figuring Bianchini to be an all-around hustler (Bianchini admits he grew up in the neighborhood pool hall), Felix said to Laura, "I think you've got a little problem here.'"

But Donald Boudreau remembers Laura being ecstatic about her new love, never looking happier or more beautiful. Early on in the relationship, she decided that this was the man she wanted to marry and told Bianchini so. He remained reluctant, however. When Nyro invited him to travel with her to Japan, he demurred, instead renting a house on Nantucket Island, south of Cape Cod. Supposedly no one knew where he was, but Nyro proved either prescient or just persistent.

"About two in the morning I got a call from an overseas operator in Kyoto," Bianchini remembers. "I don't know how she found me, but she did. She said, 'Meet me in Ireland. Come to Howth, a little fishing village.'"

So he met her in scenic Howth, just northeast of Dublin and over-looking Dublin Bay and the Irish Sea. "She said she wanted to get married," he continues, "but first she wanted to get out of Ireland, because she hated the food there."

They went to Switzerland for a couple of weeks, staying in Zurich, then took a train through the mountains to Lugano. "We were both reading Hermann Hesse [author of the novel *Siddhartha*, then popular with baby boomers], and I said, 'Well, I know where Hermann Hesse lived,' so we went to a little town above Lugano called Montagnola," says Bianchini. "I took a beautiful picture of Laura sitting in front of Hermann Hesse's grave."

Then they were off to Portofino, Italy, hoping to be married there, but were unable to get the proper paperwork because of a mail strike. "You know what they do in Italy when they have a mail strike? They burn the mail!" he laughs. After visiting a friend of Bianchini's in Bologna, Italy, the couple returned, unmarried, to New York City.

Still uncertain about tying the knot, Bianchini ventured off to Colorado to think about it, staying with a friend near Boulder. Once again, Nyro tracked him down. "I get a call from downtown Boulder that Laura's there, crying," he says. "So I drove down and saw her. She said she had found a place where we could get married in a few days, in Alexandria, Virginia."

This time, Nyro got her way. She talked Bianchini into a wedding as quick and inelegant as her parents' had been. "We flew to Alexandria, got out of the taxi, used the taxi driver as a witness, and got married in front of a judge," he says.

They later held a fancy wedding celebration for family and friends on a chilly late October night, at a hotel near Central Park. Dan Nigro, eight years old at the time, gave cousin Laura purple nail polish as a wedding gift and she insisted on painting her toenails right then—she was wearing open-toed shoes, despite the temperature. Nyro also performed at her own party, doing a tongue-in-cheek rendition of "Wedding Bell Blues" and other numbers. Afterwards, guests were offered horse-drawn carriage rides through the park.

Although Nyro kept her apartment in Manhattan, she moved with Bianchini to a little house on the water in Gloucester. Lee Housekeeper remembers a particularly entertaining evening when he and his girl-friend visited the Bianchinis while they were still honeymooning in a Winnebago camper on the edge of a picturesque Gloucester stone quarry. They built an outdoor fire to cook a huge lobster, and in the course of dinner Housekeeper raved about the then-popular film *King of Hearts*. Before they finished the meal, Nyro insisted, "I've got to see it, I've got to see this movie *tonight!*" Housekeeper, being a road manager, found a car to drive them to Cambridge, nearly forty miles away and there he bribed the projectionist to keep the theater open and screen *King of Hearts* while they munched on popcorn and lobster leftovers.

Most of the time, life in Gloucester wasn't nearly as exciting. "Although it was physically beautiful, she was unhappy in Gloucester," says Barbara Greenstein. "She had nobody there to relate to. She said to me, 'Bar, all they're interested in is recipes.' "

To balance out the quiet life there, Nyro ventured to New York for socializing and culture. Friends from that time remember someone who loved to laugh—quite different from the mysterious, sensual woman with the Kim-Novak-via-the-Bronx whisper who her fans saw onstage.

"Boy, when she got excited and laughed, she was a kick in the pants, she really was," says Kay Crow. "She was so funny, and that lighthearted giggle she had was so infectious," adds Harriet Leider. "I think she liked having people around her who made her laugh. I would say to Peter Dallas, 'I am so in love with this woman,' and Dallas would say, 'How could you not be?' "

Just as David Geffen had, Leider often looked askance at Nyro's choice of clothing. Like a Jewish mother, she'd say to Nyro, "You're going out like *that?*" "Oh, but I love these colors!" Nyro would respond. And Leider would fire back with, "What is your philosophy—if you don't know what color to wear, wear them all?"

"She came from that 'I'll have a scarf around my waist and one around my neck' philosophy," says Leider. "I'd say, 'No, Laura, *one* scarf is fine.' "

Aside from attention-getting outfits—which worked quite well for her onstage—Nyro also had a penchant for strongly aromatic perfume. In later years, her scent of choice would be Zen by Shiseido, but at that time Leider discovered that Nyro used an inexpensive brand from Woolworth's called Blue Waltz, which came in a tiny heart-shaped bottle.

"The smell from the bottle almost knocked me over—it was like cheap Shalimar, magnified twenty-five times," says Leider. "She said, 'This is the only thing I can put on in the morning that will last me all through the day.' I said, 'Through the day? It'll last you into the next *decade.*' "

They giggled over this, and Leider hatched a plan to gather up every bottle of Blue Waltz she could find in Manhattan. After two weeks, she had a case of the stuff delivered to Nyro's doorman with the note "Can I have this blue waltz? This should last you 'til the next decade." Nyro's reply, in a sweetly handwritten note, was "Every time I open my heart, there you are."

Nyro's friends describe her as an extremely generous person with her newfound wealth. For example, she would call Crow from New York in the middle of the night to tell her she had written a new song, but when Crow asked her to play it, Nyro said, "No, I want you to come to New York. I'm sending you a ticket."

"So she'd fly me out to New York and I'd hang out with her for a week or two," says Crow. "It was wonderful."

Barbara Greenstein, too, remembers Nyro giving her unexpected trip tickets. "She'd call and say, 'Where in the world should we go?' What an offer, right? One February, Russia was in the running, but because of the time of year we went to Carnival in Rio instead and had this fabulous time."

With her friends, Nyro could be playful and mischievous—certainly not a "dark madonna," as the press tended to characterize her. "She didn't mind getting in trouble," says Crow. "Sometimes she almost invited it."

Fans who only saw the serious artist anchored to her piano bench would certainly be hard-pressed to imagine Nyro belly dancing, yet when Crow moved to New York City in 1972 to work for artist Peter Max (also a follower of Swami Satchidananda), Laura implored her to take belly dancing lessons with her at Serena's Stairway to Stardom in Manhattan. (On one trip to Japan with Barbara Greenstein, she signed the two of them up for Japanese dance lessons, so she was covering an international spectrum.) Back at the Beresford they'd practice their moves accompanied by Middle Eastern music and finger cymbals Nyro had bought. But the singer was no threat to leave music for a job in a Moroccan restaurant: As one Los Angeles friend put it, after he saw Nyro and Crow display their terpsichorean talents on a visit at the Chateau Marmont hotel, "They were terrible."

When she wasn't dancing, Nyro carried herself with a sort of royal dignity, an effect enhanced by her long dresses and sashaying walk. "She didn't walk—she floated," says Richard Denaro, a San Francisco hairdresser who would become friends with Nyro in the late 1980s.

The times when she temporarily lost that dignity seemed hilarious to her pals. Kay Crow remembers a weekend visit to Felix Cavaliere's house when she and Nyro smoked pot in an upstairs bathroom— "with the window opened, like little kids, because Felix by then had become a full yogi and didn't get stoned, so we weren't supposed to either." When Nyro floated down Cavaliere's polished wood staircase, she missed a step and bounced down the rest of the way on her behind.

"When she got to the bottom, she just picked herself up and kept walking as if nothing happened!" says Crow. " 'You hurt?' I asked. 'Just my pride,' she said."

Nyro's New York cultural life included frequent movie-going, and when she saw a film she liked she returned again and again. One of her favorites was the 1970 documentary about the festival she had not played at, *Woodstock*. "She had a secret crush on Carlos Santana," says Crow. But Santana wasn't the only one in the film who caught her eye. "I never felt so much love for my fellow artists," Nyro told Vicki Wickham. "If you speak to the Who, tell them they really moved me in that picture."

Another Nyro film favorite was Woody Allen's *Bananas*. "We had to watch it twice," says Crow. "She was hysterical." On a more serious note, she also couldn't get enough of Ingmar Bergman's 1972 film *Cries and Whispers*, the gut-wrenching psychodrama about a dying woman, her repressed sisters, and a loving servant.

"It was like a miracle of a movie for both of us," says Nyro's friend Carman Moore, a composer and, at the time, the music critic for the *Village Voice*. "We couldn't get enough of that picture. We'd just sit back and let that thing pour. She told me later she had seen it maybe seven times."

■ ■ ■

At the beginning of her married life, Nyro still did some touring as a performer, including a trip to Japan with Bianchini. "She loved Japan—the architecture, the different little things," says Roscoe Harring, who was with her on one Japanese trip where she performed in just five concerts but stayed six weeks, primarily in her favorite Japanese town, Kyoto. "When the line of Hello Kitty [Japanese] toys came out, she bought every piece that she could find." Nyro's Japanese concerts were well attended, with a lot of young girls showing up who "knew all the words to the songs," Harring says. A Japanese fan, Norio Kuronumo, saw both of her Tokyo appearances in 1972, one at Shinjuku Kosei Henkin Kaikan, a popular 500-seat theater in the Shinjuku ward, and the second at the larger Yuubin Chokin in Gotanada, in the Shinegawa Ward. He remembers that Nyro complained of having a cold during the second show, but felt relaxed enough to sing an inordinate number of oldies, including the Shirelles' "Will You Love Me Tomorrow," Martha and the Vandellas' "Come and Get These Memories," the Moments' "Love on a Two-Way Street," and the Diana Ross version of "Ain't No Mountain High Enough." She even said a few words to the audience in Japanese, much to her fans' delight.

Not long after the Japanese engagement, Nyro decided to take a break. She had certainly earned one, having produced five stunning albums in just five years and having toured much of that time. Yet when Nyro decided to retreat from recording and performing, the move was somehow characterized as a retirement. Now, such a decision would have been seen as a survival strategy, since many singer-songwriters regularly take two or three years off between albums. But in Nyro's heyday, her treadmill schedule was par for the course. Creedence Clearwater Revival, as an example, released six albums in the even shorter span of July 1968 to December 1970, featuring over forty original songs by John Fogerty.

Such intense workaholism had consequences. In 1970 and '71, three of the brightest flames of the rock era—Jimi Hendrix, Jim Morrison, and Janis Joplin—had already immolated themselves with drugs. After the mid-seventies, Creedence's Fogerty didn't release another album for nine years. Nyro herself would later tell *Rolling Stone*, "When I work, I guess I'm an intense person, and the music is intense. But to add to that the prolific part, I don't think you can maintain that your whole life."

Even if Nyro wasn't a sweaty, shrieking rocker, and her drug use was benign, her writing and performances had been as raw and intense as any artist's. Moreover, the demands of both business and art were particularly hard on women. As Joplin had put it in a recorded 1970 conversation with fellow female rocker Bonnie Bramlett, "[Women] sing their fuckin' insides, man. Women, to be in the music business, give up more than you'd ever know . . . you give up a home and friends, children and friends, you give up an old man and friends, you give up every constant in the world except music. That's the only thing in the world you got, man."

And Laura Nyro wanted more. Now that she had an "old man" and financial resources, she could afford to leave behind the machinations of the business and just *be* for a while. Her early success had felt like "living inside a hurricane," she would later say, and that's why she decided to move away from the hubbub and experience life "without a bunch of people breathing down my neck." Says David Bianchini, "I think she needed to recharge herself."

Even if she faded temporarily from public view, she didn't become reclusive hermit, as she has often been mischaracterized. Her life with Bianchini was filled with entertaining adventures, many in foreign locales. They took several trips to Japan, and during one of them Laura paid for her Japanese flower-arranging teacher's fiancé to fly out from America and marry her. Laura and David (along with Barbara Greenstein and her then-boyfriend Jan Nigro, who had come along) wore kimonos that had been made for them to the ceremony, but much to their surprise they were the only ones other than the bride in Eastern garb.

Another time, Laura and David lived for a month on an elaborately carved houseboat moored on the shoreline of Lake Dal in Kashmir, the paradisiacal territory northwest of India near the base of the Himalayas. Even though they were ostensibly vacationing, Nyro was working on her music. "It was amazing—she always worked, no matter what," says Bianchini. "I could be driving down the road at eighty miles an hour trying to catch a plane for us, and I'd look over and see her writing. She carried this book with her, always."

David would take Laura each day to a one-room English schoolhouse that contained "the only piano in Kashmir," along with a stove and a Christmas tree. "I would fill the stove and get the room all warm for her, and then I'd go outside and smoke hashish with the Pakistani groundskeeper," he says. Laura imagined that she'd call her next album *Red Lantern*, so she asked Bianchini to photograph a Kashmiri man in a boat on the lake—holding a red lantern—to use as the album cover.

That was a simple request for her husband compared to the one when, living back in the United States, she asked him to become her captain. Thinking she was referring to the sort of captain she had sung about on *New York Tendaberry*, Bianchini responded, "Laura, I *am* your captain, don't worry about that."

"No, you don't understand," Nyro responded. "I want us to live on a boat and I want you to *really* be my captain."

"What kind of boat?" he asked.

"A tugboat," she replied.

Maybe Laura had been inspired by knowing a real tugboat captain, Helen Merrill's father, Frank—a Popeye-like character with a tattoo of an anchor, a knife, and a snake on his forearm. In any case, Bianchini took his wife seriously and began searching the East Coast and New Orleans for such a craft. "They're monstrous, you know—like ninety feet long, and you need a crew," he says. "But it was hard *not* to try and please her. She was pretty convincing, and pretty difficult to argue with."

Finally, he narrowed the choices down to a vessel in Florida and one in Boston. Nyro had only looked at the various tugs from docks, but in Boston she boarded a vessel for the first time. "And she gets seasick in, like, six minutes," says Bianchini. "This is on the dock!" As quickly as Nyro had come up with the notion of David's being her tugboat captain, she dropped it.

■ ■ ■

As her union with David Bianchini was being formed, the union with the other David in Laura Nyro's life was dissolving, both personally and professionally.

Nyro's first Columbia contract had expired after *Christmas and the Beads of Sweat*, and while she was recording *Gonna Take a Miracle* David Geffen had been negotiating a new contract for her with Clive Davis. But the talks took a unique twist: Rather than being primarily about Nyro as an artist, they focused more on Nyro the songwriter. Geffen wanted to sell Tuna Fish Music to Columbia, and Clive Davis wanted to buy it. The record company was attempting at the time to build up its music publishing arm, April-Blackwood, so in Davis's mind it made perfect sense to discuss the renewal of Nyro's recording contract in the context of purchasing her valuable catalog.

Indeed, Columbia would be buying only Nyro's publishing, while her services as a recording artist, for five more albums, would essentially be thrown in for free. That is, Columbia would pay her no advance royalties, which made the deal quite a shrewd one for David Geffen. He owned half of Tuna Fish, and thus would be paid half of its sale, whereas if the deal been structured purely as a recording contract he would have been entitled to only a 15 percent share as Laura's manager.

Columbia offered 75,000 shares of its stock for Nyro's previous compositions, plus the next sixty songs she would write. At $40 a share, the deal was thus worth $3 million, a reasonable figure for a publishing catalog considering that a couple of years earlier Joni Mitchell had reportedly turned down $1.25 million for hers—and she hadn't written as many hits as had Nyro. Other artists were getting equally large recording contracts in those days. Clive Davis noted that Warner Bros., for example, had given singer Dionne Warwick more than $3 million in advance royalties, while in the next year Davis would pay Neil Diamond $5 million and Sly and the Family Stone $1 million for single albums, and he offered Grand Funk Railroad $8 million to sign with Columbia. Of course, all those artists were proven hitmakers, while Nyro had only proven that her songs would be hits for others. None of her previous three albums for Columbia had reached $1 million in sales.

Clive Davis felt he was getting a bargain on Nyro's publishing, since he was taking little risk on her album sales while reasonably banking on the potential of her catalog, which had already earned over half a million dollars. David Geffen, though, considered that he was getting the best of the deal, because he believed that Nyro's chart-topping days were already behind her.

"She never wrote another successful song," says Geffen with an "I beat Clive" chuckle. "By the time she finished that third album for Columbia [Christmas and the Beads of Sweat], I think she had exhausted . . . well, gone into major decline in the quality of her work."

Nyro became, in a sense, a forgotten party amidst the wheeling and dealing between Geffen and Davis, and as facts and figures about her contract began circulating in the music press she felt a growing discomfort. She was particularly disturbed to read that she would be leaving Columbia Records.

That possibility arose in the midst of the year-long negotiations, when Geffen decided to form his own record company. He had already metamorphosed from Nyro's agent into her manager, and into (along with his partner, Elliot Roberts) other top acts, including Joni Mitchell and Crosby, Stills, Nash and Young. Now, at the urging of the head of Atlantic Records, Ahmet Ertegun, he decided to start his own label, and he wanted Laura on it.

He even gave the press tidbits to the effect that it was a done deal. In June of 1971, Rolling Stone reported that both Nyro and Joni Mitchell ("two ladies of two canyons," as the magazine called them, playing on the title of Mitchell's 1969 album Ladies of the Canyon), were rumored to be leaving Columbia and Reprise, respectively, to join the label Geffen and Roberts were about to start. "The label will be called either Phoenix or Benchmark, Atlantic distributing, and others already signed include David Blue, Jackson Browne and Julee [sic: it's Judee] Sill, all solo-folky writer singers," the magazine wrote. By September, *Rolling Stone* noted that *Gonna Take a Miracle* wasn't necessarily a Columbia product—it was being done "for David Geffen," he was paying for the recording sessions. Just a couple of weeks later, the music magazine reported that the first releases on Geffen and Roberts's new label—now called Asylum Records—would include albums by Browne and Nyro.

But Nyro had grave doubts about switching from Columbia, where she had been treated with great respect and given almost unlimited artistic freedom. Alan Merrill and his mother, Helen, both remember Nyro agonizing over what to do when she visited them in Tokyo during one of her trips there with Barbara Greenstein. "I was noncommittal and didn't advise her one way or the other," says Alan Merrill, who did suggest she put money into a Swiss bank account (which turned out to be a good financial move). Helen Merrill, too, didn't give her any firm advice other than to say that Columbia's offer "sounds like a lot to me." Greenstein remembers Nyro talking on the phone with David Geffen during that trip, telling him how upset she was that he had released to the media how much her new contract would be worth.

Back in the States, Nyro decided to test Clive Davis's loyalty and interest. In Davis's version of the story, Nyro sent him an unexpected letter saying that she had always wanted to be with the label but felt that perhaps the company was no longer willing to fight for her. Davis said he called her immediately and spent several hours on the phone, ultimately convincing her to re-sign.

Lee Housekeeper remembers it differently. "I was at a Columbia Records convention at the Century Plaza Hotel and I got a call from Clive," he says. "He asked if I knew about Laura leaving CBS and going to Asylum Records. There he was, hosting his big annual CBS convention, and it was going to be a huge slap in the face."

Housekeeper knew nothing, but offered to help Davis reach Nyro, who hadn't returned Davis's calls. "This is the part where I feel bad," Housekeeper continues. "She answered my call and I told her. She was absolutely taken aback. She was very loyal to Clive. He had done a ton of things way beyond the call of duty of any business relationship and Laura had appreciated that." Nyro told Housekeeper that, in contrast, Geffen had not been forthcoming with her in certain areas.

"A lot of it was that they were a coast apart, and as David's career started to explode on the West Coast there weren't the three- and four-hour-a-night telephone calls with Laura," says Housekeeper. "I'm sure David felt she should just trust him, but I think Laura missed the attention."

Nyro's relationship with Geffen had been changing in ways that probably frustrated both of them. As Geffen became more successful, he was less devoted to Nyro; as Nyro felt more powerful, she was less likely to listen to him. "He dominated her, for her own good, but she was the kind of person you just could not lead," says Charlie Calello. "Laura was stubborn and would not be moved."

Above all, Nyro felt safe at Columbia, while Geffen's new company—which he planned to locate in California—was an unknown, faraway quantity. "She wanted to stay in New York, and I think she wanted the security of Columbia Records," says David Bianchini. "Geffen was just starting out with Asylum."

"For her to have left Columbia would have been a total breach of honor," says Stephen Paley, "and Laura was more honorable than David Geffen. Columbia treated her like they treated Simon and Garfunkel, even though Simon and Garfunkel were their biggest-selling artists. As it happens, though, Laura would have been better off with David. Columbia could get the records into the stores, but David was a starmaker. Artists rose to his belief in them—that's his greatest gift."

Road manager Richard Chiaro adds yet another twist, having been with Nyro in Philadelphia while she was recording *Miracle*. "Clive had gone to her with the points that David wouldn't agree to, and she was put in the middle and felt really invaded," he says. "Any time a business decision invaded her privacy, she shut down and turned away from it. She got angry with the whole deal and wanted it to blow up. We'd drive back to New York from Philadelphia on weekends, and on one of those drives she asked me to take her off Columbia and go to any other label. At the time, she wanted to go to A&M Records."

When Nyro had been in Europe with David Bianchini on their pre-wedding trip, she was "hiding out" from both Geffen and Davis, according to Chiaro. Nonetheless, Geffen implored Chiaro to find her and encourage her to sign the contract. Even if she wouldn't join him at Asylum, he wanted the lucrative publishing sale to go through. Chiaro, agreeing that the deal was in Nyro's best interests, flew to Europe and met with the couple in Bologna. He returned to Geffen with the signed contract.

Bianchini had encouraged his wife to sign the foot-thick document. It gave her complete artistic freedom and would hold the CBS stock in escrow for her and dole it out in 20 percent increments each time she released an album. "I thought that would be great, because it would protect her money and she wouldn't blow it," says Bianchini.

Nyro could have had all the money at once, though: She just had to take a doctor's physical for a life insurance policy that CBS required. The company wanted protection, since it would be paying out a substantial sum for sixty songs Nyro hadn't yet written. But she refused the exam. "She thought it was an imposition on her women's rights, which I could understand," Bianchini says.

The brouhaha over Nyro's contract tore apart Geffen and Davis's once-rosy relationship, at least for the next year. For one thing, Geffen "complained bitterly" that Davis had called Nyro directly rather than dealing with him. More significantly, Geffen argued with Davis over money. While the contract had remained unsigned, CBS stock had dropped precipitously from about $40 a share to $25, and Geffen wanted an adjustment made. The CBS brass agreed to it. But when the temperamental stock then soared back to 48, Geffen didn't want to make an adjustment in return.

The final deal, as reported in Rolling Stone, was for a tax-free exchange of the 75,000 shares of stock, calculated at $40 per share. The recording agreement called for an album a year from Laura for five years—a time requirement that she wouldn't even come close to meeting.

Even with millions of dollars coming to her, Nyro felt ripped off by Geffen. "She felt she had been sold out and lied to," says Chiaro. "She wasn't ripped off in the conventional sense—everything was explained to her, options were explained." But Nyro didn't judge events in conventional terms. In hindsight, Chiaro realized that the contract changed Nyro's relationship to her art. "From that point on, she saw that her relationship with songwriting had become different," he says. "I think it was really hard for her to have already been paid for songs she hadn't written."

Nyro and her bookkeeper mother Gilda—who vehemently distrusted Geffen and questioned everything he did—also didn't like the fact that fully half the proceeds of her contract went to her manager. Her composer/journalist friend Carman Moore remembers that just the name Geffen would raise her hackles.

"Laura felt he had made his fortune on her back," he says. "She felt their relationship had been betrayed, and for her that would be much worse than anything having to do with money."

From Nyro's viewpoint, the whole deal treated her as a piece of flesh. She would later take revenge in the only way she knew how: She'd write a song called "Money" on her next album, in which she complained, "Money money money / I feel like a pawn in my own world / I found the system and I lost the pearl."

For David Geffen, however—yet another voice in the *Rashomon*-like tale—the betrayal had been Nyro's, not his. "After we announced that she was going to be the first artist on Asylum Records, she changed her mind and behind my back signed with Columbia Records," he says. "She wanted me to continue to be involved as her manager, but she didn't want to record for Asylum Records [Geffen says she hated the company's name, among other things]. But that was the end of our relationship. I was mad at her."

Geffen felt that he had been entirely supportive of Nyro's career and now she was trying to derail his. "It was one of the most disappointing experiences I had in my life up to that point," he says. "I was devoted to her, and devoted myself to her. And let's not kid ourselves, to be Laura Nyro and have a guy like me devoting himself to you is quite a thing."

"He *was* devoted," agrees Ellen Sander. "She was artistically, thematically, and stylistically out of the mainstream of rock music, so she really could have fallen off the edge of the earth but for David, who believed in her with a zeal and a passion. I don't know what it is she did to finally throw him off the train, but I know it broke his heart. He was miserable for weeks. I remember Elliot Roberts had to go to New York and get David to go somewhere, because he was so depressed."

Laura Nyro had helped launch Geffen's career, although the money from the sale of Tuna Fish did not finance Asylum Records, as some have continued to believe. Rather, Asylum was financed by Atlantic Records, and Geffen says he didn't even sell his CBS stock until many years later. The Tuna Fish deal did earn Geffen the first of his many, many millions. More than that, Nyro had given Geffen "an air of respectability," says Stephen Paley.

Geffen, in return, helped make Nyro a small fortune. "He made her wealthy and independent *and* he sold her out," says music biographer and Nyro's long-ago campmate, Marc Eliot. "That's what those guys do, that's what they're *supposed* to do. Geffen creates, then he sells out. If you get into bed with a Geffen, that's the kind of 'sex' you expect to get."

Geffen spoke to Nyro only a handful of times after their falling out. Nyro recalled one such conversation for journalist Michael Watts, saying they had casually talked about their lives. She knew that Geffen was unhappy with her behavior, but she explained their breakup simply as "We were just growing in different directions." In a nutshell, Geffen's life had gravitated toward the pursuit of huge amounts of money, while Nyro had begun to find the business of music oppositional to her art.

Geffen says that the humiliation he felt spurred him to "throw myself into Asylum Records and turn it into what it became"—a label successful artistically and financially, with artists such as Mitchell, Browne, and the Eagles (all of whom were managed by Geffen and Roberts) on its roster. He later, not surprisingly, sold Asylum as well, earning $7 million for it from Warner Bros. in 1972.

One of the last times Geffen spoke to Nyro, she was in L.A. doing a concert in the late 1980s. By that time, he was mega-rich, having started Geffen Records—which he would then sell to MCA in a 1990 deal that made him more than half a billion dollars. Nyro, in sharp contrast, had been out of the limelight for over a decade.

"I can't help but believe that the loss of me in her life, in terms of her career, was extraordinarily significant," says Geffen. "I think she never recovered from it." In their brief conversation, he felt that Nyro seemed sad that he still hadn't gotten over his feelings of anger and betrayal. But in his mind, she had never made amends to him that he considered meaningful.

"And she didn't have to," he says. "Our lives were the answer to it all. She knew it, and I knew it."

12
SMILE

During their second summer together after they wed, Laura Nyro and David Bianchini decided to spend several months in New Orleans, renting a two-bedroom apartment in the French Quarter where Nyro wrote music. "She wanted to listen to some gospel stuff and some jazz," says Bianchini of their new venue. While Nyro composed, he would paint or create sculptures in the studio he kept across town, which he'd drive to on a Vespa motor scooter.

But the marriage had begun to fray. When Housekeeper and his girlfriend came to visit, the scene wasn't nearly as gay as it had been during their honeymoon in Gloucester. "They were on the skids," he says. "They were arguing; it was bitter."

Housekeeper had another late-night adventure with the couple, along with Bette Midler (in New Orleans for a concert) and her boyfriend-manager, Aaron Russo. All three couples had shaky relationships, and when they got together for dinner the women banded together to complain about their mates, Housekeeper says. That led the three men to go out drinking on their own, and by evening's end they had landed in jail for vandalizing the bar's restroom and then tussling with police. "The idea," says Housekeeper, "was that the old ladies had to bail us out—that was our revenge."

Bianchini had taken on the "captain" role in Nyro's life, working for her as all-around protector and adviser, but perhaps the role didn't allow him enough of his own life. "The feeling I got was that this man was not real clear on who he was," says Kay Crow. "Laura was clear on who she was, but he was trying to find himself."

He may also have found it hard to reach Nyro when she was writing. "Most artists I've worked with who were really good songwriters, they shut everything else out when they're working," says Richard Chiaro.

"They love you, and then they say they have to go write a song and you don't see them for two days. But they have no idea that two days have passed. If you're slightly insecure, you think you've been abandoned.

"Laura and David had that kind of problem," he continues. "He put up with a lot—and she put up with a lot. He did take off sometimes, and he was spending her money. On the outside it looked like a real opportunistic thing for him to marry this wealthy woman and have this fast Mercedes convertible, but I think he actually loved her in his own way."

Bianchini blames much of their marital problems on post-traumatic stress from his Vietnam experience, which included excruciating cluster headaches. "I remember being in a movie theater with her in Boston, and I had such a headache as I came out of there that I ripped the railing off the wall," he says.

By 1973, Nyro was ready for another series of moves. "I'm not very territorial toward one place," she later told *Rolling Stone*'s John Rockwell. First she moved out of the Beresford and into a less opulent apartment at 100 Riverside Drive, near Eighty-second Street. It had high ceilings, huge windows in its spacious main room, and a tiny balcony with a beautiful view of the Hudson River.

Nyro also wanted to find a place in the country, where she could be surrounded by trees. Crow remembers taking a puddle jumper with Nyro to rural Vermont to see a piece of land. Nyro proceeded to tell the seller—a straitlaced sort who Crow thinks was a retired sheriff— that she was looking for five hundred acres "with a stream where I can wash my hair in the summer, and a donkey to take me to the market to get my vegetables."

All the while she talked to the seller, Nyro was playing with fuzzy hand puppets that she had bought at LaGuardia Airport. "This man thought we were whacked," Crow continues. "He said, 'I'll be right back,' and we found out later that he went next door to run a credit check on her. She was eccentric, she was a dreamer, but it was all reality for her."

Nyro ended up settling not in Vermont, but on a hilly, winding road in Danbury, Connecticut, a Colonial-era town that was once known for its beaver hat industry. She had already spent time there at Felix Cavaliere's fifteen-acre estate, which had a large waterfall and a pond on which she could feed ducks. Cavaliere let her know about another property available on Zinn Road, one that had been owned by Swami Satchidananda's Integral Yoga Institute (which had moved to a larger yoga village in the state). Satchidananda's students had lived in a large house on the multiacre Danbury compound, while he lived in a smaller cottage situated over a pond and small waterfall, connected to the lawn of the main house by a small wooden bridge. For the rest of her life, Nyro would mostly live in that cottage.

Nyro's land wasn't far from downtown Danbury, but remained isolated by a wealth of trees. The single-story contemporary main house was built around a central brick fireplace that almost bisected the long central room, and a wall of windows faced the pond. As she had done at the Beresford, Nyro kept furnishings to a minimum, particularly in the cottage. "There was nothing there," says record producer Joe Wissert. "Talk about sparse! There was a small gas range. There was a piano, a bench, and a little cot bed. It blew me away."

"People would be astonished at just how simply she lived in her home space," says her sister-in-law, Janice Nigro. "She had an unusually small home, considering what she could have had, and very simple furniture. She was not one to accumulate and hang onto junk at all."

The city of Danbury offered little cultural activity but did harbor a bit of musical history: It had once been home to another famous American composer, Charles Ives (1874–1954). Considered a maverick and an eccentric, Ives "cared little for the musical styles and fashions of his day." Not unlike Nyro, he combined fragments of familiar folk music with unconventional compositional techniques into a "uniquely American" style. Coincidentally, in an article written about Nyro, Carman Moore compared her "innocence" to that of Ives, asserting that such innocence came across in Nyro as emotional courage.

Nyro bought the Danbury property while she was still married to David Bianchini, and he remembers spending time there with her. "I taught her how to ride a bike there, and I taught her how to drive," he says. "That was a trip—she didn't want to drive. But she was pretty good on the bike." He also discovered that the otherwise unathletic Nyro was good at one sport: "She was a vicious croquet player," he says. "She liked to hit the other person's ball into the woods."

Their marriage, likewise, went out of bounds. "We separated a while, got back together, separated a while, got back together," says Bianchini. According to court papers, they separated for good in the middle of March 1974, but it wasn't until July of 1976 that Rolling Stone reported Bianchini suing Nyro for divorce, charging "utter desertion."

"When the divorce came through, she didn't even go to court," says Cavaliere. "She just said, 'Give him what he wants.' He did very well for being together that short period of time." According to Bianchini, though, he was given only a small settlement.

But the next year, Nyro sued Bianchini in Manhattan Supreme Court, declaring herself sole owner of a $200,000 account held by the Zurich branch of Bankers Trust. She took the action in order to keep the money away from Bianchini, who was supposedly demanding half of it or else he would sue for alimony. ("I never threatened her with anything like that," he maintains.) The suit stated she had deposited the money on June 5, 1972, and two days later had cosigned a letter with her husband saying the cash belonged only to her. When they separated, she had withdrawn the money from the account.

The very private Nyro must have been horrified to read the February 26, 1977, article in the New York Post headlined "Nyro Sues to Keep $$ from Hubby." Under an unflattering close-up of the singer was the caption " 'Picnic' no more."

Despite the suits, after their final split Nyro and Bianchini remained in touch, but not close. Nonetheless, she kept the name Laura Bianchini. It provided a disguise for her, an alias under which she could navigate with some anonymity. Besides, says David, "She thought it was a beautiful name."

Nyro would rarely mention her ex-husband to friends, but once, years later, she brought out a scrapbook to show Keith Decker, who was working for her at the time. "It was like sixth-grade school-girl-crush stuff—cutout hearts, pictures that she drew for him," says Decker. "Something nice and sweet. When she showed it to me, she said, 'I'm a real softy.' "

David Bianchini eventually remarried and had a daughter. But in 1990, Nyro's name was once again linked to his in the newspaper: She was identified as his ex-wife in a Boston Globe report of how he and two other men were caught cultivating large crops of marijuana in two rural Vermont barns. Investigators had been led to the barns because of their excessive use of gas and electricity during the winter months.

Bianchini, who ironically was not a marijuana user himself ("it gave me a headache"), unsuccessfully offered post-traumatic stress disorder as his defense. He says he refused to cooperate with prosecutors and implicate others, and that's why he ended up with a harsh twenty-one-year sentence. He was released after nine years, in 1999, and moved back to the Gloucester area.

■ ■ ■

During her marriage, Nyro didn't record any new material, but Columbia reissued her first album in 1973, retitled The First Songs. "While other young girls poured their hearts into their diaries, Laura Nyro changed the course of pop music," read the advertising copy.

With Nyro's fame came a glowing reappraisal of her early work. "Nyro's music reflects an originality and tone that is almost totally apart from most of what is being done these days in pop music," wrote Robert Hilburn in the Los Angeles Times. Critic Myles Palmer wished that rock music criticism "hadn't devalued the English language so much that I have to struggle for convincing superlatives, because these 12 songs have ambience, variety, soul to spare, sparkling arrangements and flawless engineering."

It's not surprising that the album reached only No. 97 on Billboard's charts, considering that most Nyro fans already owned copies of her first LP. Columbia's re-release of "Wedding Bell Blues" as a single made even less impact: Although it was listed as one of Billboard's Pop Picks, the record didn't chart.

In some circles, the absence of Nyro from the public eye had made hearts grow fonder. In 1974, thinking that the singer was perhaps permanently out of circulation, Ian MacDonald of the British music paper New Musical Express offered a premature encomium to her five years of "high-pressure creativity squeezed through the tightest focus available to anyone who isn't actually a certifiable monomaniac." Some critics, MacDonald said, had written her off as too intense, too repetitious, and too egocentric, but in his mind her supposed faults were actually strengths. Her "special clichés," for example, were simply a form of "personal punctuation," as they were for other great songwriters. Nyro, he offered, was "the single most powerfully original woman performer in rock . . . and totally wiping out most of both sexes on her songwriting."

As Laura Nyro had edged away from the business, other women singer-songwriters had begun receiving public attention far beyond what she had attained, at least as a singer. Carole King put out her immensely successful Tapestry in 1971, and Carly Simon began a string of hits with "Anticipation" in that year and "You're So Vain" (the latter produced by Streisand hitmaker Richard Perry) the next. In 1974, Joni Mitchell made her biggest splash to that point with the album *Court and Spark*—on David Geffen's Asylum Records—which yielded such popular songs as "Help Me" and "Free Man in Paris," the latter written about Geffen.

By 1975, when poet turned punk rocker Patti Smith emerged as a seminal figure, the scene for women artists began to shift toward harder-edged rockers who played electric guitars rather than acoustic ones (or piano) and who sang at a spotlighted mike with all the fury of their male counterparts. Being a poet, though, Smith was seen more as an heir to Nyro than to, say, Janis Joplin.

After her marriage ended, Nyro was ready to retake the spotlight herself. Her return certainly wasn't predicated on a renewed imperative to make it in the record business, however. "She would talk about 'my music, my music,' " says Carman Moore. "Music was her religion. She liked to live in her next piece, her next song, her next musical idea and let the world go by."

In the record company bio released with her next album, Nyro's version of her time away sounded like a fairy tale:

> At age 25, feeling drained and alienated by the high-pressure world of the money-fame entertainment business, she withdrew from the scene to seek renewal as a person and as a musician. She went to live in a small New England fishing town on the Massachusetts coast. Confused and ever-wondering at first, she led a simple life, meeting new people, getting back in touch with nature and a more natural rhythm, learning through books and friends the enlightenments of the feminist movement, and slowly writing music far from the spotlights and pressures. . . .
>
> At the end of a three-year marriage, she returned to New York and wrote "Stormy Love." She received a warm homecoming from family and friends, and new love. During the following months, new melodies and words continued, and she recorded a few songs, then a few more, and a new record, *Smile*, was created.

As the rather sanitized bio pointed out, Nyro had indeed been enlightened by the feminist movement while away, and had returned to the music business with a more politically charged sense of herself.

"I realize now that I've been trying to reach out . . . to speak all along," she told Moore in his 1976 interview. "The first feminism I expressed was long ago through melodies and rhythms, and a few years later my life caught up."

The women's movement had picked up considerable steam in the years Nyro was out of the limelight, including the birth of "women's music" festivals that included artists singing lesbian love songs and female fans taking off their shirts while they listened. When Georgia Christgau reviewed the second annual National Women's Music Festival, held at the University of Illinois in Champaign in June of 1975, she noted that Nyro had not performed there but was nonetheless "into feminism."

Nyro's take on feminism seemed rudimentary but heartfelt. "People should be encouraged to believe in themselves—not to be a lady but to stand on their own goddamned two feet," she told *Rolling Stone*'s John Rockwell. "I believe in love and I believe in work and that they should go together." Such beliefs, even if they sounded simplistic, would substantially change the personal mythology of her lyrics. The "soft and silly" Lilianaloo would entirely vanish, and in her place would emerge a resolute woman who had dropped the masks that once protected her. The destructive force she had once called the Devil would now be called war or prejudice, and the man she sought as her captain would now be required to be an equal partner. As writer Patricia Romanowski put it, Nyro began mixing social issues and personal concerns in a way that was "seamless, logical, natural."

She hadn't stopped searching for love, of course—and she found it again with Gregory Royce Bennett, a carpenter, musician, and guitar-making friend of Bianchini's whom she had met in Gloucester. Journalist Michael Watts of *Melody Maker* described him as a "quiet, lithe man" with a ponytail, and Nyro referred to the Ohio-born Bennett as a "gypsy man." She encouraged his own singing and songwriting during their relationship and, according to Barbara Greenstein, helped finance his guitar-making shop in Woodstock. Nyro even let the public know about Bennett in interviews, exceedingly rare behavior for her.

"He was very handsome," says Patty Di Lauria (then Patty Newport), who met Nyro through Bennett on New Year's Eve 1974 (he had worked on commercial fishing boats out of Gloucester with her then husband). "He had dark brown eyes, nice cheekbones; I think he was part Native American. He also had a very lovely speaking voice, sort of like her brother Jan's. He'd sing to Laura, she'd sing to him, then they'd do duets with beautiful harmonies. Greg was a huge, passionate love in her life, and justifiably so." Di Lauria was quite fond of Bennett, as were other close friends of Nyro's.

Some of Nyro's songs for her new album had been in the works for several years, such as "I Am the Blues," but others weren't completed until just before she recorded them. She admitted to interviewer John Rockwell that she wasn't as prolific as she had been in the past, getting the feeling for her songs at a "slower rhythm." While her previous work had been mostly inspired by the city, her new album would be more reflective of the patterns she found in nature, which she related to both sexuality and music. "Like, I have windflights," she said enigmatically. "They keep me up at night."

To produce her new album, Nyro returned to someone from her past: Charlie Calello. He believes that the record company encouraged their reunion, but Nyro told Rockwell that she had simply met him again. Michael Watts in *Melody Maker* reported that the two engaged in a casual phone conversation, Calello suggesting she try out a couple of her new songs with him at Columbia's New York studios to see if they wanted to work together.

They created a comfortable but very different production partnership this time around. With three albums under her belt since *Eli*, Nyro no longer invited the kind of artistic input Calello had provided eight years earlier. "If you catch artists early enough in their career, they listen," he says. "After they have success, they really don't want to hear anything. You sense when you can tell them what to do and when you can't. Laura had gained a degree of confidence in what she was doing. Though my input was there to a certain degree, she really dominated the making of the record. The only song I had a lot of say in was 'I Am the Blues.'"

Calello visited Nyro in Danbury to start working out arrangements and found that she still described music synesthetically, likening sounds to anything but other sounds. He especially recalled one interaction, a story retold so often among New York musicians that it has become Nyro apocrypha:

"She played me a song on acoustic guitar—she wasn't a very good guitar player, but the song was very simple—and I said to her, 'Laura, how do you hear this record sounding?' She got all excited and enthusiastic and silently stared out into space for maybe two complete minutes. Then all of a sudden her eyes popped wide open and she said, 'Like my chair!' "

With a Nyro album under his belt, Calello could quickly decode her. "I knew I was a very sick person because I totally understood what she was talking about," he says. "It was a very plain wood chair—we were sitting in the kitchen—and she wanted a very organic, plain kind of record that had wood as part of the ingredients."

Will Lee, who played bass on the album (he's a longtime member of Paul Schaeffer's band on *The Late Show with David Letterman*), has a similar chair tale, which suggests that either he or Calello turned the chair story into their own, or that chairs had become one of Nyro's favorite musical metaphors. Says Lee, "I'm sitting in this cold room [a recording studio], steel folding chairs, and she came over to me and said, 'I want this to sound like an old wicker chair I have in the country.' My joke always was 'Show me a picture of the chair so I can hear what it sounds like!' "

Given that Calello understood the chair metaphor to mean organic ingredients, he hired esteemed jazz stand-up bass player Richard Davis, then forty-five, to provide an acoustic bottom for several cuts on the album. Davis had played for everyone from Peggy Lee to Van Morrison (on his seminal *Astral Weeks* album). "Richard is a great, *great* musician, and just a lovely man, and Laura fell in love with him," says Calello. The feeling was mutual for Davis, who would soon tour with Nyro as well. "I loved being around her," he says. "She had a kind of voluptuous female appeal, too—dark hair and a kind of plumpness, but a solid kind of appearance. And those eyes! I never told her, but I just liked looking at her," he laughs.

The rest of the recording cast was equally accomplished in the jazz world, including Joe Farrell on soprano sax and sax and flute player George Young (both had also played on *Eli*), trumpeter Randy Brecker (a member of the first-album incarnation of Blood, Sweat and Tears), his saxophonist brother Michael Brecker (who, with Randy, formed the jazz-funk Brecker Brothers band), and guitarists John Tropea and Hugh McCracken (another *Eli* alum). "These players were friends of mine I had done records with," said Calello. "I always wanted to use guys who were the best."

Nyro hadn't specifically asked for jazz players but did want a bluesy, slick sound for the album. Even if her musicianship on piano wasn't up to their elite standards, the players appreciated her as a composer and artist. "Guys at that level don't always have tolerance for musicians who don't play as well as they do, but I think they respected Laura for what she did and as a result were a little more tolerant," says Calello.

By doing a more jazzy record, Nyro was also tapping into the musical zeitgeist: Jazz rock (which incorporated jazz flourishes or improvisations into rock-based songs) and fusion jazz (jazz played with a harder, swirling, rock-oriented beat) had become popular crossover forms, pioneered in 1969 by Miles Davis on *Bitches Brew* and in the early seventies by groups such as Weather Report, Mahavishnu Orchestra, and Return to Forever (with which Farrell had played). Other singer-songwriters, including Tim Hardin and Joni Mitchell, had begun their own crossover by using jazz musicians on their albums or in their touring bands. The folk-based Hardin, who like Nyro was known more for others' renditions of his songs (especially Bobby Darin's version of "If I Were a Carpenter"), had been incorporating jazz players into his musical mix since the mid-1960s, even playing at Woodstock in 1969 backed by the jazz group Oregon. Mitchell began her long affair with jazz in her 1972 album, *For the Roses*.

The recording of Nyro's album in mid-1975—at Columbia's 30th Street studio—went fairly smoothly, according to Calello. Harriet Leider sat in on a session where Nyro recorded piano and vocal for "The Cat-Song," playing "an incredible grand piano with an incredible embroidered piano shawl over it," she recalls. Nyro, Leider, Calello, and Peter Dallas then spent the afternoon listening to playbacks, eating, and laughing uproariously.

"She would turn to me after a playback and say, 'What do you think?' " says Leider. Flattered even to be asked, Leider replied, "Works for me!" Indeed, she told Laura that despite the fact she had always been a dog person, Nyro's song celebrating the uncomplicated life of a feline named Eddie made her want to get a cat.

But in the midst of the easygoing recording sessions for the album, there were tears as well as laughter: Both Nyro's beloved mother, and Calello's father Pat, who had played on *Eli and the Thirteenth Confession*, passed away.

Gilda Nigro had suffered from ovarian cancer, the same illness that had killed her mother and her mother's youngest sister, Minnie. She had been diagnosed just a year and a half earlier, after having complained of stomach upsets. At first her symptoms seemed related to stress, since Gilda and Lou had been involved in protracted legal problems over a large vacation house Laura had purchased for them in New York's Ulster County town of Ellenville. It had been Gilda's dream house, built to her specifications, but the contractor had done shoddy work that led to water leakage, and Lou felt their only recourse was to sell it.

As in a preponderance of ovarian cancer cases, Gilda was diagnosed too late for effective treatment. The best she and Lou could do was go to Mexico to obtain laetrile, the then popular (but medically unproven) cancer remedy made from apricot pits, even smuggling some of the medication back into the States. But it was to no avail. When Gilda died on August 13, 1975, she was just forty-nine.

A few days after Gilda's passing, Nyro called Patty Di Lauria to tell her, and although they hardly knew each other Patty drove out that weekend to comfort her. "I drew her a bath, made her take a nice long soak," says Di Lauria. "I heated up the soup I brought with me, I made her some warm milk with honey and I put her to bed. The next day she ferreted out things her mother had written her, little notes, and she showed me a few photographs of her mother and she cried a bit. We just passed a few quiet days, with me cooking and cleaning, letting her have the space and company. I just looked after her."

In other words, Patty cared for Nyro as Nyro had once cared for another Patti (LaBelle), and they thus began a friendship that lasted till the end of her life. That November, Nyro would treat her new friend to a two-week trip to Tokyo and Kyoto, and while there she asked Di Lauria to photograph her. Di Lauria's casual images of Nyro in a rosy-pink sweater, which Nyro had purchased in Japan and carefully removed the beading from, would adorn the rose-colored cover of her new album.

Nyro was devastated by Gilda's death, yet took little time off from recording. As she told journalist Michael Watts, "I could've broken all the windows in the studio, but I went back to work." She had never lost anyone she loved so much, and she said it made her feel both more angry and more loving.

■ ■ ■

Despite the loss of her mother and the breakup with her husband, Nyro's album would counterintuitively be called *Smile*, titled for its concluding track. She set an impish tone before the first note of music, speaking the word "strange" to open the album. Then the music starts with the strumming of an acoustic guitar, sweet as a smile, and Nyro sings the only cover song of the collection, "Sexy Mama," written by Harry Ray, Al Goodman, and Sylvia Robinson. "Mama" had been a minor 1973 hit for Ray and Goodman's male vocal group, the Moments ("Love on a Two-Way Street") but Nyro gives the song a gender-bending twist, imagining a man singing to her: "He said, 'Come on, sexy mama / lay back and let me soothe you.' " There's ultimately a confusion of who's singing to whom, though, when Nyro exhorts, "Give it to me now baby." Nyro is warmly sensuous in her inviting come-on; The Moments, in comparison, sounded lascivious.

Nyro smoothly segues from that opener into "Children of the Junks," a song she had written in Hong Kong and had performed in an earlier version at the Fillmore East in 1970. "Junks" sounds like a stereotype of chinoiserie, with its "oriental" chords, its lyrical reference to the nearby city of Kowloon (whose name Nyro just loved saying, says Barbara Greenstein), and a rather unfortunate allusion to "slant-eyed children." Nonetheless, Nyro effectively invokes an Asian experience, using spare instrumentation dominated by Davis's bass, while somehow making a bustling foreign harbor seem not unlike her familiar Hudson River.

From there, she goes into the most upbeat song on the album, "Money," inspired by "cylinder rhythms—the turning of the city, the turning of business." The percolating groove, fueled by Michael Brecker's insistent sax solo and her own multitracked vocals, drives a downbeat message: In her thinly veiled stab at Geffen, she sings, "A good friend / is a rare find. . . ." The bitter Nyro had "found the system and lost the pearl," and here she retaliates against those who may have stolen it from her oyster.

She switches gears for "I Am the Blues" (a song she had performed a variation of around 1970), for which Calello crafted a close harmony, Gil Evans–style arrangement using four French horns, trombones, and Randy Brecker's muted trumpet. The song finds Nyro in a bluesy mood, "all alone with my smoke and ashes," but soon she's off "like superfly" on a fanciful flight through the night sky. As Carman Moore described it, "Laura creates a setting totally devoid of anchors to earth; all is ephemeral, smoky, glowing but not flaming."

Side Two of Smile begins with "Stormy Love," taking Nyro back to earth and the reality of her failed marriage. She's rueful about a man who "could make me sing," but she's ready to love again though she's never "gonna be the same." Like other cuts on the album, this one is textured by acoustic guitar rather than piano (Nyro is credited as one of the album's guitarists) and is embellished by George Young's flute solo.

In "The Cat-Song," Nyro returns to the syncopated spirit of earlier albums. She takes on the role of Eddie, a cat who sleeps "with one eye open," then looks for a breakfast fish tail to "turn it into a fishscale." Nyro obviously wants to steal a moment of Eddie's less complicated life, rather than being one of those people who, as Eddie describes it, "wheel and you war and you whitewash your day away."

On the next cut, Nyro again embraces a "blue" mood with "Midnite Blue"—often confused with Melissa Manchester's 1975 song of the same title. Passionately but defiantly she sings of a man who makes her both laugh and tremble. Since she describes this character being "shy, sly gypsy high now," one assumes that she's writing about her "gypsy man," Greg Bennett, who plays guitar on the cut.

The album closes with "Smile" ("I'm a non-believer / but I believe / in your smile"), a dreamy love song for a snowy winter's night. Nyro wanted a Japanese sound, and Calello convinced her that employing a Japanese harp, or koto—a six-foot long wooden instrument with thirteen silk strings—would turn the whole band Japanese.

"That was a major event to have koto players on a record session," says Calello. "It's hard to use that kind of music, because it doesn't deal in the same kind of tonality. Laura was very, very impressed, and worked out the parts with the players." The song begins with two kotos playing, then ends with an extended East-meets-West jam between the jazz musicians and kotoists Reiko Kamota and Nisako Yoshida.

With only eight songs and about thirty minutes of music, Smile was much thinner than Nyro's previous efforts. Calello felt that her compositions for the album were just okay. "I thought she was in a creative mode, but not an exceptional creative mode," he says. "I didn't think she had the goods."

Most critics agreed, at least in part. Janet Maslin characterized Smile as a postcard more than an album, with Nyro substituting a pensive serenity for the fire of old. Maslin liked "The Cat-Song" and "Money" best, because to her they contained the most exciting refrains.

In Creem, James Wolcott noticed that Nyro, like Mitchell, had come to spark in her audience a sense that they weren't just watching her grow, but were shaping that growth—"that a collective autobiography is being written," he wrote. But then he snapped that Smile was a dull, too-tranquil chapter in that book. In an all-too-familiar lament, he found Nyro's voice offensive, deciding it sounded "as if a starving cat were trapped in her ribcage."

Likewise, Dave Marsh in Rolling Stone gave with one hand and took away with the other, admitting that Smile had a grows-on-you charm but calling Nyro's lyrics "sententious babble" and Calello's arrangements forced ("like trying to merge Alice Coltrane and Carole King"). He suggested Nyro "knock it off and go back to being the crazy kid from the Bronx we all used to love." It's hard to know who "we" were, since Rolling Stone critics had never showered much affection on Nyro.

British journalist Charles Shaar Murray, on the contrary, praised Calello's arrangements for integrating Nyro's piano more seamlessly into the mix than ever before. In the past, he had felt "as if only Nyro and her piano were real and that the other instruments were but phantasms." Fellow Brit Penny Valentine had perhaps the most empathetic take on Smile, seeing it as the work of a woman who finally showed optimism about life and confidence about love. Nyro still needed the blues as a musical resource, she wrote, "but they are no longer an integral part of her existence."

Finally, John Rockwell judged Nyro's music to be as strong as ever, with "I Am the Blues" matching her best work. He deemed the poetry of Smile as lesser in quality than that of Nyro's "inspired adolescence," but expected she would reach a far wider audience than before with the album. Having "paved the way for Joni Mitchell, Janis Ian, Dory Previn, and Phoebe Snow, . . . now they've paved the way for her," he predicted. The album did not meet such lofty expectations, however, despite being played widely on album-oriented FM stations after its release in March of 1976. It reached only No. 60 on Billboard's album chart.

Critics and fans had hoped that the Nyro who returned from her self-imposed retreat would be the same Nyro who left. But as a woman who always did things on her own terms—let alone someone who had married, moved from the city, discovered feminism, and lost her precious mother—she was bound to disappoint. She was in the same no-win situation that Joni Mitchell would describe a few years later in an interview with Rolling Stone's Cameron Crowe. Any artist, said Mitchell, gets crucified for too-often repeating the formula that brought them initial success, yet is equally criticized for upending that formula and going in another direction.

"But staying the same is boring," said Mitchell. "And change is interesting. So of the two options, I'd rather be crucified for changing."

So, too, would Nyro. And even though she had changed, the concert tour she'd soon embark on would prove that her audience was waiting with welcoming arms rather than hammer and nails.

13

SEASON OF LIGHTS

By 1976, Nyro had been off the stage for four years, except for a brief appearance in May 1975 at the Harkness Theater in New York. That night, her former backup trio, Labelle, summoned her from the audience to sing harmony on their huge hit "Lady Marmalade." While Nyro had been away, Labelle had transformed themselves into *Star Trek*–garbed rock divas. In comparison, onstage at the Harkness Nyro wore a plain black shawl as she sang along with the racy lyrics *"Voulez-vous coucher avec moi ce soir."*

Before hitting the road again on her own, Nyro needed a new manager. Richard Chiaro had stuck around for a while after she moved to Gloucester, but then realized she was going to take a longer break than he imagined. Felix Cavaliere suggested that Nyro consider hiring the former manager of the Rascals, Sid Bernstein.

Known for bringing the Beatles to Carnegie Hall in 1964 and to New York's Shea Stadium in 1965, the Bronx-raised Bernstein was described by *Melody Maker* as having a "bonhomie . . . as expansive as his person." He had actually met Nyro in 1967, but he hoped she had forgotten. That's because when he'd come to hear her play at her 888 Eighth Avenue apartment, invited by David Geffen, he had fallen asleep and started to snore. "Obviously I had worked late the night before and was quite tired," Bernstein says. (In his autobiography, *The Making of Superstars*, he came off as more egotistically flippant: "I was probably tired from running to the bank with Rascal money.")

Geffen, who had known Bernstein while he was still working in the William Morris mailroom, nudged him awake. "I didn't think Laura saw me, but I guess she'd heard me over the playing," says Bernstein, who felt mortified. The next day Geffen called and said he'd upset her, and that was that.

Flash forward to 1975, and one day while Bernstein was visiting Felix Cavaliere in Danbury, the Rascal suggested they drop over to see his neighbor, Laura Nyro. Being familiar with Bernstein's embarrassing tale, Cavaliere soothed him with, "I think she's forgotten about it, Sid." Indeed, Bernstein received a warm greeting and forgiveness. "He has a good heart," Nyro would say.

"I liked her so much, she was such a good girl," says the avuncular Bernstein, who soon began planning Nyro's tour. He remembers her as a "special, soft person. The musicians loved her. She was not like a leader, she was an inspiration." He also grew fond of Grandpa Mirsky. "This elderly gentleman was her charge, her buddy, her pet person," he remembers. "She took care of him as if he was her grandchild. I liked the way she supported him and loved him and cared for him."

For Bernstein, managing Nyro had the ring of an artistic investment more than a purely financial one. "I want her out there, reclaiming the audience that is rightfully hers," he told *Melody Maker*. But Nyro wasn't an easy client to manage. "She's probably the sweetest person I've ever worked with, but she has her rules which I find a little uncomfortable: no TV appearances, no interviews, no hustle—but this is her style," he wrote shortly after he came into her employ. "I can live with that because she's such a superb artist. I must compromise because this is her life, a private life, and I respect her for that. Even though it kills me! . . . At this point, she's been working longer than she ever worked at one time and enjoying it, so I'm optimistic."

Part of Bernstein's strategy was to make Nyro accessible to the press again, but she'd grown increasingly wary of the media. "I say what's really important in my music," she had told Vicki Wickham back in 1971, "and I find that most of the time words are just a lot of ———, unless you get into a really humid conversation with someone and you take off your mask and say what you truly feel." She would later tell an interviewer, "In some stories it's their image of you that dominates, rather than you. Also, sometimes the press wants a more conservative show-business consciousness from me, and that's not my reality."

Nyro had felt particularly burned by a 1969 feature written by Robert Windeler for the short-lived Hollywood trade magazine *Entertainment World*. Windeler had been invited to dinner with Nyro in Greenwich Village by his friend Stephen Paley (Leonard Bernstein's daughter Jamie was also there), and wrote his piece based on the evening's conversation, never telling Nyro that she was "on the record." Besides feeling betrayed by this lapse of journalistic ethics, Nyro may also have been annoyed by the fact that Windeler misspelled her birthname as "Negro" and wildly editorialized about her dress being grabbed by a female fan as she came off the stage at the Troubadour. He wrote that Nyro shouted, "Don't touch me!" in a voice "as stern as it would have been if the woman had been wearing a sign: 'I Am a Lesbian.' " Nyro was so upset by the article that she insisted Geffen buy and then destroy each offending copy he could find on Los Angeles newsstands. Paley—whom she held responsible for having introduced her to Windeler in the first place— was ordered to drive around Manhattan and do the same.

For the rest of her career, Nyro would cautiously pick and choose her interviews, trying to suss out the "vibe" of the interviewer before agreeing to do a story. That vibe took precedence over the prestige of the publication, which often led to her doing interviews for lesser known magazines and newspapers.

Since Nyro refused most requests for interviews, she ran the risk of inaccuracies being printed and reprinted. Having chosen not to speak with Sheila Weller of Ms., for example, Nyro surprisingly wrote a letter to the editor complaining of Weller's mistakes in her mostly positive November 1975 essay.

"Sheila Weller's biographical lines about me are imaginary and misleading," Nyro groused. She pointed out, for example, that Gilda Nigro held jobs other than "housewife," that Nyro was not forming an all-woman band, and that she couldn't recognize herself in the "pitiful 'life-soiled' picture" that was created. Nor did she appreciate the "sad, bad photograph" that accompanied the piece (a dark-eyed, broody image taken by Stephen Paley).

But Nyro's reading could have been more careful: Weller had written only that Nyro hoped to use mostly female musicians on her next album, and when Weller spoke of "life-soiled women," she was talking about the characters in Nyro's songs, not Nyro herself. In reply, Weller claimed the erroneous material had come either from an unidentified business associate who had spoken to Weller on Nyro's behalf or from two articles to which the associate had referred Weller.

Nyro also criticized the article's headline, and on that she hit the mark. "Seclusion from what?" she asked of the title "Laura Nyro: Out of Seclusion." "I do have a life other than on a vinyl record."

In fact, once interviewers met Nyro face-to-face, the mystique vanished and a well-rounded, fully grounded woman emerged. John Rockwell, who interviewed her in 1976 for Rolling Stone, found her to be charming and charismatic, even if her conversation could be frustratingly poetic for a "practical-minded person." Her hearty laughter showed him that she was earthy rather than spacey. Nyro knew she was much warmer than she had usually been portrayed, but when she felt invaded she would become aloof as a form of self-protection.

■ ■ ■

With a new manager in tow and selected members of the press beginning to trumpet her return, Nyro next auditioned a touring band to reproduce the jazzy sounds of *Smile*. She ended up choosing some of the best studio and performing musicians in New York—Richard Davis on bass, John Tropea on guitar, vibraphonist Michael Maineri, drummer Andy Newmark, and flutist/saxophone player George Young. Davis, Tropea, and Young had all played on *Smile*, as had the new band's percussionist Carter C. C. Collins. Nyro's pal Nydia Mata rounded out the ensemble.

Maineri, a longtime admirer of Nyro's music, had been invited by his old friend Roscoe Harring to play percussion at an early rehearsal but brought along his vibraphone as well. Nyro loved the instrument, so Maineri wound up playing it on nearly every tune in concert. Nyro and Maineri connected on several levels: He had grown up just a neighborhood over from her in the Bronx, he too had a Jewish mother and Italian father, and like Laura he loved to watch films at the nearby Loew's Paradise—the 4,000-seat movie palace on the Grand Concourse and 188th Street where the ceiling came alive with twinkling "stars" and drifting mechanical clouds.

Drummer Andy Newmark auditioned after most of the band had been assembled. He thought perhaps that Nyro had planned to use only percussionists, "because she wasn't too keen about the drums being too dominant or too loud." But Newmark says she proved willing to match her idiosyncratic rhythms to a steady tempo: "I think she tried to adapt to the band rather than have the band adapt to her kind of free piano-playing style."

Tropea, who was a busy studio musician as well as a "smooth jazz" recording artist, saw it differently. "We had to fit into Laura's rhythms," he says. "She went with the lyrics and the rhythm of her voice, and they weren't always in four-four. She wasn't the best piano player for the gig, but if we had a real good pianist he might not have gotten the right feel for her music. It was hard, but we made it work, and in the end the band sounded great."

Although George Young started the tour, he soon left, and with the salary Nyro would have paid him she was able to hire three young horn players as replacements: saxophonist Jeff King, flutist/saxophonist Jean Fineberg, and trumpeter Ellen Seeling. Fineberg and Seeling, then attending Indiana University, had been recommended by Mata, who had played with them in the mid-seventies all-woman rock band Isis. Their tryout was at an early tour stop in Philadelphia. "It was pretty nerve-wracking," says Seeling. "We bought Smile at a store in Bloomington, learned a couple of tunes, and flew to Philadelphia to play the sound check onstage at Symphony Hall with guys like Richard Davis and Mike Maineri, who we'd been listening to for years as students. That was our audition, and we played the show that night."

The important thing was not simply how they played, but how they fit in with the band—which was now half studio pros and half less-experienced players. "Laura wouldn't put up with someone who was a pain," says Fineberg. "She picked personnel based on ability and personality." Those who worked best with Nyro understood and accepted her bohemian outlook.

"She was a total free spirit, a hippie still living on into the seventies," says Newmark. "A flower child. She never grew up or changed. She was very gentle and wispy. Not trying to manipulate whatever was around her, just flowing. I only have nice memories of her."

The band members gave input on the arrangements, especially Maineri and Tropea, although Nyro had the final say. She would continually refine each song with the band until she got what she wanted. "There were no written charts at all, and she wouldn't provide horn lines," says Fineberg. "She wanted horn players but hadn't done a whole lot of thinking ahead of time as to what they'd do."

The well-schooled jazz stalwarts in the band ultimately appreciated Nyro's way of working. Says Newmark, "She just knew certain chord changes and licks—she wasn't really a strong player—and as long as we didn't step on her or get in her way, she encouraged people to do their own thing. It was just her voice and her songs, and that's kind of timeless. It would have worked today, it would have worked twenty years before."

"It wasn't just a gig for us—we loved the music," adds Maineri. "Most pop shows you play the same things every night. Laura didn't want you to play the same thing every night, so that was a jazz musician's ideal gig."

Nyro would start each concert in a way most unusual for her: by strumming the guitar while singing "Stormy Love." That proved the calm before the musical storm, as the band would then kick into a high-energy version of "Money." The set included several other songs from Smile, along with rearrangements of what were now Nyro's oldies, such as "And When I Die," "Sweet Blindness," "Sweet Lovin' Baby," and "Emmie."

Maineri took the spotlight during "The Cat-Song," opening with an improvisation on a small wooden baliphone (a primitive vibraphone). One night he embellished his solo by wearing a startling cat mask that a fan had given Nyro, and the crowd "went nuts." Michael the Cat thus became a regular part of the show, until Maineri felt it was just too corny and retired the mask.

The tour, which lasted into July, was full of laughs, good food ("huge amounts of sushi," says Fineberg), top hotels ("She wanted to stay in beautiful places," says Seeling), generous pay, and an easy weekend schedule that allowed the New York players to return to the city for lucrative weekday recording sessions. Obviously Nyro hadn't designed the tour as a moneymaker. "I think she just about covered the cost of the band," says Bernstein.

When the band played dates on the West Coast for a couple of weeks, going as far north as Vancouver, British Columbia, Nyro and the women players traveled in a GMC Palm Beach van nicknamed the Green Hornet (the men flew). Nyro, Mata, Mata's partner Ellen Uryevick, and Barbara Greenstein rode the van cross-country up and back from California, awakening each morning to spectacular new surroundings that the hired chauffeur had driven them to during the night. "We learned for the first time what 'purple mountain majesty' means," says Greenstein.

"She was enamored of the van, she loved the lifestyle," says Fineberg. Adds Seeling, "She was very down to earth; she wasn't real taken with herself. She was a total artist and totally obsessed with what she was doing musically. She lived and breathed that stuff—with time out for sushi and ice cream."

As with the album Smile, reviews of the concerts were both thumbs up and thumbs down. Robert Hilburn of the Los Angeles Times continued to rave about Nyro, calling her show at the Santa Monica Civic Auditorium "simply stunning." He wrote: "In an age in pop of increasing theatrics and reliance on electronic effects, Nyro is one of the few artists who can captivate an audience with simply the glory and majesty of her own voice and music."

The Christian Science Monitor marveled over Nyro's more relaxed, less iconic demeanor onstage: "She danced, smiled, laughed, and in general acted unmysterious and simply, wholly talented," wrote Madora McKenzie. Before playing a third and final encore at her Boston concert, Nyro even cracked a joke: "Okay, I'll play one more song and then we can all go home and watch *Mary Hartman*," she quipped, referring to the cult-favorite late-night television series.

Critic Janet Maslin, though, felt Nyro was "taking it easy" at her March 5 tour-opening concert in Hartford. "Once-galvanizing songs like 'Sweet Blindness' and 'The Confession' were now calmed down and smoothed over, delivered without the shrieks, yelps and wildly unpredictable tempo changes . . . that had originally made them so torrid," she wrote.

Life magazine's Maggie Paley, too, remembers finding Nyro's performance disappointing in comparison to the "totally dramatic" shows she had watched at the Fillmore East five years earlier. "There wasn't anything new," says Paley. "Or there was something new, but it seemed pale."

Rolling Stone was surprisingly gushy about Nyro's four-encore Carnegie Hall appearance on March 31. Although the "surface exuberance" of her music was gone, it had been replaced by other qualities, wrote critic David McGee: "The music was ethereal, trancelike, piercing, introspective." Nyro, he concluded, had brought meaning back to "that misused, overused word: magic."

Carnegie Hall took on some visual magic as well, as Sid Bernstein arranged for yellow daffodils to be handed out to audience members as they arrived. "When she stepped out on the stage"—in a bright red floor-length dress—"she saw an ocean of flowers. It absolutely floored her, because she was such a nature child," says Bernstein.

The Carnegie concert was broadcast live on New York radio station WNEW-FM and on WBCN-FM in Boston, and several other shows on the tour were taped by a mobile CBS recording unit to use for a live album. As far as record companies were concerned, live albums were low-cost, profit-taking ventures that allowed popular artists to capture new sales on old material. They had proven to be career boosters for artists such as the Allman Brothers (*Live at the Fillmore East*, 1971) and Peter Frampton, whose career-making 1976 live set, *Frampton Comes Alive*, sold six million copies. Nyro's closest musical peer of the era, Joni Mitchell, had put out a jazz-inflected live album in 1974, *Miles of Aisles*, so Nyro was following her lead as well.

Nyro was as painstaking in cobbling together the live album as she had been with her studio projects. Fineberg remembers listening to tapes of a previous night's concert in the van, then later spending "untold hours" at Nyro's house listening to the recordings, trying to decide which version of a song was best. "It was completely, totally obsessed," says Fineberg. "Finally, we came to decisions—but then, when they put out the album, half the tunes weren't on it!"

Columbia had planned to release a two-record set, as was common at the time, and had even sent promotional copies of it to American disc jockeys in January 1977. But the company changed its mind and released just a single album with a gatefold cover that spring. Only ten of the originally scheduled sixteen songs made it to *Season of Lights*, and several tracks were shortened by editing out their instrumental jams.

The version of *Season of Lights* that made it to record stores opens with "The Confession," Nyro sounding in good voice but backed by a too-bouncy arrangement that lacks the original's intensity. Contrarily, she sings the second cut, "And When I Die," more slowly and darkly than the 1966 recording, finishing the song by vocalizing along with Jeff King's abstract saxophone solo.

On "Upstairs by a Chinese Lamp," Fineberg's flute is given prominence, creating a sort of opium-den atmosphere, but the band makes the song sound more R&B than the orientalized album version. Nyro next performs "Sweet Blindness" in a more downbeat, poignant style than it appeared on *Eli and the Thirteenth Confession*, similar to the rearrangement of "And When I Die." Nyro's voice sounds huskier than it had a decade before, and she reaches more tentatively for high notes, often avoiding them entirely.

Side One concludes with "Captain Saint Lucifer" from *New York Tendaberry*, again at a somewhat slower pace and with a couple of lyric corrections. Nyro changed the line "early *bloomers* made of earth and lovelace" to "early *summer* . . ." One can only guess why "summer" now made more sense to her than "bloomers," which themselves could have been flowers, old-fashioned women's pants, a girl who develops at a young age, or just a word that sounded good to Nyro. She also substituted "tiger" for the word "jangle" in the line "a jangle from a congo lovechase." It may have been more literal in its meaning, but it sounds less interesting.

Side Two opens with "Money" and "The Cat-Song," both with arrangements similar to those on *Smile*. Before the latter, however, lis-

Louis Nigro, playing the trumpet at a Catskills resort in the 1950s.
(*Courtesy of Dan Nigro*)

Laura, at about age three.
(*Courtesy of Louis Nigro*)

Baby Laura with mother Gilda and
father Lou, 1948.
(*Courtesy of Jan and Janice Nigro*)

Laura's junior high school graduation portrait, 1962. (*Courtesy of Dan Nigro*)

Laura and brother, Jan, c. 1963. (*Courtesy of Jan and Janice Nigro*)

The Nigro family, c. 1970 (*clockwise from top left*): Lou, Gilda, Jan, and Laura. (*Courtesy of Louis Nigro*)

Nyro singing "Poverty Train" at the Monterey Pop Festival, June 17, 1967. *(From "The Lost Monterey Tapes" by D. A. Pennebaker; courtesy of Pennebaker/Hegedus Films)*

Nyro and her new agent, David Geffen, New York City, 1968. *(Photo by Stephen Paley, courtesy of Michael Ochs Archives)*

New York Tendaberry by candlelight: Nyro and coproducer Roy Halee during recording sessions, 1969. (*Photo by Stephen Paley, courtesy of Michael Ochs Archives*)

"You did it already"—Nyro with trumpeter Miles Davis, *New York Tendaberry* recording session, 1969.
(*Photo by Stephen Paley, courtesy of Michael Ochs Archives*)

OPPOSITE PAGE: Nyro taking a dance break during *New York Tendaberry* recording sessions, 1969.
(*Photo by Stephen Paley, courtesy of Michael Ochs Archives*)

Nyro with composer Stephen Sondheim in his Manhattan apartment, listening to music, c. 1969.
(*Photo by Stephen Paley, courtesy of Michael Ochs Archives*)

Nyro at the Fillmore East, December 1970.
(*Photo by Sherry Rayn Barnett*)

Rock 'n' roll boyfriends: Nyro kissing Jim Fielder (1968); hugging Jackson Browne (1970); and holding hands with Dallas Taylor (1969).
(*Photos by Stephen Paley, courtesy of Michael Ochs Archives*)

Crosby, *Nyro*, Nash, and Young: Laura visiting a CSNY rehearsal session at Warner Bros. in Burbank, with (*left to right*) David Crosby, Neil Young, and Graham Nash. (*Photo by Henry Diltz*)

Nyro (*holding hat*), with Swami Satchidananda (*center, in robe*) and Felix Cavaliere (*right, in jacket*), Hartford, Connecticut, 1974. They were going to a ballet performance by Rudolph Nureyev. (*Courtesy of Integral Yoga Institute*)

David Bianchini in Vietnam, c. 1970. (*Photo by Alan R. Bingham*)

Nyro with husband David Bianchini, c. 1972. (*Copyright © David Gahr*)

"Gypsy man"—boyfriend Greg Bennett as drawn by Nyro, c. 1974–75. (*Courtesy of Patty Di Lauria*)

Nyro with *Eli* and *Smile* producer
Charlie Calello, c. 1975. (*Courtesy of
Charles Calello*)

Nyro on *Season of Lights* tour, Santa Monica Civic Auditorium, 1976.
(*Photo by Sherry Rayn Barnett*)

"Tiny child, you're a miracle to me...": Laura with her infant son, Gil, and (*bottom*) with Grandpa Isidore Mirsky, 1978. (*Courtesy of Jan and Janice Nigro* [top], *Barbara Greenstein* [middle], *and Louis Nigro* [bottom])

Laura on the bed in her Danbury cottage with her puppy Ember, c. 1981.
(*Courtesy of Jan and Janice Nigro*)

Gil and Ember in front of the pond in Danbury, with Nyro's cottage and the "Gypsy"
trailer in the background, c. 1981.
(*Photo by Terry Golash, M.D., courtesy of Barbara Greenstein*)

Gil, c. 1982. *(Courtesy of Louis Nigro)*

Grandpa Mirsky, c. mid 1980s.
(*Courtesy of Jan and Janice Nigro*)

Jan Nigro, Janice Nigro, Laura, and
Gil in Stewart Park, Ithaca, New
York, c. 1989–90.
(*Courtesy of Jan and Janice Nigro*)

Laura and Maria Desiderio in Long Beach, Long Island, with Maria's dog Scootie, c. 1989. (*Photo by Janice Nigro*)

Nyro onstage with singer Diane Wilson (*left*) and percussionist Nydia Mata, Philadelphia, 1988. (*Photo by Linda Johnson*)

Portrait of Laura Nyro, 1990. *(Photo by Pat Johnson)*

A world to carry on: Gil Bianchini at age twenty-two, New York City, 2001.
(Photo by Linda Johnson)

teners could catch the rare sound of Nyro's *speaking* voice, as she banters with the audience.

"You're beautiful!" someone yells out.

"So are you!" she responds. "It's good to see you again."

Nyro performs the next song, "When I Was a Freeport and You Were the Main Drag," solo at the piano, using her familiar chords and syncopation but again ending with wordless, rhythmic vocalese. She also made another minor lyrical change, substituting ". . . *and this is* my due time" for "I'm a woman / *waiting* for due time." That elicited a burst of applause from women in the audience, who obviously enjoyed hearing a "sisterhood is powerful" statement from Nyro.

The album closes with two more piano-accompanied numbers, "Timer" and "Emmie." Neither add much to their incarnations on *Eli*, although the latter showcases Nyro's unadorned concert style.

Melody Maker judged the album harshly, calling it "one of the most disappointing releases of the year," especially coming after what the reviewer called her "memorable (and curiously underestimated)" *Smile*. The review found the new versions of her songs, except for those featuring just Nyro and her piano, to be perfunctory, with leaden arrangements and "insensitive" drumming by Newmark.

Stephen Holden's review in *Rolling Stone* lacked the magazine's usual cynical edge, but he didn't show much enthusiasm either, suggesting that as Nyro softened the emotionalism of her delivery, the impact of her artistry had diminished. Her early songs, he said, were "torn right out of the moment," and her art then seemed a "desperate act of survival," but her new versions felt cool and detached. Holden acknowledged that Nyro had grown more disciplined in her work—a quality some critics had felt she lacked—but contended that discipline was no substitute for passion. Critic Ariel Swartley, in *The Village Voice*, pretty much agreed, writing that *Season of Lights* only confirmed "the terms of Laura Nyro's comeback: She won't set herself on fire for us anymore."

Nyro's voice *had* lost some of its impact as she softened her delivery, but there was no winning for Nyro with certain critics. If she was passionate and unbridled, she was called undisciplined and shrill. If she simplified, softened, or showed more emotional detachment, she was deemed bland and was considered to have lost her wizardry.

In the British publication *Sounds*, Mike Davies angrily pointed out that the single-disc version of the album was bound to be unsatisfying. "What you lose is the feeling of coherence that the full running double set can convey," wrote Davies, who had obviously heard the promo version. He concluded, " 'Season of Lights'? Not at CBS. Maybe it's time she found a label that cares."

It wasn't until 1993 that Sony Japan finally released the "complete version" of *Season of Lights* on CD, and as Davies had suggested, it proves far more engaging than the truncated 1977 album. Besides the original set of songs, the Japanese release includes "Sweet Lovin' Baby" from *New York Tendaberry*; "I Am the Blues," "Smile," "Mars," and "Midnite Blue" from *Smile*; and a new Nyro composition that never appeared on another album, "Morning News."

With a fetching minor melody, "News" decries the evil quartet of war, corporate greed, sexism, and the exploitation of native peoples. The song feels more a fragment than a whole, but its last verse contains an insightful couplet that expresses an emblematic dilemma for Nyro: "Two worlds spin in time / One around you, one inside." More and more, she would find that the outside world, with its warring and prejudice, belied the peace and love she was searching for within herself.

Columbia's decision to shorten the album by cutting recently released songs seems logical, but it's hard to know why the company would also cut Nyro's only *new* song. Also, some lovely riffing by the band was lost in the editing, including Maineri's baliphone excursion on "The Cat-Song," a percussion explosion in "Timer," and a funky horn jam and Tropea guitar solo in "Captain Saint Lucifer."

The truncated *Season of Lights* made little impact on record buyers, spending only five weeks on the *Billboard* album charts and reaching just No. 137 on the albums chart. The complete *Season of Lights* comes much closer to achieving the actual feel of Nyro's concerts. On the shorter album she seems to fit uncomfortably into the band's arrangements, but she comes off more successfully as ringmaster in the complete version. Even if the jazz-fusion arrangements sound a little busy—especially compared to the more spare production on her studio albums—Nyro is obviously having fun as a member of a horn-flavored band, something she had wanted to be part of since the outset of her performing career.

Maybe Sid Bernstein could have spoken on her behalf to CBS about releasing the complete album, but after a year of working with her he was out of the picture. After he was particularly disappointed that Nyro turned down an interview he'd arranged with *The Village Voice*, she asked to meet with him at her grandfather's.

"I don't mean to frustrate you, Sid, but I don't feel like working," she told him. "I really just want to record and not tour again for a while, and that means you won't make any money with me. Why don't we forget about management and interviews and just remain friends?"

From then on, Nyro would mostly eschew professional management. More often than not, she asked friends like Roscoe Harring—who was primarily her road manager—to act de facto as artist's manager as well.

"I don't like being called a manager," says Harring, who nonetheless held that role for Nyro on and off for over a decade. "It was a friendship and not a business thing. When she needed to be represented to the record company, she would make me go to things. She never yearned to be like a star. She was very satisfied being a good songwriter. She never would do anything for money—on purpose." He laughs.

"I can laugh about that now, but that's why a lot of manager-type people who thought that they could make her a rich person never succeeded. It would make them crazy. Me, not being a business type, I didn't care. We'd just sit there and laugh."

14
NESTED

After she finished her *Season of Lights* tour, Nyro took Patty Di Lauria to Japan with her for the second time. Di Lauria thinks her friend may have needed a break from her relationship with Greg Bennett, which wasn't going well. "She told me he had difficulty with her being so wealthy and he being essentially a poor carpenter-musician. She did have an awful lot of money at the time, and that made him feel inadequate or something. I liked Laura's take on money—if there was some, great, let's share it; if there isn't, then we won't have any."

When they returned to the States, Di Lauria even spoke privately to Bennett (with Nyro's permission), telling him, "The money thing doesn't matter—she's crazy about you. Everything will even out, so just be glad it's there and enjoy it." But Bennett never got comfortable about not being the breadwinner. Also, Nyro very much wanted to have a child, and he did not. Shortly after the Japan trip, the couple broke up.

"He was a very major love; he broke her heart," says Di Lauria. "And she drove him crazy, needing what she needed. Sometimes with Laura there wasn't compromising. They just came to loggerheads, and that was that." Barbara Greenstein says that shortly afterward, Nyro invited her on a trip to Mexico to "recuperate" from the painful split.

The next spring, Di Lauria spent several months with Nyro in Danbury, painting the cottage where Nyro would then live. "While we were there it was a very quiet existence—I don't remember anyone coming to visit while I was painting the cottage," says Di Lauria, who by that time had split with her husband and had met a man she would marry, Andy Uryevick, the brother of Nyro's friend Ellen Uryevick. They had met in Danbury while he was designing the *Season of Lights* cover. A new man would soon enter Laura's life as well.

Harindra Singh—known as Hari—was tall, dark-haired, handsome, and about ten years Nyro's senior. Jan and Janice Nigro had met him in India, where he said that his father was a raja, with many wives and children, and that he was some sort of prince. Jan and Janice found Hari to be funny, charming, smart, and interesting, and soon became fast friends. "People met him and instantly liked him," says Janice. They thought he'd be a good match for Laura, who had spent time in India and followed the teachings of Indian guru Swami Satchidananda. "I remember writing some glowing testimonials from India, and they must have been persuasive, because Laura and Hari started corresponding," says Jan. He soon came to visit her in Danbury, and not long after that Nyro became pregnant.

Her relationship with Singh wasn't as high-keyed as her love affair with Greg Bennett, says Patty Di Lauria: "With Harindra it seemed more grounded, more mature, less emotional." Did Nyro choose him mainly because he would provide her with a child? "To say that she just saw him as father material is too harsh," says Di Lauria. "I would never say that."

Nyro had been thinking and talking about motherhood for a couple of years. "One thing I take seriously is having a baby," she had said in 1976. "That's part of my feminism." Laura's good friend Anne Johnson—who had met her in 1973 when Janice Nigro had been a student of Anne's husband Charles at Goddard College—thinks that the birth of her own second child in 1976—named Laura in Nyro's honor—may have helped stoke Nyro's maternal urges.

Nyro already seemed to be an angel of conception, at least where her friends were concerned: Patti LaBelle's son Zuri had been conceived on her trip with Laura to Japan, and Laura Johnson was conceived while Anne and Charles were visiting Nyro in Danbury.

Nyro's pregnancy would prove inspirational to her music and she'd record, her new album, Nested, at her own nest in Danbury (thanks to Dale Ashby's mobile recording unit). Roscoe Harring would act as producer, and he called in Felix Cavaliere to help.

"They were going around in circles," says Cavaliere. "She was pregnant at the time, there was a tour pending, and nothing was happening on the album—there were guys laying all over the house instead of doing their sessions. I went in and got it going. She was not a person who could control a room musically. She really needed an outside source to come in and snap the whip a little bit."

"Everything with Laura musically was slightly haphazard and loose," says *Season of Lights* drummer Andy Newmark, who rejoined Nyro for the *Nested* sessions. "Whatever happened happened. Not that she was unprofessional—she just wasn't bothered about it all being right and perfect and showing people what to do, like most artists. She was kind of wispy and ethereal. If we got something, that was all right, and if we didn't get something for a day or two, that was okay, too."

Bassist Will Lee also remembers *Nested* as a slow, disorganized project. "But in a way that was kind of good because it got more loving care than a lot of quick in-and-out projects would get," he says. "It was organic in its conception, because we would just build these arrangements from scratch."

Nyro's style was particularly challenging for a bass player like Lee, who needed to find the right bottom line for each song. "She would play these odd chords on the piano—they were just sort of big clusters of notes—and I'd have to try to decipher what the root of these chords were supposed to be," he says. "A lot of times, no matter where I would place the root, it never felt grounded. I would say something like 'Is this the root?' and she would say, 'I don't know, try it.' She wouldn't really commit, so it was very artsy, that whole process. Usually I would have to make an executive decision myself. She wasn't really forceful about saying which was right and which was not right."

For a producer, Nyro's easygoing attitude—combined with a perfectionism about her own recorded performance—could be crazy-making. "You had to really love her to put up with her," says Cavaliere. "We hear stories about how difficult movie stars are, and I'm sure it's the same mentality, to a degree, but I felt her [perfectionism] was genuinely rooted in this musical world she was in, which tortured her. Everything, every word that was in a song, had to pass her test. She was brutal on herself. I had heard of artists who destroyed their paintings, and she was like that. You had to stop her before she destroyed it. She would go past the point of brilliance, and I'd try to intervene at that point: 'This is great, this is great, let's stop, let's do it now, let's do it *now*.' "

Despite Nyro's less than assertive nature as a bandleader, Will Lee remained in awe of her as a songwriter and found her personally delightful. He remembers one particular incident when he, Newmark, and guitarist Vinnie Cusano (who went on to play with Kiss under the name Vinnie Vincent, thus making *Nested* a collector's item for Kiss completists) were struggling over a certain arrangement.

"We finally got a good tape, and right on the last note of this four-

or five-minute song, Laura's German shepherd Chestnut [Beautybelle had died] barks. Right at a real sensitive moment." In response, Lee started to sing, 'Chestnut's roasting on an open fire,' and Nyro dissolved into girlish giggles: "Oh Will, *stop!*"

"She was just extremely cute," says Lee. "She had the heart of a little girl and the will of a very strong woman."

Nyro liked to begin recording sessions with a sing-along of her favorite oldies, and Lee obligingly joined in. "She always had a big vocabulary of Motown-type songs. That's where she comes from, you know—that was the soundtrack of all of our childhoods. I didn't know if she was warming up or just having some fun, but I was happy to play along," he says.

Nested, which was released in June of 1978, has quite a different feel from Nyro's past efforts. It's more breezy and certainly more homegrown-sounding, as befits the casual setting for the recording sessions. Nyro would later tell a journalist that she was not unlike a visual artist who would go through "a blue phase, a green phase, a rose phase," so considering Adger Cowans's cover photo of Nyro with a red flower in her hair, *Nested* might be attributed to her rose phase. However, it contains thematic elements drawn from her whole colorful songwriting career.

Nested opens with another blue-titled song, this time "Mr. Blue (the song of communications)." Greg Bennett was Mr. Blue, according to Patty Di Lauria, a man looking bemused by Laura while she ponders various forms of communication, including extraterrestrial. In a sly spoken rap, she reports that he says to her, "I mean, I've heard of liberation / but sweetheart—/ you're in outer space." Despite the title, the subtly humorous, self-deprecating song isn't the blues, however: It has a beautiful winding melody on which Nyro showcases most of her vocal range.

The next cut contains even more blue: "Rhythm and Blues." Catchy, but a bit old hat, it's a syncopated roadhouse romp, with the Lovin' Spoonful's John Sebastian (a friend of Nyro's) supplying a rollicking harmonica line.

"My Innocence" finds Nyro thinking of her mother, as she certainly would have been just before becoming a mother herself: "My innocence, my innocence comes from my warm earth mother . . . / the sky is speechless." She also leaves another clue about her love life, singing that she's given her innocence to "my cold, cold lover," whom she describes as a man with the Indian hair. That could mean Hari, the man of East Indian ancestry, or Bennett, with his American Indian heritage and long dark hair (Di Lauria believes it's the latter). Nyro concludes that she's facing "unknown future / it's me and you now." Could she be contemplating a life with her soon-to-be-born child that would not include either lover?

On "Crazy Love," Nyro is accompanied just by her piano, giving the song the simplicity and power of a live performance. Its gorgeous melody evokes love's majesty and melancholy, as she recalls a "gypsy man" from "midwest plains and rivers," who sang catfish blues. She's certainly referring to Bennett, her guitar-playing gypsy who hailed from Ohio. In the song's third verse, she sings about the child she didn't have with Bennett, as she had hoped to: "Oh my lover / father of my unborn star."

In the closing cut on Side One, "American Dreamer," Nyro is an ingenuous believer disappointed by the realities of greed and incompetence. Like "Money" on *Smile*, she complains about those who have taken advantage of her (or others), whether in marriage, management, or health. "Autumn's child is catchin' hell," sings the October-born Nyro, "for having been too naive to tell / property rights from chapel bells." The second verse complains about a smiling manager who made the singer sign a contract with "transparent lines." In the last verse, doctors tell a patient that she's imagining things. Could that be about Laura's mother not being diagnosed until her cancer was too advanced to treat? Through all the disappointments expressed in the song, Nyro keeps a sense of black humor, knowing that she's destined to keep dreaming despite it all.

Side Two begins with acoustic guitar strumming. "She would tune the guitar to a chord and put her finger across the strings," says Will Lee of Nyro's rudimentary technique. "She wasn't exactly Django Reinhart." But guitar, on which Nyro had written several of the album's songs, gives a radiance to the song "Springblown," as she reflects soft feelings toward a lover whose face is "like a warm embrace to me." This may have been about Hari, considering how she shyly whispers, "I worry / worry maybe / I'm calling your name / you know / seeds of our baby."

The next song, "The Sweet Sky," is one of the overlooked delights of Nyro's repertoire. With its shuffle beat, delicious harmonies, and irrepressible, repeating coda ("Sweeter than the sweet sky"), it's reminiscent of some of the catchiest Nyro compositions of the past, such as "Save the Country" or "Time and Love." But here the topic is summery and light: Nyro knows she's supposed to follow rules, stay in line, but she's "like a teenager / gone like the 4th of July / for the sweet sky."

She follows that song with the electric piano–accompanied "Light," a sort of New Age musing ("In your flight / send your love out / to the planet's soul"). It's subtitled "Pop's Principle," in reference to a recording engineer with whom Nyro would discuss physics, according to Di Lauria. The sentiments of the song are simplistic, but Nyro overcomes any treacle with her sincerity and lush harmonizing.

The second-to-last cut on the album, "Child in a Universe," offers another transcendent melody. One can forgive Nyro being in an extraterrestrial mood as she's about to give birth, because she can't help but see herself as just a small part of the grand cosmos. She addresses the first verse to a star, the second to the sun, and the third to the moon, to whom she sings: "I saw your light on . . . can we talk a while / you see I lost my smile." While searching the sky, Nyro pleads for some peace to be sent back down to earth, to a "child in a universe."

She closes Nested with "The Nest," returning to an Oriental sound, created here by piano, bass, guitar, and Felix Cavaliere's organ. "Brown shiny nest / up in a tree / maple and warm / like the nest in me," she sings. Rarely in pop music has a woman so openly expressed the excitement and trepidation of impending motherhood.

Equally rare would be Nyro's decision to tour that summer while visibly pregnant. Patty Di Lauria remembers her shopping for "sexy" maternity clothes at a store called Lady Madonna, and choosing several colorful long dresses that wouldn't so much hide her figure as celebrate it. In performance at intimate clubs such as the Roxy in Los Angeles, San Francisco's Old Waldorf, Park West in Chicago, the Great Southeast Music Hall in Atlanta, and the Bottom Line in Manhattan (her first of many subsequent appearances at the latter), she was, as one fan described her, so pregnant that her fingers seemed to barely reach the piano keys. Nyro didn't dwell on her state, but did say to the audience in between-song patter, "We're both really happy to be here."

Her final gig of the tour was on a hot July night at the Dr Pepper (formerly the Schaeffer) Music Festival in Central Park, which that summer also featured her old friend Todd Rundgren and the first group that had covered her music, Peter, Paul and Mary. Journalist Paul Colford fondly recalled that Nyro's performance was "as languid as the night itself."

Harring still chuckles at the memory of what happened before Nyro took the Central Park stage. At the sound check, she had noticed that she wouldn't be able to see the first three rows of the audience, nor they her, from her perch on the fifteen-foot-high stage. "Can you lower the stage?" she asked Harring.

He responded, "Laura, it would take a week to lower this stage!"

"Oh, I can't do this, it's impossible," she said. "I can't move closer to the edge, and it's just so high." She urged Harring to talk to promoter Ron Delsener, and he did so only to appease her, coming back with the same answer: *impossible.* Nyro thought about it for another minute, then made a final unanswered plea:

"Then could they raise the audience?"

■ ■ ■

Reviewers were split about both the *Nested* tour and the album. Alan Jones in *Melody Maker* compared the album favorably with *Christmas and the Beads of Sweat*, praising its "similar balance of introspection and exuberant celebration, the same melodic authority and confidence." The reviewer pointed out that Nyro was once again preoccupied with the "fragility and transience" of relationships, plunging herself into the pain of separation in one song, but emerging with renewed spirit and optimism in another.

On the flip side, Paul Ramball in Britain's *New Musical Express* considered *Nested* uninspired. "It'll blend in fine with your wallpaper," he wrote. Similarly, Eliot Wald in the *Chicago Sun-Times* suggested that the songs themselves were beginning to blend together, "as if the original idea that made her unique was the only one she's ever had." He admitted that it might be inappropriate to require an artist to keep blazing trails, but still opined that "what was so refreshing in 1968 seems to have tired in 10 years."

Village Voice writer Richard Mortifoglio gave a blunt review of the album that failed to consider it in the context of Nyro's pregnancy. He condescendingly claimed that she had commanded adoration from middle-class college girls of the late 1960s because she represented "the poetics of their hysteria." Furthermore, although he had appreciated Nyro's "vocal equipment," her "great melodic gift," and her improved professionalism on *Smile*, he found *Nested* to have little evocative imagery, "dopey and weak" science references, banal lyrics, and nondescript (but "effectively pretty") tunes. "Deeply flawed," he concluded, "Laura Nyro was and remains an amateur erratically touched by some outrageous genius."

He was equally tough on her Central Park appearance, praising only her "marvelously sexy" versions of Dr. John's "Mama Roux" and her own "Man in the Moon" (which would appear on a subsequent Nyro album). But he wondered whether those same college women who had loved her "celebration of needful feeling" viewed her now as a domineering friend from high school whose influence they resented.

Conversely, Robert Palmer in The New York Times enjoyed Nyro in performance much more than he had in the past. "The songs emerged clearly from the haze that has so often seemed to billow around the singer," he wrote, "and a commanding, delicate but sensual performer emerged along with them." Crawdaddy's equally enthused Daisann McLane saw Nested as a confident effort, both vocally and instrumentally. "It's homegrown, but it jumps," she wrote.

McLane also considered Nyro's new lyrics in light of the complex, scary feelings associated with pregnancy. The nest, McLane intuited, wasn't just the home Nyro was fashioning for her child, it was also the insularity she had fashioned to protect herself. "I like Laura Nyro precisely because she's so remote from anything but the torments and joys of her own soul," she concluded. Perhaps a male critic like Mortifoglio, rather than appreciating or identifying with her isolation and singularity, felt personally excluded.

Nyro did seem to be coasting somewhat at this point, in the sense that she was restating old themes and images rather that creating new worlds with each subsequent album. But if her work is read as an ongoing journal of self-discovery, rather than as the career path of a commercial artist who continually reinvents herself, it makes more sense. No longer the tortured teenager striving to comprehend life and love, Nyro had now deliberately chosen to have a child and settle into her earthy world—and thus her music logically reflected more peacefulness than the emotional roller-coaster ride of an Eli or New York Tendaberry. Taken on its own terms, Nested is a thoughtful, tuneful, and charming Nyro album, albeit with less lyrical magic than some of her past efforts. The public, though, didn't respond enthusiastically: Nested didn't crack the Top 200 albums on Billboard's charts and has long been out of print.

■ ■ ■

By the time Laura Nyro was ready to give birth, Hari Singh was out of her life. "Nice guy, but he just didn't stand up to her qualifications," says Roscoe Harring. "Never knew what hit him. Laura was a very powerful woman, don't forget. She wanted to have a child, and that's what happened."

Felix Cavaliere says that Singh had gone back to India to speak to his family, and perhaps to his guru, about the fact that he had impregnated a woman and wondered whether or not to marry her. "It was an interesting situation for him, because the man was a religious guy," says Cavaliere, who became fairly close to Hari because of his own interest in Eastern religion. "Laura's religious beliefs were completely different from his. He was basically a Hindu, a yogi, and she had sort of an earth goddess type of religion. He came to an environment that stripped him down to bare bones. He wore a turban when he met her; when he left her, he had a T-shirt on."

To others around Nyro, Hari had seemed "jive," as Helen Merrill, who briefly met him in New York, describes him. "The so-called prince," she says skeptically. "There are about a billion princes in India." Patty Di Lauria, who spent the previous New Year's Eve in Danbury with Laura, Hari, and Andy, wasn't crazy about him either: "He was a very charming person, but he was also a pontificator. He was pretty full of himself." As Patty remembers it, Hari actually asked Laura to marry him—out of a sense of duty, if nothing else—but when she said she didn't want to, he abandoned ship.

Knowing that Singh would not be there for the birth, Nyro engaged family and friends to help out. She planned a natural childbirth and chose a birth center in Manhattan, but at the beginning of her ninth month came to feel that this center was not going to provide the sort of birth experience she wanted. So she made a last-minute switch to a birth center in Reading, Pennsylvania—a five-hour drive from Danbury.

The plan was to leave for Pennsylvania before she went into labor, but her water broke not two minutes before starting the journey, so she was in light labor throughout the ride. "It was actually very fun and exciting," says Janice Nigro, who drove her sister-in-law to Reading. Nyro's plans for a natural childbirth went somewhat awry, because after over twenty hours of labor it was suggested she have a cesarean section for the baby's safety. When Nyro called her friend Patty in Colorado, where she and Andy Uryevick now lived, to give her the good news that she'd finally delivered a healthy dark-haired son on August 23, she sounded exhausted and weak. But suddenly she summoned up the strength to deliver a loud declaration on the rigors of labor: "AND MEN SHOULD BE ON THEIR KNEES!"

■ ■ ■

In Ashkenazi (Eastern European) Jewish tradition, a child is named after a deceased relative to honor that person. Whether by tradition or desire, Laura named her son Gillian, after her mother Gilda. From the outset, most people called him simply Gil or Gilly.

Just as he had pointed out that people would mispronounce Nyro, Lou Nigro told his daughter that Gillian was an English woman's name and that his grandson would be the butt of jokes growing up. "But she had a stubborn streak," says Lou. However, when Gil entered nursery school, Nyro decided to formally change his name from Gillian Singh to Gil Bianchini. She had been using Bianchini as her own surname; he now would share that moniker.

Singh never met his son, and Nyro never publicly revealed who had fathered Gil. The closest the information came to being in print was in a mid-1980s interview with Patti LaBelle in *Interview*. She inaccurately pieced together what she'd heard about Nyro's life: "I know she married a guy and they divorced, and then she married an Arab prince. . . . Somebody like that, who had some other wives. And she had a baby . . ."

15
MOTHER'S SPIRITUAL

As Laura Nyro settled into motherhood in the quiet environs of Danbury, women in pop music were making more noise than ever in punk and New Wave bands, especially those originating in England, such as Siouxsie and the Banshees, the Raincoats, the Slits, and the Pretenders (led by American-born Chrissie Hynde). This latest group of women artists were tougher-shelled than a Nyro or a Joni Mitchell, infusing rock with poetry and attitude. Singer-songwriter no longer seemed a fitting moniker: Their music was more combative than confessional.

But a new generation from the dramatic-confessional school began emerging as well, most notably Kate Bush from England and Rickie Lee Jones from the United States. Both were daughters of Nyro, so to speak, and Jones—although at first compared more to Mitchell because of their long, straight blond hair—has never hesitated to credit Nyro as a prime influence.

Nyro's world, in stark contrast to the slashing guitar sounds of early-eighties female musicians, was filled with the quiet daily dramas of single motherhood. It was hard not to have her own mother there to provide guidance, but Gilda's friend Flora stayed with Laura a while after Gil was born, as did Patty, and Jan and Janice lived in Danbury for about six months during Gil's infancy. Nyro also had the companionship of a new Belgian Tervuren puppy—a shepherd with a soft fawn-and-charcoal coat—that she named Ember. He would remain one of her best friends for the next fifteen years.

Motherhood pushed Nyro even further into feminism, which she embraced with the fervor of a religious convert. She became as intrigued by the metaphorical qualities of certain goddesses as she once was by the God/Devil dichotomy. While the popular stereotype of feminism was that it was dreary and humorless, Nyro saw a feminist world as somehow more fun. "Feminism is a bright color in a gray reality," she would tell *Woman of Power* magazine in a 1985 interview.

She also saw *women* in terms of color—at least in a phone conversation she had with Melissa Manchester about men's and women's roles. "Women are red, and they just get redder as they get older," Nyro told Manchester, who had met her early heroine while visiting a recording session for *Smile* with songwriter Carole Bayer Sager (whose piano Lou Nigro tuned). Nyro and Manchester ended up having several long phone chats in the late 1970s about integrity, songwriting, and poetry.

"Laura *spoke* in poetry—that was what I found most interesting and dazzling," says Manchester. "One can put on a 'writer's hat,' but she actually spoke the way that she wrote."

The "red" comment inspired a lyric in a Manchester song, "Through the Eyes of Grace." "I ended up writing 'Women don't get older / just a deeper shade of red.' That was directly out of my conversation with Laura," she says.

Nyro's feminist beliefs also included a vision of utopian communities with central kitchens to feed the needy, and places for older people to connect with youth and animals rather than live in "separate, lonely spaces." Perhaps she was thinking of Grandpa, whom she had moved into a garden apartment near the McDonald's in downtown Danbury. Mr. Mirsky, now in his eighties and nearly deaf, still delighted in cleaning her house on his frequent visits.

"I remember one day he was on his hands and knees in the cottage scrubbing the floor," says Keith Decker, a former Head Start teacher hired by Nyro in early 1981 to care for Gil, "and Gil just ran across the room and jumped on Grandpa's back. Everyone thought he was going to die, but fortunately he was okay."

With men like Decker, Roscoe Harring, Grandpa, brother Jan, father Lou Nigro, and Andy Uryevick around, Gil didn't lack for male role models. But there weren't many men around Nyro in terms of love interest. Decker does remember a short-term relationship she had in the early 1980s with a man named Guy, who worked as a groundskeeper at a Berkshires resort near Amherst, Massachusetts.

"I never saw what she saw in him," says Decker. "He wasn't very bright. He had Incredible Hulk good looks—big-browed, dirty blond hair. I drove her up there once to pick him up, and then she kind of sent him packing after a week. I'm not sure he even knew who she was." Decker and his brother Michael, who began doing maintenance on Nyro's property in the early eighties and later lived in the main house for a decade along with his partner Ralph, would later joke that Laura's very last boyfriend had been "a guy named Guy."

■ ■ ■

Although Nyro remained at a remove from the record business, the business had not entirely forgotten her: In 1980, CBS in England released a greatest hits collection called *Impressions*, containing thirteen songs from her first four albums. Not long after that, with Gil almost two years old, Nyro began planning her next album of original material. She would call it *Mother's Spiritual*.

The idea for the album, she told *Guitar* magazine, had come to her in a minute, then took years to manifest. "The relationships and responsibilities that were inspiring the music were also pulling me away from it in terms of time," she said. Nonetheless, Nyro felt abundant with musical ideas—"like the Goddess of Creativity," she would say.

She did much of her writing during the night, an experience she described to one writer as "swimming in a cool, dark river—kind of shiny and exhilarating." She'd jot down her ideas rather than taperecord them, and if paper wasn't nearby, she'd scribble on a matchbook cover or even her hand. Sometimes she'd hear a particular instrument—gypsy violins, for example—accompanying the song in her mind.

Roscoe Harring remembers Nyro at first having just fragments, as she called her incomplete songs. "She'd have two choruses of one song and play them on the telephone to me, and we'd go do it in her home studio, putting this with that and that with this to see how it sounded," he says. Even later, in the process of recording the album, Nyro would transfer a section of one song to another as the creative spirit moved her.

Nyro's subject matter was right there at home. She wanted to reflect "a new world," she said, because that's what she felt she had entered. "*Nested* was from a one-to-one vision of romantic love, but with *Mother's Spiritual* the theme of love went *zap*, toward a sense of all of life, all of creation."

The new world took her further from the struggles of the city; it was rooted in the landscape around her. "I could feel the spirit of nature and elves, and I'll always feel that anytime I'm around the trees," said Nyro, whose property was filled with maples, white birch, mountain laurels, oaks, weeping willows, white pines, cedar, poplar, ash, and Nyro's favorite, a pink-and-white flowering magnolia. The trees influenced even the form of her new songs, she told *Woman of Power*—the new compositions followed the energies of outreaching branches, while her city songs bounced off streets and skyscrapers.

She would dedicate her album to the trees, and write two songs about them. Some critics chided her for being such a tree hugger, but her pantheism was real and heartfelt. "I sometimes feel more in common with the trees around my house than with the society I live in," she confessed. She had even written a youthful poem entitled "Trees" in 1961, reading in part, "And golden times catch up with us / and we find a haven among the trees / For we know and trees have seen / What no man has found but we."

Nyro was tapping into a zeitgeist on *Mother's Spiritual* that would be deemed New Age, but up to that point New Age music had primarily been instrumental—blending classical, jazz, folk, and ethnic sounds. Nyro, as always, wasn't thinking about labels, except perhaps the label of "mother." More than anything, her new work would be about the mother that she had become, and the one she had lost and still longed for.

"I remember walking into the Danbury house and noticing all these small little shrines that I knew were dedicated to her mother, and Laura confirmed it," says bassist Elysa Sunshine, who would play on the album. "It might have been a photograph of her mother and a couple of objects on a shelf. Little devotional places. I think she missed her mother terribly. Especially having her own kid, it made those feelings that much stronger."

In *Woman of Power*, Nyro told a story about Gilda and Lou Nigro's ill-fated house in Ellenville, remembering the pleasures of it and not the troubles. Nyro particularly recalled a glassless, wood-shuttered window in her parents' second-floor bedroom that opened onto a view of the inside of the house. When Gilda looked out that window, her daughter imagined, she was looking at the people and the things she most loved.

"The spirit of that window never really left me," said Nyro. "You could say that *Mother's Spiritual* is a celebration of my mother's window."

Over the next year and a half, while Roscoe Harring handled the business end of Nyro's life and Keith Decker babysat Gil and did chores, Nyro "wrote music like crazy," Decker says. "She paid absolutely no attention to worldly events, largely because she was so focused on the music and the album. She lived in Laura Land." Indeed, one day in 1981, Nyro said to Decker, "Did you know that President Reagan was shot?" Replied Decker, "Yeah, Laura—*six months ago!*"

Drawn by the lure of the open road, Laura and Gil would take off frequently on long weekend trips, with Decker driving her large recreational vehicle, nicknamed the Gypsy. They might head for Ithaca, New York, to visit Jan and Janice, or down to Hilton Head Island in South Carolina, where Nyro at one point rented a house for a month on the beach. Not surprisingly, the song Decker remembers her composing there, on a portable electric piano, became known as "Roadnotes." It includes the lyrics "Me and my friends / somewhere on the road / child and dog play / winds they blow."

Even before Gilly had turned a year old, Laura also had driven out to Colorado, with Roscoe Harring, leaving her young son with Patty and Andy for five days while she and Roscoe tooled around New Mexico. It then became an annual tradition for Nyro to bring Gil for a stay of a couple of weeks at a time with the Uryevicks, while she took time for herself and her work.

Despite her love of car travel, Nyro was not much of a driver herself. David Bianchini tried to teach her, then Roscoe Harring, who says that Nyro finally got her license around 1980. Michael Decker remembers her taking lessons from Sears Driving School, located at the Danbury mall.

"They would come by the house and pick her up in a white Chevrolet Cavalier, and she just loved that little thing," says Michael Decker. "She graduated and they felt she was ready to take her driving test, but she didn't think she was ready—so she signed up and took the whole course all over again. This time she took the test and passed the first time. Now she had her license and had to buy a car, so what did she buy? A Chevy Cavalier! A wagon, though—a little white Cavalier wagon."

"God, I don't know how, but she passed her test," adds Harring. "She wouldn't make lefthand turns, only righthand ones. She couldn't drive to the city, or to anywhere but the 7-Eleven near her house. That was it. She got a license and then never drove." When she did get behind the wheel, Nyro didn't inspire much confidence in those around her. "She was a terrible driver," says Michael Decker. "One day she nearly drove over my foot."

Young Gilly was a sweet and energetic boy, a normal kid of that age who loved to wrestle and be tickled, says Keith Decker. Nyro was a devoted mother, trying to keep him away from eating sugar and watching inappropriate TV shows. But when it came time for her to put together an album, her focus sometimes turned more toward her art than child-rearing.

"I was the one who toilet-trained Gil, for example," says Keith. "She was just so focused on *Mother's Spiritual*. She would sometimes get so frustrated with Gil that she'd leave and go to a hotel, and I'd have him for the whole weekend. To be honest, if there's any negative thing about Laura, it's that she was not more hands-on with Gil back then. But my brother Michael says that Laura was not that way later on with Gil."

"When she was recording and writing, that was all she did, one hundred percent," says Michael Decker. "That's all she could do. She was so easily distracted by emotion. Someone's [bad] energy could ruin her afternoon. That's how vulnerable she was when she was in that hyperfocus. She truly needed to control her situation, the energy that was around her. Gilly was a distraction, like any of us were. It wasn't about love; it was about her art. She didn't multitask at all; she just didn't have the capacity."

Nyro told *Sojourner* magazine that the writing process, for her, was "uncivilized." Songwriting rearranged her everyday life, because it became such a priority. "It beckons you away from your other responsibilities," she said. But when she had no projects or wasn't answering the phone, "She was the consummate mother," says Michael Decker. "She truly adored Gil. That's the bottom line."

Even with her intense focus on the project, *Mother's Spiritual* required a lengthy three-act recording process to reach fruition. Act One took place in Danbury, beginning around the spring of 1982. There, Nyro would demo songs on studio equipment Harring had installed in her former bedroom in the main house. Because she had decided to develop the new compositions slowly and organically, Nyro had to find musicians who would work more patiently—and less expensively—than the clock-watching New York studio pros. Compatibility was once again key in choosing players: Drummer Terry Silverlight, for example, remembers taking a quiet walk with Nyro around the Danbury property just so she could "see what kind of a person I was."

Manhattan-based Silverlight came recommended by Nydia Mata, while bassist Elysa Sunshine—like Nyro, the mother of a young child—was suggested by a friend of Harring's. "I guess I got the affirmative action chair," laughs Sunshine, who was told that Nyro wanted a balance of genders in the band. Her surname couldn't have hurt, either, as the band ended up blessed with Sunshine and Silverlight. Completing the core group was Connecticut-based guitarist John Bristow, suggested to Nyro by her real estate agent, of all people. Nyro had dropped in unannounced at a local club to watch Bristow play with his jazz-fusion band, then invited him over to jam.

All three musicians had been fans of Nyro's music. Bristow had performed "Beads of Sweat" and "Upstairs by a Chinese Lamp," while Silverlight, as a preteen, had idolized Nyro and even tried to find her phone number. He eventually tracked down David Geffen, who deemed the request cute, but wouldn't divulge any information. (When Silverlight later told Nyro that story, he expected a similar "that's cute" response, but instead it made her nervous that he had pursued her, even fifteen years after the fact.)

For the next nine months, Nyro and the band came together two or three times a week to practice and record, with Harring engineering. Silverlight remembers Nyro working from her "woman's book," a lyric-filled notebook with a flowery cover. "The songs were all pretty much there, but some of the bridges weren't written yet and the tempos weren't set," says Silverlight.

"We were trying to find soft but fiery arrangements, and it wasn't easy," adds Bristow. "She wasn't absolutely sure what she wanted, but we experimented with ideas she gave us and ideas we put to her." A rehearsal tape from those early sessions, when compared to the final vinyl, shows how much Nyro restructured songs over time: One song is missing a bridge and contains a verse that would later be dropped, while a second has different lyrics in its chorus, and a third has a coda that would later be cut and pasted onto another song.

As she had while recording *Nested*, Nyro frequently began sessions by singing sixties oldies, insisting that Bristow and Sunshine provide harmonies (Silverlight doesn't sing). Sunshine says that some sessions consisted almost solely of playing Motown favorites with Nyro, or just having a meal together. Even though she expected the unexpected at rehearsals, Sunshine could bank on Nyro's soft-spokenness. "There were times I wanted to just get out of there and make a loud noise!" she laughs. But the bassist came to appreciate Nyro's quiet, slow-as-erosion process, even as it frustrated her:

"Whatever I initially came up with as a bass part, my first idea was summarily rejected, and usually my second. It took a while to give her what she wanted, but it was actually a good creative experience. One thing that impressed me so much was that Laura always sang beautifully. Her style and emotional delivery never wavered. I always loved just listening to her."

For the drummer, the challenge—as always with Nyro—was to

speed up or slow down according to her whim. "Her sense of time breathes a lot," affirms Silverlight. "It's so emotional, it's beautiful. But to put a drum set with that is a little risky."

The demo making lasted until the end of the year, according to Sunshine. Then Nyro found what she thought would be the perfect relaxed situation in which to record the finished songs: an old Victorian house–turned–studio known as the Boogie Hotel, located in Port Jefferson, Long Island. To produce, Nyro hired old friend Joe Wissert, whom she had recently reconnected with. Wissert, who now lived in California and had achieved great success with Boz Scaggs's *Silk Degrees* album in 1976, originally hailed from Philadelphia, where he acquired old-school R&B tastes similar to Nyro's. He didn't feel that *Mother's Spiritual* would necessarily be a commercial album, but he thought it was "great stuff . . . just in the artistry of what she says, and what she was putting together."

The recording didn't get off to a good start, however. For one thing, the Boogie Hotel didn't have the right vibes. Says Bristow, "The engineers hadn't a clue where Laura was coming from. They didn't have the patience that we all did to work with her in the way she needed to be worked with. They were used to rock acts like Meat Loaf coming in there, partying their asses off and bangin' out a record. I think she detected, at least subconsciously, the quiet mockery she was getting from some of the people there.

"Laura was very soft, like a breeze," he continues. "She may not have been able to put her discomfort into words, but she was searching for a spiritual mood that wasn't there."

Wissert may not have been the best match for Nyro either. "He was very sensitive to her and his method was not to take over, but maybe where he went wrong was that he wasn't very authoritative," says Silverlight. Adds Sunshine, "He was a very sweet man, but Laura was not easy to work with, as sweet as she was." Sunshine summarizes the Boogie Hotel experience as being three weeks of misery for Nyro. "She was away from home, it was wintertime, and she wasn't feeling well—she had congestion and some throat problems—so she wasn't vocally where she wanted to be. I don't think being away from her nest, so to speak, was very good for her."

Wissert remembers only that Nyro was frequently ill and had to keep postponing sessions. Finally, he had to return to California, with the album in limbo. Nyro then informed her faithful musicians that she was going to build a serious studio in her house to record the album.

She'd call them when it was ready, she said. Silverlight figured that the project was over.

But true to her word, about five or six months later Nyro called the three musicians back to Danbury. Recording engineer Art Kelm had indeed built a studio in the main house, which cost Nyro in the range of $150,000 to $200,000. Nyro would refer to it as the Cauldron, and Bristow began to think of Nyro as the Good Witch. "She didn't make brews or cast spells," he says, "but she was kind of a gypsy. Her mannerisms, the way she looked, and her spirit gave her a Good Witch presence."

When the musicians returned to Danbury, the new studio was not the only change. An attractive, long-dark-haired female painter named Maria was there much of the time. "I wasn't going to ask too many questions, but there was obviously this very significant person in Laura's life," says Sunshine.

None of Nyro's close friends are certain how she met Maria Antonia Desiderio, who was seven years her junior, but it may have been backstage after one of Nyro's concerts. Nyro may also have visited the Magic Speller, a women's bookstore in Newport Beach, California, which Desiderio co-owned with her lover at the time. Considering that Nyro was an avid reader, her bookshelves filled with volumes on spirituality, art, women's liberation, animals, and Native American and Japanese culture, the bookstore connection was probably quite a plus. Desiderio would later tell Jan Nigro that Laura—who friends say had not previously been with a woman lover—pursued her.

Wendy Werris, a bookseller's rep and Nyro fan who did business with Desiderio's store, had always thought that Maria resembled Laura. Imagine her surprise then, when on one sales visit she found Desiderio gone and her partner explaining with some disdain, "Oh, Maria moved to Connecticut to live with Laura Nyro."

Their relationship remained almost entirely hidden from Nyro's public. Even if Nyro never spoke directly to the press of her affectional preference—and she never would in her lifetime—two songs on *Mother's Spiritual* strongly suggested that she was now relating with a woman. In "Melody in the Sky," she describes a new affair that she's taking a day (and a night) at a time. "And I like you," she sings, "I'm not looking / for Miss or Mr. Right." If nothing else, those lyrics make a bold statement of bisexuality.

The lustful song "Roadnotes" may also be directed toward a woman. "Hold me tight / angel of the night / hold me right / 'cause my love is the ocean," she sings in a bedroom voice. An angel can certainly be a man, but the song is redolent of female sensuality, the chorus being shorthand pillow talk that's unspecific as to gender: "Lover / that's right / lover." Nyro addresses this and other songs on the album only to "lover" or "baby," rather than to a captain or her man. She would continue to degenderize love lyrics for the rest of her career, a telling gesture for someone who had so specifically written about men in the past.

Nyro's fans—particularly lesbians—had long speculated about her sexuality, pointing first and foremost to the lush, female-centered romanticism of the song "Emmie." But Nyro maintained that "Emmie" was about universal womanhood and was a favorite of her mother— hardly the endorsement one would expect for her daughter's paean to a female lover. Nonetheless, lesbians continued to scan for clues to Nyro's sexuality, hoping that a confirmation of her romantic attraction to women would explain their own strong attraction to the singer.

"The first time I think I thought Laura was a lesbian," says Harriet Leider, her lesbian friend from the mid-seventies, "was when I heard her sing 'December's Boudoir' from *Eli and the Thirteenth Confession*. Not 'Emmie'—I didn't go there with that one—but when I heard 'December's Boudoir,' a chill ran up my spine. It evoked some kind of very erotic fantasy that could only be played out with another woman."

Though Leider had known Nyro during her marriage to Bianchini and her relationship with Greg Bennett, she wasn't surprised by her friend's eventual change of heart. "She *loved* women. Women were her joy and her passion. The biggest thrill Laura had was laughing with the girls. So it was no surprise when she came out."

Some of Nyro's friends suggest she may have entertained the notion of bisexuality even earlier in life. "When we were in high school I remember she kind of mentioned to me that it was an option to her," says Carol Amoruso, her junior high school friend. "And I was, at that point, freaked out by it." Roscoe Harring, too, says that he and Laura often discussed her strong emotional feelings toward women.

But after she got together with Desiderio, Nyro would not have appreciated being called a lesbian or having been described as "coming out." She preferred to be called "woman identified," according to Janice Nigro. Richard Denaro, her San Francisco hairdresser friend, remembers a long conversation with her about her abhorrence of labels.

"She made very clear to me that she would never allow herself to be labeled anything by anyone," he says. "She felt that to say someone was gay or lesbian or bisexual was merely another form of separatism, and there was enough separatism without that. She felt the world was too vast and too open to limit oneself."

"Laura's take on relationships was 'Love is where you find it. Be open to it,' " says Patty Di Lauria. "Just as long as it's a good relationship between two people, love is beautiful. She was basically bisexual. Laura would get down talking about a fellow just as easily as she'd get down talking about a woman, in terms of thinking someone was physically attractive. She might have gone back and forth if she hadn't settled with Maria."

Choosing to be with Maria seemed part of Nyro's feminist evolution, as well as reflecting her desire to find a caring partner after her disappointments with men. "I thought that the men Laura chose were just not sensitive enough," says Harring. "I think that over the years she just turned, and it worked out for the best for her. I think she was finally very happy with Maria. They had a very nice companionship." Nyro would even write a song called "Companion," characterizing herself as wanting "a very special trust / a very special lust."

"I think maybe the idea of being with a woman meant having more of a friendship available than you could have with a man," says Nydia Mata. "Even though there was so much passion with Greg, it was hard for her with him."

Louis Nigro comfortably accepted Laura's new relationship. "She was like another daughter, a lovely woman," he says of Desiderio.

Michael Maineri, the vibraphonist on the *Season of Lights* tour, remembers Nyro's own words on the subject when he came to visit her in Danbury. "I said, 'So what's going on here? How's your love life?' And Laura answered, 'Well, it's right here—Maria and I. I found my soulmate. I'm happy.' "

■ ■ ■

In Act Three of the *Mother's Spiritual* recording drama, Nyro and Harring acted as the album's producers. At one point, Nyro's old friend Todd Rundgren helped out for a few days as well, much as Felix Cavaliere had done on *Nested*. "I came in and kick-started the project and made sure that she got all the tracks done," he told Swedish journalist Dan Backman in 1999.

Silverlight remembers Rundgren doing production only on the cut "To a Child." "My take on it, from overhearing his conversations with her, is that he thought there should be a hit on the record, thought that was the best thing for her," says Silverlight. "He said, 'Look, you're just writing songs about trees and the wind, and the record's just not going to go anywhere.' " Nyro herself quoted Rundgren, after he first heard the tracks, as asking her, "Is this mom's rock or something?"

Elysa Sunshine asserts that Rundgren had about as much impact on Nyro as Wissert had had: "Every suggestion he made was one hundred eighty degrees from what she wanted. She wouldn't take any suggestions, really, except what she had already decided she wanted."

Columbia executives didn't fare much better with Nyro. Silverlight overheard her arguing with someone from the record label on the phone, saying, "I want to do it the way I want to do it, and I don't necessarily care if there's a hit on it. I just have this material, written for this project, and that is the most important thing, just the music."

"Obviously the person on the other end of the line was saying, 'We're not going to sell any records with this, you have to have a hit,' " Silverlight imagines. "But Laura stood up for what she believed in."

A few other musicians contributed to the final mix of Mother's Spiritual—Rundgren is credited with playing synthesizer on two cuts, Nydia Mata played some percussion, Julie Lyonn Lieberman played violin, and brother Jan Nigro, who had often jammed with his sister, added some guitar parts, especially on the song "Sophia."

Jan and Laura collaborated on another musical project around that time: He had sent out some of his compositions to various artists, and Kenny Rankin responded to the ballad "Polonaise," which Jan had written a decade earlier. As it turned out, Rankin decided to do it as a duet with Nyro, whom he knew from the late sixties. "It was a huge thrill for me," says Jan. "Their voices sounded incredible together, and there was a certain excitement in the music business about the coupling of two great singers. There was even talk about the possibility of its release as a single, although it didn't seem like mainstream single music." Then the dream crashed down: The small record company Rankin was signed to went bankrupt, and the record—in which Rankin's silky alto and Nyro's soulful soprano fetchingly intertwine—was never released.

■ ■ ■

After Mother's Spiritual was finally completed, Bristow, Silverlight, and Sunshine expected they would be hitting the road with Nyro. "I thought maybe we'd go out for two weeks here, two weeks there, and it would be very child friendly, mother friendly, and musician friendly," says Sunshine. But when the album wrapped up, Nyro decided to stay put.

"I will never forget sitting outside her house and her saying to me, 'I know I should go on the road and promote the album, but I don't feel like it,' " Sunshine recalls. "I said to myself, 'Well, that's the end of this gig!' And it was. Laura was soft-spoken, but you didn't budge her. She didn't feel like it, so no tour." Five years later, Nyro would tell *Musician* magazine, "At the time, [touring] just wasn't convenient for the rest of my lifestyle."

Despite their shared experience as mothers with young children, Sunshine and Nyro hadn't connected outside the music. "I mean, we were friendly, but we're just sort of stylistically different," she says. She did bring her daughter to Danbury a few times to play with Gil, and thought Laura looked at the little girl almost wistfully. Perhaps Nyro imagined for a moment how motherhood may have been different with a more sedate girl child rather than her "elf on speed," as she would characterize her son in the *Mother's Spiritual* song "To a Child." "He was very much a three-year-old boy, and she was just so mellow. I remember saying that I never saw a mother and kid so rhythmically mismatched," says Sunshine.

Nyro expressed that rhythmic mismatch—indeed, the full spectrum of a mother's mixed emotions—in "To a Child," which she declared "Gil's song" on the lyric sheet. While singing of her love and hope for him, she also lays out the difficulty of being both mother and artist. "I'm a poet without a poem," she writes. A subtle jokester, Nyro laments that while Gil is a miracle to her, "I'm so tired / and my miracle is not."

She called "To a Child" the most "realistic" song she ever wrote, and laughingly told interviewer Paul Zollo in 1994 that when she finished writing it she thought, "I'm finished hassling with this world. I'm finished having children. This is my final statement. . . . But I didn't keep that commitment."

On *Mother's Spiritual*'s second song, Nyro sarcastically thanks the patriarchy for "The Right to Vote," suggesting that there are no good options on the ballot. While men expect a woman "to wait and serve," the singer believes her place "is in a ship from space / to carry me / the hell out of here." Nyro sings the spunky melody with verve and amusement, the song arising from her "sense of humor when it comes to pain."

Keith Decker says she wrote the song one sake-fueled night when a few girlfriends were over. It originally contained another verse (which she later replaced with a bridge): "All America is on a diet / Fat and skinny on a diet too / Whoever you are trying to impress / Is probably a bigger fool than you." That, too, showed her humor about pain, since Nyro had a lifelong love affair with food (her library was filled with self-help books, some about compulsive eating, according to Michael Decker) and a concomitant struggle with her weight. Maria chucked the self-help books the week after Laura died, says Patty Di Laura. "Laura was one of the most glorious human beings I have ever known, and she had all of these self-help books that less-glorious people wrote," Di Lauria adds.

The next cut on *Mother's Spiritual*, "A Wilderness," again focuses on Gilly, who makes a cameo appearance pretending to be a crocodile about to eat up both his mother and her bed. Though a Freudian might find other symbolism there, the crocodile fantasy is also a good metaphor for Nyro's desire not to crush "the wilderness in you child / or the wildness in me."

The fourth cut on the album, "Melody in the Sky," turns to romance and, probably, Maria: "Lover / I'm your friend / and tonite your melody / and you own yourself / I belong to me," Nyro mixed desire with a strong sense of feminist independence, and she and Maria affirmed that sentiment throughout their life together, almost always maintaining separate living spaces.

Nyro stays with the love theme in "Late for Love," posing questions both serious and waggish about the nature of the beast, such as whether love is sex, "Can you fly it? / Is it made in Japan?" She finally concludes, "Love is where you are." The queries are feminist in nature, but the melody remains lacy and the mood amorous.

She asks more unanswerable questions in "A Free Thinker," a song with a classically engaging Nyro melody but the rather self-evident proposition that women should think for themselves. With lines such as, "Are you a consumer / a mere number / on a supermarket line?" Nyro trades her once elusive poetry for overspecific didacticism. "She grew up and her mother died—she didn't have to hide as much," suggests Nyro scholar Patricia Rudden. Unfortunately, Nyro's lyrics proved less magical as she grew more direct about her social concerns.

But on the last song of the album's first side, Nyro returns to prime form. In the gorgeous "Man in the Moon," she may be speaking either to a former lover or to the moon itself when she expresses the desire to "to melt the arctic beat / in my breast / next to yours." Her subsequent dream of a new world comes across as enchanting rather than preachy, and as she repeats "new-ew-ew world" in a rising arpeggio, she carries listeners willingly along with her.

Nyro had performed a somewhat different version of the song in 1978, and the way she changed it shows how *she* had changed. Its second verse used to read: "Face in the moon / dish ran away with the spoon. . . . Since I brightened my night with yours / baby baby." She even sang this version in early rehearsals for *Mother's Spiritual*, but by the time the album was finally recorded she had replaced the playful nursery-rhyme sentiment with her latest notions of feminism and motherhood—declaring that she yearns "to make a new world / I wanna raise my babies / in a new world." For Nyro, the man in the moon had become the *old* world; she and her baby embodied the new.

Side Two opens with Nyro's two tree songs. In the lightly rocking "Talk to a Green Tree," she describes herself as a working mother who turns to trees for wisdom. Maybe the trees can even teach her about child-rearing, especially since she can't turn to her mother, of whom she sings, "I need your wise words / but you died before he was born." Nyro mixes her tree love with polemics about a world full of war and of men who shirk child care. With sly wit, she suggests that if a man did take on housework, he'd be hard-pressed to have the energy women can still summon "for the midnite hour."

The other arboreal song, "Trees of the ages," is a lilting evocation of green spirits. One can imagine Nyro ambling through her woods, finding trees to be stolid companions: "they toss, shimmer in the wind . . . / they know everything." To some, such sentiments might seem unbearably corny, but in a noncynical mood one can feel comforted by Nyro's expression of "the great green harmonies."

She returns to the more politicized aspect of her nature-based feminism in "The Brighter Song," directed to a "sister" whom Nyro urges to "believe in your happiness." As in "A Free Thinker," the rather heavy-handed lyrical message is much leavened by the music, but it's not one of Nyro's stronger efforts.

"Roadnotes" follows, and finds Nyro more sensual than ever in this meditation on traveling and lovemaking. "Gypsy fever / I've been here many times / the motels / the trailers / the netted tents / of the road." she sings. On that road, as she celebrates her birthday, she whispers sultrily, "Baby I want everything." As Michael Decker points out, that's as good a description of Nyro's guiding life principle as anything she ever wrote.

Next up is "Sophia," in which she implores the goddess of wisdom to "shine your light / for a gypsy queen / in a midnite dream." Nyro also speaks to the goddess Hecate (who rules over the night's demons and ghosts and is considered a guardian of crossroads), asking her to "shine your light / down the open road." Nyro had obviously become interested in Wicca, the benevolent witchcraft that became a popular alternative spiritual practice in feminist circles from the seventies on. Nyro deemed goddess spirituality to be lusty and joyful, calling it a practice that "teaches you to love the cycles of your life." That's not to say that Nyro was necessarily a goddess worshiper; she instead described herself as a "spirited" woman, defining her spirituality in terms of "joy, connection and nature."

It's not surprising that Nyro connected with Sophia and Hecate. The latter provides protection in the darkness, which someone as drawn to the moon and the stars as Nyro would have appreciated. The former goddess not only brings wisdom, but symbolizes women's struggle to be taken seriously. In *Sophia: Goddess of Wisdom*, author Caitlin Matthews points out that Sophia has historically been allowed to be a messenger, a mediator, a helper, and a handmaid, but rarely allowed to be fully self-possessed and creatively operative. In other words, the mythic Sophia has been treated like most woman artists—denigrated as well as exalted.

Moreover, Sophia represents a woman's special form of wisdom, which Nyro increasingly honored in her songs. Writes Canadian author Marion Woodman of Sophia, "Her wisdom is rooted in experience, in compassion. She thinks with her heart and is more concerned with the processes than with the products of a life lived fully. She does not value the presence of power but the power of presence." The same words could have been written about Nyro, who was known for being very present with her friends and making them feel carefully listened to.

Mother's Spiritual closes with the title song, a soothing lullaby that knits together memories of Nyro's beloved mother with her own motherly concerns. She first pictures a street corner straight out of the Bronx, "where the kids boogie all nite," then imagines a band of angels arriving to bring salvation—which is perhaps the peace, love, and protection only a mother can give. The enigmatic phrase "mother's spiritual" suggests the inherited wisdom and power of both Gilda Nigro *and* of a great mother goddess. With its luscious melody and heartfelt lyrics, "Mother's Spiritual" remains a creative highpoint of Nyro's career.

In its final verse Nyro sings "each one's a lover / to this winter nite star / a pilgrim—a pioneer / that's who you are." For the pilgrim image, Nyro drew inspiration from poet-writer Jain Sherrard, who pictured motherhood as a "foot soldier's pilgrimage." In her extensive interview with the feminist magazine *Woman of Power* in 1985, Nyro pointed out that Sherrard—whose 1980 book *Mother Warrior Pilgrim: A Personal Chronicle* she'd obviously read—likened child-rearing to an unusual kind of warfare in which "both sides have to win." Nyro had appropriated Sherrard's notion of the warrior aspect of motherhood in "A Wilderness," singing, "Mama's puttin' on some warpaint / for a little bit of combat." Like Sherrard, Nyro had turned to poetry (and song) as a way to reclaim her separate life even as she gave herself over to her child's needs.

Nyro closes the album with a brief reprise of several elements—the line "What is life?" from "To a Child," the line "Love is really you" from "Late for Love," and some laughing baby sounds. It's a lovely tribute to the object of her own motherly love, her son Gil.

Overall, *Mother's Spiritual* has a warmth, expressiveness, and soothing quality that engenders a sense of healing: a purpose for which New Age music was specifically designed. Nyro had naturally gravitated toward that sound, her voice showing a newfound depth, clarity, and effortlessness. Gone is the straining for high notes or extra intensity; instead, she stays most often in her lower register, venturing upward only in soothing bell tones. Even her sense of rhythm had changed, the syncopated shuffle beat replaced by steadier, calmer cadences.

Nyro certainly was proud of the album's feminist message, since her subsequent press kits always mentioned that "the lyrics were presented at the Chicago Peace Museum as a feminist vision." Actually, the handwritten lyrics from just three of her songs—"Mother's Spiritual" and "The Right to Vote" from *Mother's Spiritual* plus "Child in a Universe" from *Nested*—were part of the exhibit *Give Peace a Chance: Music and the Struggle for Peace* at the Chicago museum. Running from September 1983 through January 1984, the show celebrated various musicians who had contributed to the peace movement, including John Lennon and Yoko Ono (whom Nyro loved) and the group U2.

The artwork on the gatefold cover of *Mother's Spiritual* imparted its own feminist message. Nyro had undertaken a nationwide search for women's art, putting the same unrelenting effort into the visuals as she did into the music, finally choosing Oregon artist Jo Mannino Hockenhull's painted tiles and "lite sculptures" for the album's inside cover and record sleeve. "Nothing ever was complete until the last t was crossed," says Patty Di Lauria of Nyro's work process. "Laura was very hands-on. She had a very clear vision of what she wanted and worked hard for it."

Andy Uryevick designed the cover, as he had *Season of Lights* and *Nested*. For the former, Nyro had insisted on using paintings by Japanese artist Rokuru on the cover package, and Andy remembers that it was difficult to obtain permission and involved a hefty fee. "But she just loved the work and wanted to include it in the overall design," he says.

Because Nyro had creative freedom at Columbia, the company let her do as she wished with her album covers, even after trying to convince her otherwise. The biggest argument, says Andy Uryevick, was over whether Nyro's name should be at the top of her album's front cover, where buyers could see it more easily as they flipped through record bins. "Laura didn't want her name on the top because she didn't want it to be the main emphasis [she wanted to emphasize the album's title]," he says. "She was always anti-establishment. What was important to her was the work." (For the record, Nyro's name is on top of *Mother's Spiritual*'s cover, but on the bottom of *Nested*'s).

Mother's Spiritual was released by Columbia in January of 1984. An ad for it in *The Village Voice* acknowledged the season: "Stay Warm This Winter with Laura's Latest 14 Original Songs—About the New World." Columbia may not have otherwise known what to say about the album, which was so different from Nyro's past work. Staying off the road certainly didn't help boost the album's sales, and it spent only three weeks among *Billboard*'s Top 200 albums, peaking at No. 182.

With some reservations, a number of critics embraced Nyro's new direction and style. *Musician*'s David Fricke liked the album even if "Nyro's romantic caress is now more of a matriarchal hug than the brash tenement soul squeeze of her early records." He pointed out, though, that it would be hard to get a hearing for such music at a time when brash New Wave, not New Age, was the day's popular sound. Nyro's songs, he ventured, would probably only be understood by "the ex-hippie audience now facing those middle-age realities, like Ann Beattie *New Yorker* stories set to a chamber pop soundtrack."

Don Shewey in *Rolling Stone* complimented Nyro's "flamboyantly passionate voice," "brooding piano," and "liquidly textured" songs. He also offered kudos to "Man in the Moon" for its Pat Metheny–like guitar and singable refrain, and to "The Right to Vote" for being "more tuneful and amusing than the prosaic title might suggest." But he complained that the allusiveness of Nyro's lyrics had given way to didacticism and preachy rhetoric, and suggested that her song about talking to trees sounded "downright cuckoo."

In *The New York Times*, Stephen Holden averred that Nyro's "liquid instrumental textures . . . restless harmonics and blurred song structures really *do* suggest a natural paradise of brooks, trees, and moonlit communions between people and supernatural forces." On the other hand, he complained that instead of fully developing her lyrical ideas, she "contorted" them with "febrile, quasi-biblical diction and preachy broadsides." Were she not a pop music legend, Holden suggested, the album could have been released only on one of the small independent, lesbian-oriented "women's music" labels such as Olivia Records that had emerged in the mid-seventies.

Similarly, Eric Levin in *People* felt that Nyro's infusion of pantheism and feminism didn't serve her music well. "Her invertebrate melodies are little more than mood riffs lifted from the stockrooms of jazz, blues and soul," he wrote. He also complained that her lyrics were "flaccid"—a revealing word choice from a man who then criticized her "tiresome sex-role preaching." Levin closed the review by quoting Nyro's "Right to Vote" line about taking off on a spaceship, snidely adding, "If you insist on leaving, Laura, take this album with you."

Georgia Christgau in *The Village Voice* joined the negative chorus, deeming the album "politically tame and musically passé." She did, though, credit Nyro for melodies that "climb and roam and float" and lauded the "effortless drama" of her phrasing, declaring that "she has better timing than Mary Tyler Moore."

Nyro was well aware of the negative remarks. "I've read some terrible reviews," she laughingly told *Musician* interviewer Laura Fissinger (who called the album passionate and beautiful). Christgau's review particularly rankled, probably because she suggested that Nyro's songwriting royalties had protected her from the need to compete in the workplace, and thus Nyro didn't need feminism until she had a child.

"I consider her article—disguised as a music review—plain ornery, and I discredit any references she made about my life as she does not know me or the spirit of my music," Nyro wrote in a rebuttal letter to the *Voice*, not unlike her earlier letter to *Ms.* Nyro expressed feelings many artists harbor about critics—that they're presumptuous, that they wouldn't appreciate mean critiques of their own work, and that they maintain little credibility if they haven't created art of their own. But she also tried to impune Christgau's feminist credentials by addressing her as Mrs., incorrectly believing she was the spouse of *Voice* music critic Robert Christgau.

Nyro concluded her missive by saying, "In truth, *Mother's Spiritual* has an independent, free-thinking spirit, and yes—an independent, free-thinking and soulful audience." Her fans, in another words, would nurture her music and serve as the best antidote to harsh criticism.

Christgau and others still expected Nyro to have an edge; others were more accepting that motherhood and a mellower lifestyle had sanded it down. In the essay "Female Identity and the Woman Songwriter," British journalist Charlotte Grieg noted that Nyro, having chosen to raise a child, had taken the opposite path of Joni Mitchell, who as a very young woman gave up a daughter for adoption. Grieg noticed how Nyro bravely tried to express the complexity of maternal feelings, from elation one moment to "crying by the washing machine" (in "To a Child") the next. "She finds nothing to mirror her feelings in the culture," wrote Grieg, "and we are left with the picture of a totally isolated woman, the mother, with this tumult of emotion going on inside her."

Writer Patricia Romanowski has pointed out that when a male songwriter such as John Lennon ponders fatherhood, critics bend over backward to praise his sensitivity, but women whose work is informed by parenthood are often misunderstood or disparaged. Combine motherhood with a career and you're dealing with an enormous amount of societal prejudice about women's roles. The ever-insightful Joni Mitchell unmasked that particular dogma, refusing to take the bait when *Rolling Stone* interviewer Cameron Crowe suggested that Nyro simply hadn't been "tough enough" to survive in the record business.

"Laura Nyro made a choice that has tempted me on many occasions," Mitchell demurred. "And that was to lead an ordinary life. . . . Which is brave and tough in its own way."

"Growth is the nature of the creative process," Nyro herself said to an interviewer in 1984. "You have to accept it, respect it, and move on." It was a sentiment that some of her fans might not have wanted to accept, especially the baby boomers who weren't ready to slow down and "mellow out" quite yet. Nyro had perhaps matured faster than they had, but like other great artists, she couldn't wait for everyone to catch up.

16
ROADNOTES

Just as Laura Nyro had traveled extensively during her relationship with David Bianchini, settling for months in different locales, she took up a peripatetic lifestyle with Maria Desiderio as well. They usually maintained separate abodes, or at least a separate studio for Maria. "Maria was very proud and had her own identity as a painter," says Di Lauria. "She wasn't just Laura's significant other, a hanger-on—she had her own stuff going."

Around 1986 the pair relocated to Amherst, Massachusetts, a town known for its proximity to five colleges, being home to such literary stalwarts as Emily Dickinson and Robert Frost, and having a large population of lesbians. Nyro told her guitarist friend John Bristow that she liked Amherst's sixties-style, college-town vibe, and the presence of its many artists and musicians.

In contrast, Danbury seemed a cultural wasteland. "Laura brought all the culture to Danbury there was," says Nyro's friend Anne Johnson. Nyro could not be wholly satisfied with a too-quiet country existence. "I must have the city and the country in my life to be complete," she told one journalist.

Nyro and Desiderio had been taken by Amherst on a weekend excursion there, and shortly after that rented a huge studio apartment in an old school building. "It had floor-to-ceiling windows," says Michael Decker, "and the ceiling was about fifteen feet high. I struggled for hours to get a big red couch from the main house into the place, but we made it fit. And Laura put in some low Japanese paper lamps [which she also used to illuminate the Danbury cottage] and a couple of futons. That was it—Laura did not go for extravagance at all."

Desiderio rented part of another house nearby for her art studio.

Then, after some months, the couple bought a house and Maria took over the second floor while Laura and Gil had rooms on the first. Michael Decker, who built a kennel in the back for Ember, continued to care for the Danbury property, driving back and forth to Amherst a couple of times a week to do Nyro's shopping and banking.

Throughout their years together, Desiderio worked as seriously and consistently on her artwork as Nyro did on her music, with Nyro quite supportive of her efforts. In a conversation between Laura and Maria which was included in Nyro's 1989 press kit, Laura answered "you" to the question of which artists inspired her.

Desiderio worked mainly in oils, but also employed watercolors and did some sculpting in clay. "She was an abstract artist, with roots in realism," says Michael Decker. "She would do still lifes and anatomical paintings of hands and such. Aside from that, she mostly painted impressionistically. Just beautiful work; I enjoyed it very much." Maria's portrait of Nyro was one of the few artworks in the Danbury house, hanging over the armoire in Laura's bedroom.

"They were the most artsy people I ever met," says guitarist Jimmy Vivino, who would soon be in Nyro's backup band. "They didn't give a shit about the everyday things people think about. They lived with different priorities. They were, to me, very similar. They were great for each other."

In 1987, Laura, Gil, and Maria left Amherst for a rented house in the upstate New York city of Ithaca, another bookish college town and the home of Jan and Janice Nigro. Grandpa had just died, and Patty Di Lauria speculates that Nyro wanted to be close to kin. "She had visited before and knew that Ithaca was a special place, with a lot of culture and beautiful nature and art," says Jan Nigro. "We shared some wonderful times—music and dinners and a lot of fun." It was also close enough that Michael Decker could continue to travel back and forth as Nyro's factotum.

Di Lauria remembers Ithaca as the place where Nyro colored her hair for the first time. "She was turning gray and didn't want to look gray at that point in time," she says. "Her shiny black hair wasn't as glorious as it had been, so that's how I talked her into it, and she liked the result. She left one piece of gray in the front."

Ultimately, Ithaca felt a little too far from New York City, music-wise, so the family moved back to Danbury after about a year. But they'd still take breaks from the countryside (usually when Gil had a school vacation) to spend a month in a house in Hilton Head, South Carolina, or a month in Key West, Florida. "She loved being a gypsy, loved that pulse," says Decker.

"She was always going places," agrees Nydia Mata, who thinks Nyro's travels were of a piece with her lifelong soul searching. "I felt like Laura was looking for something that she already had. She was one of the most enlightened people I knew, yet she was always trying to get that."

Amid her various moves, and mostly out of the public eye, Nyro continued to write and record. Having finally fulfilled her Columbia publishing deal after *Mother's Spiritual*, she formed her own publishing company again, first dubbed Sashimi ("she went from Tuna Fish to Sashimi," quips Di Lauria) and then Luna Mist Music (which, coincidentally, rhymes with Tuna Fish).

One of her first projects after *Mother's Spiritual* was composing and performing the title song for the 1985 feature-length documentary film *Broken Rainbow*. Produced by Victoria Mudd and Maria Florio, who were introduced to Nyro by their mutual friend Charlie Calello, it dealt with a subject dear to Nyro's heart: the mistreatment of native peoples. Back in 1970 she had bemoaned the "homeless Indian / of Manhattan Isle" (in "Christmas in My Soul") now she could put music to her feelings about the forcible relocation of the Navajo people from their tribal homelands in Arizona.

"I was just praying that I could write a decent song," Nyro said in a radio interview, "because I knew that it was going to be a beautiful documentary. . . . I think that the empathy just created the song." Nyro must have felt particularly proud of her efforts, since she would include the song on her next two albums, and the film itself went on to win an Academy Award for best documentary.

Los Angeles recording engineer Mark Linett, who had engineered several albums for Rickie Lee Jones in the early 1980s, ran the board at Nyro's home studio for the "Broken Rainbow" session. He'd been contacted for the job by Barbara Cobb, a bass player and former member of the women's band Isis (along with Nydia Mata and *Season of Lights* band members Jeanie Fineberg and Ellen Seeling) who had begun to informally act as Nyro's business representative. Sometime after the "Broken Rainbow" session, Linett worked again with Nyro when Cobb hired some "big-time" rhythm sections to demo new material with her friend. "My feeling was that she had to have only the very best musicians playing with her, because her talent was so ferocious," says Cobb.

The group of musicians who came to Danbury included well-known drummer Steve Gadd, percussionist Lenny Castro, guitarist Hugh McCracken (who had played on Eli), and legendary bass player Chuck Rainey, who had played on the song "Eli's Comin' " back in 1968 and had also recorded with Nyro acolyte Rickie Lee Jones. "You have to have the kind of musicians around those women who care to go deeper than read a chord chart, because it's very sensitive, very special," Rainey says of Nyro and Jones. "It's very iridescent music: It is and it ain't, it could be but it don't have to be." (Not surprisingly, the metaphysically inclined bassist enjoyed talking pyramids and Egyptology with Nyro rather than merely music.)

Despite connecting with Nyro, Rainey found the Zinn Road sessions to be rather disorganized. "Laura spent a lot of money on that session, and as I understand she turned right around and a few weeks later had [bass player] Nathan East and someone else from California come out and do the same thing," says Rainey. (Cobb says she had always wanted to hire East, because she thought his soulful playing would be a good match for Nyro.)

Guitarist John Bristow came to play at one session with Gadd and East. "We toyed with ideas," he says. "Those guys were the highest paid musicians in the business at the time, and I don't think you used them unless you could get the project done quickly. Laura, at least from what I saw, didn't get things out that way."

Rainey concluded that Nyro hadn't kept up with current recording techniques and styles. "It happens to a lot of artists who isolate themselves; they forget that there's a world going on," he says. Roscoe Harring agreed.

"Laura didn't have an extensive record collection, but I'd make her listen to a few things to get her to be technically better on her records," says Harring. "She refused to do a lot of things with a track, or she wanted to do things live, or she wanted to do it her way, which was not always technically the right way and frustrated many producers and engineers. The context was fabulous; the sound was not the best."

Although Linett remembers that some nice arrangements emerged from the Zinn Road sessions, overall they didn't work out to Nyro's satisfaction. Rainey and Gadd are credited for their arrangement of the song "Roll of the Ocean," which would appear on Nyro's next album, but as it turned out that album would be done live, with an entirely different group of musicians. Doing it live, says Linett, "sort of solved a number of problems in terms of getting it done, rather than trying to get it done perfectly."

Linett hadn't been a particular fan of Nyro's music before he worked with her, so he had a fresh perspective on her work at that time. "It seems that when she got her life in focus, her artistic focus got kind of scattered," he suggests. "I don't think she cared about writing another 'Wedding Bell Blues,' trying to craft a pop song. She got to this stage where she was just setting her life to music. Not doing a finished song, but just a postcard."

Nyro still wasn't interested in the *business* of music, and where it fit in her esteem is indicated by the place where Linett saw her framed award from BMI honoring a million plays of "Wedding Bell Blues": Nyro had stored it in a cupboard under a sink. In general, she felt distanced from the early work that made her so successful. When a fan of hers, Frank Dalrymple, approached her in the mid-eighties with the idea of writing a theater piece based on her music, she told him she didn't want to include any songs she'd written before *Smile*. "She said something like, 'Please, no early songs, they're very male-centered and don't represent what I feel or stand for now,' " he says.

"I don't know if she got burnt out and didn't feel she could write commercial pop music anymore, or if she could have written it and didn't want to," says Annie Roboff, now a Nashville songwriter but then a New York–based musician. Roboff and fellow musician Stephanie Stein worked with Nyro to prepare a songbook of her post–*Christmas and the Beads of Sweat* compositions, but although a section of Nyro's 1989 press kit was subtitled "Excerpts from New Songbook," the book never materialized.

Being purposefully out of the mainstream also kept Nyro unaware of how important she remained to other artists. At one point in their collaboration, Roboff mentioned some well-known industry people who said they'd love to work with Nyro. "Really?" She responded in surprise. "I think part of her knew the impact she had on artist after artist, songwriter after songwriter, and a part of her didn't," says Roboff. "And I think she wanted to get back into the thick of things, but I don't think her heart wanted to be where the thick of things would have taken her."

■ ■ ■

Besides all her address changes over the course of the eighties, Nyro made a number of lifestyle changes as well. Most significantly, she quit smoking. It was something she had been trying to do at least as far back as the recording sessions for *Mother's Spiritual*, when drummer Terry Silverlight remembers her sneaking cigarettes. Michael Decker, too, recalls her coming over to the big house on the Danbury property to cadge an occasional smoke from his partner Ralph. "Marlboro Man?" she'd greet Ralph flirtatiously, and he was too helpless with amusement to refuse. Then she'd go out behind her garage to light up, trying to conceal it from Maria. "It was a whole act," laughs Decker.

Nyro was so proud of finally kicking the habit—she'd been a seriously addicted, pack-a-day smoker since her teens—that she made her triumph the centerpiece of a delightfully odd new composition, "The Japanese Restaurant Song." It's Nyro's "day in the life"—a humorous report of a visit to a Japanese restaurant where the singer gets high on plum wine, imagines herself a geisha, is greeted by her lover with "a sweet hello" kiss, and tries to keep kids in line. When the cook tells her "children not exactly well behaved," Nyro replies, "Well, you can't have it all." In a spoken break, Nyro then reveals that she's just quit smoking and thus finds it hard to control her appetite. So she asks the waitress to bring her a great big—she pauses here for maximal effect— "bowl of chocolate ice cream." As Nyro would tell journalist Susan Cole, audiences needed only to listen to this song to "figure out what I've been doing the last couple of years."

With smoke no longer roughening her vocal cords, Nyro took a newfound delight in her singing. "Ever since I was a teenager I never knew my instrument as a nonsmoker," she said to Cole. "So now when I sing I deal with the true timbre of my voice."

Around the same time, Nyro also decided to become a vegetarian. She had long considered taking that step, saying in 1984 "There's a sticker around now that says: 'Peace begins with nonviolent eating.' This is very provocative for people like myself who haven't yet fully made that commitment."

Her beloved Grandpa Mirsky had long been a vegetarian, having become disgusted by the sight of animals being slaughtered when he was a child, but Nyro had not considered avoiding meat when she was younger. "I was one of those people who kind of enjoyed all that food," she said. She had even been willing, twenty years earlier, to try elephant meat, serving the canned "delicacy" to *The New York Times*'s William Kloman while telling him that her fondness for the animal made her curious about how it tasted. The Laura Nyro of 1988 would have been horrified by such a notion; by that time, she had decided she wouldn't eat anything that had a face, let alone a creature that she loved.

Nyro's vegetarianism emerged out of her newfound identification as an animal rights activist. She first came in touch with that movement at a sidewalk information table where she saw images of animal exploitation. "I almost walked away from it, but I just made myself look," she said in a radio interview. From then on, she began to think about where her food and clothing came from. "I started to look into it just like I had looked at women's rights," she said. People asked her why she wanted to focus on "animals instead of people," but she responded, "I don't see the difference."

While her staunch support of animal rights led her to offer literature about various organizations at her concerts, Nyro did not speak out about another potent social issue of the time: gay rights. However, Nyro made a private gesture toward one of her most ardent fans that showed the depth of her compassion about the scourge of AIDS. Bart Gorin, who worked for a New York art dealer, was so enamored of Nyro that he used to hire Lou Nigro to tune his grand piano, hoping to hear tales of his daughter (a strategy that a number of Nyro fans, including singer-songwriter Desmond Child, also employed). Gorin had even learned Nyro's address on Zinn Road and had shared it with author Charles Kaiser, a close friend who had attended many Nyro concerts with him.

Kaiser found reason to use that information when Gorin was judged terminally ill with AIDS in 1991. That's when he wrote to her,

Dear Laura,

Bart Gorin is the greatest fan you've ever had. He has been to every concert you've ever given within 200 miles of New York City, and he needs you now more than he's ever needed you before. Please call him.

Three weeks later—it may have taken that long for the missive to reach her from Zinn Road—Nyro called Kaiser from where she was now living, on Long Island. "Where's Bart?" she asked. The next morning, Gorin picked up his phone to hear Laura Nyro's voice. They chatted for about fifteen minutes, "though Bart later pretended it had been an hour," says Kaiser.

"That was the greatest thing that has ever happened to me," Gorin told Kaiser. For the rest of his life—he died just a few months later—his spirits lifted and a certain faith was restored. Said Gorin, "Maybe everything is working in Divine Right Order after all."

■ ■ ■

In 1988, after ten years off the stage, Laura Nyro was finally ready to return to live performing. Yet another new bevy of women artists had begun to get attention, and Nyro hadn't failed to notice and appreciate new arrivals on the music scene, such as the cool-and-jazzy Sade and folk-bluesy Tracy Chapman (whose work Nyro characterized as "real songs"). Given their success, Nyro may have felt that a welcome mat would be out for her, too, although she insisted that their popularity had no influence on her. "It just so happens that there is more of an open attitude out there toward creative woman artists, and that's wonderful," she said to one journalist. "But whether there was or wasn't, I would be out there singing right now."

One thing that inspired her to be out there again was the passing of Grandpa, who had died in December 1986 at the age of ninety-one. "I think that if a close guardian of yours like that dies, you feel like you've lost your port and you grieve until you decide to build a strong bridge between yourself and the world and give of yourself," she would say in a press kit interview.

Nyro had stayed home to provide stability for Gil, but having done that for a decade she now decided, "It's time for Mom to get out there and sing." And with Gil approaching his teens, Nyro seemed to be recapturing hers. She talked about how her revitalized voice had evoked both her pure love of singing and her teenage joie de vivre. "There are different crests, and these two times stand out," she said.

As she had felt as a teenager, everyday life wasn't enough for her anymore because it didn't allow a full expression of herself. "Sometimes only poetry can say it," she told radio interviewer Ed Sciaky. "I think there's just this deeper language, and a way of putting your world back together again and breaking through barriers."

Nyro was serious enough about her latest "comeback" to even hire professional management. Roscoe Harring hooked her up with Beverly Hills–based manager David Bendett, who had worked with such acts as Ike and Tina Turner and John Sebastian, and Bendett's associate Geoffrey Blumenauer would do Nyro's booking. True to his word,

Harring had promised Blumenauer back in 1983 (while Harring road-managed Sebastian) that when Nyro returned to the road he could book her.

Nyro also decided to put together a band, albeit a smaller and less expensive ensemble than her 1976 group (the only holdover would be percussionist Mata). The key player would be guitarist Jimmy Vivino, yet another Italian-American in the New York/New Jersey mold of Calello, Cavaliere, and Maineri. Vivino was a friend of Cavaliere's, and was playing with him at the Lone Star Café in Manhattan when Roscoe Harring brought Nyro to a winter's night gig.

"I saw this small woman in the audience with a ski hat on, really incognito, totally dressed down," remembers Vivino. "I couldn't believe it was Laura Nyro, she looked so pedestrian. I'd always pictured her as this, like, *goddess* behind the piano. Sort of attached to the piano, as if they were one thing."

It wasn't surprising that Nyro and Vivino immediately hit it off: He had recently worked with artists who were very much part of Nyro's musical heritage—Darlene Love, Ronnie Spector of the Ronettes, and Ellie Greenwich, cowriter of such songs as "Be My Baby," "Da Doo Ron Ron," and "Let It Be Me." "It was like I was being groomed for this position, since Laura is really a culmination of that [era]," says Vivino.

At one of their first rehearsals in Connecticut, Nyro wrote down her musical ideas for Vivino on a paper plate, beginning at the center and spiraling outward. "Then I knew she was really thinking a different way," he says. "On the other hand, I *got* every word that I read, because it took a certain determination to get around this thing. Playing with her is the closest I'll ever get to Art. Everything else, including the job I have now [he's a charter member of the Max Weinberg Seven band on NBC-TV's *Late Night with Conan O'Brien*] is work."

To complete the ensemble, Vivino suggested his friend Frank Pagano on drums, and Nyro hired Dave Wofford, formerly of the fusion group Spyro Gyra, to play bass. Vivino and Pagano could also sing harmonies, but to add another female voice Nyro hired singer Diane Wilson. Once again, Nyro's selection criteria wasn't simply musical. "She really had to get along with everybody," says Vivino.

In an almost shocking break from her own performing tradition, Nyro decided to play an electric keyboard on the tour. "I'm like every other fan—I want to see Laura behind the acoustic piano, where she belongs," says Vivino, "but she felt liberated, like she didn't have this big thing in front of her."

"All of a sudden, she wanted to face the audience rather than be sideways," adds Harring. "When she played the acoustic piano, her hair would hang down and nobody could see her. So we searched half a year for a piano. We went to music stores, and she'd wear glasses and a scarf and a hat to disguise herself." (Harring was surprised by the number of people who recognized Nyro in public places, her long, thick hair being "a dead giveaway.")

Despite her long break, Nyro had not been forgotten, as Blumenauer quickly found out: Within weeks of announcing the tour, which Nyro formally dedicated "to the animal rights movement," he received interview requests filling fifteen single-spaced pages. The TV magazine 48 Hours even wanted to interview her about how quitting smoking affected her singing, and both David Letterman and Johnny Carson wanted her to appear on their late-night programs. But Nyro turned down such offers, being particularly sensitive about her appearance on TV.

Knowing of Nyro's relationship with Desiderio, Blumenauer asked how he should answer questions about her love life—specifically, what should he say if anyone asked if she was a lesbian? "Tell them I'm a lover of people," she responded. Few did ask, but when Richard Cromelin of the Los Angeles Times directly inquired as to her personal situation, she answered coyly: "It's me and my son. And my dog. . . . And then we have others whom we love and who participate in our lives . . . I think right now I'll just express it that way."

It wasn't that she was being particularly guarded, Nyro insisted— after all, she did not sing superficial music: "I get down. I talk about it." But at a certain point she liked to draw boundaries because the other people in her life had a right to their privacy, she said. Those who knew Maria Desiderio say that she was even more private than Nyro, but Nyro's own sense of discretion—and her unwillingness to have a label slapped on her sexuality—was more than enough to keep certain topics off-limits.

■ ■ ■

The new band's first gig, in June 1988, was at the Red Creek Inn in Rochester, New York. Vivino still had a lot to learn about working with

Nyro: "I was so used to musical-directing showbiz acts, and as the star would leave the stage I'd say, 'Ronnie Spector!' or 'Darlene Love!' Sort of emceeing. So when Laura's getting up to leave the stage, I said, 'Laura Nyro!' Well, she took me backstage after the show and said, 'Jimmy, since people are here to see me, it's not necessary to tell them who I am.' It was a very nice way of saying, 'Don't ever do that again.' After that, we would come out onstage and nothing would be said, she would just start. When we were done, we'd just leave. There was a certain amount of dignity attached to this gig. She had a vision of doing things."

Nyro's vision extended to stagewear as well, especially since her vegetarian and animal rights beliefs included an avoidance of leather goods. "She'd say to me, 'Do they make guitar straps out of cloth?' or 'Can you play without wearing a belt, is that possible?' " Vivino remembers with a laugh. One time, Nyro insisted that the tour bus stop at a mall, where she bought Vivino three pairs of Converse canvas sneakers. "She never was preachy about it," he says. "It was more like, 'Jimmy, I think these sneakers are for you, aren't they great?' "

(Nyro unsubtly encouraged Vivino toward a vegetarian diet as well, praising him when he made a mushroom sauce for ziti. "See, you really don't need to have meat in the sauce!" she said. She later insisted that he name his black Scottish terrier pup Ziti.)

Nyro didn't put on artistic airs, but did ask a few specific things from the nightclubs she played, expressed in the "Laura Nyro Rider" to her contract. It stipulated, for one thing, that if there was a dance floor adjacent to the stage, the club had to place a barrier of at least two rows of tables and chairs in front of the stage so that the audience would have an unobstructed view (and the musicians and their equipment would be protected from the dancers). She also asked to be provided strictly vegetarian meals backstage, preferably Middle Eastern food such as hummus, pita, and babaganoush. For her road crew of Roscoe Harring or Martin di Martino, she requested a six-pack of Heineken beer; for herself she asked for a six-pack of Coca-Cola, with which she made an occasional post-show rum-and-Coke.

Most important, says Geoffrey Blumenauer, Nyro wanted a description of "every step she'd have to take, from the bus to the dressing room, from the dressing room to the stage, from the stage back to the dressing room, and from the dressing room back to the bus." She didn't want to pass through the audience to her dressing room or to the stage, as she had often done in places such as the Troubadour, and that proviso required some creative and amusing reconfigurations at certain clubs. The Nightstage in Cambridge, Massachusetts, fashioned a small room out of curtains on the stage, where Nyro could stay prior to and between shows. And at the tiny, 100-seat Stephen Talkhouse in Amagansett on Long Island, the proprietor cut a door for her in the back of the stage—which thereafter was known as the Laura Nyro Door.

Throughout June and July, Nyro and her band toured clubs and small concert halls along the East Coast, from New Hampshire to Miami, playing mostly on weekends. They traveled in a large van, which Vivino says made it easier for Nyro to make frequent stops. "We drove enough now, let's take a walk," she'd say, or "Wait, pull over, there's a mall!" In August, they headed west for shows in Taos, Boulder, New Orleans, San Jose, and Los Angeles. Their set typically opened with the thrilling harmonies of "The Wind," then offered old favorites such as "The Confession," "Emmie," "Wedding Bell Blues," "And When I Die," and "Stoned Soul Picnic."

She had reworked her oldies, however. "My show is not about nostalgia," Nyro asserted to the *Chicago Tribune*'s Chris Heim. When she performed an older composition, it was only "because I can get down with the song as a musician and enjoy singing it." The revamped versions often gave new meaning to the originals. "Wedding Bell Blues," for example, made her appear to *Hartford Courant* rock critic Frank Rizzo as "a determined woman who knows what she wants, not just some love-starved woman begging to be taken to the altar." Similarly, Rizzo felt that her slowed-down interpretation of "And When I Die" gave Nyro more space to reflect on the lyrics she had written as a teenager.

The *Tribune*'s Heim echoed that opinion. "After the mauling ["And When I Die"] has gotten over the years, it would seem impossible to resurrect it," he wrote. "Yet Nyro did just that by singing to a spare keyboard and [Vivino's] mandolin accompaniment. The song took on the air of a timeless mountain melody, an approach that heightened the ageless and universal sentiments of the lyrics."

Nyro's set didn't include any songs from her masterpiece, *New York Tendaberry*. When someone backstage at a concert asked her why, she replied, "Let me put it this way: Why don't we go jump off a bridge?" She elaborated to her friend Richard Denaro that one couldn't live forever on the edge—and the *Tendaberry* songs were those of a "teenage wild banshee."

"When she wrote those songs, they were about what she was feeling then," says Vivino. "Later, it was, 'Well, I don't feel that way now, so I can't sing it.' It no longer meant anything to her."

Her new compositions meant the most to her, so after warming up the crowd with familiar melodies she would say, "Now that I have a captive audience, I want to play some new songs." Those included "Roll of the Ocean," "Down South," "Companion," "The Wild World," "Park Song," "Women of the One World," and "The Japanese Restaurant Song." When she performed the latter, she heightened the mood by fanning herself with a Japanese paper fan. At one Bottom Line show, she further amused the crowd after this skit by asking, "You know where I take my acting lessons from? The old Anna Magnani movies!"

For an encore, Nyro would return solo. "At last I've got you all to myself," she'd say. Then she'd sing a couple of the classic soul songs she'd loved as a teenager, blending them in a medley with her own, "Trees of the Ages." When she finished, she'd tell the audience, "It was my dream to go out and sing for you this summer. Thank you for sharing it with me."

Even if most of her stage patter was scripted and rehearsed, Nyro proved to be less shy as a performer than she had been. She proved adept with ad libs, too, as when she found the lights too hot at San Francisco's Fillmore West that August. "Could I have a fan onstage?" she asked, and with that a man began walking along the front set of tables toward the stage. Nyro held her hand out in a "stop" gesture and said, "No, I didn't mean that kind of fan—but thank you." She also joked in San Francisco, when introducing "Wedding Bell Blues"— the song that opens, "Bill, I love you so"—that she had written it for Bill Graham, the famous Fillmore West entrepreneur.

As always, Nyro's performances in Los Angeles and New York were tour highlights. In L.A., she sold out a five-night run at the Mayfair Music Hall in Santa Monica, an intimate 333-seat venue that dated back to 1911. The stars came out in force to see her, including Joni Mitchell and then-husband Larry Klein, Al Kooper, Melissa Manchester, and Peggy Lipton. They all went backstage to greet her afterwards. "She sat like a queen, graciously soaking it all in," says Geoffrey Blumenauer.

With no complimentary seats left for the shows, Blumenauer found himself selling seats to some VIPs who requested them, including Los Angeles Times music critic Robert Hilburn and, of all people, David Geffen. "Geffen called me to ask whether Laura would mind if he came," he recalls. "She told me she didn't care—and I told Geffen he had to pay for the tickets." When Geffen failed to show up at the Mayfair, Blumenauer still expected him to fulfill his financial commitment. "I called him the next day at his beach house in Malibu and said, 'You will send over the forty dollars, won't you?' And he did."

Hilburn, despite also having to pay for his seats, deemed Nyro's performance "a reminder of just how unique her musical vision remains, even after all this time." He noticed how much her shyness had diminished, writing that she now related to the audience rather than retreating from it. Nyro's strategy of facing the audience from her electric piano obviously had worked for this critic, but many of her fans missed the richness of the grand piano's sound.

In July and again in September, Nyro played Manhattan's Bottom Line, where she'd last performed a decade earlier. Singer Phoebe Snow remembers an ecstatic audience at one of the July shows: fans, family (a group of about a dozen Nigros filled one long table), and musical luminaries from a range of genres, including Dion DiMucci, Paul Stanley of Kiss, Paul Schaeffer of the David Letterman show, Suzanne Vega, Patty Smythe, and Peter Allen (who furiously shook Nyro's hand backstage while telling her that she was the person who inspired him to be a songwriter).

"I was with [singer-songwriter] Brenda Russell and she almost had a breakdown," says Snow. " 'It's Laura!' Brenda said. People were just having, like, a religious experience." "The excitement in the air was overwhelming," agrees Nyro's cousin Dan Nigro. "People who didn't even smoke were going outside for a cigarette!"

Critics responded enthusiastically. "She's lost a few of her top notes, but her voice is still an instrument of exceptional texture, sweetness, depth and expressiveness," wrote Chicago critic Albert Williams. Similarly, although *Variety* felt that Nyro's "exhilarating" approach had been tempered, she now "sang everything in an unhurried, almost deliberate manner, as if taught by life to enjoy and share the richness as much as the frolic and virtuosity of her pipes."

Those pipes, wrote Barbara Shulgasser in the *San Francisco Examiner*, were "clearer, fuller and more acute" than ever, thanks to her having given up smoking. But the critic also credited the accumulated "cigarette damage" for giving Nyro "a new depth, a swirling purity reminiscent at times of Dionne Warwick."

After the July gig at the Bottom Line, Stephen Holden restated Nyro's position in the pop music constellation: "No other pop music cult figure of the era has had a more lasting influence on urban music," wrote the critic from *The New York Times*. Calling her backing quintet "excellent," he remained more descriptive than judgmental, pointing out that Nyro's "mystical, feminist vision has helped provide her with an emotional platform from which she can relate to an audience more directly than she used to."

For *Newsday* columnist Stephen Williams, the Bottom Line show felt a bit like a college reunion, as he noticed how Nyro had changed yet remained the same: "Her voluptuous, earth-mother figure is no longer draped in black—she wore a sprightly red-and-white blouse printed with a butterfly—but she was in character in other ways: coy and pouty expressions, waves of long hair that she swished back regularly, and a voice that walks the line between anguish and pure buoyancy."

The 1988 tour was almost a complete sellout for Nyro, says Blumenauer. She drew especially well in cities known for an open-minded intelligentsia and a large gay and bisexual population. Nyro felt exuberant about the whole experience, telling Chicago journalist Heim, "My whole 'tribe' came out [at the Bottom Line]"—"tribe" being an endearment for her die-hard fans—"and it was just delicious . . . I'm on Cloud 9."

"I just think that it's a very soulful connection," Nyro would say to Cromelin about the relationship with her audience. "Maybe the cult of the mother, the call of the wild . . . Whatever it is, it's really beautiful."

Blumenauer considered Nyro fun and easy to be with. "We connected," he says. Bendett, though, as other managers had, found Nyro unmanageable. "She was very hands-on, very critical of things," he says. "No one was going to take the reins away from her. She was driving things, one way or another, and everyone was just giving her input—that was the take she had."

That was the business side of things—never the best part of the music experience for Laura Nyro. For a fellow musician, such as Jimmy Vivino, working with Nyro was pure joy. "I just looked over at her every night and loved her," he says. "She was the kindest soul, and the sexiest woman ever. She got me every time she sang. You can do gigs and it just gets routine, but with Laura it never got routine. She had a very communal feeling about the people she was working with. It was, 'Don't you think we could all live here?' It was never I—it was always *we*. Everywhere we went, she'd say, 'Let's stay another day.' "

17
THE BOTTOM LINE

Nyro was buoyed by the positive response to her tour and had more than a half-dozen new compositions at the ready, so it would have seemed obvious for her to begin cutting a new studio album. She did in fact do some recording in her home studio with the Vivino band. "Everything was great," says Vivino of the sessions, "but not good enough for Laura." According to Geoffrey Blumenauer, Columbia Records offered Nyro a $400,000 recording budget for a new album and the services of producer David Kershenbaum, who had recently produced Tracy Chapman.

Nyro instead decided to go live. "My mood was for a live record: the warmth, the spontaneity," she told *Musician*. "I don't feel much of that when working on a studio record unless everything goes very, very smoothly and quickly." She had already recorded her first set of comeback shows at the Bottom Line, the venue at which she felt the most relaxed, and decided to record her late-summer appearance there as well. "This was something she did with no record label, with her own money, no support," says Vivino. "If she had an idea and record companies started acting like jerks, she'd just say, 'Forget it, I can do this myself.' "

Columbia, which had waited five years for a new Nyro album, did not want her next release to be a live set. So Nyro's manager David Bendett—"a genius negotiator" according to Blumenauer, as well as being a former school chum of Nyro's Columbia A&R person, Don DeVito—worked a "one-off" deal with Nyro's label. She would be allowed to sign with another record company for the live album, then return to Columbia for her next studio effort.

Bendett and Blumenauer sent out her live tapes to various top-line record companies, hoping to spark interest, but though all responded warmly, according to Blumenauer, they passed. Blumenauer finally approached Lori Nafshun at Cypress Records—a boutique label distributed by A&M Records—which had recently put out Jennifer Warnes's admired album of Leonard Cohen songs, *Famous Blue Raincoat*. Cypress offered $60,000 for the album, plus standard royalty points. "Not bad for a double live CD," says Blumenauer.

The album did not prove a financial success, however. "I would bet a million dollars that Laura never reached the profit zone with *Live at the Bottom Line*," Blumenauer says. "I know that she herself paid $18,000 for a quarter-page black-and-white ad to promote it in *Rolling Stone*. Cypress did little."

Nonetheless, Nyro professed pleasure with the 1989 release, *Laura: Laura Nyro Live at the Bottom Line*, a two-record set in a single sleeve decorated with concert photos. "It tells you where I'm coming from right now as a writer, what's on my mind, and it draws from way back to when I was a teenager," she told radio interviewer Ed Sciaky in 1989. "I also feel that it's just . . . there's no frills. That's me not in the studio, just live, just as it was happening."

As if to illustrate that spontaneity, the first of the four album sides begins with words of welcome and an evocation of the season: "Hi, how are you?" says Nyro. "I'm here to celebrate this summer night with you."

Then she launches into her new version of "The Confession," driven by Pagano's pounding snare drum and Vivino's percolating guitar. Nyro changed one section of lyrics in the song, from "I keep hearing mother crying / I keep hearing daddy / thru the grave / little girl, of all the daughters / you were born a woman / not a slave," to, "I keep hearing mother crying / thru the grave / little girl, my daughter . . . " She thus took it from the realm of fiction into more concrete autobiography, as if she heard her own mother sending a feminist message from the beyond.

Without ending the first song, Nyro and band segue into "High-Heeled Sneakers," the rocking blues standard by Robert Higginbottom. Perhaps the two songs just sounded good together, but Nyro more likely saw a lyrical connection between the sexual abandon of "The Confession" and the bravado of a woman telling another woman (or being told by someone) to "Put on your red dress mama / 'Cause we're goin' out tonight."

Still feeling sexy, Nyro switches to the jazzy "Roll of the Ocean," singing, "I want Coltrane in the moon / Just that starry aching tune."

In the next cut, the country-soulful "Companion," Nyro marries one of her warmest melodies to lyrics expressing what she's looking for in love: not the old Sturm und Drang of youthful passion, but the companionship of someone who will provide "laughter in the dark" and that "lovin' lovin' spark." "When I was very young I was looking for trouble," Nyro would explain. "I didn't know I was. But now I have too many important things to do; I don't want to be drained and I don't want trouble."

"Companion" is almost commercial-sounding tune, but remains unresolved, its flow interrupted by Nyro's introduction of her band. Also, at the end when she lists things she "lusts" for, she includes such unromantic items as "peace on earth." Nyro had become unable to talk about one-on-one love without immediately universalizing it into her hopes for humanity.

On "The Wild World," she turns again to pure politics, this time bewailing the killing of endangered species: "Sister whose back / Does that fur belong on?" Carried with a rock-hard beat, the harmonized chorus of "wild world / wild world / oh it's all around you / wild world" makes it one of her more appealing protests.

Side Two of the first disc opens with an interwoven medley of "My Innocence" from *Nested* and "Sophia" from *Mother's Spiritual*. Their themes—the sense of innocence she had gained from her mother and the nurturance she now sought from goddesses Sophia and Hecate—had obviously merged for her. At this point in her career, Nyro often combined songs, but while that may have been intriguing thematically, it caused the separate songs to lose their individual identities.

She follows the medley with a wearier version of *Mother's Spiritual*'s "To a Child," informed now by ten years of motherhood. She ends the song with a new line, "I wish you harmony," which rings out as her hope for Gil as he approaches his teens. During the applause that follows the song, Nyro remarks to the audience, "All the mothers have given me a standing ovation."

She closes Side Two with the "timeless mountain melody" version of "And When I Die," with Vivino on electric mandolin. Nyro at forty sings her teenage anthem with resignation, rather than with a youth's fantasy of immortality.

The third side of the double set opens with a gorgeous new Nyro original, "Park Song," that seems tantalizingly unfinished, containing only two verses and one round of the chorus. "Park Song" takes Laura and Gil outside, where "autumn leaves / drift by like angels." She sees her child illuminated in joy, "laughin' & whirlin' / his love is a ten piece band / That child throws sparks / Across the park / Across this whole crazy world." In the chorus, Nyro and her harmonizing cohorts pray to the leaves to give a mother strength, asking them to "cool the tired / Renew the weary / As you float down / in wonder."

The next cut, "Broken Rainbow," had become an integral part of Nyro's live show, its meandering melody almost a chant. In its simple chorus, Nyro takes the viewpoint of both the "Native American nation" and, perhaps, herself: "At the edge where I live / At the very edge where I live / Home sweet home America." As she had twenty years before, Nyro was still searching for her America, where compassion would take precedence over insensitivity and greed.

The following song, "Women of the One World," again feels like it's missing a verse. Nyro would describe "Women" as being about the moments where the everydayness of being a mother meets the mystic. She sings, "We are dancers sweepers bookkeepers / We take you to the movies," and one can't help but think of her own bookkeeping mother. Nyro also points out, "We oppose war," sporting herself among those women who would take care of their kids *and* fight injustice. At the end of the live version, she sarcastically tells the audience, "That's our hit."

The third side ends with "Emmie," for which Nyro completely changed the ending. She now emphasized spectacular harmonizing on an "ooh la la la / ooh ooh ooh" chorus, and replaced the line "She got the way to move me, Emmie . . ." with a listing of *all* the women (mother, daughter, sister, lover) Emmie might be. The song now sounded loving, nurturing, and sexy, all at once.

The final album side begins with a perky arrangement of "Wedding Bell Blues" that owes more to the Fifth Dimension than to Nyro's original. "It was her fun song," says her cousin Dan Nigro. It seems almost a return to the showbizzy form in which she sang it at the Monterey Pop Festival, thus making it more of a nostalgia trip than a restatement of themes, as her other oldies had become.

"The Japanese Restaurant Song" is *Live at the Bottom Line*'s tour de force. Throughout the rest of her career, Nyro would annually update her mid-song rap to report how long she'd been without a cigarette. She'd also invent new teases about what she ordered from the restaurant waitress, changing from a bowl of chocolate ice cream to a bowl of strawberries (after she went on a nondairy vegan diet). As Nyro gained weight in subsequent years, she would say to the audience with a wink, "If it's not one thing, it's another."

For the next cut, Nyro returns to her Top 10 catalog with a slowed-down version of "Stoned Soul Picnic," again skewing the arrangement in a more pop-ish direction. At the end of the song, though, Nydia Mata launches into a percussion solo, which leads to a raucous jam that better captures the mood of a *real* stoned soul picnic.

The album ends, as did her concerts, with Nyro soloing at her electric keyboard. "I finally have you all to myself," she says, then performs a medley of the Delfonics' 1968 ballad "La-La Means I Love You" along with "Trees of the Ages" and "Up on the Roof." In combining them, she honors three loves: a romantic one, nature, and the catch-it-where-you-can paradise of the city. She coats all three love songs in her syrupy-slow, heart-wrenching vibrato; the effect is mesmerizing.

Reviews of the album, as had become standard for Nyro's work, ranged from kudos to jeers. *People* called it "terrific," the reviewer assuring readers that it was no "mothball marathon," but "a comeback to care about." Reviewer Bob Sarlin, though, found Nyro's new songs self-indulgent and lacking focus. "It's a little hard to hear the same woman who tore the head off the sucker with songs like 'Stone Souled Picnic' [sic] singing a bright little ditty about taking her kids to a restaurant," he wrote. Nyro, he felt, had gotten lost in "quirkiness" and "lightheaded hippiedom."

Without Columbia behind it, the album did not garner as much attention as her previous recordings, and that led Nyro to try some homegrown marketing techniques. Before appearing on the Mountain Stage radio show in 1990, she obtained an 800 number for gathering phone orders. Lee Housekeeper, who was doing some work for her again, remembers her complaining that the message he recorded sounded too "K-Tel" (referring to the infamous TV-hawked record collections), so they spent four hours re-recording it.

Housekeeper believes Nyro sold only about six hundred copies over the phone, but sales weren't her primary concern. "She didn't care about the money side of it," he says. "She just wanted to know the album was out there and being promoted and being available to fans." Nyro herself, in her now-familiar credo, said, "I love art, not show business, and I've accepted the fact that the two are very different things. I'm not singing again with some kind of mega-success thing in mind. There's nothing vaguely romantic in that. It wouldn't feel right."

The best way for her to have the album heard, let alone purchased, was simply to go back on the road as a performer. She also found another good reason to continue touring in the summer of 1989: Her voice had improved even more. "I can hold my notes twice as long this summer as last summer," she told Stephen Holden.

Nyro had relocated yet again, following her gypsy pulse to Long Beach, New York, located on a spit of land on the South Shore of Long Island. She rented a shorefront house at 9 Pennsylvania Avenue while Maria rented a nearby place a couple of blocks inland. "I think it was just time that she wanted to live by the ocean," says Roscoe Harring. "She loved the water." As she had written in "Roll of the Ocean," "I want the roll / the roll of the ocean / I want the sweet deep / Elemental roll." Nyro would later say that the nature of the ocean, with its waves and ebbs and flows, "is like my attraction to music."

Gil, who variously attended a public school, a Hebrew school, and a Catholic school on Long Island, still operated at a much faster pace than his sedate "Mama," as he called Nyro. "He was like a gnat buzzing around her," says musician Vicki Randle, who would tour with Nyro that summer. "And Laura only had one speed—slow. No, she had two speeds: The other was off." Nonetheless, Randle found Nyro to be totally engaged with her son. "Laura would appear helpless in a lot of situations," she says, "but she wasn't helpless with Gilly. I think she really excelled at being a mother."

Nyro considered the relationship with Gil a "great romance." Describing their interaction to a Chicago journalist, she mixed images of a favorite actress, slapstick humor, and a musical soundtrack: "It's like a romantic Italian comedy with Anna Magnani and this little Harpo Marx guy, kind of chaotic, with a violin running through it," she said.

Randle had joined the Vivino-Pagano band lineup so that Nyro could save money by taking only three musicians on the road. As a percussionist, bass player, and vocalist, she could replace Nydia Mata, Dave Wofford, and Diane Wilson. (Nyro even suggested, without success, that Randle play tambourine with her foot while plucking the bass strings.) But it proved too taxing for Randle and Vivino to split duties on bass guitar as well as playing their prime instruments, so partway through the tour bassist Wofford was rehired.

Since Nyro was in Long Beach, Randle—who has toured with such artists as George Benson, Lionel Richie, and Jeffrey Osborne and since 1992 has been the percussionist-singer on *The Tonight Show* with Jay Leno—relocated from Los Angeles to the main house in Danbury. Soon after she arrived on the East Coast, Roscoe Harring pleaded with her to try and interest Nyro in playing the Korg M1 (a popular state-of-the-art electronic keyboard that could produce different instrumental sounds and play more than one musical track). Randle had brought one with her from California. "See that beat-up Casio with the crack in it?" Harring said to her. "That's what's she's going to use on this tour unless we can get her to use the M1."

By this time, Nyro had gathered a collection of inexpensive Casio-type keyboards, big and little. "She'd sling one over her shoulder and bring it when we'd drive somewhere, like from Danbury to the city," says Harring. "She wrote a couple of different things in the front seat of the car." Nyro didn't care that the instrument she was about to take on tour had a rinky-tink, guitarish squawk—she wanted that guitar sound, says Vivino. "We also had a portable fan blowing gently on-stage, just because it felt good to her. I think the fan had been at rehearsals. We took our environment and moved it to the stage."

But the keyboard Nyro had been using didn't even have an "out" port for channeling its sound into the P.A. system, leaving Harring with the unenviable task of miking its inadequate little speaker. "The thing is, she likes the way it sounds," Harring told Randle, "so here's my plan: If you can program a sound on the M1 that will come close to the sound that she's playing on the Casio, maybe I can talk her into taking the M1 out on the road."

Randle, not yet expert at programming the equipment, spent a feverish night trying to duplicate the sound, and presented it the next day at rehearsal. Nyro went for it, much to everyone's delight. "For the tour I was on, she used the M1," says Randle. "She eventually started loosening up a bit and trying a piano sound. She wasn't really interested in any of the other sounds. She had an idea in her head of what she wanted. She didn't argue—she just didn't agree with you."

Randle's first experience with Nyro's fabled stubbornness didn't change her affection for the artist. "She was the most guileless person I've ever known. You just wanted to make her happy. I didn't get her at all, but I totally respected her and I totally loved her."

With Randle's voice added to the mix, Vivino found the second incarnation of the band to be a little tougher and funkier than the first. "The first band was more velvet-like, maybe," he says. "Diane has a quality to her voice that worked great, while Vicki brings an Oakland thing to it. She's like all of Sly and the Family Stone in one person."

While Gil stayed with Mata's mother, Nina Maza (whom he considered a grandmother figure), the band began its tour in June of 1989, first along the Eastern seaboard. By July, they ventured out for weekends in midwestern cities such as Toronto, Madison, Wisconsin, Indianapolis, and Chicago, and then in August played dates in the western United States.

"We did small shows in small clubs, because she really liked that," says Randle. "She had this fanatical following, so she didn't have to worry about selling out clubs. She had to worry about selling a lot of tickets at small theaters, though, because she didn't really have a new audience, and she totally wasn't interested in doing anything that would result in her getting a new audience."

Nyro's set in 1989 wasn't much different than it had been in 1988, and not much had changed in her staging requirements either—although she now insisted that she play only on stages that were level. That rule emerged from her experience of playing the otherwise charming outdoor Shakespearean stage of the Mary Ripon Theater at the University of Colorado, Boulder. The stage was built higher at the rear than the front, causing Nyro to have to lean during her performance. In 1989, she insisted that the promoter even out the stage, which cost about $800.

One of Nyro's more unusual engagements that summer was at the Michigan Womyn's Music Festival in the countryside of Hart, Michigan. She played the gig solo, but couldn't have brought the males in her band anyway, as the annual event allows only women. The five-day camp-out, which features lesbian-oriented performers, touchy-feely workshops, and thousands of fans wearing little or no clothing, was a seemingly odd choice of venue like Laura, who had chosen to remain ambiguous about her sexuality. Nyro had, however, attended the festival once before as a visitor, in 1981, and her decision to perform there made perfect sense to Vicki Randle.

"It seemed she'd been waiting her whole life for this moment," says Randle, who had performed there herself two nights earlier. "Her whole sense of spirituality pointed at these people—women who would feed their dogs vegetarian diets [as Nyro did]."

Unfortunately, Nyro wasn't particularly on that night, perhaps bothered by the huge mosquitoes buzzing around her head, which necessitated that she wear a bandanna. The Michigan audience was respectful, if subdued, and one observer was particularly impressed by Nyro's emotional rendition of the Cole Porter classic "Every Time We Say Goodbye."

On other nights of the tour, Nyro's stage magic was in full force. In Los Angeles, she again drew a celebrity-packed crowd, this time to the Wiltern Theater. The nearly sellout audience at the 1,800-seat Art Deco palace included Barry Manilow, David Byrne, and Madonna, who came with Sandra Bernhard and Warren Beatty. Geoffrey Blumenauer, who was sitting behind that trio, overheard Bernhard expounding on Nyro's songs to Madonna while Beatty sat silently. Finally, when Nyro launched into "Wedding Bell Blues" near the end of her set, the famously single (at the time) Beatty leaned over to Madonna and said, "Now there's a great song."

Turnout-wise, the Wiltern engagement proved to be the pinnacle of Nyro's comeback. After the initial excitement of her return, her audiences dwindled to a core faithful over the next few years. She had, after all, been away from the stage for ten years, and that cost her a decade's worth of fans. "You pay in generations," explains singer-songwriter Janis Ian. "If you're not touring for five years, you've just missed a generation of listeners." Nyro had thus missed two generations.

But just as her music had changed to reflect her life, Nyro relished her new role as a working artist. She had formerly been a mysterious diva, floating across glittery concert halls and being the toast of the pop music world; now she was more of a cultural laborer, fulfilling the progressive social legacy passed down to her from her grandparents. As a union musician, she was also reliving her father's early career.

"I'm kind of like those thousands of musicians that just go out and . . . hit the road and do their work," she would tell Chicago writer Richard Knight Jr. "I'm just your wild working musician."

Having a smaller audience didn't particularly bother her. "Laura was always ambivalent about fame," says Patty Di Lauria. She liked the accolades, the respect for her work, but found the "fame trip" to be shallow. Perhaps she solved her ambivalence by purposefully letting her circle of fans shrink over time. As she once told her cousin Dan Nigro, "I have a limited but quality audience—and that's the way I want to keep it."

18

WALK THE DOG

Onstage, Laura Nyro remained a goddess to her fans. Offstage, she led an earthy, unremarkable life. "She had a tremendous joie de vivre, a feeling of exuberance," says her friend Barbara Cobb. "She was like this ancient woman and a little child at the same time. And she was so fun-loving. It was like being on a hayride with a teenager."

Onstage, Nyro moved with a hypnotic, sensual indolence, as if she couldn't possibly go any faster. Offstage, she did her own version of power-walking early every morning, traveling up and down her long dirt driveway for about fifteen minutes, wearing in her unique workout garb of long dress and sneakers. "She was so cute," says Michael Decker. "She'd walk really fast and pump her little arms, and *maybe* break a sweat."

When she lived in Long Beach, Nyro would take her exercise with Maria along the seaside boardwalk, using hand weights while briskly walking from where they lived to the boardwalk's end. Before turning back, she'd reward herself—with ice cream. Decker says her reasoning probably ran along the lines of, "Oh, we deserve this."

It's much easier to imagine Nyro eating than exercising, especially after hearing her "Japanese Restaurant" tale. "Imagine her holding a peach in front of her mouth and closing her eyes—luscious," says Decker. "It was elegant, it was sensual. She truly loved food."

Except when she was a vegan, Nyro especially adored ice cream. "She was heavily addicted to Häagen-Dazs chocolate chocolate-chip ice cream," says Michael's brother Keith. "I used to have to go run out for that." Adds Michael, "When she was on a self-proclaimed diet, she would call me over and whisper, 'Mike, want to run to 7-Eleven? Get me a little Häagy? Don't tell Maria.' " If Decker could sneak the chocolate treat in past Maria—who would, like any spouse, give Nyro a hard time about breaking her diet—Laura would eat the entire pint.

Her workouts, then, were a rather futile attempt to counterbalance the siren call of fattening food. Ever since her teens, Nyro had battled against being overweight, but by the early 1990s the struggle had been compounded by hypothyroidism—a thyroid deficiency that typically causes fatigue, weakness, and weight gain. For the rest of her life, she would have to take a synthetic thyroid medication to correct the imbalance.

Nyro may have wanted to stay in shape in order to handle her busy life as a musician and a mother. Even though she had begun to tour again, she tried to limit her engagements to weekends so she could be home with Gil during the school week. She would even write a song about her life as a working mom, in which she instructs her child to "Walk the dog & light the light / I'll see you Sunday / 'Cause I'm workin' on Saturday night."

Nyro and her family had returned to Danbury around 1990, after briefly considering both a move to Greenwich, Connecticut, and getting a place in Manhattan. Her next tour—this time solo—would begin in March of 1990, just a few months after the last tour had ended, and would extend all the way through August.

Early on in this tour, Nyro received some long-overdue recognition: On March 31, she was inducted into the New York Music Awards Hall of Fame. The eclectic awards, hosted that year at the Beacon Theater in Manhattan by M. C. Lyte, honored artists from rock to rap to Broadway who were either born and raised in New York or established themselves there. Nyro qualified under both standards.

Her friend John Sebastian of the Lovin' Spoonful inducted her, and then Nyro came onstage to perform "The Wild World" with a reunited band of Vivino, Pagano, Wofford, and Randle. She followed that with a solo rendition of "And When I Die," and offered a brief thank-you speech in which she reiterated her solidarity with the animal rights movement. The message is all about love, she said.

In the next couple of months, Nyro further supported her beliefs by making a couple of charitable appearances. On April 22, that year's Earth Day, Nyro was videotaped singing "Broken Rainbow," and the tape aired on VH1's weekend Earth Day programming. A couple of months later, on June 10, she performed on the steps of the U.S. Capitol at the conclusion of a first-ever March for the Animals event. Her long hair swirled about her face as she sang in front of one of the most potent symbols of America—a word and ideal she had so often evoked in her sungs. "It was quite dramatic," says her cousin Dan Nigro.

Nyro could no longer fill large auditoriums on her own, but among her admirers she remained much in demand. When she appeared at the intimate McCabe's Guitar Shop in Santa Monica—which became her Los Angeles–area performance home for the rest of her career— she was visited backstage by singer Natalie Cole, who asked her to contribute a selection to Columbia's *Acoustic Christmas* album. Nyro readily agreed to the benefit project, which would be released that holiday season, and soon after recorded a medley of the Everly Brothers' classic "Let It Be Me" and a song made famous by Cole's father, Nat, "The Christmas Song."

Nyro was also visited at McCabe's by actress-singer Katey Sagal, a longtime Nyro fan, and by actors Sissy Spacek and William Peterson. According to Geoffrey Blumenauer, Spacek and Peterson wanted Nyro to be the voice of the romantic comedy they were making, *Hard Promises*, and eventually offered her an advance of $80,000 for each song she would write for it. But Nyro passed on the project after reading the script. "She said it contained too much violence," says Blumenauer. "She feared the film would not sit right with the feminist movement."

Nyro had parted company with David Bendett after the 1989 tour, and after her 1990 solo tour grew unhappy with Blumenauer as well. Roscoe Harring then introduced her to booking agent Steve Martin at the William Morris Agency, the place where she'd been represented by David Geffen.

"One of the reasons we got along is because she said I was like an *anti*-agent," says Martin. "When we debated issues it was for good reason—the right thing to do, the right place to play. It wasn't about money or anything like that." Martin, in turn, found Nyro to be "one of the sweetest, most sensitive people you ever want to meet in your life. Incredibly warm and funny, great sense of humor. Loved to laugh—and could laugh at herself."

Martin found her a new manager, Jeff Kramer, who also managed, Bob Dylan—still one of the most prestigious artists at Columbia (now Sony/Columbia) and one of the few artists who had been there even longer than Nyro. Being Dylan's manager, Kramer had a lot of "juice" with the label, and since Nyro was gearing up to do her first studio album in nearly ten years—and her first album not done either live or in her home studio in nearly twenty years—he seemed like a good choice to run interference.

But first, Nyro would go on tour with her early hero, Dylan. That summer of 1991, he was playing large outdoor venues, including Great Woods Center for the Performing Arts in Boston; Tanglewood in Lenox, Massachusetts; the Garden State Art Center in Holmdel, New Jersey (where Nyro had played in 1970); and the 10,000-seat Jones Beach amphitheater in Wantagh, Long Island. Nyro would open the show, the first time she'd been an opening act since her stint at the hungry i.

She played solo at the electric piano, in her now-familiar new style, and one fan who saw her on a hot July night at Tanglewood marveled at how she created a soothing, intimate feeling even at such a large venue: "It was if she had just invited a few of her friends in to hear some music of a summer evening." But the fan also recognized the incongruity of Nyro's gentle music—which "rarely rose above the mid-tempo pace of a rippling brook," as a reviewer put it—being followed by Dylan's electric rock assault.

"She was so naturally endearing onstage," says Steve Martin, who felt that Nyro's short set went over well with the Dylan-oriented crowd. Then again, he noted puzzlement among Dylan's fans when she performed "The Descent of Luna Rosé," a song that would appear on her next album.

"I suppose a lot of them said, 'Who is this odd woman up there singing songs about her period?' " he laughs. "But when Laura would do one of her hits, they'd go, 'Oh, yeah.' "

Martin says that Kramer, who otherwise adored Laura, felt particularly frustrated that she wouldn't play many of her easily recognizable songs. Martin would tell her, "Laura, these people have to connect the dots between the songs and you!"

"It got Jeff crazy, and she enjoyed that it got Jeff crazy!" says Martin. Nyro was being mischievous, not mean—she just delighted in confounding those who expected she'd let the business hold any sway over what she felt like doing.

Nyro told the Los Angeles Times that it was "different" for her to open for someone else, but she did enjoy the tour and thought it went pretty well. At a couple of the shows, though, beer-drinking fans in the front rows proved too raucous for her gentler music. "I left my ballads out of those shows," she laughed.

■ ■ ■

When it came time for Laura to record her next album, in June 1993, her son Gil was nearly fifteen years old. Perhaps that's why she could finally leave her nest to create what would become *Walk the Dog & Light the Light*.

Nyro had gathered only half a dozen new originals for her first CD-only recording, and would fill out the rest of the CD with two songs she'd previously recorded and three "teenage primal heartbeat songs of my youth," as she put it in the liner notes. "That music is about real singing," she would say. "There's a passion for melody, for phrasing. It's sweet, it's street, it's wonderful."

The addition of old and reinterpreted material may have indicated a slow period in her writing, but perhaps they also helped her express themes she couldn't realize with only her recently penned songs. *Walk the Dog* certainly can be read as a diary of Nyro's concerns: She sings about her everyday life as a working artist and mom, her maturity as a woman, her love relationship with Maria, and her distress about the mistreatment of women, minorities, native peoples, and animals. She remained unabashedly old school in her politics as well as her musical tastes, even as a backlash against feminism was gaining steam. It took a certain courage for Nyro not to color her songs with a cynical, post-feminist sensibility.

"The peace movement was never a fad to me," she told writer Harriet Kaplan. "Feminism is not a fad. The animal rights movement is not a fad. These things are essential and always will be. Likewise, I'd like to think the same about my music."

To coproduce the album with her, Nyro chose an old friend from the New York music scene, Gary Katz. Best known for his polished, sophisticated work in the 1970s with Steely Dan, Katz had met Nyro in the late 1960s and had even sung some background dates with her for their mutual friend, the eccentric singer-songwriter Thomas Jefferson Kaye. "We rekindled our friendship some years ago," says Katz. "I can't remember how it happened, but I think through our mutual friend Tommy again [who subsequently passed away]."

Nyro felt comfortable about working with Katz because he loved old soul music, he made clean and professional records, and he wouldn't impose his style on her. As she told him, "I ain't no chick singer who just comes in and sings and that's it!" Nyro also thought Katz had "this really nice studio," River Sound, on 95th Street between First and Second Avenues in Manhattan. It had been set up for him and for Steely Dan's Donald Fagen by engineer Wayne Yurgelun, who would engineer Nyro's album as well. Its digital 32-track recording system was state of the art—and light-years from the four-track analog setup used for Nyro's first album.

Katz chose the musicians for *Walk the Dog*, but Nyro "knew most of them and she trusted me on that," he says. They included some of New York's finest, including old compatriots Bernard Purdie on drums and Randy Brecker on trumpet. One of the guitarists Katz hired, who had played on many of the Steely Dan records, turned out to be Nyro's long-lost high school buddy Elliott Randall. When they first saw each other, "It was so warm I can't tell you," says Randall. "I remembered her, absolutely—she's very hard to forget—and we rekindled a friendship. She and my wife really enjoyed each other as well. I wished we had gotten together earlier. She was such a deep woman, in so many different ways—someone you'd want to have as a friend all your life."

Unlike her last studio album, *Mother's Spiritual*, Nyro didn't take her *Walk the Dog* musicians on a long, exploratory process of working and reworking the material. "Laura was a very complete artist—she had her songs and she knew the arrangements for the most part," says Katz. Nonetheless, she remained open to the players' input. "The mood was really great—it was about communication," says Randall. "I always say that vibes go on tape. You can tell when people have had fun making a record. It makes you smile even more."

Engineer Wayne Yurgelun remembers Nyro as "absolutely refreshing" to work with. "I came into the project at a period when I was dealing with a lot of crazy artists, and Laura was very pleasant, very easygoing," he says. "She had her idiosyncrasies in perfectionism, but most artists do."

The perfectionism centered around her vocals. "She would create these outrageous harmonies in which she sang all the parts, and the sound was just tremendous," says Yurgelun. "She'd take a tape home, work on it, and then try different things in the studio. That can be really, really painstaking for an engineer, because you're just going over and over and over something. Painstaking it was with Laura, but enjoyably so. Laura had a certain thing she wanted to hear, and she wouldn't stop until she got it to that point."

Coming from the Steely Dan school of notorious perfectionism, Katz patiently weathered Nyro's desire to constantly redo tracks, even if they sounded fine to him. "We worked really well together," he says, perhaps forgetting some of their tougher moments. "Laura was very particular about how she worked, and I pretty much have the same attitude. She was just so good. She was very self-conscious about her voice and this and that, so she would redo vocals until she felt really satisfied with them, but they really didn't take that long."

"Gary can be strong, and when he wants something he's even stronger than Laura," says drummer Purdie, who laid down a steady groove into which Laura fit herself, for a change. "But he knows how to do it tactfully." Adds Elliot Randall, "I'm trying to be diplomatic about this—I think Laura had a bit of a struggle with Gary, but not as much as she might have had with other people." In fact, Nyro amusedly described herself and Katz as "two independent thinkers," expressing amazement that they "came out of it alive."

Most of the tracks were cut with drums, bass, guitar, and Nyro's piano and vocals (she was isolated in a windowed booth, within view of the musicians). Nyro would later redo her lead vocal over the rhythm track and add harmony vocals. Studio manager Scott Barkham liked to just sit and listen. "She had such a great tone to her voice," he says. "I was blown away by her ability to just hit it, pretty much every single time. Huge, lush background vocal things. It was pretty impressive."

Purdie recalls that Nyro's piano parts had to be on the mark before the band would complete a rhythm track, because she couldn't duplicate her own playing as easily as the studio pros could fix their performances. "If her voice wasn't right, at least she could fix it. But the piano always had to be right. That's one of the main reasons we had to do many, many tracks, because she might miss something on the piano while trying to do something with her voice."

Yurgelun felt that the song Nyro laid down the quickest, "Broken Rainbow"—which she had previously recorded both for the documentary film's soundtrack and for her live album—captured her at her best. The recording was done late at night, with just Bashiri Johnson on percussion, Freddie Washington on bass, and Nyro on piano and vocal. Although Nyro usually wanted to rerecord her original vocal, Yurgelun felt she should leave this one as is in order to capture the immediacy of a live Nyro performance. "That night I did a rough mix, because I really wanted her to hear it, and I gave it to her to take home," he says. "She came in the next session and said she liked it."

According to Yurgelun, when the brass from Sony made a rare visit ("Laura didn't want them around much; she wanted to make her record the way she wanted it"), "Broken Rainbow" was the track they liked best. "That's the way we want *all* the vocals to be," he heard someone say.

Mixing the album took longer than the initial recording, as Nyro, Katz, and Yurgelun tried to mesh their ideas of what it should sound like. "I had to forget about being sweet at certain times," Nyro laughingly told interviewer Dan Backman. After about four months of on-and-off work, the album finally was completed. "We loved the record," says Katz, speaking for Nyro and himself. "Both of us were totally satisfied with what we did."

■ ■ ■

Walk the Dog opens with a lesser-known oldie, "Oh Yeah Maybe Baby (The Heebie Jeebies)," a Phil Spector/Hank Hunter composition recorded in 1961 by one of Spector's famed girl groups, the Crystals. It was a tune Nyro had long enjoyed playing and singing. "It kind of has a spirit to me of a new beginning—just something being born," she told radio interviewer Fred Migliore. But Nyro infused the song with her own romantic spirit: Having done it from memory, she hadn't recalled how hyper the Crystals had sounded. After she heard the old record again, she hilariously mimicked it for her cousin Dan Nigro, making her voice sound like one of the Chipmunks.

The next song on the CD, Nyro's own "A Woman of the World," is propelled by one of Nyro's finer melodies. A smooth, soulful tune, it's reminiscent of her earliest work. "This song is reaching for . . . healing. A healing in the relationship," Nyro told Migliore. "Friends and lovers can give the sun to each other / Not this rain," she sings, and one can't help but wonder if she was reflecting on up-and-down times with Desiderio, with whom Nyro sometimes had a "confrontive" relationship, according to Nydia Mata.

As in "The Japanese Restaurant Song," Nyro once again showed a sense of humor—and unblushing immodesty—in the CD's next cut, "The Descent of Luna Rosé," a song she dedicated in the lyric sheet "to my period." "It may seem odd in the music business, but feminist poets"—whose work Nyro frequently read—"always write about their periods," she said. "So I felt a bit of an obligation." The song seems directed more towards her lover than her "flow," as a premenstrual Nyro requests, "Tell me a joke / Make sure it's funny / By the bedroom lite / Baby don't look at me like Freud / That could create a void / And get you thrown out."

Nyro's friend Richard Denaro remembers discussing the song's title with her during a long late-night call. "She wanted to know if I understood the song, as a man," he says. "I said, 'Laura, you're the first person, I'm certain, who has ever written a song about waiting for her period!' And she said, 'Baby, you've got it!' She was bent on naming the whole album 'The Descent of Luna Rosé,' but I said, 'People will think it's an opera.' "

In the CD's next two songs, Nyro moves from the personal to the universal. "Art of Love" is a wish for peace, while "Lite a Flame (The Animal Rights Song)" argues that prejudice against animals ("like the elephant of the plain") is no different from that against women or people of color. It was obviously a significant song for Nyro, since she made sure it was included on the greatest hits collection that Sony/Columbia would release a few years later.

The next cut, "Louise's Church," begins like a primer in women's cultural history: "Sappho was a poet / Billie was a real musician / Frida drew the moon / I'm goin' by Louise's church / She built in the city." A poet (the woman-extolling Greek from Lesbos), a singer (jazz goddess Billie Holiday), a painter (Mexican surrealist Frida Kahlo), a sculptor (American scrap-wood fabricator Louise Nevelson)—they're cornerstones of Nyro's artistic inspiration. The song can be heard as an incantation to her muses, as she asks the "goddess of life and music" to "shine on me awhile."

Louise's church is a real place, its formal name being the Erol Beker Chapel of the Good Shepherd. It's a meditative oasis located smack-dab in midtown Manhattan, in the modernistic St. Peter's Church on Lexington Avenue at Fifty-fourth Street. Nyro's nickname for it comes from the white-painted wood sculptures by Louise Nevelson that grace its interior walls.

Nyro had long admired Nevelson and her approach to color. "She works basically with black, gold and white," Nyro had explained to *Sojourner* magazine. "She sees black as containing the silhouette, the essence of the universe, and gold gives the shining edge to the world, from the sun and moon."

It's not surprising that a musician who saw her own work in terms of colors, and used many color references in her own songs (from green trees to midnite blue to red yellow honey), would relate to an artist so attuned to the visual spectrum. Nyro fan Paul Laub also suggests that the dual nature of Nevelson's works—which often rise in spire-like forms like city skyscrapers, yet are built from what is essentially street refuse—echoes Nyro's early inspiration to elevate the most base nature of the city into a thing of intense beauty.

Nyro had a family connection to Nevelson as well: Her great-uncle and great-aunt, William and Theresa Bernstein Meyerowitz, had been Nevelson's first important art teachers in the 1920s. Nevelson had taken weekly drawing lessons from them in their studio in the Hotel des Artistes on West 67th Street in Manhattan, and received their encouragement. Laurie Lisle, in her biography of Nevelson, quotes Bernstein as saying, "I think that the single element that we gave her was the feeling that the language of art was the prime language of a human relationship with life." Nyro, too, spoke that language.

"Louise's Church" is followed by the title song, "Walk the Dog & Light the Light" (subtitled on the lyric sheet "Song of the Road"), in which Nyro sees herself as a gypsy everyworker who "make their livin' / Their independence / Dawn thru moonlight / On both sides / Of that ribbon of highway." "In this case," Nyro explained to Fred Migliore, "the working person is also a mother, and she's like, keeping an eye on both things. She's watching the work, and she stops along the way to call her kid."

Gil figures again in the last Nyro original on the CD, a new version of "To a Child" sung to the spare accompaniment of her piano, with a solo flourish by a flute at the beginning and end. This recording had initially been done for the 1992 Columbia project, *'Til Their Eyes Shine: The Lullaby Album*, produced by singer-songwriter Rosanne Cash and Columbia's Don DeVito, with royalties earmarked for a program in Louisville, Kentucky, that exhibits the art and poetry of children living in areas of conflict. Nyro contributed to the CD's booklet a photo of herself as an infant being held by Gilda.

Her third presentation of the song on *Walk the Dog* indicates another rededication of herself to her son. She may be extending that loving message to Gil in the last cut on the CD as well, a nostalgic medley of two early-sixties classics: the Impressions' "I'm So Proud" and the Shirelles' "Dedicated to the One I Love."

Opening and closing the album with R&B oldies echoed Nyro's habit of warming up with her musicians by playing favorite music of the past. On *Walk the Dog* she also seemed to relish the challenge of combining her sociopolitical songs with the pure sentimentality of a lovelorn teen (and a loving mother). The primal longing for love in her life had meshed completely with her universal longing for, as Elvis Costello once sang, "peace, love, and understanding." She explained in her record company bio, "When I was young, I would write songs where either someone was breaking my heart or I was breaking theirs. That's what almost every writer wrote about, as if that's all a heart can do. But I see life differently now and love has changed and so has music—it's all fuller and more real."

The CD was released on September 7, 1993. After such a long wait for it, Sony/Columbia's hopes had to be somewhat high, and a media advisory from the label predicted that the mere act of releasing Nyro's new work would "generate massive amounts of press." Among other strategies, the marketing department planned a "Columbia Radio Hour" to showcase the recording, and an advertising campaign designed to "reach the old fans as well as targeting a new audience for this soulful songstress." As Columbia's director of marketing, Mason Munoz, told *Billboard*, the company was hoping the Nyro CD would attract older listeners who were still "relevant and vital and cool, who want more than A/C [adult contemporary, or "easy listening" music]."

But a series of events worked against a large promotional push for the album. Nyro didn't do the radio show because of a personal conflict on the day it was scheduled. She also decided to fire her manager, Jeff Kramer, at just the time she could have benefited from his clout.

"We set up a show for her at the Bottom Line [in September 1993] to showcase the new release and all the Sony people were there," says Steve Martin. "I went backstage before the show to say hello, and I said, 'Gee, where's Jeff?' She said, 'Oh, I fired him. It just wasn't working out.' "

Martin had also hoped to have Nyro appear on *Late Night with David Letterman*, where he had a close contact and "they were dying to have her on." But she put him off until the album came out, then decided against it. "I just don't like the way I look on television," she told the booking agent. "I think she was afraid of succeeding, at some level," he speculates. "She was very reticent about her own career. It wasn't that she didn't want exposure, but she wanted it on her terms."

Reviews of the album were generally excellent. *People* found her work "as patently seductive as ever." *Pulse!* wrote that she had recaptured the fusion of "Tin Pan Alley craft, confessional intensity and jubilant sensuality that made her best work live up to the most positive implications of the term 'white soul.' " And *Stereo Review* featured the album in its Best of the Month section, writer Steve Simels asserting that while Nyro's new songs weren't as "consistently tuneful" as the best of her oeuvre, they still showed a "reassuring authority" that more than compensated. He noted that the album made clear Nyro's looming influence: "A whole generation of smart, eclectic (and, truth be told, self-absorbed) female songwriter/performers seem to have sprung up in the last decade or so—and their debt to Nyro is suddenly obvious," he wrote.

Even Rolling Stone joined the bandwagon, calling the album "utterly irresistible, if slight . . . In a New Jack [the popular R&B style of the time] world in which synths, samples and rhythm boxes prevail, Nyro's piano-based soul music, so retro and spare, and her remarkable singing voice, so exuberant and expressive, sound transporting."

For Nyro, the album culminated her long, slow reentry into the musical mainstream. "I'm more disciplined with my writing now," she told Billboard's Jim Bessman. "It's back at the top of my list, along with concentrating on my show and practicing it."

As she was about to turn forty-six, Nyro had reached a stage in her personal development that felt balanced and strong. Perhaps that's why she reconnected so positively with the joys of her teen self, rather than memories of her former angst. "I'm at a point where I see more clearly and better understand life," she said to Bessman. "I'm growing spiritually, and have more compassion. And I'm a better singer now."

But quite soon she would not have a record label. By 1994, after twenty-five years together, she and Sony/Columbia severed their ties. While Nyro had continued on her inexorable path of artistic freedom, the corporate record business had become more and more wedded to the bottom line. "Earlier on, the business was serving the music; now the music is serving the business," she told Barbara Cobb.

Singer-songwriter Desmond Child, who after decades of being a Nyro fan had been befriended by her, says he unsuccessfully encouraged Columbia executive Don Ienner to resign Nyro. "I couldn't imagine Laura Nyro not at Columbia Records," he says. "They wouldn't break even, but who cares? It was Laura Nyro—the cachet, the credibility factor! It really hurt her that they didn't want to resign her—she was devastated, like someone who had been disowned. She still had her godfather there, A&R man Don De Vito, but when the new regime took over, she lost many of her ties. They weren't used to dealing with artists who were that eccentric and had their own way of doing things."

At times Nyro even doubted herself, especially when Walk the Dog didn't sell in large numbers. "At her weaker moments she would question how strong her material was," says Michael Decker. "I remember her asking me to be reminded that her old stuff was genius.

It wouldn't take much to get back on top of the wave, but she would sometimes get dragged down by the undertow."

Ultimately, Nyro would resurface with confidence. "Someone out there will have a sweet tooth for my music," she told writer Harriet Kaplan in 1994. "They'll say, 'Laura, we're going to give you support. Why don't you go into the studio and create the music you want.'

"I feel like a soul mother in my prime," she concluded, "even if Columbia doesn't."

19
ANGEL IN THE DARK

After having toured solo for three years, Nyro went to take female musicians along for her post–*Walk the Dog* engagements. At first she looked for women who could both play and sing, but while holding two weeks of auditions at a Tribeca loft she decided she just wanted harmony vocalists.

"She was working out a lot of the arrangements during the auditions," says Diane Garisto, one of the singers Laura hired. "It was a collaborative, organic experience. She really respected the singers."

Nyro initially chose eight women (all except Garisto were African-American), including her 1988 backup vocalist Diane Wilson, and performed with them on Long Island and in San Francisco. But a group of that size proved expensive. By the time Nyro appeared on November 13, 1993, at the Mayfair Music Hall—site of her triumphant return to Los Angeles five years earlier—she had narrowed the group down to six women, and later would reduce it to three.

The effect of Laura and her Harmonies, as she called them, was stunning—like being in a room with a band of angels, was how her friend Richard Denaro put it. Not since her days with Labelle had Nyro found such consummate companions for her own voice, which had become richer than ever.

"When you're in your forties, it can be the best time or the worst time for a singer," says Garisto, who had previously toured with Steely Dan and George Benson. "You can get this color in your voice, or this horrible quavering vibrato. Laura's voice—the colors in her voice—were just so beautiful."

On Christmas Eve, the six-woman harmony group accompanied Nyro at the Bottom Line, reliving her early-seventies tradition of doing a New York Christmastime show. "She did a Christmas Eve show with almost no Christmas music!" laughs Alan Pepper, co-owner of the club. "It was a chance for her to share the traditional warmth of the season with her 'tribe'—not an opportunity to sing Christmas songs," explains Dan Nigro. "Christmas was a very special time to her—my cousin the Jewish girl. It was a time to really connect."

Nyro wanted the singers to surround her at the grand piano—not the electric this time—but to accommodate them, the nose of the instrument had to be pushed over the edge of the stage. "If you put the piano the way she wanted it, about seventy or eighty people were literally sitting under it, so you sure as hell couldn't see her [from those seats]," explains Pepper. "I said to her, very diplomatically, 'Laura, I kind of think this ain't gonna work.' And Maria said to her, 'It's not gonna work.' Laura tried it a couple of different ways, but the only way it felt right to her was to have the piano hanging over the audience."

So Nyro came up with a Solomonic solution: She brought in a box of her latest CDs and instructed Pepper to give a copy to anyone who sat in the obstructed seats. But he was not to tell people about the prize beforehand. "Well, lo and behold, those seats filled in rather quickly, because people just wanted to be close to her," says Pepper. "Then we gave people the CDs and said, 'It's a gift from Laura, because of the inconvenience.' They were very appreciative."

Booked once again by Geoffrey Blumenauer (Steve Martin had drifted out of the picture), Nyro continued to perform throughout 1994, sometimes with three harmony singers and other times solo. She wanted to continue touring while her energy for performing remained high. "Oh, I've got a few good years left," she said to writer Richard Knight. "I just think of it like a stove and . . . it's, like, on the front burner."

One of the more spectacular numbers she did with the Harmonies was a new version of "Save the Country," a song she thought she'd never perform again. But a friend nagged her to sing it until one day she sat down at a keyboard and connected at once with it again. "I sing it totally different, just completely different, yet the essence of the song is there," she told Knight. Instead of the pounding, "Save the country NOW!" ending, she instead chanted the lines "in my mind I can't study war" and "there'll be trains of blossoms / there'll be trains of music"—from "Stoned Soul Picnic."

"It's almost like my philosophy in a nutshell," is how Nyro explained the odd juxtaposition. "In my mind I can't study war because there'll be trains of blossoms, there'll be trains of music. I still feel that."

A particularly memorable moment on the 1994 tour took place back-stage at the Fairmont Hotel in San Francisco. A fan had approached Roscoe Harring to display a remarkable foot-long thigh tattoo: Laura's long-hair-blowing likeness from the cover of *Walk the Dog*. On the op-posite leg he had tattooed his other favorite singer, Joni Mitchell. Har-ring, who usually kept fans out of Nyro's dressing room, couldn't resist letting this one in to show off his epidermal tribute (as the fan had already been doing for other audience members). Without hesitation, "the guy dropped his drawers to show her," said Harring. "That flipped her out—she could not stop laughing. Fell off the couch."

When Nyro's friend Richard Denaro later came to her dressing room, she retold the story. " 'What did you say to him?" Denaro inquired.

"I asked, 'Didn't my hair hurt?' " said Nyro, and once again dissolved into laughter.

Nyro's 1994 tour extended across the ocean for the first time in more than twenty years, as she returned to her beloved Japan, appear-ing at 200- to 400-seat clubs in Tokyo, Osaka, Kobe, and Nagoya. "She had all these really young fans—fifteen, sixteen, seventeen years old—who were discovering her for the first time," says Diane Garisto, one of the Harmonies who accompanied her. "Laura loved that and dubbed it the Puppy Love tour."

She also performed again in London at the Union Chapel, a former church located in the hip suburb of Islington. Despite Nyro's long absence from Britain, the chapels' pews were filled to capacity on the rainy night of November 11, and she received a warm and lengthy greeting when she entered wearing a red cape. Her long hair now was streaked with gray, and her figure was much more amply proportioned, but "her voice was still opulent and strong and wonderful," says one fan in attendance.

The chapel's domed roof proved as good as a subway station in providing the right echo for her and three Harmonies. For an encore, Nyro performed solo, including a melancholy reading of the Rodgers and Hart song "He Was Too Good to Me," which she announced she had learned at age fifteen from a Nina Simone album. Not surprisingly, she de-genderized the lyrics, changing the title line to "*You Were* Too Good to Me."

When the audience insisted on a second encore, Nyro admitted she hadn't practiced anything else. "She must have been sincere," says the London fan, "because she doodled with 'Stoned Soul Picnic,' fumbled the chords, and then segued into a wonderful 'Walk On By' to finish."

Those last songs, raved Mick Brown in the *Daily Telegraph*, "seemed to float upwards to the vaulted rafters of the church like prayers. Who says there are no such thing as angels?"

For Phoebe Snow, the most transcendent Nyro show of 1994 took place in the Oak Room of New York's Algonquin Hotel, at a songwriters' roundtable for a primarily record-business crowd. Desmond Child opened for Nyro, ending his set with a moving, homoerotic version of her song "The Man Who Sends Me Home." Then Nyro came to the grand piano with two backup singers and proceeded to enrapture the packed room. "I had never seen Laura as I saw her that night," says Snow. "She was touching God. Her voice was pristine and perfect, and when the singers harmonized they all sounded like one voice. The tears were streaming down my face. Laura came back for, like, four encores; we wouldn't let her leave. Everyone in that room had sort of a communal moment where we all knew that this was as good as live music gets."

(Nyro had befriended Snow in the late 1980s; she was a huge fan of Snow's powerful voice and had asked their mutual pal Jimmy Vivino to hook them up. Snow remembers conversing with Nyro about how to protect one's heart and spirit from the crassness of the music business. "Laura was trying to be a total support person," says Snow. "I was mending my own creative broken heart in those days, and she was so encouraging, saying, 'Come on, you don't have to put up with this shit. I have some ideas, I have a studio, I would love to hear your writing.' She extended a hand to me—that's how she was.")

Nyro completed 1994 with another Christmas Eve show at the Bottom Line, this time with three Harmonies. As she had the previous Christmas, she taped the show, with her *Walk the Dog* engineer Wayne Yurgelun at the controls.

Around the time she was completing *Walk the Dog*, Nyro had put in a call to documentary filmmaker D. A. Pennebaker, whom she had seen once or twice since he made *Monterey Pop*, about possibly doing a video for her. Coincidentally, Pennebaker was then transferring his Monterey footage onto digital video in order to archive it. He invited Nyro to come down and see her own performance again.

"I said, 'You weren't booed at all—they were cheering for you,' " says Pennebaker. "She said, 'Oh, I don't believe it!' " Perhaps she took his word for it; she never did make it to his studio to see the video, nor did she follow through with the idea of making the video.

■ ■ ■

While continuing to tour, Nyro was polishing a new collection of songs. The act of writing was joyful for her, she told music journalist Paul Zollo. "So many songwriters moan about the process, but she wasn't like that at all," says Zollo, who, after "nine years of pestering and pleading," had finally been granted an extended interview (he promised it would cover only songwriting). "She loved writing songs."

Nyro had even been writing a song about songwriting, called "Serious Playground," in which she characterized her work as a sort of architecture: "I make my living / building homes / I build them out of music / with my imagination . . . my boss is / The Muse." To Nyro, the serious playground of music making was a space to both work and play.

She did face a certain conflict, though, when it came to touring and writing. Laura tended to rise at dawn, then be in bed by 9:00 P.M. During a tour, she had to discipline herself to sing at night. "It throws me off the schedule," she said to Zollo. She wasn't joking when she sometimes told audience members that they had kept her up past her bedtime.

According to Michael Decker, Nyro would start writing early because it was her clearest time of day. She would be hyperfocused on her work then, demanding absolutely no distractions. "You wouldn't go into the cottage if you heard her playing piano," he says. But by about 2:00 P.M., she would be wiped out. "*Overload* is a word that often was uttered in late afternoon," he says. At times like that, Nyro might seem completely disfocused. "She could truly disconnect and just float," he says.

Decker ascribes Nyro's behavior not to any sort of artistic temperament, but to her possibly experiencing an adult version of attention deficit disorder (ADD), which he considers himself to have. Common among creative people, it's simply "a variation of brain style, no more no less," says Lynn Weiss, Ph.D., a psychotherapist in Austin, Texas, and author of six books on ADD, including *ADD and Creativity*. People with ADD, says Weiss, don't organize details in a linear way, but operate more out of feelings, intuition, and a total immersion in what they're doing.

"First-level creative people—the person who truly invents, the visionaries—are ADD," she claims. "They aren't popular. It's the followers who are popular." ADD or not, Laura Nyro perfectly fits such a description.

But ADD can also make a person seem scattered and spacey, which might explain how Nyro in interviews could sometimes sound vaporous and poetically opaque. Then again, Nyro's daily speech, as Melissa Manchester had noted, sounded poetic about even the most mundane topics. Says her brother Jan, "In everyday life, she would say things that were strikingly beautiful and profound."

The hard part for Nyro, Decker suggests, is that when she wasn't "writing or playing mom or lover or friend or just floating for the day," she could fall prey to a whole series of distractions—from talking endlessly on the phone to eating compulsively. Nyro herself showed some willingness to embrace the ADD explanation for her dramatic swings between focus and disfocus: Decker says that he, Laura, and Maria all pored over the ADD book *Driven to Distraction: Recognizing and Coping with Attention Deficit Disorder from Childhood Through Adulthood*, by Edward M. Hallowell and John J. Ratey, finding much of its perspective "right on the money."

On the other hand, Nyro's longtime friend Barbara Greenstein, who's a psychoanalyst, doubts the armchair diagnosis. "She absolutely did not have a touch of ADD, not at all," she says. "That doesn't ring true. Laura was one of the most focused people, and she was able to screen out stuff. She may have been reading up about it in regards to someone else."

■ ■ ■

Although Nyro did not yet have a contract with a music label in 1994, she wanted to begin recording new material. So she decided to do it on her own—not an uncommon strategy for independent artists, who then sell their masters for distribution. "The big companies are set up to support the mega-moneymakers," she told journalist Harriet Kaplan. "The alternative artists don't have this strong support system from record companies."

Besides putting her new songs to tape, she also wanted to record a collection of oldies and classic pop standards for a sort of *Gonna Take a Miracle 2*, a project she had been considering since at least 1988. Nyro did not have the money for studio time, however. Having received bad financial advice, she owed back taxes to the IRS. That's why she decided to accept money from her dad Lou, and an offer to help finance recording sessions from a fan she'd become friendly with, Eileen Silver-Lillywhite. A college professor and respected poet with two young sons, Silver-Lillywhite also paid for Nyro to record her 1993 and 1994 Christmas Eve concerts at the Bottom Line.

To produce the oldies, Nyro turned to old friend Peter Gallway, a singer-songwriter with whom she had recently reconnected and invited to open for her at some engagements. With Gallway, she recorded the Gershwin pop standard "Embraceable You," the little-known Burt Bacharach/Hal David composition "Be Aware," and four sixties soul classics: "Ooo Baby Baby," "Will You Love Me Tomorrow," "La-La Means I Love You," and "Walk On By." They first worked together at Gallway's studio in March 1994, then at Manhattan's Power Station studio in late August. For the Power Station sessions, Gallway put together a rhythm section that included a familiar face—bass player Will Lee—along with drummer Chris Parker, percussionist Carol Steele, and guitarist Jeff Pevar.

The recordings remained unfinished, though. In a familiar refrain, Gallway says, "She was never quite satisfied—she's always been very picky about what she liked and what she did not, and she was never quite able to take them to completion."

Earlier in the year, Nyro had recorded another version of the dreamy "La-La Means I Love You," this time as a guest vocalist with the Manhattan Transfer. The quartet's female vocalists, Janis Siegel and Cheryl Bentyne—both longtime Nyro fans—had met her backstage at Mc-Cabe's in Los Angeles when she appeared there in April.

"We've sung with Ella Fitzgerald and with Sarah Vaughan, but meeting Laura Nyro we were both tongue-tied," says Bentyne, who had performed torchy early-Nyro songs such as "Buy and Sell," "Lazy Susan," and "Lonely Women." "But she was just adorable, so sweet. We said, 'We'd love to work with you someday, yada yada,' and we left."

Coincidentally, the group was then recording Tonin', a series of collaborations with legendary pop artists, and Bentyne was looking for another song on which to feature her voice with a guest's. Asked who her dream partner would be, she said Nyro, and the song that popped to mind was "La-La," which she and Siegel had heard Nyro sing in a medley that night at McCabe's. When Bentyne nervously called the singer in Connecticut about the idea, her immediate answer was, "I'd love to."

Laura must have been intrigued to hear who was producing: her coproducer from Christmas and the Beads of Sweat, Arif Mardin. "It was such a wonderful feeling to have her in the studio," says Mardin. After she laid down her vocal, Nyro said to him, "Why don't we do this again?"

"She put the feel down, and we just let her sing—that's the kind of respect you have to pay people like her," says Bentyne of the New York recording session, where Nyro accompanied herself on electric piano. "She kept saying in this little voice, 'Is that okay, Arif?' I'm going, Oh my God, it's *Laura Nyro*—what do you mean, is it okay?"

Bentyne did, however, suggest one lyric correction: In the Delfonics' version, the opening line reads, "Many guys have come to you / With a line that wasn't true," but Nyro had changed it to, "Many *ones*." Bentyne thought "ones" sounded grammatically incorrect, and had Mardin quietly suggest that Nyro try "Many *loves*"—which she did.

The production on *Tonin'* is more lavish and middle of the road than Nyro's typical recording style, but her vocal remains strong, if slightly buried in the mix. She flavored the song with a soulfulness reminiscent of both her earlier work and the original recording, making it one of the album's best cuts.

Not everyone was as lucky as Bentyne in getting Nyro to participate in their projects. Around the same time, Frank Stallone—Sly's brother and a client of Geoffrey Blumenauer's—wanted Nyro to cowrite the title song for his brother's movie *The Specialist* and sing it with him as a duet. As she had earlier with the film *Hard Promises*, Nyro turned down the lucrative opportunity because the script contained violence, and also because she didn't collaborate as a writer.

A year or so later, filmmaker Allison Anders tried to recruit her to write a song for *Grace of My Heart*, her 1996 movie about a Carole King–like sixties songwriter. Although Anders managed to corral some of the country's best songwriters for the project—Burt Bacharach, Lesley Gore, Carole Bayer Sager, Gerry Goffin, and Joni Mitchell (whose ex-husband Larry Klein oversaw the music)—Nyro passed. Perhaps she couldn't imagine writing within the film's parameters.

In late October 1994, Nyro recorded two more oldies, this time at River Sound studios, where she had done *Walk the Dog*. Wayne Yurgelun, her *Walk the Dog* engineer and a Connecticut neighbor, served as producer for "You Were Too Good to Me" and "Let It Be Me." The former had been recorded not only by Nina Simone but also by Nyro's childhood jazz singer friend, Helen Merrill, in an arrangement by someone Nyro much admired, Gil Evans.

At the end of April 1995, Nyro returned to the Power Station, this time to demo three of her new compositions—"Triple Goddess Twilight," "Serious Playground," and "Animal Grace"—with Dan Gellert producing. "Animal Grace" is probably a tribute to Ember, her adored dog. "I love my dog / I rest my case," she sang, ending the song by amusingly singing of earth as an "interspecies affair" to the tune of Sly and the Family Stone's "Family Affair."

"Triple Goddess Twilight," which she had performed at some 1994 concerts, is a poignant reflection on the two lodestars in her life, her mother and grandfather. Nyro pictures being carried through the park by her mother (the "park" image figures in several songs about Gil) and then being left her mother's "twilight colors" of rosé, burgundy, and coral mist. Nyro recalls Grandpa as a streetwise, urbane, working-class man who "painted houses on a ladder in the sky" while teaching his granddaughter that she could change the world.

In the chorus of the song, she evokes the Triple Goddess, an archetype common to many cultures, embodying the three phases of a woman's life—maiden, mother, and crone (Hecate, whom Nyro had sung about in "Sophia," is considered a triple goddess). Nyro had already sung about the wildness of the maiden ("only now am I a virgin I confess") and the nurturance of the mother. Now she was contemplating her approaching cronedom, the time when a woman begins to impart her hard-earned knowledge. The twilight in the song's title perhaps symbolizes that moment of passage, from the lightness of day to the rich darkness of night, and while entering that dimming light Nyro evokes her beloved ancestors as guides.

■ ■ ■

Nyro played McCabe's in Los Angeles again on February 11 and 12, this time solo. During the engagement, she invited a few local women poets to come meet with her, including Wanda Coleman. Coleman remembers a warm encounter, during which she shared Chinese take-out with Nyro and discussed her poem "Sapphire as Artist in the World," which had appeared in a couple of early-nineties poetry anthologies as well as in Coleman's own book, Hand Dance.

"We had a really lovely visit, it was very moving," says Coleman. Nyro told her that the poem had inspired her to pick up songwriting again after a dry spell. She especially liked the line "Rhythm is a state of concentration / So complete it leaves you defenseless / Opens to all in tune with it." "That sentence reached out and grabbed her," says Coleman. "Because she was a musician, I think she sensed the music under the language."

Coleman intuited that Nyro, who had gained more weight since her previous Los Angeles appearances, was ill. Her poem thus seemed to be a harbinger of Nyro's upcoming struggle, since it was about the refusal to give in. "You do what you have to do in the face of unbeatable odds," says Coleman. "And here she was, facing the most unbeatable odds of all."

When Laura came out to visit Patty and Andy in Colorado in the early spring of 1995—Gil had been staying with them during his school break—Patty, too, recognized that Nyro wasn't well. "She usually wore only lipstick; this was the first time I ever saw her put on foundation makeup," she says. They discussed whether Nyro's thyroid problem was acting up or whether she could be anemic. "I never thought about cancer," says Di Lauria, "because she walked so much while she was there. She loved to walk. I made her promise that when she went back home she'd go to a doctor."

But Nyro wasn't diagnosed until the summer, when she went to see a doctor in the Los Angeles area. He sent her to an oncologist, where she received the worst possible diagnosis: stage 4 ovarian cancer.

The risk of developing ovarian cancer—which usually occurs in the cells that make up the ovary's outer lining—is fairly low in the general population, at 1.8 percent (about 25,000 cases annually). However, when two or more first-degree, or first- and second-degree relatives have had the disease, the risk for an individual increases to 50 percent. Nyro's mother, Gilda, her maternal grandmother Sophie, and her great-aunt Minnie (Sophie's youngest sister) had all died of the disease.

If this cancer is diagnosed promptly, the five-year survival rate is 80 to 95 percent, but it's rarely discovered in its first stages. Ovarian cancer has been dubbed the silent killer because those early symptoms—weight gain, bloating, back pain, fatigue, and vague abdominal and pelvic discomforts—are subtle and easily ignored. The late comedian Gilda Radner, one of the most famous sufferers of the disease, showed those symptoms for a year before her diagnosis. The CA125 blood test can spot the disease in its early stages but is not a foolproof diagnostic tool, since it also registers positive for certain benign conditions.

By stage 4 of ovarian cancer, the malignant cells have spread outside the ovary and abdomen, usually to the liver. The chance for survival beyond five years for stages 3 and 4 is only 25 percent.

Ironically, around the time Nyro was diagnosed, scientists discovered that mutations in two particular genes, BRCA 1 and BRCA 2, are strong predictors for almost all familial ovarian cancers. A genetic test can now determine whether or not a woman has inherited a mutated gene. Even without such a test, Nyro had considered the familial connection to ovarian cancer.

"Laura definitely felt she was going to get it," says her brother Jan. "I remember more than once when she made some dark comment about it, and I scolded her about being depressing. But in the end, she was right." Had she chosen to, Nyro might have had a preemptive oophorectomy (removal of the ovaries) or a complete hysterectomy to lessen her risk, but this is a difficult decision for anyone to make. Only in retrospect does it seem a tragically missed opportunity.

Lou Nigro remembers Nydia Mata coming over to his apartment with Gil, who at the time was about to turn seventeen, and telling him that Laura was going to call from California. When the call came, Nydia and Gil quietly left the room as Laura gave her father the devastating news. A week later, she would have a hysterectomy, then stay for months at Maria's mother's house in Torrance, California, while undergoing chemotherapy.

Despite the drain of chemo, Nyro remained determined to complete her recording projects. In the midst of her treatment, she returned to the Power Station, with Wayne Yurgelun as producer and several players from *Walk the Dog*. "There was Freddie Washington on bass, Bernard Purdie on drums, Laura on keyboards, and me on guitar," says Elliott Randall. "Which was the way she liked to cut anyway—the more live the better. She was basically saying to us, 'Whatever feedback and ideas you have, don't hold back.' "

In order to get such top-flight musicians to work on a limited budget, Yurgelun secretly informed them that Nyro, who was wearing an unobtrusive wig that matched her normal hairstyle, was ill. "I said, 'Look, she may not have too many more sessions—how about just helping out here?' " Yurgelun particularly credits Randall with helping to pull everyone together by writing charts and playing cheerleader for the project.

The band recorded four Nyro originals at the session: "Angel in the Dark" (which she had performed at the Bottom Line in 1994), "Gardenia Talk," "Don't Hurt Child," and "Sweet Dream Fade." "Gardenia Talk," an atmospheric love song Nyro had performed in concert in the early nineties, was originally scheduled to appear on *Walk the Dog*, but she hadn't been satisfied with it then, says Yurgelun.

In "Angel in the Dark," Nyro returned to her soul music roots, with a slow, finger-snapping groove. In light of her illness, the lyrics are particularly poignant, even if they were written before her diagnosis: "I don't know how / I don't know where / I'll be dreamin' and on my feet again / cuz I can't laugh no more / without an angel / so if you're there / come back to me."

In "Don't Hurt Child," one of the last songs she wrote, Nyro deals with her teenage son's late-adolescent struggles, telling Gil that she can identify with his pain because she too had been young and wild. She urges him to "heal your wild wing / and fly."

"Sweet Dream Fade" was the last song of the session. It may have reflected a time, before she became ill, when Nyro and Desiderio had separated for a while. "Their relationship had its ups and downs, but mostly ups," says Patty Di Lauria. In the song, Nyro suggests they try again: "Do you wanna make a sweet dream fade / After all the sweet tries we made / Never mind perfection / Heroes or heroines / Tonight / Let's be lovers again / Tonight."

Having gotten down the basic rhythm tracks and Nyro's vocals, the songs still needed harmonies and embellishments. But Nyro would never return to the studio to finish the project.

Back in California, even as she was finishing up her chemotherapy, Nyro tried to maintain a semblance of normal life. One long weekend she ventured up to San Francisco, looking for a Belgian Tervuren puppy to replace Ember, her adored dog who had recently died. It was shocking to see her wearing a beret on her hairless head, says her friend Richard Denaro, whom she spent a day with, but he otherwise found her "as beautiful and spirited as ever." When they drove out to meet the Tervuren breeder, Nyro turned the afternoon into a picnic, bringing sushi along in a cooler.

She also brought an impromptu picnic when she met with Che Johnson, her friend Anne Johnson's son, and his partner Jeffree on the Redondo Beach Pier in January 1996. "I remember that she was deeply concerned that the hummus she brought wasn't soulful enough, because she had to buy it rather than make it herself," says Jeffree.

Nyro returned to the East Coast by the end of winter, and blood tests showed she was in remission. But by August, when Laura and Maria came to visit the Johnsons at their summer house in Vermont, the cancer had returned. Doctors told Nyro that she might live six months with no treatment, while another round of chemotherapy would add about a year to the prognosis. At that point, as Gilda

Nigro had twenty years previously, Laura decided to undertake alternative treatment because she couldn't bear the thought of more chemo.

One of the unorthodox alternatives she explored was the Revici program in New York City, developed by the Rumanian-educated physician and oncologist Emanuel Revici. He proposed that cancer was associated with an imbalance between different classes of the body's lipids, or fats, and his treatment regimen included the use of various chemical formulations, including the element selenium. Revici's theories remain controversial and unproven by conventional medical research, but Nyro found comfort in his program.

"Laura tried everything she could alternatively," says Anne Johnson. "She battled, I tell you, she really battled. It was just incredible. When I was around she was very upbeat, but Maria told me that she went through periods when she was extremely angry. Laura would say, 'What did I do? Why am I being punished?' "

Few people around her knew she was sick. "We talked a little about it—I knew she'd been going to treatment," says Elliott Randall. "She was convinced she would beat it. I don't think it was until the very end that she figured out she couldn't. If there was any way she could have, by mind over matter, she would have been the one."

When Phoebe Snow heard that Nyro was ill, she called with the notion of offering assistance. But Nyro's opening line was predictably, "Are you okay? Do you need anything? How's your daughter?"

"I thought, 'Damn, I called to talk to her about her problem!' " says Snow. "But she was not forthcoming about that, and nobody wanted to pry or coerce her."

■ ■ ■

Nyro's last project with Sony/Columbia, it turned out, would not be Walk the Dog but a "best of Nyro" package. In 1996, the Legacy division of the company, which handles reissues, decided to put together a retrospective of her career. Although record companies have been known to release material they own without the artist's consent, Columbia involved Nyro from the outset.

"My understanding of it was that she definitely wanted to do it," says project director Mark Feldman. "The whole point was to put out a record that Laura was happy with, because it was her music."

But Columbia's initial list of songs weren't to Nyro's taste, and thus began a long negotiating process. As Laura told one journalist, "I strongly felt it needed a woman's touch and an artist's touch." She also wanted to be sure the collection included socially conscious songs from her later career. To help represent her interests, Nyro called on Lupe De Leon, a booking agent who she'd become friendly with after he hired her to play the Fairmont Hotel in San Francisco. "She offered to give me a couple of [royalty] points on the album," says De Leon, "but I said, 'Forget about it, let's just do it.' For me, it was a real honor working with her."

So, from December 1996 through March 1997, De Leon ran interference between Nyro and Columbia. "She was very much the perfectionist, very much the 'things have to be right or I can't put my heart into them' kind of person," he says De Leon. "Man, I was amazed at what she got Columbia to do—which is to their credit. She picked a lot of the songs and had approval on everything." According to Feldman, the project took an entire year from initiation to completion—about twice as long as a typical two-CD set requires. "There was definitely a lot of back and forth," he says. "It was hard for her to let go and say, 'Okay, this is it.' "

Compromises were hard-fought, but ultimately agreeable to both parties. Nyro allowed the inclusion of the Bones Howe–produced version of "Save the Country," while Columbia added Nyro and the harmony group's unreleased live takes of that song and of "And When I Die." Columbia also agreed to add a couple of Nyro's most political songs, "Lite a Flame" and "Broken Rainbow."

"To be honest," says Feldman, "a lot of those songs were not her most well known, which is why they weren't suggested at the beginning of the project. But they were important to her, so we wanted them to be there." Nyro could not, however, untangle contractual problems with now-defunct Cypress Records that would have allowed the collection to include "The Japanese Restaurant Song," which had appeared on *Live at the Bottom Line.*

Nyro had input on the packaging of the CD as well, from the photos to the inclusion of song lyrics in the booklet (which Sony/Columbia felt would take too much space). "We fought and fought with them and they finally agreed to list some of the songs," says De Leon, "and use the jewel box for the lyrics of 'New York Tendaberry' and 'Save the Country.' One day I got in a kind of heated discussion with Mark Feldman about something, and he said, 'Man, we can't do any more.' Yet they would—they would go a little further."

When they began working with Nyro, neither Feldman nor De Leon knew she was terminally ill, but it gradually became apparent. "She never told me she had cancer—she told me she had a major illness—but I figured that's what it was," says De Leon. "She sounded weak on the phone towards the end, but she was still talking about getting well and playing. We'd talk about her making another record." In retrospect, Nyro's perfectionism about the project, including a half-dozen daily calls to De Leon, took on a completely different meaning. "This was going to be a record of her life's work," he says.

The two-CD album, entitled *Stoned Soul Picnic: The Best of Laura Nyro*, was released in March 1997, and Nyro was pleased. "She called and said, 'I like this, I like the package,'" remembers De Leon. Adds Feldman, "She told me she was really happy with it, and she put in this little personal dedication to me that was real sweet."

In *People* magazine's review, Tony Scherman gave the collection a B, saying that Nyro had "talked her label into including a bigger chunk of her recent work than deserves to be on a best-of set." He found the second disc to be meandering, but the first "glows, lit by six songs from *Eli*, one of the greatest albums from the brief era when music was a religion, a communal rite." Steve Futterman of *Entertainment Weekly* graded Nyro's effort an A, suggesting, "Fans of today's visionary female popsters would profit from a good listen to Nyro, the shamefully overlooked singer-songwriter who paved the way for them 30 years ago."

■ ■ ■

Around the same time as her greatest hits were being compiled, a tribute album to Nyro was also in progress. Its producer was Peter Gallway, although the idea had come from Steve Plotnick, the president of the concept-oriented label Astor Place. It was Gallway, though, who suggested the album be done solely by women artists.

"I thought it would be a twist to the tribute concept, and uniquely appropriate to Laura, because I consider her one of the first groundbreaking feminist pop artists," he says. Gallway wanted a cross section of musical styles, but ended up with a somewhat homogeneous roster whose best-known names included Phoebe Snow, Suzanne Vega, and Rosanne Cash.

Gallway suggested songs for each artist to perform, but ultimately each made her own decision. "To my disappointment, no artist really felt that it was appropriate for them to do 'Emmie,' which is one of my favorite songs," says Gallway. No one chose any recent Nyro compositions, either. Gallway had hoped Nyro herself would participate, contributing a song she had never put on disc. "We talked about it, but I don't know if she was comfortable with it, and I think she was probably too sick to do it even if she wanted to."

When the recording was nearing completion, Gallway sent Nyro a copy. "I think she was pretty sick by then, though even in my last conversation with her she was not presenting to me how sick she was," he says. "She was telling me she was optimistic, she was hopeful. I was asking her if she'd be willing to do interviews about the record, do a show. She was sort of hedging, saying maybe it was possible and how she hoped to tour the following summer."

Nyro had also been exploring various options for putting out her new music. Eileen Silver-Lillywhite has written that she and Nyro planned to release the music under their own label, Luna Mist Records. But Lillywhite isn't the only person Nyro discussed a new record label with. Los Angeles–based Gail Gelman—who manages singers Vonda Shepard and Valerie Carter and at one time managed an artist Nyro much admired, Joan Baez—talked with Nyro in 1996 about joining the independent record label she planned to start.

"I said, 'I would love you to be able to make the record you want to make,'" says Gelman. "She said, 'Well, that would be a real treat. I would love to get together with you.'" Although they talked frequently on the phone over a few months, they didn't meet. "She never talked about her illness, but I knew from somebody else. The only thing she told me was that she had a lot of serious issues in her life at the moment. If she had lived, I probably would have ended up being her manager, and I know I would have signed her to my label—there was no question in my mind.

"You know what was interesting?" adds Gelman. "In every conversation—and it still haunts me to this day—Laura said to me, 'You sound too good to be true—are you still going to be around?' She always came around to that issue, making sure I wasn't going anywhere and that I was telling her what I really believed. The irony of it is that I didn't go anywhere—but she did."

Gelman was able to carry a torch for Nyro's memory in another way: She gave David Kelley—producer of the TV show *Ally McBeal*, on which

Gelman's client Shepard sings every week—a copy of Nyro's greatest hits album. The next week Kelley asked Shepard to record "Wedding Bell Blues" for a fantasy sequence between Ally and her former boyfriend—named Billy, of course. Over the next couple of seasons, Shepard would also perform "Stoney End" and "And When I Die" on the show, as Kelley worked Nyro's songs into his storylines.

■ ■ ■

By the end of February 1997, Nyro knew she was in the final stages of her illness. That's when she called Patty Di Lauria, who had promised to fly out from Colorado whenever she was needed. Di Lauria spent the next six weeks with Laura and Maria, camped out on a futon on the floor of the cottage, where they all stayed.

Nyro was relatively free of pain, thanks to a morphine patch, but she frequently battled nausea. Despite everything, she was "a true delight," says Di Lauria. "It was a pleasure to be with her and to be looking after her, if you could possibly say such a thing." She remembers one particular sunny day when Nyro was feeling pretty good and didn't have any doctor appointments. To amuse the three of them, Di Lauria suggested they peruse a small book called *Art and Nature* and choose pictures that represented each other's souls.

"I set the rules—it didn't have to be representational in terms of form, but something about the color and the dynamics had to represent each person's soul," she says. "When we were all done"—she won't reveal which pictures they chose—"Laura just looked at me and said, 'That's a great use for a book.' The point is, we tried to find nice things in the midst of it all."

Maria and Patty also set up indoor picnics with people Nyro wanted to see in her last days, including Lou Nigro, Anne and Charles Johnson, and Roscoe Harring. Cousin Steve Marcus visited a couple of times and tried to humor Laura with his spot-on imitation of Grandpa. "Lauretchka!" Marcus would say in Grandpa's unmistakable growl. "You look beautiful. I've been meaning to tell you."

"I could sort of channel him," says Marcus. "And Laura wanted to feel his presence, in a way." The last time Marcus saw his cousin, he made plans to come again the next weekend and sleep on a futon. They would watch movies. But it was not to be.

The day before she died, Jan and Janice Nigro and their almost-two-year-old son came to see Laura. She had applied red lipstick for their visit and sat in a chair while they gathered around and listened to the Gallway tribute album. Nyro had little to say about it, but Jan noticed that she had assumed an uncritical state of grace about everything. Engraved in both his and Janice's memory of that day was a moment when Laura said, very clearly and despite all the pain she had suffered, "I have no complaints."

Nyro was lucid at 5:30 that evening, but soon after began to fail. Maria and Patty stayed up most of the night with her. At 5:15 A.M. on April 8, a windy Tuesday morning, Laura Nyro passed away.

■ ■ ■

Her memorial service, held at the Danbury house on the dreary, wet Saturday that followed, reflected a personal legacy more than a musical one. "The people who were there were essentially this humble collection of friends and family," says Peter Gallway. "They weren't superstars, they weren't movie stars, music stars, none of that."

Most of the mourners were drawn to the cottage, where they held each other and shared recollections in library-quiet voices. Many recalled Nyro's generosities. Misha Masud, her old friend from camp days, drew comfort from memories of being in that house with her and just singing.

After a time, the hundred or so mourners sloshed through mud to a large tent that had been set up on the meadow, where each was given a candle with a red ribbon tied around it. By then, the rain was pouring and the day had grown quite dark. There were more stories, more tears, and even some laughter. Anne Johnson described her longtime friend as someone who cast a spell. Cousin Steve Marcus did his impersonation of Grandpa. And Roscoe Harring recounted Nyro's suggestion that they raise the audience when she performed in Central Park. Maria didn't talk, but John Bristow, who attended with his *Mother's Spiritual* compatriot Elysa Sunshine, remembers her looking "beautiful, even in her sorrow."

A month earlier, at Laura's request, Patti and Maria had selected a Japanese maple tree to plant outside her bedroom window, just across the brook. Her ashes would be buried underneath that tree, along with those of Ember.

Nyro had long loved things Japanese, including haiku poetry, and the Japanese haiku poets were known to write poems about their own impending deaths. Gozan, a poet who died in 1733 at the even younger age of thirty-eight, wrote a verse that Nyro herself might have composed as she anticipated leaving the world that early spring:

> *Ka ya hiraki*
> *Nori toku tori no*
> *Kirabiyaka*
>
> *Blossoms fill the sky*
> *a carefree birdsong*
> *echoes truth.*

20 A WORLD TO CARRY ON

Because her illness had been a secret to all but an inner circle of family and friends, Nyro's death shocked longtime acquaintances and fans alike. Singer-songwriter Melissa Manchester's reaction was typical. "I remember driving home from dropping my kids off at school and heard her music on the radio and an announcement of her passing, and I was socked in the stomach," she says. "I had to pull over and I just cried and cried and cried. Then I came home and put on *Eli*, people started to call me, and we all just cried. It was unbelievable."

Although Nyro had been out of the limelight for much of the past couple of decades, all the major American newspapers and magazines— as well as TV and radio news shows and British, Japanese, and Swedish journals—published substantial obituaries. Most remembered her primarily for her first fevered years of creativity. *Time* called her an "intense and lyrical singer-songwriter whose freeform musical emotionalism captured for many the passions of the 1960s and 1970s." The Associated Press's Polly Anderson, whose report was excerpted in various publications, mused nostalgically about those same days, in which "her music could be heard coming from college dorm rooms across the country."

A number of memorialists assessed her place in pop music history, with Stephen Williams in *Newsday* ranking her in importance with Bob Dylan and Joni Mitchell. In *The Boston Globe*, Steve Morse characterized Nyro, along with Mitchell and Carole King, as "among the first singers to write in an authentic women's voice after years of industry decrees that men write for them."

Vince Aletti credited Nyro not only for inspiring her more obvious progeny, such as piano-playing confessionalist Tori Amos, but even the most outré alternative artists such as Björk or Courtney Love, whose existence he couldn't imagine without Nyro having come first. "She was our Garland, our Streisand, our moody, messy diva, and she blurred all boundaries," he wrote in The Village Voice. Richard Harrington, in The Washington Post, concluded, "Lots of people were later compared to Laura Nyro. Nyro herself was never compared to anyone."

A number of critics made a point to honor Nyro's singing as much as her songwriting. Newsday's Williams argued that while her songs were often hits for others, it was her own "tenuous, spooky vocals . . . that were indelible." Similarly, Reuters's Matthew Lewis noted that Nyro "was shamefully overlooked as a solo artist, especially during her creative heyday from 1966 to 1972."

Her former record company gave full due to her legacy. Sony Music Entertainment president and COO Tommy Mottola told Billboard's Jim Bessman, "Laura Nyro was a true original. When she burst on the scene in the late sixties, no one had ever heard songs or singing like that before—and they haven't since. She laid the groundwork for an entire generation of female singer-songwriters."

Other memorialists offered more personal tributes. "She wrote about the world I lived in, but infused it with so much passion that ordinary things—the weather, the river, the streets, the kids—glowed with a spiritual energy," wrote New York–born singer-songwriter Suzanne Vega. "Though we were plain ordinary nasty kids, when she sang she made us beautiful."

■ ■ ■

On the radio, Nyro received her finest obituaries from NPR (National Public Radio). Weekend Edition host Scott Simon, who had interviewed her in 1989, delivered a five-minute tribute, calling her a curious cross between Martha Reeves (of the Vandellas) and Leonard Cohen. On Terry Gross's NPR show Fresh Air, Cambridge-based music critic Milo Miles reconciled Nyro's transition from "urban sorceress" to "devoted tree hugger" by saying, "But I think her ideals were consistent: Because she swept all the sounds she loved into her music and made them work harmoniously, she was always practicing an ecology of the spirit."

Ironically, considering Nyro's once-huge audience as a hit songwriter, local radio music programs were the least likely place to hear more than a quick eulogy. Although Fred Migliore, host of the Melbourne, Florida, public radio show Another Unusual Sunday Morning, offered a three-hour Nyro tribute to other NPR affiliates on the national satellite, few ran it. One of those who didn't, Chris Douridas, then host of the trend-setting Morning Becomes Eclectic on Los Angeles NPR affiliate KCRW, seemed largely unfamiliar with Nyro and her impact on cutting-edge singer-songwriters. However, his guests that week—eclectic record producer and musician Don Was, and Phoebe Snow—both talked about Nyro.

Don Was asked Douridas to play Nyro and LaBelle's "The Bells." "For an artist just to be able to lift a thing to this emotional point that she gets to in the middle of the song, to have that kind of feeling inside to propel a performance like that, is staggering," said Was. "But to have the chops also to pull it off! They don't make 'em like this anymore."

Snow requested her favorite Nyro cut from her college years, "Captain for Dark Mornings." "The phones lit up like a Christmas tree," she recalls. "It was college-age listeners going, 'Who is that, where can I get that record?' Laura Nyro is timeless. She works now, she worked three decades ago."

At least one local radio station got Nyro exactly right. On the Wednesday night after Nyro's passing, WFUV, out of New York's Fordham University, simply played Eli and the Thirteenth Confession in its entirety.

■ ■ ■

A month after her passing, the Gallway-produced tribute album Time and Love was released. People's Billy Altman praised it for working on a variety of levels, "all of them solidifying Nyro's legacy as one of American pop's more underrated masters," but British critic Ian MacDonald expressed a more common sentiment, especially among Nyro's fans: "Next to the immensely alive and mostly celebratory originals, these remakes are bloodless: indeed, sometimes even incongruously sinister."

The album as a whole lacks the passionate, upbeat energy that infused Nyro's work, substituting instead a postmodern weariness. A raucous song like "Eli's Comin'," for example, becomes a dirge in Lisa Germano's version, and even the gospel-based Sweet Honey in the Rock drain the life out of "And When I Die." At least performers such as Dana Bryant, in her spoken-word version of "Woman's Blues," and Jill Sobule, in her cheery take on "Stoned Soul Picnic," capture Nyro's sense of bliss.

"That's another important thing to stress about Laura Nyro's music— the fact that you can just baldfacedly be *happy* in a song," says singer-songwriter Wendy Waldman. "Happy music, music that expresses joy, the naive celebration of another day above ground. Who does that now? Who just goes, 'Man, good to be alive!'' '

Phoebe Snow, who recorded "Time and Love" for the tribute, felt that the project had been rushed. "No money, no budget," she says. "They called me at the last minute, and under those circumstances it was amazing we could do anything." Snow suggests that the project should have included male artists and singers more contemporaneous with Nyro. "There are so many people who are survivors of this industry who hold Laura in such high esteem," she says.

Peter Gallway, though, felt that the project's lack of commercial appeal may have reflected Nyro's own drift away from the mainstream of pop music. That may be his defense for an off-the-mark result, but his analysis of Nyro's uneasy relationship with commerce seems right on:

"Maybe the music business was truly something that Laura Nyro didn't believe in, or really didn't want to ultimately be part of," he says. "Can we say she's right or wrong? Those of us who cherish her voice and her spirit and her talent hungered for her to get what we perceive as her just desserts and the ongoing recognition that she deserved, but that wasn't the case. People really do remember her more as a younger person with that fire, those records, those shows, all of that mystery, all of that excitement, all of that emotion. Her greatest risk was stepping away, being a mother, doing the things that were important to her."

The oversimplification of pop music over the decades of Nyro's career also worked against the richly complicated artist. "For a songwriter, she does some fairly complex harmonic things, which is why her stuff is probably not popular now," jazz pianist/composer Billy Childs, for whom Nyro had been an early inspiration, told interviewer Paul Zollo. "I mean, what is popular now is beyond being simple; it's nonexistent, you know. Like, harmony doesn't exist."

■ ■ ■

Six months after Nyro's death, on October 27, 1997, Maria Desiderio staged a Laura Nyro Memorial Concert, held at Manhattan's majestic (but shabby) Beacon Theater, where Nyro had been inducted into the New York Music Hall of Fame in 1990 and where, in one of her last outings, she had enjoyed watching Chaka Khan perform. Coproduced by Lisa Vogel of the Michigan Womyn's Music Festival, it served as a belated wake for Nyro's fans.

The concert featured artists Nyro had worked with and been admired by, including Kenny Rankin (her friend from Verve/Folkways days), Tuck and Patti, Phoebe Snow, Patti LaBelle, Sandra Bernhard, Rickie Lee Jones, Desmond Child and Rouge, and Alice Coltrane (who, with her son Ravi Coltrane, played John Coltrane's "After the Rain" in Nyro's honor). Pianist Steve Gaboury directed the backup band, which featured Nyro's longtime drummer friend Bernard Purdie, *Season of Lights* horn players Ellen Seeling and Jean Fineberg, and Harmonies Diane Wilson, Diane Garisto, and Frieda Williams. Even *New York Tendaberry* arranger Jimmie Haskell contributed to the proceedings, working out an arrangement of Nyro's song "Angel in the Dark" for Patti LaBelle.

Most of the artists offered verbal as well as musical paeans. Bernhard recalled first hearing *Eli and the Thirteenth Confession* on a kibbutz in Israel and deciding, "I want to be just like Laura Nyro." From Nyro, she said, she had learned "to reflect the love of the universe back to the audience." Kenny Rankin deemed Nyro "the salt of the earth," as well as a friend who had once cradled him while he cried. "For that one moment in time, my name was Billy," he said, then sang a touching, guitar-accompanied version of "Billy's Blues."

In the most stunning performance of the night, Rickie Lee Jones, who had once called Nyro "America's greatest songwriter," performed two particularly difficult, downbeat Nyro compositions, "You Don't Love Me When I Cry" and "Been on a Train." When Jones reached the part in "Train" where Nyro screams, 'No, no, damn you mister!' she reproduced the anguish with such goose-bump-raising exactitude that she seemed to be channeling her progenitor's spirit.

The concert would be Desiderio's last public commemoration of her lover. During the spring of 1998, in an irony too cruel to imagine, Maria too was diagnosed with late-stage ovarian cancer. Having seen the toll chemotherapy exacted on Laura, she decided not to undertake any treatment for the disease. Reclusive by nature and not wanting to burden anyone, she took an apartment in New York City for a time before returning to Danbury, where Michael Decker and his partner tended to her. She passed away on November 26, 1999, at age forty-five. Her ashes were buried under the Japanese maple alongside Laura's and Ember's.

■ ■ ■

In the years since Nyro's death, the artist has popped in and out of public consciousness.

Several honors have come her way: The Recording Academy recognized her contributions by naming *More Than a New Discovery* to its Grammy Hall of Fame in 1999, and music TV station VH1 counted her as No. 51 on their Top 100 Women in Rock list. On May 10, 2001, the Connecticut Women's Hall of Fame inducted Laura into its ranks at a ceremony attended by her father, son, brother, sister-in-law, and friend Patty Di Lauria. The evening included a medley of Nyro songs sung by a four-woman a capella group organized by Diane Garisto, and a solo rendition of "And When I Die" by Jan Nigro.

There have been several new covers of Nyro songs (besides those of the tribute album), including an Irish folk version of "And When I Die" by Kevin Burke's Open House, Tuck and Patti's "Captain for Dark Mornings," and several remakes of the torchy *More Than a New Discovery* songs by jazz artists.

"Many of the tunes on that first album are extremely jazz friendly," says New York–based Mary Foster Conklin, who recorded "Billy's Blues." "I could not hope to produce Nyro's 'money notes,' but what I could do was address the heart of the tune—add my perspective to her passion."

Nyro's name also pops up as a reference point for other artists. Jill Cuniff, lead singer and songwriter for the punk- and hip-hop-influenced women's band Luscious Jackson, told a journalist a few months before Nyro died, "People speak detrimentally of [Joni Mitchell] and Laura Nyro as those 'confessional women songwriters,' but I say thank God someone was confessing something, because those shared experiences are what I feed off."

In the 1999 book *Listen to This: Leading Musicians Recommend Their Favorite Artists and Recordings*, Nyro surprisingly made the lists of two male rock and rollers—Louie Perez, drummer and lyricist for Los Lobos, and Peter Buck, guitarist for the band REM. "I was obsessed with Laura Nyro when I was a teenager," Buck said. "Those first four records, no one's ever made music like that. . . . I don't think she ever got the respect she deserved."

Perez listed Nyro's first album as No. 2 on his all-time Top 10 list, saying "What [Jimi] Hendrix did with a guitar, Nyro did with her voice and her songs."

Two British journals have also praised Nyro's oeuvre in the past several years. Robert Sandall in the *Sunday Times* of London, writing about *Eli and the Thirteenth Confession*, insisted that "If musical talent was the sole criterion by which pop musicians were judged, Laura Nyro would be up there with the Beatles and Frank Sinatra. [But] innovation and originality on the scale she preferred do not always get their just rewards." Just a month later, the pop culture magazine *Uncut* celebrated *New York Tendaberry* as a "classic album revisited," and writer Ian MacDonald called Nyro one of the twentieth century's "major sisters."

Even Joni Mitchell, a woman not known to credit anyone short of Mozart or Picasso as having influenced her art, has paid homage to Nyro. In a 1998 interview with the British music magazine *Mojo*, Mitchell said that Nyro was the only female artist with whom she'd accept any artistic linkage. "Laura Nyro you can lump me in with, because Laura exerted an influence on me," said Mitchell. "I looked to her and took some direction from her."

■ ■ ■

Nyro's music has recently become the source for several theatrical reviews. Two were coincidentally produced in May 2000: *Stoned Soul Picnic: A Celebration of the Music of Laura Nyro*, in Vancouver, British Columbia, and *Soul Picnic* in Austin, Texas. But it was the third production, this time in New York City, that garnered the most attention. *Eli's Comin'*, which played at the Vineyard Theater in Union Square from May through mid-July of 2001, featured four female singers, a male dancer, and a live combo performing over twenty Nyro compositions. Creators Diane Paulus and Bruce Buschel linked the songs together, without dialogue, into a loose narrative about a young girl finding love, trouble, and redemption in the city.

Reviews were cool toward the extrapolated story line, but warm about Nyro's music. "When the singing is allowed to stand front and center," wrote Associated Press drama critic Michael Kuchwara, "*Eli's Comin'* convincingly makes the case for putting the work of Laura Nyro on a stage." The show's four female principals—Anika Noni Rose, Mandy Gonzales, Ronnell Bey, and Judy Kuhn—were honored with Obie Awards for their performances, and Deirdre Murray received an Obie for the show's vocal and instrumental arrangements.

Audiences seemed to love the show, allowing the Vineyard to extend it for over a month beyond its planned run. But once again, the public was drawn to *other* people singing Laura's songs, perhaps soothed by an imposed story line less demanding than the ambiguous complexities of Nyro's originals.

Shortly before *Eli's Comin'* hit the stage, Nyro's final recordings were released by Rounder Records under the title *Angel in the Dark*. It was a bittersweet moment, as the vocals had not been completed to Nyro's satisfaction, but it was thrilling to hear her poignant renditions of old classics and new originals.

Eileen Silver-Lillywhite, who reportedly mortgaged her home to pay for the Nyro recording sessions, had gained possession of the master tapes, then sued Maria Desiderio for the right to release them, citing a contract that Nyro had signed with her. With Desiderio ill from cancer and the legal defense becoming a drain on the estate, Desiderio had settled the case. Silver-Lillywhite claimed in the CD's liner notes that Nyro had wanted the music released, but Patty Di Lauria insists that she didn't: "Laura did not wish any of this music to go out," says Di Lauria. "She wished it to be destroyed. Her relationship with Eileen had soured."

Scott Billington, who produced the Nyro project for Rounder Records, didn't know about the legal conflict until his work was nearly done. He handled the melding of the various songs and recording sessions with sensitivity and few musical additions, asking John Tropea to add guitar parts to some of the songs and write horn charts for Michael and Randy Brecker to play.

"I had tears in my eyes when I listened to the final mixes," says Tropea, who had played with Nyro on *Smile* and the *Season of Lights* tour. "I felt I was playing along with her. I even played the same guitar I had used with her in the seventies—a hollow-body L5 Gibson, which gives more of a round, jazz sound."

Nyro had matured into a jazz singer in her final recording. The standards she chose fit perfectly her mature range and sensibility, and blended well with her beloved oldies and engaging new compositions. Perhaps the most stunning song on the collection is Bacharach-David's "Be Aware," which expresses a concern for humanity perfectly in line with Nyro's lifelong values. Her sweet but powerful rendition of the little known classic draws tears.

Despite being an unfinished work, the album received excellent reviews. Brett Milano of *The Boston Phoenix* wrote that, sadly, the songs felt like a fresh beginning for Nyro: "The mix of cosmic and earthy elements will be familiar to her fans—she was blurring sexual/spiritual lines long before Prince got the idea. But there's a playfulness here that hadn't been around since her seminal '60s albums, and these unpolished piano demos capture her natural charm better than the tight production on her last few official releases."

Entertainment Weekly, while judging the work not as "consistently dazzling" as Nyro's best, nonetheless gave it a B+ rating, praising the "resonance of the late artist's deeply personal vision" and singling out "Angel in the Dark" and "Triple Goddess Twilight" as "intoxicating." On Amazon.com, Carl Hanni called *Angel in the Dark* "nothing short of a magnificent final kiss blown from the other side." And in London's *Guardian*, Richard Williams concluded, "It will be a big surprise if any singer-songwriter, of whatever gender or generation, releases anything this year remotely as accomplished and affecting as these last offerings from an artist of genuine and enduring originality."

■ ■ ■

Unfortunately, Nyro's "enduring originality" continues to be overlooked in places where she should be part of the canon.

She's neither a member of the Rock and Roll Hall of Fame nor the Songwriters Hall of Fame (although Desmond Child has vigorously lobbied the latter for her conclusion). She was also ignored at Lilith Fair, the women's music festival whose first incarnation occurred the summer after her death. By all rights the festival should have been dedicated to Nyro, but her name wasn't even mentioned, though her legacy was everywhere present in the poetic songs of Paula Cole, Jewel, and Lilith Fair's founder, Sarah McLachlan. At a remove of thirty years, most of these singers had not been directly influenced by Nyro but by her acolytes, so they remained oblivious to her pioneering role. As writer Patricia Romanowski has put it, "Any woman who soared to emotional heights on a less-than-perfect voice or dared to be a woman musician rather than a lady or a girl owes Nyro a tremendous debt." Adds Nyro scholar Patricia Rudden, "Laura Nyro and Joni Mitchell divided the world between them in 1968; thirty years later you can trip over all the female singer-songwriters."

As Nyro's work receives more attention from stage shows such as *Eli's Comin'*, the inattention to her may be remedied. Indeed, when the show *CBS Sunday Morning* did a seven-minute TV tribute to Nyro on July 8, 2001, sales of *Angel in the Dark* and other Nyro albums immediately spiked, as did ticket purchases for the New York play.

Nyro's legacy may also be boosted by future music releases, both from Rounder (which next plans to release a recording of Nyro at the Bottom Line with her harmony singers) and from Nyro's estate, which hopes put out a live Japanese recording by Laura and the Harmonies, as well as cover songs and originals that Nyro recorded at her home studio in the early 1980s. Those covers include the Cole Porter classic "Every Time We Say Goodbye" and a Dr. John song, both of which Nyro was known to perform in concert. Di Lauria, who also served as executor of the estate for a time after Maria's death, also hopes to have Nyro's out-of-print albums *Mother's Spiritual* and *Nested* re-released.

"People in the music industry regard Laura very highly as an artist," says Di Lauria, "but aside from her relatively small coterie of fans, nobody else knows who the hell she is. My goal is to assure her rightful place in pop history."

To administer Nyro's publishing, Di Lauria engaged Cherry Lane Music—a well-respected New York music publishing operation owned by Nyro's first producer, Milt Okun. Having never spoken with Nyro after her lawsuit against him and Artie Mogull over thirty years ago, Okun had been astonished to hear from Maria Desiderio after Nyro died.

"She said that Laura told her that I was the only adult at the time who treated her fairly and understood her music," says Okun. "I always considered Laura my one failure in business, because we didn't continue recording together. That really bothered me throughout the years, so this gives me a sense of completion." Among other ventures, Cherry Lane hopes to encourage new covers of Nyro's songs and recently published a new collection of Nyro's compositions, *Time and Love: A Laura Nyro Songbook*.

As for those in Nyro's world who "carry on," her father, Louis Nigro—who turned eighty-six in February of 2002—still occasionally tunes pianos. He was *Eli's Comin's* biggest fan, attending nearly thirty performances and becoming friendly with the cast and theater staff. He often stood at the door as the audience filed in, answering questions about his daughter or asking people where and when they had first heard her music.

Laura's son, Gil Bianchini, attended the opening-night performance. Now a tall, handsome twenty-three-year-old, he's been working as a barber in Harlem and attending business classes at a local college. His primary aspiration, though, is to become a hip-hop artist, and in the summer of 2001 he began cutting his first demos. Although not a singer, he writes poems and short fiction as well as the rhymes of rap music.

Part of Gil's legacy from his mother, he says, is her spirit of kindness. "It's not like she sat down and told me, 'Be kind to people,' " he says. "It was just something I saw from her all the time. She always put out harmonious vibes. She was a rare person—she never gossiped, she never talked down to people, she rarely got angry. If you were real close to her and got her angry, then she had, like, a warrior temper, but she didn't get angry often. She always showed a lot of care and hospitality—that's part of the reason people cared about her so much."

■ ■ ■

Perhaps *Angel in the Dark* and *Eli's Comin'* will spark a re-exploration of Nyro's remarkable catalog; perhaps this book and future releases of her music will do the same. Much of her work remains an undiscovered treasure, especially by those who never heard her songs except as filtered through the Fifth Dimension, Three Dog Night, Barbra Streisand, or Blood, Sweat and Tears.

Fortunately, as long as recordings exist, a great singer never dies. Judy Garland, Billie Holiday, Dusty Springfield—the moment we hear their voices, they're beside us. The same, too, with Laura Nyro. Every time her songs are played, if only for those moments when we're embraced by the plangent timbre of her voice, she is alive once again.

AFTERWORD

This is the first biography of Laura Nyro; it is *a* story of her life, not *the* story. She probably would have insisted that her biography (or autobiography) is in the songs she wrote. If you want to know her, I imagine her saying, go to the music.

So I echo that sentiment: Go to her music. Most of her albums are currently available on CD. The complete version of *Season of Lights* is available as a Japanese import. Her out-of-print albums can sometimes be found on Internet auctions, through music dealers and in fan-to-fan trades. Hopefully those albums, too, will soon be re-released.

If you're unfamiliar with Nyro's work, it would seem easiest to start with one of her greatest hits collections. That's not, however, the best way to understand and appreciate her music. She wrote albums more than individual songs. Be brave: Start with *More Than a New Discovery* (now called *The First Songs*) and work your way album by album, song by song, to *Angel in the Dark*.

SELECTED BIBLIOGRAPHY

The main focus of my research was interviews from original sources. However, the following books, articles, and other media provided a wealth of information, opinion, and Nyro's own quotes. Printed sources that were used for only a couple bits of information are included with their complete reference in the Notes.

Albertson, Chris. "Laura Nyro: From the Heart." *Down Beat*, April 2, 1970.

Backman, Dan. Telephone interview with Nyro. City (Sweden), October 20, 1993.

Bessman, Jim. Unpublished liner notes for Nyro's greatest hits album, 1997.

Black, Johnny. "Finale." *Hi-Fi News & Record Review*, April 1997.

Clein, Harry. "Laura Nyro: Rock Madonna from the Bronx." *Coast FM & Fine Arts*, October 1969.

Cole, Susan G. "Laura Nyro: Child of the City Comes Back with Grown-Up Vision." *Now* [Toronto], July 13–19, 1989.

Cromelin, Richard. "Laura Nyro Returns for a Soulful Connection." *Los Angeles Times*, August 11, 1988.

Critique. PBS-TV, January 1, 1969.

Davis, Clive, with James Willwerth. *Clive: Inside the Record Business.* New York: Morrow, 1975.

Douglas, Susan J. *Where the Girls Are: Growing Up Female with the Mass Media.* New York: Times Books, 1994.

Etchison, Michael. "Soul . . . For Laura Nyro 'Love Is Surely Gospel.' " *Los Angeles Herald-Examiner*, October 8, 1968.

Fissinger, Laura. "Organic Feminism." *Musician*, September 1984.

Flanagan, Bill. "The Luscious Life." *Musician*, September 1, 1989.

Goodman, Fred. *The Mansion on the Hill: Dylan, Young, Geffen, Springsteen, and the Head-on Collision of Rock and Commerce.* New York: Vintage Books, 1997.

Heim, Chris. "A Season Veteran: Laura Nyro Is Back—and It Feels Like Spring." *Chicago Tribune,* July 31, 1988.

Johnson, Pete. "Better Than Eli: Pete Johnson Reviews *New York Tendaberry.*" *Coast FM & Fine Arts,* October 1969.

———. "Purple, Tuna, and Laura Nyro." *Teenset,* February 1969.

Kaplan, Harriet. "Shine On." *Village View* (Los Angeles), April 1994.

King, Tom. *The Operator: David Geffen Builds, Buys and Sells the New Hollywood.* New York: Random House, 2000.

Kloman, William. "Laura Nyro: She's the Hippest—And Maybe the Hottest." *The New York Times,* October 6, 1968.

Koplewitz, Laura. "Laura Nyro's Songwriting and Artistic Transformation." *Sojourner,* August 1984.

LaBelle, Patti, with Laura B. Randolph. *Don't Block the Blessings: Revelations of a Lifetime.* New York: Boulevard Books, 1997.

MacDonald, Ian. "The Five-Year, Five-Album Span of High-Pressure Creativity." *New Musical Express,* June 29, 1974.

Maslin, Janet. "Singer-Songwriters." *The Rolling Stone Illustrated History of Rock & Roll,* Jim Miller, ed. New York: Rolling Stone Press/Random House, 1976.

Migliore, Fred. Radio interview, "FM Odyssey," November 17, 1993.

Moore, Carman. "Laura Nyro Comes Back (Yay!)." *The Village Voice,* March 1, 1976.

Nyro, Laura. "Notes from an Interview on 'Envisioning a Feminist World.' " *Woman of Power,* Spring 1985.

Paley, Maggie. "The Funky Madonna of New York Soul." *Life,* January 30, 1970.

Pollock, Bruce. "On Songwriting/Laura Nyro." *Guitar,* October 1984.

Reed, Rex. "Laura Nyro's *New York Tendaberry.*" *Stereo Review,* February 1970.

Rockwell, John. "A Drop-Out Sings of Her Tangled Life." *The New York Times,* February 29, 1976.

———. "Laura Nyro: From City Girl to Natural Woman." *Rolling Stone,* April 8, 1976.

Romanowski, Patricia. "Laura Nyro." *Trouble Girls: The Rolling Stone Book of Women in Rock,* Barbara O'Dair, ed. New York: Random House, 1997.

Saal, Hubert. "The Girls—Letting Go." *Newsweek,* July 14, 1969.

Sciaky, Ed. Radio interview, December 1989.

Snyder, Michael. "Q and A with . . . Street Diva Laura Nyro." *San Francisco Chronicle*, December 1994.

Sontag, Deborah. "An Enigma Wrapped in Songs." *The New York Times*, October 26, 1997.

Thomas, Michael. "Laura Nyro." *Eye*, May 1969.

Valentine, Penny. "An Exclusive Interview: Laura Nyro." *Sounds*, February 20, 1971.

Ward, Ed, Geoffrey Stokes, and Ken Tucker. *Rock of Ages: Rolling Stone History of Rock and Roll*. New York: Rolling Stone Press/Summit Books, 1986.

Watts, Michael. "In from the Cold." *Melody Maker*, February 7, 1976.

Weller, Sheila. "Laura Nyro: Out of Seclusion." *Ms.*, November 1975.

Joel Whitburn. *The Billboard Book of Top 40 Hits*. New York: Billboard Books, 1989.

———. *Joel Whitburn's Top Pop Albums 1955–1992*. Menomonee Falls, WI: Record Research, 1993.

Wickham, Vicki. "Laura's Music Says It All." *Melody Maker*, February 6, 1971.

Wilson, F. Paul. "Nyro Fiddles," 1989. On www.lauranyro.net.

Windeler, Robert. "Laura Nyro: New Queen of Contemporary Music." *Entertainment World*, December 19, 1969.

Zollo, Paul. "Laura Nyro: Inside the Oneness." *SongTalk*, vol. 4, issue 2, 1994. (Reprinted in part in *The Performing Songwriter*, May/June 1997 and in the liner notes for *Stoned Soul Picnic: The Best of Laura Nyro*, Columbia/Legacy, 1997.)

NOTES

Unless otherwise noted, quotes are from my interviews. Commonly used print sources are listed by the author's surname as it appears in the Selected Bibliography. A full reference is provided for print sources not listed in the bibliography.

1. ONE CHILD BORN

1: "Laura": Written by David Raksin, the song was played as an instrumental in the film; later, Johnny Mercer added lyrics and the song became a band and vocal standard.

1: "Fish gotta swim": "Can't Help Loving Dat Man," by Jerome Kern and Oscar Hammerstein.

2: U.S. Army band: Famous trumpeter Al Hirt was a fellow band member.

2: a small town near Naples: Interview with Michael Nigro.

3: the Bronx: The borough emerged from the land that Jonas Bronck purchased and began to farm in 1639, taking its name from Bronck's River. Hence it's called the Bronx, since the names of rivers are generally preceded by "the" (Mississippi, Nile, etc.). From Lisa Garrison, *The South Bronx and the Founding of America* (New York: The Bronx County Historical Society, 1987), p. 7.

3: Gezelitz, Ukraine: Gezelitz was a village near the larger city of Ekaterinoslav, which is now called Dnepropetrovsk.

3: daughter of a cantor: Information on Laura's great-grandfather Gershon and great-uncle, William Meyerowitz, from Theresa Bernstein Meyerowitz, *William Meyerowitz: The Artist Speaks* (Philadelphia: The Art Alliance Press, 1986), pp. 14, 19–20.

3: His work, and that of his wife: Meyerowitz died in 1981. As of the summer of 2001, Teresa Bernstein Meyerowitz was still very much alive in New York City, at age one hundred and eleven.

3: In one painting: Owned by Louis Nigro.

3: paintings of musicians: "Painter Theresa Bernstein, 110, regains fame in her second century," *Jefferson City (Md.) News Tribune*, February 26, 2001.

3: critic Stanley Olmstead: From Meyerowitz entry in *Current Biography 1942*, pp. 588–589.

4: from Vilna: Vilna is now known as Vilnius.

4: Pale of Settlement: From Joan Comay, *The Diaspora Story: The Epic of the Jewish People Among the Nations* (New York: Random House, 1980), pp. 210–11. In 1897, nearly 5 million Jews lived in the 386,000 square miles of the Pale, which included portions of Lithuania, White Russia, Bessarabia, and the Ukraine. The years 1907 and 1908, when Gilda's parents arrived in the United States, were the height of Jewish immigration from czarist Russia.

4: red-diapered childhood: From Amy Swerdlow, "A Child of the Old, Old Left," *Red Diapers: Growing Up in the Communist Left*, Judy Kaplan and Linn Shapiro, eds. (Urbana: University of Illinois Press, 1998), p. 256.

4: Harlem: That part of Manhattan was once a stronghold of the Jewish community. During World War I, Harlem's Jewish population grew to 178,000. From David C. Gross, *The Jewish People's Almanac* (Garden City, N.Y.: Doubleday, 1981), pp. 50–51.

5   "painters have to drink": Interview with Esther Marcus.

5: parental figure and even a soulmate: Interviews with Steve Marcus and Anne Johnson.

5: "I feel the genes": Mary Campbell, "I Chased the Devil and Then I Made It," Associated Press, April 22, 1969.

5: probably Jewish: About 50 percent of the population in the Grand Concourse neighborhood was Jewish, according to Gary Hermalyn and Lloyd Ultan, "Bronx," *The Encyclopedia of New York City* (New Haven, CT: Yale University Press, 1995), pp. 142–146.

5: "kind of dirty . . . poverty and harmony": Harry Clein, "Laura Nyro: Rock Madonna of the Bronx," p. 20.

5: The numbers: Interview with Nyro by Scott Simon on *Weekend Edition*, National Public Radio, 1989.

6: One of its main tenets: From Felix Adler, "Eight Commitments of Ethical Culture."

6: boring and corrupt: Nyro, *Woman of Power*, p. 35.

6: "God is earth": Valentine.

6: "We learned about people": Watts.

6: opera (as did Grandpa): Sciaky.

6: loved . . . Ravel and Debussy: From the liner notes of *Stoned Soul Picnic* (Columbia/Legacy, C2K 48880, 1997).

6: dark songs of love and loss: Interview with Jan Nigro.

6: reading poetry: Flanagan.

6: an "Indian song": Watts.

7: "my first language": Greg Goth, "Laura Nyro: Solo, Soul to Soul," Gannett News Service, May 4, 1990.

7: "Laura and Elvis": Interview with Jan Nigro.

7: a figure revered: Interview with Jan Nigro.

8: "Laurie, I'm your mother": Watts.

8: a certain naivete: Interview with Laura's first cousin Estelle (Nigro) Meyer.

8: "My father was very protective": Clein, p. 21.

8: needed a breather: Interview with Esther Marcus.

8: "mystery modern" element: Moore, p. 124.

9: "sad little girl": The quote appears in Thomas, p. 74, and in her Columbia Records biography from 1969, where Thomas may have found it.

9: close herself into her room: Critique.

9: "I had friends . . .": Clein, p. 21.

9: "Creative Writing" notebook: Courtesy of David Bianchini.

10: preeminent summer resort: From Irwin Richman, Borscht Belt Bungalows: Memories of Catskill Summers (Philadelphia: Temple University Press, 1998), p. 4.

10: A typical bungalow colony: From Michael Strauss, "A Bungalow in the Hills," The New York Times, June 10, 1956, sec. XX, p. 9. Quoted in Richman, Borscht Belt Bungalows.

11: 'Never on Sunday': Theme from 1960 Jules Dassin film of that name, written by Manos Hadjidakis. It won the 1960 Academy Award for Best Song.

12: The music for Sing Night: E-mail from Laney Greenberg.

12: "her first masterpieces": Quotes about Sing Night and Color War from interview with Jan Nigro and from remarks he made at the Laura Nyro Memorial Concert, October 27, 1997.

2. TEENAGE PRIMAL HEARTBEAT

13: urban-based music: "The cornfields of Nebraska didn't give good echo," wrote Anthony J. Gribin and Matthew M. Schiff in Doo-Wop: The Forgotten Third of Rock 'n Roll (Iola, WI: Krause Publishing, 1992), p. 86.

13: "The Wind": Rock critic Dave Marsh ranked this record No. 67 in The Heart of Rock & Soul: The 1001 Greatest Singles Ever Made (New York: Da Capo Press, 1999).

13: "earthy, romantic music": Snyder.

13: the first two 45s: Pollock, p. 29.

13: neo doo-wop: From Barry Hansen, "Doo-Wop," The Rolling Stone Illustrated History of Rock & Roll, Jim Miller, ed. (New York: Random House, 1976).

13: "four guys and me": From Bob Shelton, liner notes for More Than a New Discovery.

13: "sitting at the top of the steps": Zollo.

14: girl-group music: Douglas, pp. 83–90.

14: "I Sold My Heart to the Junkman": The original recording was actually sung by the Starlets, but erroneously credited to the Blue Belles by an unscrupulous record executive. The actual Blue Belles then did a cover version of what was supposedly their own record. From LaBelle, p. 96, and David Nathan's liner notes to Golden Classics, Patti LaBelle and the Blue Belles (Collectibles, 1994). Nathan refers to Joel Whitburn's Top R&B Singles reference book.

15 "Envy": Cameo Records. The similar Nyro song is "Blowin' Away." Thanks to Gary Levine for pointing this out.

15 Jaynetts: Interview with Alan Merrill.

15 to Mayfield's records: Backman.

15 Joan Baez: Kaplan.

15 Billie Holiday . . . Sarah Vaughan: Pollock.

15: "the great mother-musician-teacher" . . ."Strange Fruit": Zollo, p. 42.

15: "dark woman" . . . "As a woman": Nyro, Woman of Power, p. 34.

15:   "he wasn't kidding me": Paley, p. 47.

15:   After the trumpeter died: *Rolling Stone*, November 14, 1991.

16:   "off the beaten track": Zollo.

16:   "the real language of life": Sciaky.

17:   zaftig: (Or zaftik). From Fred Kogos, *A Dictionary of Yiddish Slang and Idioms*. (New York: Castle Books, 1966), p. 87.

18:   music was . . . the language: Zollo.

18:   five-mile ride: Interview with Ed Ziegman.

18:   not the *Fame* school: The two separate schools became one organization in 1961, and in 1984 joined in a single facility behind Lincoln Center in Manhattan. It's now known as the Fiorello H. La Guardia High School of Music and Art and Performing Arts. The building that housed Music and Art in Harlem is now A. Philip Randolph High School.

18:   Laura . . . applied . . . as an art major: Interview with Louis Nigro.

18:   operatic singing: Watts.

19:   "I felt this thunderbolt": Pollock, p. 29.

20:   Toni Wine: She wrote the 1965 No. 1 hit by the Mindbenders, "A Groovy Kind of Love."

20:   "Society's Child": The record rose to No. 14 on *Billboard*'s Top 40 in June 1967, according to *Billboard's Book of Top 40 Hits*. Alan Merrill says that Nyro felt competitive with Ian after she scored her hit, saying, "If she can make it, so can I— I'm better than her!" Adds Merrill, "I think Janis Ian was good for Laura; that competition was just one of the many sparks that propelled her forward."

20:   three-week leave: Paley, and interview with Barbara Greenstein.

20:   "the type of hooky player": Albertson, p. 12.

20:   Gilda went to the principal's: Interviews with Louis Nigro and Esther Marcus.

20:   Laura refused to accept: Interview with Louis Nigro.

21:   a domestic: Clein, p. 21, and Albertson, p. 12.

21:   "Blindman's Bluff" . . . "Hi": Lyrics in Nyro's own hand. Thanks to David Bianchini.

21:   more as a songwriter: However, Elliott Randall says that although he has no independent memory of it, Helen Stokes recalled to him that Laura, Elliott, Helen, and her twin sister, Phyllis, went on an audition as singers at Roulette Records.

21:   "Stand Straight, Die Right": "Laura agonized at the last minute whether to end it "Die Right" or "Fly Right," says Alan Merrill. "She was afraid of the former title sounding negative, but that the word "fly" would be taken as a possible drug reference. The music biz was still pretty conservative in the mid-sixties."

22:   very daring: Albertson, p. 12.

22:   "simple melodies": Clein, p. 23.

22:   Trinity Music: From Dodd Darin with Maxine Paetro, *Dream Lovers: The Magnificent Shattered Lives of Bobby Darin and Sandra Dee by Their Son* (New York: Warner Books, 1994), pp. 189, 192.

22:   Darin was cute: Interview with David Geffen.

22:   *Stop the World*: The 1961 stage musical had recently been released in a film version. From www.allmusic.com.

22: "What Kind of Fool Are You": From Clein, p. 23, and interview with David Geffen. "I know it's a true story," says Geffen, "because I [later] knew Bobby Darin, and we laughed about it."

22: different names: Black, p. 122.

23: settled instead on Nyro: In the area of Italy where Laura's grandfather was raised the name Nigro would actually sound more like "nero," with the g aspirated and the r rolled. Told to Pat Rudden by Nyro's cousin Michelle Meyer.

3. MORE THAN A NEW DISCOVERY

24: Tin Pan Alley's: The Alley was both a sophisticated style of early twentieth-century pop music and the actual place (West 28th Street between Broadway and Sixth Avenue in Manhattan) where the city's music publishers were centered. Writer Monroe Rosenfeld gave it the name, likening the sound of composers plunking out tunes on their pianos to the sound of tin pans striking each other. From www.allmusic.com.

24: except as demos: Carole King's demos were so good that singers such as Dusty Springfield collected them.

24: Essra Mohawk: Although she emerged independently of Nyro's influence, the piano-playing Mohawk sounded more like her than any other woman of that era. She began recording as a fifteen-year-old, in 1964, and in 1970 released her most stunning album, the Nyro-esque *Primordial Lovers* (Reprise Records). Mohawk (born Sandy Hurvitz) even hung out briefly with Nyro and her manager David Geffen in Los Angeles in 1968 and thought she would be signed by Geffen (she was then under contract to Frank Zappa), but the deal was never made. Mohawk believes she was abandoned because she'd be competition for Nyro; Geffen says she was too difficult for him to want to work with her.

25: "She chose homeliness": Kathy Dobie, "Midnight Train: A Teenage Story," *Trouble Girls: The Rolling Stone Book of Women in Rock,* Barbara O'Dair, ed. (New York: Random House, 1997), p. 233.

25: Nyro listened to Simone: From stage patter by Nyro at Union Chapel, London, November 11, 1994. Nyro may have heard Simone's version of the song on the 1961 live album *Nina Simone at the Village Gate.*

25: be just a songwriter: By June 1966, Nyro had already copyrighted a number of songs, including several that she would never record: "Enough of You," "Moon Song," "Lady's Spell," and "Bossa Nova, Please" (listed as "Bossa Nova Baby" on BMI's list of Nyro compositions). She supplied only the lyrics for the latter (the music was by Murray Conwesser), which was copyrighted on October 21, 1965. (This information comes from research by Patricia Rudden at the copyright office in Washington, D.C.)

26: tape of that session: Courtesy of Stephen Paley. The tape was given to him in the 1970s, incorrectly identified as being from Nyro's audition for Mercury Records. Artie Mogull has identified it as the demo session he organized.

26: "The Moon Song": Title and lyrics from Nyro's own lyric sheet, c. 1966 (thanks to David Bianchini).

27: Dusty Springfield's: Nyro continued to admire Dusty's music throughout her life. In 1994, she would tell writer Richard Knight that her desert-island CDs would include music from Springfield, Van Morrison, John Coltrane, Billie Holiday, and Phoebe Snow (Knight transcript, June 18, 1994).

27: *Die Meistersinger:* Nyro's history contains two minor connections to the Wagner opera: Her great-uncle William Meyerowitz played an apprentice in the opera at the Metropolitan, and the prelude to the opera was played as entrance music for Nyro's high school graduation ceremony at Carnegie Hall.

29: 'Society's Child': It wasn't until Ian appeared with Leonard Bernstein on his 1966 television special about popular music that the song gained acceptance. From Jason Ankeny, www.allmusic.com.

30: mostly at Bell Sound: Some sessions were held at Mirror Sound and at A&R studio on Seventh Avenue. All according to Herb Bernstein.

32: she sounded bitter . . ."Just incredible fights": Albertson, p. 12.

33: "folk wisdom that teenagers have": Zollo.

34: four-year-old son: Interview with Che Johnson.

35: 'You're going to be a big star.': Thomas, p. 74.

36: stuffing herself into . . ."the most uptight bride": Albertson.

36: Verve's ad: *Cash Box,* February 25, 1967.

36: inane jokes: Albertson.

36: an "image maker": Thomas.

36: felt hellish: Thomas. David Geffen retold the aircraft carrier story on the *Critique* television show in 1969, describing the audience as "60,000 drunken sailors." To which host John Daly replied, "I'm an old retired naval officer, David— would you like to rephrase that? She was on an aircraft carrier, and, what, 60,000 nice young men?"

37: 84 male vocalists: In comparison, on the *Billboard* Hot 100 of June 9, 2001, the chart included 61 male vocalists and 35 females. (Thanks to Gary Levine for this and the following chart information.)

37: Miami: In *Billboard,* November 26, 1966, "Wedding Bell Blues" was reported as a "regional breakout" single in that city. The single had reached No. 19 on Miami's WQAM Fabulous 56 Survey for the week ending November 12. Those preparing the station's weekly surveys never figured out how to spell Laura Nyro's name, however, variously calling her Lord Myra, Lara Myro, and Lara Nyro.

37: No. 3: It reached that position in L.A. on the weekly survey of December 28, 1966, and No. 3 in San Diego on January 4, 1967. "Boss Radio" began at KGJ in 1965, programmed by the Bill Drake–Lester Chenault organization, then spread to other stations in California and across the country. From www.bossradioforever.com.

37: "Boss Jock": Author's recollection. Deejay Morgan obviously appreciated Nyro's talent: On a show he did October 18, 1968, he followed up the Fifth Dimension's version of the Nyro song "Sweet Blindness" by saying, "If Jimmy Webb [one of the other great songwriters of the day] and Laura Nyro ever got married and had a child, and that child wrote a song, that would probably be the last song ever written,'cause nobody else would ever want to touch it from there on out." (Thanks to Gary Levine for the sound check.)

37: The Blossoms . . . Darlene Love: The Blossoms were best known as the backup trio on the TV music show Shindig and for harmonizing behind Elvis Presley in concert. Love was Phil Spector's brilliant contract singer, whose powerful lead voice was heard on "Da Doo Ron Ron" and "He's a Rebel" as well as on solo efforts such as "Christmas (Baby Please Come Home)."

38: released in August 1966: www.allmusic.com.

4. MONTEREY AND GEFFEN

40: basement nightclub: From Joel Selvin, San Francisco: The Musical History Tour: A Guide to Over 200 of the Bay Area's Most Memorable Music Sites (San Francisco: Chronicle Books, 1996), pp. 30–31.

40: didn't mention an opening act: Herb Caen, San Francisco Chronicle, January 18, 1967, p. 27.

40: "truck salesmen" . . . wanted to do only concerts: Albertson, pp. 12–13.

41: The week that Nyro opened: Information on the other acts in town from San Francisco Chronicle. The Matrix was "the first hippie nightclub," according to Alice Echols, Scars of Sweet Paradise: The Life and Times of Janis Joplin (New York: Metropolitan Books, 1999), p. 115.

41: "San Francisco Sound": From liner notes, The Best of Laura Nyro: Stoned Soul Picnic.

41: In a caricature: From Louis Nigro's collection, seen by author.

42: Adler's personal pick: Interview with Lou Adler, and from interview with Adler by Robert Santelli, Goldmine, July 17, 1987, p. 72. For his personal selection, John Phillips chose The Group with No Name and festival governor Paul Simon chose a singer named Beverly whom he'd been working with.

42: "I'm Laura Nyro" . . . "flounced away": From Ellen Sander, Trips: Rock Life in the Sixties (New York: Scribner, 1973), p. 93.

42: off-one-shoulder creation: Alan Merrill says that Nyro was concerned about appearing overweight at Monterey, and one day at her family apartment in the Bronx sketched an idea for her and her backup singers to wear teepee dresses to hide under.

43: Chip Monck: From Bill Graham and Robert Greenfield, Bill Graham Presents: My Life Inside Rock and Roll (New York: Delta, 1992), p. 192.

43: she had been high: Black, p. 122.

43: "one of the more unusual acts": Photo caption, Teenset, October 1967, p. 40.

43: "dreadfully pretentious": Bartholomew E. Barry, Santa Cruz, California, "Letter to the Editor," The New York Times, November 16, 1997.

43: "seemed to try too hard": Ward et al.

43: "the disaster that was . . . Laura Nyro's": Unattributed review quoted in Barney Hoskins, The Sound of Los Angeles (New York: St. Martin's, 1996), p. 145.

43: Nyro characterized: Albertson, p. 13.

44: At least Michelle Phillips: From Michelle Phillips, California Dreamin': The True Story of the Mamas and the Papas (New York: Warner, 1986), p. 137.

44: "a crucifixion": Clein, p. 23.

44: "Lost Monterey Tapes": Pennebaker is eventually planning to release the Monterey material on DVD; see www.pennebakerhegedusfilms.com.

45: awkward stage patter: Kloman reported that one of the backup singers said, "Hello, all you guys out there." Nyro corrected, "There's chicks out there, too. Don't forget about them." "That's right, Laura," responded the singer. "Well, hello, guys and chicks."

45: "I learned from Monterey": Black.

45: "Up Up and Away": From Michael Tatsui's Tribute to the Fifth Dimension website, http://members.aol.com/laruemccoo/main.htm.

46: At Binder's urging . . . he was "mesmerized": Interview with David Geffen, and from Joe Smith, Off the Record: An Oral History of Popular Music (New York: Warner, 1988), p. 304.

46: twenty-four years old: Biographical information on Geffen from Goodman and from King.

46: "The human Rolodex": The interconnections between Geffen, Sander, and Holtzman include business (Holtzman put Geffen in charge of a merged Elektra/Asylum Records in 1973, according to Goodman, pp. 248–49), sex (Sander was the first woman Geffen says he slept with), and parenthood (Sander and Holtzman had a child together).

47: "a very strange girl": Paley.

47: "the biggest star": Robert Sam Anson, "David Geffen Talks a Little," Esquire, November 1982, p. 114.

47: "one interesting, unprotected place": Quoted in John Seabrook, "The Many Lives of David Geffen," The New Yorker, February 23 and March 2, 1998, p. 114.

49: "The strength of her writing": Davis, p. 98.

49: Nyro only laughed: Zollo, p. 25.

49: Nyro was signed: Davis, p. 97.

49: seventeenth-floor "penthouse" . . . "uptown downtown": Kloman, p. D32.

49: A step up in class: Description of apartment from Donald Boudreau.

50: "I wouldn't call it anything else . . .": Quote and recipe from Clein, p. 24.

5. ELI'S COMIN'

51: Soul Picnic: Verve/Forecast ad, GQ Scene, date unknown (probably late 1967). The ad is illustrated with drawings of Ian and Nyro, and the mock-poetic copy for Nyro reads: "Laura Nyro. Pronounce it 'Nero.' Pronounce her in a class by herself. Because Laura Nyro has declared her independence from the tried and trite with every gutsy note she sings. With every song. For Nyro writes her own. And her songs are 'something else.' Unlike anything else. Professional pigeonholers have described Laura Nyro as 'pop-blues-jazz-rock-soul with a dash-of-folk and a dollop-of-gospel.' Nonsense. Because Nyro is Nyro. A loner. An innovator. An unabashed original. Which is why we called her first album More Than a New Discovery FT/FTS-3020. Her second, just out, is a veritable Soul Picnic FT/FTS-3029."

52: innovative recording: Patricia Rudden points out that South African vocalist Miriam Makeba multitracked her own voice on one of her early 1960s albums.

53: Paul Griffin: The pianist had backed Bob Dylan on his first three rock albums, *Bringing It All Back Home, Highway 61 Revisited,* and *Blonde on Blonde.*

53: "Alice in Wonderland": Albertson, p. 13.

53: "Then he did a thing": ibid. Six years later, Phoebe Snow would use Sims on several tracks of her popular debut album *Phoebe Snow,* including her hit "Poetry Man."

55: "You get on a train": Interview with David Mizrahi, who grew up near the Nigros and played basketball on the same high school playground as did Jan Nigro.

55: life-altering "trip": Kloman, p. D32.

56: "love her or hate her" . . . exactly what that was: Ellen Sander, "Laura Nyro: Eli and the Thirteenth Confession," *Hit Parader,* October 1968, p. 20.

57: March 13, 1968: From liner notes, *The Best of Laura Nyro: Stoned Soul Picnic.*

57: "the parting chrysalis": Brian Van der Horst, *New York Free Press,* April 1968.

58: poetry she'd been reading: One might guess that Nyro read the work of the English Victorian poet who's considered a precursor of the Modernists, Gerard Manley Hopkins (1844–1889). Like Nyro, Hopkins delighted in colorful words, combining two words into one new one and emphasizing the seasons in his work. For example, in his poem "The May Magnificat," he included lines as lilting as Nyro's in "Stoned Soul Picnic": "Flesh and fleece, fur and feather / Grass and greenworld all together. . . . And azuring-over greybell makes / Wood banks and brakes wash wet like lakes / And magic cuckoocall / Caps, clears, and clinches all—" In another possible inspiration for Nyro, Hopkins wrote a poem called "Spring and Fall: To a Young Child," while Nyro later titled a song, "To a Child."

58: just beyond comprehension: Johnson, *Teenset,* p. 50.

59: "G chord with a C bass . . .": Calello further explains, "With a C bass, that should be a C-major 9 chord, but she eliminated playing the third of the chord [the middle note]. For example, a C-major 9 would be C, E, G, B, D. She would leave the E out, so you'd have C, G, B, D, which would be a G major chord with a C in the bass. She used to rotate chords like that, which was very unusual."

60: written about her cat: Author's recollection, from Nyro's stage patter, 1969.

60: Sondheim: Quoted in Kloman.

60: "the eternal feminine": Zollo, p. 25.

60: " 'someone else' ": Alan Merrill suggests Nyro might also have been inspired by a beautiful redheaded child at camp, Emmeline Diller. "Emmie Diller was breathtaking to look at, aesthetically perfect," says Merrill. "She was known to us as both Emily and Emmie. I think Laura was her counselor one summer."

61: "inexplicable rhythm changes": Maslin, p. 314.

61: "just finished with a man": Etchison.

61: "joyful": Despite her joyful feeling, Nyro wrote the song in a minor key. Says Patricia Rudden, "It's what they teach you about Jewish music—minor doesn't mean sad. Her cantorial genes are showing."

61: "scintillating shame": Romanowski, p. 138.

62: "The struggle in the city . . .": Kloman.

62: "less a woman yielding": Weller.

62: "my mother is going to know": Sander, *Hit Parader*.

62: "She Doesn't Explain Anything": April 27, 1968, p. 2.

62: finally reviewed the album: The lack of a review before that had prompted San Francisco musician Will Porter to send a Nyro-extolling letter to the magazine under the pseudonym Tom Wilson—which *Rolling Stone* coincidentally published in the same September issue.

62: No. 181: Whitburn, *Top Pop Albums*.

63: 125,000 copies: Saal, p. 68, reported that *Eli* had sold "some 125,000 copies" by mid-1969.

63: "The most played album": *EYE Electric Last Minute*, July 1968.

6. NEW YORK TENDABERRY

65: No. 3 on its pop chart: The record debuted on the *Billboard* charts on June 22, 1968.

65: 8,000 . . . to 17,000: Etchison.

65: At Davis's suggestion: Interview with Bones Howe.

66: No. 17: August 1, 1968. From charts collected by Gary Levine.

66: played once an hour: Etchison.

66: One of her friends: Robert Windeler, "Laura Nyro: New Queen of Contemporary Music," *Entertainment World*, December 19, 1969, p. 8. The person was only identified as Laura's "best friend."

66: "Laura Nyro is now the hippest": Kloman, p. D32.

67: *Kraft Music Hall*: Seen by author, Museum of TV and Radio archives.

67: Critique: Patricia Rudden remembers that the show was scheduled to be rebroadcast later that month but was preempted (at least in New York City) by a debate on the ABM treaty—ironic, considering how Nyro didn't want to "study war no more" in "Save the Country."

68: sought out romantic experience: Critique.

68: "Old Lady of the Year": Mentioned by Cameron Crowe in "The *Rolling Stone* Interview" with Mitchell, July 26, 1979.

68: Jim Fielder: Biographical information from bassplace.com newsgroup and from Martin Aston, "Tim Buckley: The High Flyer," *Mojo*, date unknown.

69: "screaming for joy": Ellen Sander, "Rehearsal with the New Blood, Sweat and Tears," *Hit Parader*, March 1969, p. 51.

70: In the songbook: *The Music of Laura Nyro* (New York: Warner Bros. Publications).

70: Nyro began to record . . . surrounded by ducks: Kloman, p. D32.

71: kissing a duck . . . different and stranger: Johnson, *Teenset*.

71: "my very wild time": Zollo.

71: Ashley Famous Agency: "Random Notes," *Rolling Stone*, September 28, 1968, p. 6.

71: someone to coproduce: On Columbia's CD re-release of *New York Tendaberry*, only Nyro is credited as the producer, but on the album's original credits the producers are listed as Laura and Roy Halee.

74:   "People were always frightened": Paley, p. 46.

74:   "When I record": Etchison.

74:   "She can wear them": Paley, p. 45.

75:   Gil Evans: Albertson, p. 13.

75:   "You can almost hear the crickets": ibid.

76:   "Indians on the warpath": Paley, p. 46.

76:   warm pale blue: Campbell, op. cit. Nyro also told Campbell she had written a song for *New York Tendaberry* called "When Good Men Go Bad," whose color was "a definite plum lavender." (Nyro never released a song of that title, however.)

76:   "It used to be embarrassing": In Timothy White, *Rock Lives: Profiles & Interviews* (Henry Holt, 1990, p. 336).

76:   "Nyro Fiddles": Published on the website www.lauranyro.net.

77:   "I can't play on this": Paley, pp. 46–47.

79:   she sported a callus: Etchison.

79:   "girlish giddiness": Jim Bessman, unpublished liner notes, 1997.

79:   "When I listen to it": Posting by Claire Johnson on Utne.com, Laura Nyro topic, January 27, 1999.

79:   "I tried to express": Gershwin speaking about his composition "Rhapsody in Blue" in an interview with Hyman Sandow, quoted in Edward Jablonski, *Gershwin: A Biography* (New York: Doubleday, 1987), p. 75.

80:   "jingoistic pabulum": Note to author from David Scott.

81:   "Goblin Market": I'm indebted to Nyro fan Susan Bouthillier for making this connection.

81:   *New York Tendaberry* was released: From liner credits, *The Best of Laura Nyro: Stoned Soul Picnic* (Columbia/Legacy, 1997).

81:   earlier design of the cover: Interview with Stephen Paley.

82:   "an event of major importance": Jim Bickhart, "The Notorious Ramblin' Bros. [column]," UCLA *Daily Bruin*, October 8, 1969, p. 9.

82:   "the singer who has done the most": Reed, pp. 86–87.

82:   "her best album yet": Johnson, *Coast FM & Fine Arts*, pp. 25–27.

82:   "At 22, Miss Nyro": Robert Hilburn, "Laura Nyro's Sound of the City," *Los Angeles Times*, date unknown.

82:   "Raw convulsive music": John Gabree, "Laura Nyro," BMI, November 1969, p. 17.

82:   "The elusive poetess": Don Heckman, "Nyro, Donovan, Zappa and More," *The New York Times*, November 9, 1969, p. 36.

82:   No. 32: Whitburn, *Top Pop Albums*.

7. TOP TEN

84:   Geffen had kept her away: Paley, p. 47.

84:   King Curtis: E-mail correspondence with Stephen Paley.

84: James Taylor: Interview with Lee Housekeeper, who also supplied perfor-
    mance dates and sites.

85: "underground" stereo FM radio: Discussion of the phenomenon from Michael
    C. Keith, *Voices in the Purple Haze: Underground Radio and the Sixties* (Westport, Conn.:
    Praeger, 1997), pp. 7, 19–20, 23, 27, 29–30, 33, 35.

86: "Columbia Is Underground": The other artists listed in the ad were Blood,
    Sweat and Tears, Michael Bloomfield, the Byrds, the Chambers Brothers, Leon-
    ard Cohen, Bob Dylan, the Electric Flag, Tim Hardin, Janis Joplin, Al Kooper,
    Taj Mahal, Moby Grape, Simon and Garfunkel, Spirit, Switched-on Bach, and
    Johnny Winter.

86: Even Clive Davis admitted: Davis, pp. 106–7.

86: *Teen Set:* "Rock Is a Bore (Yawn)," February 1969.

87: "She smiled silently": Reed, p. 87.

87: "indescribably powerful performer": Pete Johnson, "Laura Nyro at Trouba-
    dour," *Los Angeles Times*, May 31, 1969, pt. II, p. 6.

88: Woodstock: From "Head Staff of Woodstock Fair," *Billboard*, first week of June,
    1969.

88: sold out in a day: From Vince Aletti, "Laura Nyro: Every Number an Encore,"
    Rolling Stone, January 21, 1970, p. 14. The shows were at 8:30 P.M. and at
    midnight (according to the original program).

88: "Bravissima, Lauriska!" Cypress Records press kit, 1989.

88: "Elizabeth Taylor dress": Aletti, op. cit.

88: Russian seamstress: Interview with Barbara Greenstein.

88: the simple gesture: Also described by Don Heckman, "Riffs," *Village Voice*,
    December 4, 1969, p. 47.

88: "gentle as a razor": Nancy Erlich, *Billboard*, December 13, 1969.

88: soulful one-on-one interactions: Interview with Anne Johnson.

88: "Where I live . . .": From notes taken by Patricia Rudden at concert, and from
    Heckman, op. cit.

89: "breathless attention" . . . "rugged support": John S. Wilson, "Laura Nyro
    Comes to the Fore with Two Concerts at Carnegie," *The New York Times*, De-
    cember 1, 1969.

89: "unremittingly intense": Heckman, op. cit., p. 47. This review drew the wrath
    of one "Mannaggia Sia Fatta" of the Bronx in a December 18, 1969, letter to
    editor: "Let me be the first to congratulate *The Voice* on its policies regarding
    hiring the handicapped. It was a rare delight to see a major New York news-
    paper run a review of Laura Nyro's Carnegie Hall concerts by a man who is
    apparently both blind and deaf." Probably a pseudonym of either a friend or
    die-hard fan of Nyro's, Sia Fatta sent a series of similarly scathing letters (see
    page 295) over the next few years.

89: Songwriter Julie Gold: Bessman.

90: "primordial sense": Weller.

90: "we were pals": Stephen Williams, "Nyro, Ten Years Later," *Newsday*, July 11,
    1988, part II, p. 7.

90: "the first secret of girl music": John Anning, Laura Nyro chat room,
    www.utne.com, entry No. 1224.

90: "Nothing beat Laura": Tom Kuennen, guest book, www.lauranyro.net, March 16, 2000.

91: "a possessed woman": Allan Ripp, "The Great Sex Appeal Debate—A Man's View," *Your Place*, December 1978, p. 28.

91: *The Gay Metropolis*: New York: Houghton Mifflin, 1997, p. 196.

91: "could make you cry": Quoted in Bessman.

91: "in my queer life": Chuck Hayse, guest book, www.lauranyro.net, February 7, 2000.

92: *Three Dog Nightmare*: As told to Chris Blatchford (Los Angeles: Renaissance Books, 1999), p. 100.

93: 'come-and-see-me': ibid.

93: "Great album; no hits.": Interview with Bobby Columby.

93: went to No. 2: *Billboard* charts, October 25, 1969.

93: Sammy Davis Jr.'s later cover: Bobby Columby remembers the Davis cover with much amusement: "At the end of that album, he says, 'Thanks, Blood Sweat and Tears. Thanks, cats!' That whole album is Blood, Sweat and Tears songs. He was such a fan of the band that he did an entire album of our songs. Except it hurt us, because the more he said the band was good, the more uncool we sounded because he liked it!" Davis even insisted on introducing the band when they played the Hollywood Bowl. "I thought, Oh God, here's the guy who just hugged Nixon," says Columby. "We all loved and respected the guy, but we didn't want to be connected. But the next thing we know, he runs out onstage: 'Hey, everybody, here come the cats, my favorite band! Come on out— Jimmy Fielder, Bobby Columby' . . . It was a nightmare. The audience saw that connection, and right away we were a Vegas act."

93: longer and more baroque: This version of "And When I Die" appears on the album *Live and Improvised* (Columbia/Legacy 46918, 1991). It may originally have been released as *In Concert* in the Netherlands and Japan in 1976, according to William Ruhlmann, www.allmusic.com.

94: No. 13-charting: *Billboard*, October 26, 1968.

94: "Her melodies opened up": Quoted in Jim Bessman, *Billboard*, 1997.

94: "the most benign": From Lesley Gore interview with Dawn Eden accompanying *It's My Party* (Bear Family, 1994), a five-CD set of Gore's recordings on Mercury Records.

94: Despite a favorable review: From essay by Fred Bronson accompanying *It's My Party: The Mercury Anthology* (Mercury 532517, 1996), a two-CD compilation of Lesley Gore's recordings.

95: "basically a demo": ibid. Gore's birthdate from www.allmusic.com.

96: "If anyone does a song of mine": Wickham, p. 6.

96: great thrills of her life: Black.

96: room for different interpretations: Snyder.

96: "ice cream soda": Sciaky.

96: Tuna Fish: *Billboard*, December 26, 1970, p. T-28.

96: "Attention Fifth Dimension": Allee Willis, who would later gain success as a songwriter herself ("Boogie Wonderland" by Earth, Wind and Fire; "Stir It Up" by Patti LaBelle; "What Have I Done to Deserve This" by the Pet Shop

Boys and Dusty Springfield; the "Friends" theme), wrote this copy, along with other ads for Nyro, Barbra Streisand, and Janis Joplin.

8. SINGER-SONGWRITER

97: "one of the hottest songwriters": Front cover, *Cash Box*, December 13, 1969.
97: singer-songwriters emerged: Iain Chambers, *Urban Rhythms: Pop Music and Popular Culture* (New York: St. Martin's, 1985), p. 121.
97: "change under pressure": Maslin, p. 312.
97: "into the pop forefront": Ward et al.
98: "voyages of self-discovery": Saal, p. 68.
98: "In a male performer": Robert Christgau, *Any Old Way You Choose It* (New York: Penguin, 1973), p. 217.
99: "inside a Gauguin": Cypress Records press kit, 1989, from an interview with Maria Desiderio.
99: "anything goes": Kaplan.
99: classic tunes Nyro had loved: "I loved Carole King's songs," Nyro told Paul Zollo.
99: "Nyro's Nook": From "Weasel and the White Boys Cool" on *Rickie Lee Jones* (Warner Bros. Records BSK 3296, 1979).
100: "marking out the competition": William Ruhlmann, allmusic.com.
100: "à la Laura Nyro": From a letter posted by Schwartz, December 29, 1998, on www.stephenschwartz.com. Actually, the instruction mistakenly read, to Schwartz's embarrassment as he noted in his letter, "à la Laura Lyros."
100: Kenny Rankin: Posting in guestbook on www.lauranyro.net, January 6, 2000. Rankin also spoke fondly of Nyro when he performed at her Memorial Concert on October 27, 1997.
101: some of his early recordings: Andrew Rogers, who ran a now-defunct Nyro website, also pointed out the Nyro influence on Rundgren in two songs from the album *Nazz III* (recorded in 1968 but not released until 1971), "Only One Winner" and "Old Time Lovemaking."
101: "Baby Let's Swing": Two versions of the *Runt* album were released. On one, "Baby Let's Swing" was part of a medley and half the length. The entire song appeared on the other version of the album.
101: Rundgren has said: From transcript of telephone interview by Swedish journalist Dan Backman; from Paul Lester, *Uncut*, issue unknown, and from transcript of interview with John Sty in 2001.
101: Billy Childs: From Alwyn and Laurie Lewis, "Billy Childs Interview," *Cadence*, June 1997.
101: all-time favorite songwriter: Paul Zollo, "Inside Jazz with Billy Childs," *SongTalk*, vol. 4, issue 2, 1994, p. 30.
102: "On account of her": Interview with Mitchell by Dave DiMartino, *Mojo*, August 1998, p. 84.
102: "I love what you do": Interview with Stephen Paley. This party is also recounted in Davis, p. 89. He wrote that Nyro giggled and could barely talk, leaving Dylan, for once, to keep the conversation going practically by himself.

102: Geffen moved to California: King, p. 111.

103: "Stay with Me Baby": Ellison famously recorded the song with a full orchestra intended for Frank Sinatra, who became ill before his session. From *Beg Scream & Shout! The Big Ol' Box of '60s Soul* (Rhino R2 72815, 1997).

103: "a big love fest": Paley also produced some album tracks for Ellison in Muscle Shoals and had wanted to include Nyro's "Brown Earth." "But the sessions were disastrous," he says. "To add to my problems, Lorraine couldn't sing to a track; she only does well when she sings with live musicians. But I found this out too late. We never did get to do 'Brown Earth.' "

104: Clive Davis also noticed: Davis, pp. 85–86.

104: "Janis is neither Billie Holiday": "Random Notes," *Rolling Stone*, September 14, 1968, p. 8.

104: "I understand I'm not Aretha": "Random Notes," *Rolling Stone*, September 28, 1968, p. 6.

104: Nyro may have been sensitive: Davis, p. 89. When *Rolling Stone* mentioned the party in its "Random Notes" section (February 2, 1970, p. 4), it reported rather bitchily, "The new showbiz crowd was represented by Laura Nyro (wearing the same white prom dress she had on for her Carnegie Hall concert)."

105: "Even her detractors": Ralph J. Gleason, "Laura's Got Them Writhing," *Rolling Stone*, April 16, 1970, p. 20. A similar version of this review appeared in the *San Francisco Chronicle*, January 26, 1970, p. 40. Gleason inaccurately referred to Nyro as "the Manhattan Latin" in his *Rolling Stone* review, although not in the *Chronicle* version, which suggests that the change may have been made by editors. In any case, the reference once again drew the wrath of "Mannaggia Sia Fatta" of the Bronx. "She happens to be, in point of fact, a Bronx Italian, which is good enough," Sia Fatta wrote in a letter to the editor of *Rolling Stone* (June 25, 1970, p. 3). "By the way, since he seems to have such difficulty distinguishes [sic] tones in music that he disagrees with every other listener about the astonishing exactness of Miss Nyro's sense of pitch, the Bronx chapter of the Nun Scurda Sicilia (Never Forget Sicily) League hereby offers to send him, free of charge, the hearing aid of his choice."

105: "exercise in excellence": Robert Hilburn, "Laura Nyro in Concert at UCLA," *Los Angeles Times*, January 19, 1970.

105: Michael Cuscuna of *Down Beat*: Concert review, July 24, 1969. Sharing the bill with Nyro was Tim Hardin, whom Cuscuna also praised for his jazz singing. But the reviewer judged Hardin's stumbling, seemingly drunken/stoned performance a disgrace. "Fortunately, no one was cheated, thanks to the genius of Miss Nyro," said Cuscuna. "It seems a shame that Hardin had to interrupt the lovely communication between Miss Nyro and the audience by his appearance." About ten years later, when Alan Merrill saw Hardin in London, Hardin asked him to tell Nyro, "Hi from your asshole buddy. She'll know what I mean." He may or may not have been referring to this debacle.

106: "a goddess": Interview with Richard Denaro.

106: top campus attractions: The rest of the Top 10 were: 3) Judy Collins; 4) Joni Mitchell; 5) Joan Baez; 6) Aretha Franklin; 7) Dionne Warwick; 8) Vicki Carr;

9) Mary Hopkin; and 10) Nina Simone. The No. 1 group was Blood, Sweat and Tears (besting the Beatles), and No. 1 male vocalist was Bob Dylan.

106: hug or a friendly kiss: Reports of various Nyro fans.

9. BEADS OF SWEAT

108: nearly $2 million: From website of photographer Rod Watson, http://home.neo.rr.com/rodsphotogallery/CityLife/NewYork/HTML/Beresford.html.

108: Devil Dogs . . . sparsely furnished: Interview with Kay Crow.

109: large harp: Nyro, who never put in the time to learn the difficult instrument, would later give the $20,000 harp as a present to her friend Ellen Uryevick, and Uryevick soon became a professional harpist.

109: cat had fallen: This was Cho Cho San, a cat she had brought back with her from Japan who liked to chase pigeons around the terrace. From interview with David Bianchini, who performed the burial.

109: "resculpturing" . . . "lifeline": Albertson, pp. 13, 33.

109: "write for a market": ibid., p. 33.

110: in his mid-fifties: Satchidananda was born in 1914. From Sita Bordow and others, *Sri Swami Satchidananda: Apostle of Peace* (Yogaville, VA: Integral Yoga Publications, 1986), p. 5.

110: "An easeful body . . .": Interview with Integral Yoga instructor and Nyro fan Susan Bouthillier.

110: "I mistook her for an Indian girl": E-mail correspondence from Swami Satchidananda, 1999.

113: as high as No. 30: *Billboard*, October 24, 1970.

114: *sul ponticello*: Don Michael Randel, *The New Harvard Dictionary of Music* (Cambridge: The Belknap Press of Harvard University Press, 1986), p. 106.

115: the drag was Dallas Taylor: Interviews with Ellen Sander, Lee Housekeeper.

115: while she was recording *New York Tendaberry*: In Wilson, he describes her talking on the phone with "Dallas—could be the city, a guy, or a gal . . ."

115: taking the same limo: Dallas Taylor, *Prisoner of Woodstock* (New York: Thunder's Mouth Press, 1994), p. 52.

115: Taylor remembered Nyro fondly: ibid.

116: "general sarcasm.": Overheard by Dan Nigro and Patricia Rudden.

117: read as a poem: Fillmore East, New York City, June 17–20, 1970.

117: "time and indifference": MacDonald, p. 34.

117: *Record World*: December 12, 1970, p. 24.

118: "I hate Laura Nyro": Ed Ward, *Rolling Stone*, November 26, 1970.

118: Alec Dubro: *Rolling Stone*, February 18, 1971, p. 49.

118: *Melody Maker*: February 6, 1971.

118: "You want to proselytize": Robb Baker, "Christmas and the Beads of Sweat," *Rock*, February 15, 1971.

118: fourteen weeks: Whitburn, *Top Pop Albums*.

119: "Songs for every day": Full-page ad in *Billboard* for the single, "When I Was a Freeport and You Were the Main Drag," January 16, 1971.

119: "I believe there is a world": Valentine.

119: *The Music of Laura Nyro*: The book has no copyright date, but the publishing date can be extrapolated from "WB Print Deal on Nyro, CSN&Y," *Cash Box*, May 29, 1971, which stated that Warner Bros. had scheduled a rush release for its *Laura Nyro Songbook*. David Geffen and his management partner Elliot Roberts sold to Warner the print rights not only to Nyro's publishing catalog but to the catalogs of their other famous clients: David Crosby, Stephen Stills, Graham Nash, and Neil Young.

120: lighting for Bette Midler: From George Mair, *Bette: An Intimate Biography of Bette Midler* (New York: Birch Lane Press, 1995).

120: also a filmmaker: In 1974, Peter Dallas directed drag performer Holly Wood-lawn, star of Andy Warhol's 1970 film *Trash*, in a grainy, black-and-white, pseudo-silent-era short called *Broken Goddess*. Woodlawn plays a lovelorn young woman wandering in Central Park, her feelings defined onscreen by Nyro's lyrics, which appear as subtitles. Woodlawn reputedly has the only copy. Dallas died of AIDS in the early 1990s.

10. GONNA TAKE A MIRACLE

121: a box of red roses: Vince Aletti, "Red Roses from Laura for Miles," *Rolling Stone*, April 16, 1970, p. 20.

121: a more youthful audience: Miles Davis with Quincy Troupe, *Miles: The Autobi-ography* (New York: Touchstone, 1989), p. 301. Graham had first booked Davis on a bill with the Grateful Dead at his Fillmore West theater in San Francisco.

121: tattered elegance: Fillmore East description and performance dates from Ama-lie Rothschild with Ruth Ellen Gruber, *Live at the Fillmore East: A Photographic Memoir* (New York: Thunder's Mouth Press, 1999), pp. 9, 141–150.

121: Miles Davis Quintet: The seven-member "quintet" consisted of Davis, Keith Jarrett and Chick Corea on piano, Jack DeJohnette on drums, Airto Moriera on percussion, Dave Holland on bass, and Steve Grossman on saxophone.

121: "a very quiet person . . .": Miles Davis, op. cit., p. 302.

121: standing ovation and three encores: Bob Glassenberg, *Billboard*, July 4, 1970.

122: "must have marveled": Robert Hilburn, "Laura Nyro Sings," *Los Angeles Times*, date unknown.

122: Nico: Besides providing her with material and musical accompaniment, Browne had an affair with her in New York.

122: Browne had sent a letter: Rich Wiseman, *Jackson Browne: The Story of a Hold Out* (New York: Dolphin Books, 1982), p. 61.

122: visited Merrill in Japan: Merrill says Nyro wrote a song called "Northeast Northwest" inspired by that trip and the "jet age world link-up." He remem-bers it as a guitar-based composition in A-minor, with a strange guitar tuning he thinks she got from David Crosby. Nyro never recorded it, however.

123: "Mother Earth": Heard on bootleg tape.

123: played the Fillmore East: December 22–24.

123: kissed on the lips: In Mary DeTeresa, "Nyro Smiles," *Crawdaddy*, May 1976, p. 69. Nyro was reported at concert's end as "collapsing onto Jackson

Browne's shoulder" after receiving a standing ovation, then being led off the stage by him.

123: *Down Beat's* reviewer: Joe H. Klee, "Laura Nyro," date unknown, p. 32.

123: "new realm of excitement": Dave Finkle, "Love and Laura Nyro," *Record World*, January 2, 1971, p. 20.

123: "leaned back ecstatically": Richard Williams, *Melody Maker*, February 13, 1971.

124: "Love is the whole thing": M. J. Wilson, "Laura Nyro Made U-Turn on One-Way Street," *The Rockland County Journal-News* (Nyack, New York), March 7, 1970, p. 12. Since the author is affiliated with Newsweek Feature Service, the quotes are probably outtakes from Saal.

124: concert for the BBC: Richard Williams, "Lady Laura," *Melody Maker*, May 18, 1971, p. 9.

124: well-known soul ballads: "Natural Woman" was written by Gerry Goffin and Carole King, "Ain't Nothing Like the Real Thing" by Nick Ashford and Valerie Simpson.

125: "an institution": *A Tribute to the Fillmore*, December 1971, p. 60.

125: "a real lovefest": Rothschild, op. cit., p. 121.

125: "a dramatic flair": Windeler, p. 8.

125: Westbury Music Fair: April 16, 1970.

125: "rather than levitate": Ian Dove, "Jeremy Storch, Laura Nyro," *Billboard*, date unknown.

125: "you have to be his mother . . .": Heard on bootleg tape.

126: Streisand had been the bestselling: Davis, pp. 218–19.

126: "Naturally, he was dying": ibid., p. 220.

126: Geffen had a hand: King, p. 136.

126: crossover bridge: Another bridge existed between Nyro's and Streisand's music: Nyro's old friend Toni Wine, who had sung backup on Nyro's first album, also sang backup on Streisand's version of Nyro's songs. From Shaun Considine, *Barbra Streisand: The Woman, the Myth, the Music* (New York: Delacorte Press, 1985).

127: Peggy Lipton: Her album *Peggy Lipton* (Ode Records Z12-44006) also included Nyro's "Hands off the Man (Flim Flam Man)," and she then released a single of Nyro's "Lu."

127: " 'today' material": *Billboard*, date unknown.

127: peaking at No. 6: Whitburn, p. 406.

127: *Brown Earth*: It was first performed at Toronto's O'Keefe Centre (now the Hummingbird Centre) on April 21, 1971. Thanks to Sharon Vanderlinde, manager of education, publications, and archives, National Ballet of Canada.

127: a woman's journey: Valerie Gladstone, "The Long Shadow of Ailey's Great 'Cry,' " *The New York Times*, November 26, 2000. The ballet, which premiered at Manhattan's City Center, was written by Ailey as a birthday present for his mother.

128: *Nilsson Sings Newman*: RCA LSP-4289.

128: also known to perform: All heard in concert by the author.

128: bent them to her will: Williams, op. cit.

128: "the best record collection": Lenny Kaye, *Rolling Stone*, January 20, 1972, p. 49.

128: "revisit the place": MacDonald.

129: Nyro had been planning: Conversation between Nyro and the author after Music Center concert, December 17, 1970.

129: Patti LaBelle and the Blue Belles: They had originally been a quartet, until Cindy Birdsong left to join the Supremes after that group's Florence Ballard departed.

130: Bellvue Stratford: Vicki Wickham, "Laura Nyro: Working with Labelle," Hit Parader, October 1972, p. 14.

131: bet Leon Huff a thousand dollars: LaBelle, p. 157.

131: Not everything they recorded: "Random Notes," Rolling Stone, September 2, 1971.

132: recorded by "such notables": From the Carole King album The Carnegie Hall Concert, June 18, 1971 (Ode/Epic/Legacy EK 64942, 1996). After her remark about Nyro was met by applause, King added, "A fine lady if there ever was one," drawing even a louder ovation from the New York City audience.

133: "men can be roses too": Vince Aletti, review of Gonna Take a Miracle, Creem, March 1972, p. 55.

133: "as good as anything I've heard": ibid., pp. 19, 55.

133: took on a fresh sheen: Penny Valentine, "Nyro, in Reverse," Sounds, January 1, 1972.

133: "succeeds even through its disappointments": Lenny Kaye, Rolling Stone, January 20, 1972, p. 49. A few weeks later (February 17), in another missive from "Mannaggia Sia Fatta," Kaye was taken to task for saying Nyro's record collection was the best on Central Park West. "Miss Nyro's new record is more like East 172nd St. between the Concourse and Sheridan—strictly the Bronx— where she rehearsed most of it eight years ago," wrote "Sia Fatta," adding, "Miss Nyro does the Bronx real proud, see, and this Lenny Kaye should not be allowed to detract (even though he did say mostly nice things). We of Nun Scurda Sicilia would hate to have to detract from him."

133: graded the album: Robert Christgau, Christgau's Record Guide: Rock Albums of the Seventies (New Haven and New York: Ticknor & Fields, 1981), p. 284.

134: "too mannered": Aletti, Creem, p. 55.

134: No. 46: Whitburn, Top Pop Albums.

134: Soul LPs: Billboard, January 22, 1972, p. 48.

134: reached No. 103: Whitburn. It spent three weeks on the charts.

134: Record World: Gary Levine, an East Coast deejay, points out that Record World's charts gave heavy weighting to sales performance in New York, while Billboard was more reflective of the entire country. He remembers that when the album came out, New York City record stores such as the Record Hunter, Colony Records, and Sam Goody had stacks of Miracle on the floor. "You could literally see the piles diminishing in size while you shopped," says Levine. "I recall walking down 42nd Street on a raw, windy Sunday and spotting at least fifty of the new Nyro LP covers arranged in a big hexagon in the window of the King Karol record store."

134: "a husband like Armstead": LaBelle, p. 158.

135: "Zuri's nanny" . . . "what friends are for": ibid., p. 166.

135: "The Bells": Personal recollection of Nyro fan Diane Tavaglini.

135: "To be honest": John Duka, *Interview*, April 1986, p. 196. LaBelle continued to stay connected to Nyro, at least in the press. In 1990, when she played at City Center in Manhattan, *Newsday* reported that she entertained her friends backstage in "a silk kimono given to her by Laura Nyro" (March 15, 1990, pt. II, p. 2).

11. MARRIAGE—AND A DIVORCE

136: "three lovely girlfriends": Wickham, *Hit Parader*, p. 15.

136: "The temperature rose": Vicki Wickham, "America: From Vicki Wickham in New York," *Melody Maker*, January 8, 1972, p. 6.

136: "simply the most beautiful": Mitchell Fink, "Laura Nyro the Finest," *Record World*, January 8, 1972, p. 22.

136: thunderstorm: Wickham, *Hit Parader*, pp. 14–15.

137: "too delicate to survive St. Louis": Dick Saunders, *Chicago Sun-Times*, March 20, 1972.

141: also a follower of Swami: Amie Hill, "Peter Max and the Simple Curve," *Rolling Stone*, April 16, 1970.

141: "They were terrible": Author's recollection of conversation with Travis Jergen, the booker at the Troubadour nightclub, who knew both Nyro and Crow.

142: "I never felt so much love": Wickham.

143: "When I work": Rockwell, *Rolling Stone*.

143: "[Women] sing their fuckin' insides": From David Dalton, *Janis* (New York: Simon and Schuster, 1971), p. 80.

144: "living inside a hurricane": Pollock.

145: Popeye-like character: Interview with Alan Merrill. Merrill named his publishing company Tugboat Music in honor of Captain Frank.

145: made perfect sense: Davis, p. 100.

145: a shrewd one for David Geffen: I'm indebted to Goodman, pp. 127–129, for his analysis of this transaction.

146: Joni Mitchell had reportedly: Saal, p. 68.

146: Dionne Warwick: Davis, pp. 100–101.

146: Davis would pay: *Rolling Stone* reported: "Random Notes," *Rolling Stone*, January 20, 1972 (Diamond and Grand Funk), October 26, 1972 (Sly Stone), both p. 4.

146: None of her previous three albums: "Random Notes," *Rolling Stone*, November 25, 1971, p. 4.

146: getting a bargain: Davis, p. 101.

147: "either Phoenix or Benchmark": "Random Notes," *Rolling Stone*, June 24, 1971, p. 4.

147: "for David Geffen": "Random Notes," *Rolling Stone*, September 2, 1971.

147: now called Asylum Records: "Random Notes," *Rolling Stone*, September 16, 1971, p. 4.

147: an unexpected letter: Davis, p. 102.

149: "complained bitterly": ibid.

149: an adjustment in return: ibid., p. 101.

149: The final deal: "Random Notes," *Rolling Stone*, November 25, 1971, p. 4. Geffen's receipt for 37,500 shares of Columbia stock in return for "shares of capital stock of Tuna Fish Music, Inc." was dated October 22, 1971.

149: vehemently distrusted: Interview with Lee Housekeeper.

151: they had casually talked: Watts.

151: $7 million: Goodman, pp. 240–41.

151: half a billion dollars: Goodman, pp. 370–71; King, p. 455.

12. SMILE

152: New Orleans for a concert: Barbara Greenstein was also visiting Laura in New Orleans when Midler was in town, and she recalls seeing Barry Manilow—then Midler's accompanist—open up the second half of Midler's concert with a few songs of his own. He pointed out that one song was influenced by Chopin, then added, "Next to Laura Nyro, Chopin is my favorite composer."

153: "not very territorial": Rockwell, *Rolling Stone*, p. 15.

153: high ceilings: Description of the Riverside Drive apartment from Patty Di Lauria.

154: students had lived: E-mail correspondence from Swami Satchidananda, 1999.

154: maverick: From Jan Swafford, *Charles Ives: A Life with Music*, section of book published in *Washington Post*, 1996.

154: "uniquely American": Nancy Sudik, "Charles Ives—Danbury's Most Famous Composer," www.housatonic.org/ives.html.

154: compared her "innocence": Moore.

154: According to court papers: "Nyro Sues to Keep from Hubby," *New York Post*, February 26, 1977, p. 9.

155: "utter desertion": "Random Notes," *Rolling Stone*, July 1, 1976, p. 22.

155: caught cultivating . . . post-traumatic stress: From interview with Bianchini, and from *United States v. David Bianchini*, Crim. Case No. 90-18-01, and Toni Locy, "Metro Marijuana Flourished in Vt. Barns, Police Say," *Boston Globe*, February 16, 1990, p. 66.

156: "Nyro's music reflects": From "Hits and Misses" column, *Los Angeles Times*, 1973, exact date unknown.

156: "12 songs have ambience": Myles Palmer, review of *The First Songs*, source unknown.

156: No. 97: Whitburn, *Top Pop Albums*.

156: *Billboard*'s Pop Picks: 1973, exact date unknown.

156: premature encomium: MacDonald, pp. 32–33.

157: "Anticipation" . . . "You're So Vain": From, respectively, the albums *Anticipation* (Elektra EKS-75016) and *No Secrets* (Elektra 75049).

158: "I realize now": Moore, p. 124.

158: "into feminism": Georgia Christgau, "Does the Women's Movement Have a Sense of Rhythm?" *Ms.*, December 1975, p. 39.

158: "People should be encouraged": Rockwell, *Rolling Stone*.

158: "quiet, lithe man": Watts.

159: other close friends: Interviews with Ann Johnson, Nydia Mata.

159: Some of Nyro's songs: A press release from CBS a month before the album came out also listed "Haven't I Had Enough of You"—one of the tunes Nyro had demo'd in 1966—as being on the album, but it failed to appear.

159: "I Am the Blues": Both Alan Merrill and Kay Crow remember hearing Nyro working on that composition in the early 1970s.

159: "slower rhythm" . . . "windflights": Rockwell, *Rolling Stone*.

159: she had simply met him again: ibid.

159: a casual phone conversation: Watts.

160: bluesy, slick sound: Interview with Charlie Calello.

161: jazz rock . . . fusion jazz: Definitions in www.allmusic.com.

161: Hardin . . . incorporating jazz players: Interview with Michael Maineri, who played with Hardin in the 1960s as part of the band Jeremy Steig and the Satyrs.

162: laetrile: Information on laetrile from Barrie Cassileth, "Laetrile by Any Other Name Is Still Bogus," *Los Angeles Times*, January 1, 2001, p. S1.

162: Di Lauria's casual images: The larger photo on the album cover is out of focus, which Di Lauria says Nyro insisted upon using over her objections.

162: "I could've broken": Watts.

162: titled for its concluding track: So, too, had been *New York Tendaberry* and *Gonna Take a Miracle*, while *Eli and the Thirteenth Confession* and *Christmas and the Beads of Sweat* had used the last-track titles as part of the albums' names.

163: Harry Ray, Al Goodman: Ray and Goodman, along with Billy Brown, later formed the trio Ray Goodman and Brown, known for the 1978 hit "Special Lady."

163: Sylvia Robinson: It has often been misreported that Smokey Robinson wrote the song. Sylvia Robinson was the distaff half of the duo Mickey and Sylvia ("Love Is Strange"), later recorded the provocative "Pillow Talk" as a solo artist, and went on to found one of the first rap labels, Sugarhill Records.

163: Hong Kong: Interviews with David Bianchini and Barbara Greenstein.

163: "cylinder rhythms": Rockwell, *Rolling Stone*.

163: "glowing but not flaming": Moore.

164: postcard more than an album: Janet Maslin, "Laura Nyro's Restrained Return," *New York Times*, April 2, 1976, pp. 66–67.

164: "collective autobiography": James Wolcott, album review, *Creem*, July 1976, p. 66.

165: Dave Marsh in *Rolling Stone*: May 6, 1976, p. 62. Astonishingly, Marsh also chided Nyro for a lack of range and emotional timbre, calling Nyro's voice the least diverse in popular music except for Joni Mitchell's, which he felt it resembled in its "enervating sameness."

165: "but phantasms": Charles Shaar Murray, "Nyro, My God, to Thee," *New Musical Express*, March 20, 1976, p. 2.

165: finally showed optimism: Penny Valentine, "A Rose in Nyro's Harlem," *Street Life*, April 3–16, 1976.

165: as strong as ever . . . "paved the way for her": Rockwell, *Rolling Stone*.

165: played widely: *Cash Box*, "FM Analysis," March 6, 13, and 20, 1976, pp. 24, 24, 26.

165: No. 60: *Joel Whitburn's Top Pop Albums 1955–1992* (Menomonee Falls, WI: Record Research, 1993).

166: "I'd rather be crucified": Cameron Crowe, "The *Rolling Stone* Interview," July 26, 1979.

13. SEASON OF LIGHTS

167: "bonhomie": Watts.

167: *The Making of Superstars*: Publishing information unknown.

168: "He has a good heart": Watts.

168: "I want her out there": ibid.

168: "She's probably the sweetest": *The Making of Superstars*, p. 196.

168: "I say what's really important": Wickham, p. 6.

168: "In some stories": Fissinger, p. 28.

169: "Don't touch me!": Windeler, p. 8.

169: Nyro was so upset: Interviews with Robert Windeler, Jan Nigro, and Stephen Paley. Paley says he brought back a stack of magazines to Nyro's West 79th Street penthouse and burned them in her fireplace. He even demanded that Windeler give him copies from the *Entertainment World* office to make the pile more impressive. Luckily for Nyro, the magazine was available only on the newsstands of L.A. and New York City (and by subscription).

169: "imaginary and misleading": *Ms.*, date unknown (within a month or two after November 1975).

170: some of the best . . . musicians: Maineri had been a child star on the Paul Whiteman teen show, then headed Buddy Rich's band in the late 1950s and played with such jazz greats as Dizzy Gillespie, Billie Holiday, and Coleman Hawkins. He won the *Down Beat* critics poll as the top vibraphonist in 1961–62 and later played on Paul Simon records and produced three Carly Simon albums. John Tropea had played in Deodato and on many albums, and Andy Newmark had played drums for numerous pop artists.

170: Loew's Paradise: People who spoke to me about Loew's Paradise and/or the fact that Nyro went there were Michael Maineri, Harriet Leider, and Muriel Meyerson.

170: "smooth jazz": Tropea says that the soundman would often play his latest recording as background music when audiences filed in for Nyro's concerts during the tour.

171: Isis: In 1976, that group had recorded a paean to Nyro entitled, "I've Been Loving You Through Music."

172: "simply stunning": Robert Hilburn, "Laura Nyro at the Santa Monica Civic," *Los Angeles Times*, May 11, 1976, pt. 4, p. 7.

173: *Christian Science Monitor . . . Mary Hartman*: "Laura Nyro Returns—Mellower," April 29, 1976. The TV show's full title was *Mary Hartman, Mary Hartman*.

173: "taking it easy": Maslin, *New Times*, exact date unknown, 1976, pp. 66–67.

173: Carnegie Hall: Blues singer/guitarist John Hammond opened the show. From *Cash Box*, April 17, 1976, p. 32.

173: "The music was ethereal": "Laura Nyro at Carnegie: Magic Moments," *Rolling Stone*, June 3, 1976, p. 110.

174: promotional copies: Its Columbia numbers were JG 34331 and C 34332.

175: "one of the most disappointing": *Melody Maker*, September 3, 1977, p. 46.

175: Stephen Holden's review: *Rolling Stone*, August 11, 1977, p. 69.

175: Critic Ariel Swartley: "Laura Nyro's Slow Burn," *The Village Voice*, April 4, 1977.

175: *Sounds*, Mike Davies: "Laura Live: Double Trouble," August 13, 1977, p. 47.

176: Sony Japan . . . "complete version": In reordering songs for the Japanese CD, "When I Was a Freeport . . ." follows "I Am the Blues" rather than "The Cat-Song." Thus Nyro's spoken intro to "Freeport"—"Here's another song about a cat"—no longer makes sense.

176: No. 137: Whitburn, *Top Pop Albums*.

177: "don't mean to frustrate": Interview with Sid Bernstein.

14. NESTED

178: wanted to have a child: Nyro told Carman Moore, in their 1976 interview, that she longed to have a child with the man who inspired her song "Midnite Blue."

179: in India: Janice Nigro thinks Hari was from the Punjab area of the country.

179: "part of my feminism": Rockwell.

181: "a blue phase, a green phase": Zollo.

181: "Mr. Blue": The song also contains one of the corniest lines Nyro ever recorded, "Can we mend / transcend / the broken dishes of our love?"

182: child she didn't have: Interview with Patty Di Lauria.

182: rudimentary technique: *Scordatura* (tuning a stringed instrument to a chord) is a centuries-old technique also used by Nyro's more guitar-adept contemporary Joni Mitchell. Patricia Rudden suggests that for Nyro, tuning to a chord "was as economical and pragmatic an approach to the guitar as she took to the piano."

182: guitar, on which Nyro had written: Zollo, p. 24.

183: "We're both really happy": Columbia Records press kit, 1993, p. 3, quoting Tom Windbrandt in *SoHo News*.

183: "languid as the night": E-mail correspondence.

184: Alan Jones in *Melody Maker*: "Nyro's Spring Fever," July 8, 1978, p. 25.

184: "It'll blend in fine": Jones, ibid.

184: "the original idea": "Laura Nyro's Music a Fading Echo of Itself," *Chicago Sun-Times*, July 7, 1978, p. 54.

184: Mortifoglio: "Laura Nyro's Tame Hysteria," *The Village Voice*, date unknown.

185: Palmer in *The New York Times*: "Pop: Laura Nyro at Club" [The Bottom Line], July 14, 1978.

185: "homegrown, but it jumps": "Laura Nyro's Safe at Home," Daisann McLane, *Crawdaddy*, September 1978, p. 66.

185: *Nested* didn't crack: It's not listed in Whitburn's *Top Pop Albums*.

186: cesarean section: Interviews with Keith Decker, Patty Di Lauria.

187: "I know she married a guy": *Interview*, April 1986, p. 196.

15. MOTHER'S SPIRITUAL

189: "Feminism is a bright color": Nyro.

189: "Through the Eyes of Grace": It appeared on Manchester's 1978 Arista album *Don't Cry Out Loud*.

189: "separate, lonely spaces": Nyro.

189: Keith Decker: They started their working relationship/friendship soon after John Lennon died, and Decker remembers how they both felt emotionally raw about it. Nyro told Decker that she had joined the vigil outside the Dakota apartment on the day after Lennon was killed, and she'd begun to sketch out a song about him. Decker remembers her singing the phrase "On a starry starry night," but never heard a completed version of the song.

190: *Impressions*: See discography appendix for titles.

190: idea for the album . . . "Goddess of Creativity": Pollock, p. 29.

190: "swimming in a cool, dark river": Koplewitz, p. 11.

190: "a new world": Pollock, p. 29.

190: "a one-to-one vision": Fissinger.

190: "I could feel the spirit": Nyro.

190: filled with maples: Interview with Michael Decker.

191: followed the energies: Nyro.

191: "I sometimes feel more in common": ibid.

191: "Trees": Dated May 20, 1961. From Nyro's Creative Writing notebook.

191: "spirit of that window": Nyro.

193: "uncivilized" . . . "other responsibilities": Koplewitz.

194: rehearsal tape: Thanks to Elysa Sunshine. The songs that were restructured were "The Right to Vote," "Man in the Moon," and "A Wilderness."

196: built a studio: Interview with Mark Linett.

196: how she met Maria: I couldn't confirm the story that they may have met through musician Alice Coltrane, from whom Desiderio supposedly took keyboard lessons.

196: the Magic Speller: According to a blurb in *The Lesbian Tide*, the bookstore had opened with a general inventory in 1976 but had then expanded its holdings of lesbian and feminist titles. Desiderio and lover-partner Zoe Ananda were "particularly interested in 'the spiritual future of women.' " The two women declared themselves "the luckiest lesbians alive" because they experienced little discrimination regarding their lifestyle, even from their families. To prove the point, the article was accompanied by a smiling photo of Desiderio and Ananda—with their mothers. From "Community Focus," *Lesbian Tide*, March/April, 1979.

196: almost entirely hidden: In the 1992 update to his 1973 book, *Turn It Up! (I Can't Hear the Words): Singer/Songwriters Then and Now* (New York: Citadel Underground Press, 1992), Bob Sarlin presumptuously wrote that Nyro had emerged from a long hiatus "as a proud lesbian." Actually, it wasn't until Nyro died that a press release identified Desiderio as her life partner.

196: "I'm not looking": The lyric sheet reads "I'm not *waiting*," but Nyro sings *looking*. The literature accompanying the album includes several other inaccuracies, most egregiously the misspellings of guitarist Bristow as "Bristo" and bassist Elysa Sunshine as "Lisa."

198: "I came in and kick-started": Transcript from Backman.

199: "mom's rock": Fissinger, p. 28.

199: "Polonaise": Jan Nigro says that the master tapes have recently been found; he still hopes the recording will someday be released.

200: "just wasn't convenient": Flanagan.

200: the most "realistic" song: Koplewitz.

200: "I'm finished hassling": Zollo.

200: "humor when it comes to pain": Koplewitz.

203: Hecate: Nyro mispronounced the name "Heh-*sa*-tee" rather than "Heh-ka-tee." Keith Decker remembers her insisting on that pronunciation, despite his efforts to convince her otherwise.

203: lusty and joyful: Nyro.

203: *Sophia: Goddess of Wisdom*: HarperSanFrancisco, 1993.

203: Marion Woodman: With Jill Mellick, *Coming Home to Myself: Reflections for Nurturing a Woman's Body and Soul* (Conari Press, 1998). Thanks to Susan Bouthillier for this reference.

204: *Mother Warrior Pilgrim*: Jain Nyborg Sherrard (New York: Andrews McMeil, 1980), pp. 13, 15, 19. The exact quote that Nyro cited reads: "raising children is like combat—mothers and babies both fighting to come out alive—and that as battles go, mothering is unlike any other, for its peculiar quality is that both sides have to win" (p. 13).

204: *Give Peace A Chance*: From the exhibition catalog, edited by Marianne Philbin (Chicago Review Press). Thanks to Rosemary Meyer, Chicago Peace Museum.

204: (whom Nyro loved): Pollock, p. 29.

205: No. 182: From Whitburn, *Top Pop Albums*.

205: "matriarchal hug": Review, *Musician*, April 1984, p. 104.

205: Shewey: Review, *Rolling Stone*, March 29, 1984.

206: Stephen Holden: "Pop Disks Contrast Romantic Styles," *The New York Times*, February 12, 1984, p. 25.

206: Eric Levin: *People*, March 19, 1984, p. 16.

206: Georgia Christgau: "Ms. Mom," *The Village Voice*, April 10, 1984.

206: "I've read some terrible reviews": Fissinger.

206: rebuttal letter: "Mother's of Invention," letters column, *The Village Voice*, date unknown.

207: Charlotte Grieg: In Sheila Whitely, ed., *Sexing the Groove: Popular Music and Gender* (Routledge, 1997), p. 175.

207: misunderstood or disparaged: Romanowski, p. 141.

207: "Laura Nyro made a choice": Crowe, op. cit.

207: "respect it, and move on": Pollock, p. 29.

16. ROADNOTES

208: "I must have the city": Billy Altman, "Talking with . . . Laura Nyro: Still Savoring the '60s," *People*, August 30, 1993.

209: "you": Cypress Records press kit. Perhaps this was Nyro's subterranean way of revealing a bit of personal information about herself. She went on to mention several other favorite artists, including Paul Gauguin, Louise Nevelson, and Yoko Ono, whose performance piece involving her uncontrollable two-year-old child amused Nyro (she identified, obviously).

210: "I was just praying": Migliore.

212: BMI: The performing rights organization to which Nyro belonged. (American songwriters typically join either BMI or ASCAP to collect royalties for performance of their compositions.)

212: Nashville songwriter: Roboff cowrote singer Faith Hill's 1998 hit recording "This Kiss."

213: pack-a-day smoker: Cole.

213: "what I've been doing": ibid.

213: "true timbre": ibid.

213: "There's a sticker": Nyro.

213: "enjoyed all that food": Sommer, op. cit.

213: elephant meat: Kloman. Since the elephant wasn't very appetizing, Nyro ended up serving it to her dog Beautybelle.

214: had a face: Interview with Mark Linett.

214: "I almost walked away": Interview with Scott Simon on *Weekend Edition*, National Public Radio, 1989.

214: "I started to look": Mark Sommer, "Her Wild World," *Animals' Agenda*, July/August, 1989.

214: People asked her: Cole, p. 24.

215: "Divine Right Order": Interview with Gorin's friend and fellow Nyro fan Michael Proft.

215: "real songs": Cole, p. 24.

215: "It just so happens": Cromelin, pt. VI, p. 5.

215: "lost your port": Cypress press kit, 1989.

215: "It's time for Mom": Frank Rizzo, "Nyro on the Road Again and Loves It," *The Hartford Courant*, June 29, 1988, Connecticut Living section.

215: "different crests": Greg Goth, Gannett News Service, May 4, 1990.

215: "Sometimes only poetry": Sciaky.

217: sensitive about her appearance: Interview with Geoffrey Blumenauer.

217: "It's me and my son" . . . right to their privacy: Cromelin, pt. VI, p. 4.

219: the Laura Nyro Door: Interview with Geoff Blumenauer and from www.LIRock.com. The door was rarely used after Nyro's performance, since it had to remain closed due to local noise regulations. It was removed in the 1990s when the club expanded.

219: "not about nostalgia": "Nyro Shows Way for Young Artists," *Chicago Tribune*, August [6 or 7], 1988.

219: Rizzo: "Laura Nyro Offers Up a Stunning Evening," *Hartford Courant*, June 30, 1988.

219: "After the mauling": Heim, op. cit..

219: "jump off a bridge": Overheard by Dan Nigro at concert in Toronto, 1989.

220: Anna Magnani movies: Interview with Dan Nigro. Magnani's scene-chewing Oscar turn in the 1955 film version of Tennessee Williams's *The Rose Tattoo* was a particular Nyro favorite. "We had to watch *The Rose Tattoo* every time it was on," says Jimmy Vivino. Nyro's son Gil says she was quite fond of a couple of other Italian-related movies—*The Godfather* and the 1992 comedy *My Cousin Vinnie*.

220: For an encore: Nyro's dialogue recalled by fan Randy of Texas, from Bottom Line concerts, July 8–9, 1988.

220: "a fan onstage": Recollection of Richard Denaro.

220: for Bill Graham: Larry Kelp, "Laura Nyro Captivates with Old, New," *The Tribune* (Oakland, California), August 22, 1988.

221: "just how unique": "Nyro Returns to Public Eye with Artistry Intact," *Los Angeles Times*, August 15, 1988.

221: Peter Allen: Recollection of Dan Nigro.

221: Brenda Russell: Known for writing such songs as "Piano in the Dark" and "Get Here."

221: Chicago critic: "Laura Nyro, Cured and Content," unknown Chicago newspaper, August 12, 1988.

221: *Variety* felt: Review by "Enry," August 24, 1988.

221: Shulgasser: "Singer's Uncertain Return," *San Francisco Examiner*, August 22, 1988.

222: "No other pop music cult figure": *The New York Times*, July 14, 1988.

222: "earth-mother figure": "Nyro, Ten Years Later," *Newsday*, July 11, 1988, part. II, p. 7.

222: "My whole 'tribe' ": Heim, op. cit.

222: cult of the mother: Cromelin, part VI, p. 4.

17. LIVE AT THE BOTTOM LINE

223: "My mood": Flanagan.

224: two-record set: Despite being a double album with sixteen cuts (and nineteen songs, including those in the medleys), *Live at the Bottom Line* left out the first two songs with which Nyro usually began her concerts then: the oldie "The Wind" and another new composition, "Down South."

225: "looking for trouble": Flanagan.

226: meets the mystic: Simon, NPR interview.

226: vegan diet: Backstage conversation between Nyro and Patricia Rudden, March 1990.

227: *People* called it "terrific": Review by Scot Haller, December 4, 1989.

227: "lightheaded hippiedom": Sarlin, op. cit., p. 5.

227: Mountain Stage: Taped in Charleston, West Virginia, on November 11, 1990, and broadcast on 166 public radio stations. In 2000, Nyro's live recording was released on CD.

227: "art, not show business": Mitch Potter, "Laura Nyro's Taking Stock of New Fame," *Toronto Star*, July 13, 1989, entertainment section.

228: "I can hold my notes": "The Pop Life: Nyro at Bottom Line," *The New York Times*, August 30, 1989.

228: "like my attraction to music": Interview in Columbia Records press kit, 1993.

228: "Mama": From Dan Nigro and Gil Bianchini.

228: a "great romance": Richard Christian, "Garbo of Rock Back on Concert Trail," *Skyline* (Chicago), 1988.

228: proved too taxing: Randle had developed tendinitis in her wrist. "Playing bass wouldn't normally be difficult for me," she says, "but Laura plays everything in the key of C, all the white keys. The key you learn when you first learn to play the piano. In order to play bass in C, you have to play Cs and Fs—Laura liked the sound of the low F—and it's basically the most difficult position for your hand and arm if you're not really a bass player. By the time I finished the tour, I couldn't move my arm."

230: Shakespearean stage: Interview with Geoffrey Blumenauer.

230: attended the festival: Interview with Carol Schmidt. Singer-songwriter Schmidt and her group Jasmine were playing the festival, and she saw Nyro walking by one afternoon. She even asked, "Are you Laura Nyro?" and received an affirmative response. Schmidt then followed Nyro to a spiritually oriented workshop given by the woman Nyro had been walking with.

230: particularly impressed: Fan E-mail.

231: "your wild working musician": "Reason to Rebel," *Chicago Tribune*, August 7, 1994, section 6, p. 8.

231: "fame trip": Flanagan.

18. WALK THE DOG

233: place in Manhattan: In a conversation with Patricia Rudden in the summer of 1990, Nyro said she wanted to rent a house with a backyard and a tree—"I need that much nature still"—in an area of town "without too much crime and drugs."

233: thank-you speech: Awards event description from *Mixed Bag Newsletter*, 1990.

235: one fan who saw her: E-mail from Nyro fan Joan Ruvinsky, 1999.

235: "a rippling brook": Review of Great Woods show by Jim Sullivan, *The Boston Globe*, July 6, 1991, arts and film section, p. 16.

235: open for someone else: John D'Agostino, "The Essence of Nyro: Songwriter Takes a Topical, Back-to-Basics Turn," *Los Angeles Times* (San Diego County edition), August 6, 1991, p. F1.

236: "real singing": Billy Altman, "Talking with . . . Laura Nyro: Still Savoring the 60s," *People*, exact date unknown, 1993.

236: "not a fad": Kaplan.

236: old soul music . . . "nice studio": Backman.

236: "chick singer": Jim Bessman, "Columbia Lights the Light on Nyro's Studio Comeback," *Billboard*, August 28, 1993, p. 16.

238: "two independent thinkers": ibid.

239: "I had to forget about being sweet . . .": ibid.

239: "Heebie Jeebies": Philles Records. Info from website, www.soma.or.jp/ ~kowata/spector/discography-2.html.

239: "something being born": Migliore.

239: "This song is reaching for": ibid.

239: "a bit of an obligation": Interview with Nyro in Columbia Records press kit, 1993.

240: "She works basically with black": Koplewitz. Nyro almost certainly had read Nevelson's book of transcribed conversations with Diane MacKown, *Dawns + Dusks* (New York: Charles Scribner, 1976), in which the artist explained her concepts of black, white, and gold (pp. 144–45).

240: Nyro fan Paul Laub: From Utne Internet chat forum on Nyro, July 6, 1999.

241: "the single element": From Laurie Lisle, *Louise Nevelson: A Passionate Life* (New York: Summit Books, 1990), pp. 59–60. Nyro may have read Lisle's book, as Patricia Rudden gave her a copy in April 1990.

241: "In this case": Migliore.

241: *'Til Their Eyes Shine*: Also features performances by Rosanne Cash, Carole King, Emmylou Harris, Maura O'Connell, Kate and Anna McGarrigle, Gloria Estefan, Dionne Warwick, Deniece Williams, Brenda Russell, and Mary-Chapin Carpenter.

241: "I'm So Proud" . . . "Dedicated to the One I Love": The former was written by Curtis Mayfield and appeared on the Impressions' *Never Ending Impressions* (ABC Records, 1964); the latter was written by Lowman Pauling and Ralph Bass.

242: "When I was young": As quoted in unpublished liner notes by Jim Bessman.

242: "relevant and vital": Bessman, op. cit.

242: *People* found: Review by Billy Altman, exact date unknown, 1993.

242: *Pulse!*: Review by Harold DeMuir, October 1993, p. 89.

242: *Stereo Review*: "Laura Nyro, Back on the Street," September 1993, p. 90. The blurb in the magazine listed a subhead for the CD, "Run the Dog Darling Lite Delite," which never appeared on the actual release.

243: Even *Rolling Stone*: Review by John McAlley, October 14, 1993, pp. 117–118.

243: "I'm more disciplined": Bessman, op. cit.

244: "sweet tooth": Kaplan.

19. ANGEL IN THE DARK

246: "front burner": Transcript of interview with Richard Knight, Chicago, June 18, 1994.

246: "totally different": ibid.

247: tattoo: The same fan appeared and "dropped trou" for people at the Bottom Line in New York as well.

247: "Puppy Love tour": Garisto says that one show in Japan was a "transcendent" performance by Nyro. She has digitally enhanced a board-recorded tape of that night and it may eventually be released by Nyro's estate.

247: "opulent and strong": E-mail from London fan Martin (last name unknown) who was at the show.

247: "He Was Too Good to Me": The song was written for Rodgers and Hart's

1930 musical *Simple Simon*, but was dropped before the play's New York production.

248: "like prayers": Mick Brown, "Moved by the Spirit," *The Daily Telegraph*, November 15, 1994.

249: joyful for her: Zollo. "I'm really scared I'll have nothing to say," Nyro told the journalist before their telephone interview began, and then proceeded to talk to him for five hours over the course of the next two days.

249: *ADD and Creativity*: Taylor Publishing, 1997.

250: *Driven to Distraction*: New York: Simon & Schuster, 1995.

250: "alternative artists": Kaplan.

250: *Miracle 2*: Elysa Sunshine says Nyro had hinted about doing another oldies album as far back as the *Mother's Spiritual* sessions in 1982, and journalist Mark Leviton, in his review of Nyro at the Mayfair Music Hall, *BAM*, September 9, 1988, mentions that she planned to do an album of remakes.

250: back taxes: Interview with Patty Di Lauria.

251: "Embraceable You": Words by Ira Gershwin, music by George Gershwin. The song was first introduced in the 1930 stage musical *Girl Crazy* and made famous in 1940 by Judy Garland (who then sang it in the 1943 MGM film of *Girl Crazy*). From Judy Garland Database, www.zianet.com/jjohnson/.

251: "Be Aware": Dionne Warwick had recorded the song for a 1972 album, and Barbra Streisand sang it on the 1971 TV special, *Singer Presents Burt Bacharach*.

251: legendary pop artists: A couple of other guest artists on *Tonin'* had a particular connection to Nyro: Bette Midler, who sang the song Nyro had earlier revived, "It's Gonna Take a Miracle," and her old friend and coproducer Felix Cavaliere.

252: "Many ones": In Nyro's version of the song on *Live at the Bottom Line*, she also substituted "If there's something in this world that I needed / baby you are the one for me" for the gender-specific original, "If I ever met a girl / that I needed in this world."

252: "Let It Be Me": Written by Frenchman Gilbert Becaud, with English lyrics by Manny Kurtz.

252: Helen Merrill . . . Gil Evans: The two collaborated on the song in 1956 and again in 1987.

253: crone: *Webster's* defines a crone as "a withered old woman," but among feminists the word has come to signify a wise older woman.

253: local women poets: Eloise Klein Healy, whose *Artemis in Echo Park* Nyro had admired, also was invited to meet her.

254: ovarian cancer: Information on the disease from the Gilda Radner Familial Ovarian Cancer Registry, http://rpci.med.buffalo.edu/departments/gynonc/grwp.html, from the National Cancer Institute's PDQ statements, and from Craig Horowitz, "Time-Bomb Genes," *New York*, February 8, 1999, p. 30.

257: He [Revici] proposed . . . theories remain controversial: Office of Technology Assessment, "Unconventional Cancer Treatments," 1990 (from www.quackwatch.com).

258: "a woman's touch": Black, p. 122.

259: In *People*: Review, February 24, 1997, p. 26.

259: Futterman: Review, *Entertainment Weekly*, March 21, 1997, p. 73.

260: Luna Mist Records: Liner notes by Eileen Silver-Lillywhite from *Angel in the Dark*.

263: *Ka ya hiraki* . . . : From Yoel Hoffman, *Japanese Death Poems: Written by Zen Monks and Haiku Poets on the Verge of Death* (Rutland, VT: Charles E. Tuttle, 1998), pp. 178–79.

20. A WORLD TO CARRY ON

264: Time called her: April 21, 1997, p. 37.

264: *Newsday*: April 10, 1997, p. A6.

264: *The Boston Globe*: April 10, 1997, p. E1.

265: *The Village Voice*: Exact date unknown.

265: *The Washington Post*: April 13, 1997.

265: Reuters: April 9, 1997.

265: Tommy Mottola: Exact date unknown.

265: Suzanne Vega: *Musician*, August 1997, pp. 21–22.

266: Don Was: April 11, 1997.

266: Billy Altman: exact date unknown.

266: Ian MacDonald: "Nyro Worship," *New Musical Express*, exact date unknown.

267: Billy Childs: "Inside Jazz with Billy Childs," *SongTalk*, vol. 4, issue 2, 1994, p. 30.

268: one of her last outings: Sontag.

268: belated wake: Nyro was also celebrated after her death in Nashville, where her high school friend and former backup singer Toni Wine staged a packed-house tribute at the city's popular Café Milano. Says Wine, now a Nashville songwriter, "I knew there were a lot of New York and L.A. and Chicago people who now live here who loved her, but there were also many true-and-blue Nashvillean country artists and musicians who loved her as much as anyone could have."

268: featured artists: The lineup also included Toshi Reagon and Big Lovely, tribute album participants Dana Bryant and Jane Siberry; Innerspirit (a youth harmony group led by Nyro's backup singer Diane Wilson), HarpBeat (featuring old friends Ellen Uryevick on harp and Nydia Mata on steel drum and congas, along with three Cuban-style drummers), and comedian Reno (who appalled the audience with tasteless jokes about cancer).

268: Rickie Lee Jones: According to Desmond Child, Jones's first choice of a song for the concert had been Nyro's "Christmas in My Soul," but Child had already been assigned to sing it in a reunion performance with his former group Rouge. Nonetheless, as Child was practicing his piano part on the song backstage, Jones came by and asked if she could just sing along. "She was just so humble, loving Laura Nyro," he says.

268: "America's greatest songwriter": From Steve Anderson, "Bittersweet Heart at the Rodeo," *The Village Voice*, December 5, 1989. Anderson reported that Jones had played the opening notes to Nyro's "Map to the Treasure" at a Pier 42 concert in New York some years before and asked the audience, "You don't know that? America's greatest songwriter and they don't even know her."

268: "You Don't Love Me When I Cry": Ironically, that was the song Peter Gallway had unsuccessfully pitched to Jones for the Nyro tribute album. Diane Garisto points out that Jones, even though she knew otherwise, sang the lyric "rubies and smoke rings" the way she had always misheard it: as "rubies and snow cranes."

268: Maria . . . diagnosed: Interview with Michael Decker.

269: Patty Di Lauria: After Nyro's death, she divorced Andy Uryevick and later married John Di Lauria.

269: several new covers: Even Homer Simpson does Laura Nyro, as *The Simpsons* dad sang "Wedding Bell Blues" while driving his car during the November 11, 2001, episode of the animated TV series.

269: Jill Cuniff: From online source, exact citation unknown. The thirty-something Cuniff remains rare among younger pop music cognoscenti in her knowledge of Nyro. On an episode of VH1's *Rock and Roll Jeopardy* in November of 1999, the answer "Her albums included *Eli and the Thirteenth Confession* and the hit songs she wrote included 'Stoney End' " appeared under the category Cult Figures. None of the three Generation X contestants even ventured a guess that "Who is Laura Nyro?" was the question.

269: *Listen to This:* Alan Reder and John Baxter (New York: Hyperion, 1999), p. 323 (Perez) and pp. 64–65 (Buck).

269: Perez listed: "What's Your Top 10 List?" *Los Angeles Times,* September 27, 1998, pp. 8, 70.

270: "up there with the Beatles": "Crucial Cuts," *Sunday Times* (London), July 16, 2000, p. 21.

270: "Laura Nyro you can lump me in with": *Mojo,* August 1998, p. 84.

270: *Stoned Soul Picnic:* Created by Lisa Bayliss, Annabel Kershaw, and Bonnie Panych.

270: *Soul Picnic:* Written and directed by Shelby Brammer. Peter Yarrow (of Peter, Paul and Mary) helped Brammer obtain musical rights for the production, which she hoped to take to New York until the Vineyard Theater announced its intentions to do a Nyro project.

270: Kuchwara: "*Eli's Comin'* Is Quite a Concert," May 9, 2001.

270: Obie: The awards for Off-Broadway excellence were handed out on May 21, 2001.

271: who reportedly mortgaged: Interview with Patricia Romanowski.

272: "intoxicating": Scott Schindler, *Entertainment Weekly,* April 20, p. 73.

272: *Guardian:* "Songs in the Key of Life," April 6, 2001.

272: "Any woman who soared": Romanowski, p. 142. Romanowski's essay on Nyro for this *Rolling Stone* book didn't get assigned without an insult: The editors hadn't considered including Nyro until Romanowski suggested it, and they told the writer they had no more budget to pay for the essay—so Romanowski wrote it gratis.

272: CBS *Sunday Morning:* The loving commentary about Nyro was delivered by Bill Flanagan, who had written about her for *Musician* in 1989. He thankfully cleared up the Monterey Pop tall tale, but inaccurately suggested that it "took her friends four years" to find a record company willing to put out *Angel in* the Dark. As for the spike in Nyro's sales, Angel in the Dark reached No. 8 on Billboard's "Top Internet Albums" chart of August 4, 2001.

273: Nyro's publishing: Cherry Lane will collect the writer's share for all of Nyro's compositions, but only owns the publisher's share for her later Luna Mist songs.

274: Dusty Springfield: The great British singer died of breast cancer on March 2, 1999. She was just fifty-nine.

DISCOGRAPHY

(All songs written by Laura Nyro, unless otherwise indicated)
(In boldface: peak *Billboard* chart position/weeks on *Billboard* charts)

The Albums

1967
More Than a New Discovery (Verve Folkways FT/FTS-3020)

SIDE ONE
  Goodbye Joe
  Billy's Blues
  And When I Die
  Stoney End
  Lazy Susan
  Hands off the Man

SIDE TWO
  Wedding Bell Blues
  Buy and Sell
  He's a Runner
  Blowin' Away
  I Never Meant to Hurt You
  California Shoeshine Boys

Production credits: Arranged and conducted by Herb Bernstein; produced by Milt Okun. Musicians included: Laura Nyro, vocal; Hi

Fashions, background vocal trio; Jay Berliner, guitar; Lou Mauro, bass; Bill La Vorgna, drums; Stan Free, piano; Jimmy Sedlar, horns; Toots Thielmann and Buddy Lucas, harmonica.

1967

Laura Nyro (re-release of More Than a New Discovery, on Verve Forecast, FTS-3020, with lyrics on back cover instead of liner notes and songs re-ordered)

SIDE ONE

Wedding Bell Blues
Billy's Blues
California Shoeshine Boys
Blowin' Away
Lazy Susan
Goodbye Joe

SIDE TWO

Hands off the Man (Flim Flam Man)
Stoney End
I Never Meant to Hurt You
He's a Runner
Buy and Sell
And When I Die

1968

Eli and the Thirteenth Confession (Columbia Records, CS 9626)
(No. 181/7 weeks)

PART ONE

Luckie
Lu
Sweet Blindness
Poverty Train
Lonely Women
Eli's Comin'

PART TWO
Timer
Stoned Soul Picnic
Emmie
Woman's Blues
Once It Was Alright Now (Farmer Joe)
December's Boudoir
The Confession

Production credits: Produced by Charlie Calello and Laura Nyro; arranged by Charlie Calello; David L. Geffen credited as "agent and friend," Laura Nyro as "writer, composer, voices, piano and witness to the confession."

Musicians included: Laura Nyro, piano, vocal and harmonies; Ralph Casale and Chet Amsterdam, acoustic guitar; Hugh McCracken, electric guitar; Chuck Rainey and Chet Amsterdam, bass; Artie Schroeck, drums and vibes; Buddy Saltzman, drums; Dave Carey, percussion; Bernie Glow, Ernie Royal and Pat Calello, trumpet; George Young, saxophone; Wayne Andre, Jimmy Cleveland, and Ray DeSio, trombone; Paul Griffin, piano; Zoot Sims, saxophone; Joe Farrell, saxophone and flute.

1969

New York Tendaberry (Columbia Records, KCS 9737) **(No. 32/17 weeks)**

SIDE ONE
You Don't Love Me When I Cry
Captain for Dark Mornings
Tom Cat Goodbye
Mercy on Broadway
Save the Country

SIDE TWO
Gibsom Street
Time and Love
The Man Who Sends Me Home
Sweet Lovin' Baby
Captain St. Lucifer
New York Tendaberry

Production credits: Arrangements by Laura Nyro; produced by Laura Nyro and Roy Halee (who also engineered); conductor and consultant, Jimmy Haskell; manager and friend David Geffen.

Musicians included: Laura Nyro, piano and vocal; Gary Chester, drums; Bob Bushwell, bass; Bernie Glow and Lew Soloff, trumpet.

1970
Christmas and the Beads of Sweat (Columbia Records, KC30259)
(No. 51/14 weeks)

SIDE ONE

Brown Earth
When I Was a Freeport and You Were the Main Drag
Blackpatch
Been on a Train
Up on the Roof (*Gerry Goffin/Carole King*)

SIDE TWO

Upstairs by a Chinese Lamp
Map to the Treasure
Beads of Sweat
Christmas in My Soul

Production credits: Produced by Arif Mardin and Felix Cavaliere; musical arrangements by Laura Nyro and Arif Mardin; conductor Arif Mardin.

Musicians: On Side One, the Boys from Muscle Shoals—Roger Hawkins, drums; Eddie Hinton, electric guitar; Dave Hood, bass; Barry Beckett, vibes; Jack Jennings, percussion—plus Felix Cavaliere, organ and bells, and Stu Sharf, acoustic guitar. On Side Two, Dino Danelli, drums; Chuck Rainey, bass; Cornell Dupree, electric guitar; Ralph MacDonald, percussion; Ashod Garabedian, oud; Michael Szittai, cimbalin; Alice Coltrane, harp; Joe Farrell, woodwinds. Additionally, Duane Allman, electric guitar on "Beads of Sweat," Richard Davis, bass, and Laura Nyro, piano.

1971
Gonna Take a Miracle (Columbia Records, KC 30987) **(No. 46/17 weeks)**

SIDE ONE

I Met Him on a Sunday (*S. Owens/D. Coley/E. Harris/B. Lee*)

The Bells (*I. Bristol/G. Gaye/Marvin Gaye/E. Stover*)

Monkey Time (*Curtis Mayfield*)

Dancing in the Street (*W. Stevenson/Marvin Gaye/I. Hunter*)

Desiree (*L. Cooper/C. Johnson*)

You've Really Got a Hold On Me (*W. Robinson*)

SIDE TWO

Spanish Harlem (*Jerry Lieber/Phil Spector*)

Jimmy Mack (*E. Holland/ L. Dozier/ B. Holland*)

The Wind (*N. Strong/B. Edwards/W. Hunter/Q. Eubanks/J. Gutierrez*)

Nowhere to Run (*E. Holland/L. Dozier/ B. Holland*)

It's Gonna Take a Miracle (*T. Randazzo/B. Weinstein/L. Stallman*)

Production credits: Produced by Gamble & Huff; string and horn arrangers Tom Bell, Lenny Pakula, and Robert Martin..

Musicians: Backing vocals by Labelle (Patti LaBelle, Nona Hendryx,
Sarah Dash); Laura Nyro, piano and vocals; Jim Helmer, drums; Larry
Washington and Nydia Mata, bongos and congas; Ronnie Baker, bass;
Roland Chambers and Norman Harris, guitar; Lenny Pakula, organ;
Vince Montana, percussion.

1973

The First Songs (second re-release of *More Than a New Discovery*, on Columbia
Records, KC 31410). **(No. 97/11 weeks)**

1976

Smile (Columbia Records, PC 33912) **(No. 60/14 weeks)**

SIDE ONE

Sexy Mama (*H. Ray/A. Goodman/Sylvia Robinson*)

Children of the Junks

Money

I Am the Blues

SIDE TWO

Stormy Love

The Cat-Song

Midnite Blue

Smile

Production credits: Produced by Charlie Calello and Laura Nyro.

Musicians: Laura Nyro, piano, vocal, guitar, and woodblock; Will Lee, Bob Babbit, and Richard Davis, bass; Chris Parker, Alan Schwartzberg, and Rick Maratta, drums; John Tropea, Jeff Mironov, Jerry Friedman, Joe Beck, Huey McCracken, and Greg Bennett, guitar; George Young and Michael Brecker, flute and saxophone; Joe Farrell, saxophone; Randy Brecker, trumpet; Reiko Kamota and Nisako Yoshida, koto; David Friedman, vibes; Carter C. C. Collins, conga drum; Paul Messing, Jimmy Macullen, and Rubin Bassine, various percussion.

1977

Season of Lights . . . Laura Nyro in Concert (Columbia Records, PC-34786) **(No. 137/5 weeks)**

SIDE ONE
The Confession
And When I Die
Upstairs by a Chinese Lamp
Sweet Blindness
Captain St. Lucifer

SIDE TWO
Money
The Cat-Song
Freeport
Timer
Emmie

Japanese (Complete) Version (on CD) (Sony SRCS 6807)

Money
Sweet Lovin' Baby
And When I Die
The Morning News
Upstairs by a Chinese Lamp
I Am the Blues
When I Was a Freeport and You Were the Main Drag
Captain St. Lucifer

Smile
Mars
Sweet Blindness
The Cat-Song
Emmie
The Confession
Timer
Midnite Blue

Production credits: Musical direction, Laura Nyro.

Musicians: Laura Nyro, voice, piano, and acoustic guitar; John Tropea, electric guitar; Michael Maineri, vibes, baliphone, clavinet; Andy Newmark, drums; Richard Davis, bass; Nydia "Liberty" Mata, congas and percussion; Ellen Seeling, trumpet; Jeff King, saxophone; Jeanie Fineberg, flute and saxophone; Carter C. C. Collins, second percussion.

1978

Nested (Columbia Records, JC-35449)

SIDE ONE

Mr. Blue (the song of communications)
Rhythm and Blues
My Innocence
Crazy Love
American Dreamer

SIDE TWO

Springblown
The Sweet Sky
Light—Pop's Principle
Child in a Universe
The Nest

Production credits: Laura Nyro and Roscoe Harring ("production gang")

Musicians: Laura Nyro, vocal, piano (acoustic and electric), church organ, guitar, and string ensemble; Will Lee, bass; Andy Newmark, drums; Vinnie Cusano and John Tropea, guitars; Nydia "Liberty" Mata, percussion; John Sebastian, harmonica. Also, Felix Cavaliere, electric piano and organ; Cyril Cianflone and Tony Levin, bass.

1984

Mother's Spiritual (Columbia Records, FC 39215) **(No. 182/3 weeks)**

SIDE ONE
  To a Child . . . (Gil's song)
  The Right to Vote
  A Wilderness
  Melody in the Sky
  Late for Love
  A Free Thinker
  Man in the Moon

SIDE TWO
  Talk to a Green Tree
  Trees of the Ages
  The Brighter Song
  Roadnotes
  Sophia
  Mother's Spiritual
  Refrain

Production credits: Produced by Laura Nyro.

  Musicians: Laura Nyro, voice, harmonies, acoustic and electric pianos, and dulcimer; John Bristow, electric guitar; Lisa Sunshine, bass; Terry Silverlight, drums; Todd Rundgren, synthesizer; Nydia "Liberty" Mata, percussion; Jan Nigro, acoustic guitar; Julie Lyonn Lieberman, violin.

1989

Laura: Laura Nyro Live at the Bottom Line (Cypress Records, YL6430; CD: YD6430)

DISC 1, SIDE ONE
  The Confession
  High-Heeled Sneakers (*Robert Higginbottom*)
  Roll of the Ocean
  Companion
  The Wild World

SIDE TWO
My Innocence/Sophia
To a Child
And When I Die

DISC 2, SIDE ONE
Park Song
Broken Rainbow
Women of the One World
Emmie

SIDE TWO
Wedding Bell Blues
The Japanese Restaurant Song
Stoned Soul Picnic
Medley: La-La Means I Love You (*Thomas Bell/William Hart*)/Trees of the Ages/Up on the Roof (*Gerry Goffin/Carole King*)

Production credits: Produced by Laura Nyro; coproduced by Jimmy Vivino

Musicians: Laura Nyro, voice and keyboards; Jimmy Vivino, guitar, harmony, and electric mandolin; Frank Pagano, drums and harmony; David Wofford, bass; Nydia "Liberty" Mata, percussion; Diane Wilson, harmony.

CDs

1993
Walk the Dog & Light the Light (Columbia, CK 52411)

Oh Yeah Maybe Baby (The Heebie Jeebies) (*Phil Spector/Hank Hunter*)
A Woman of the World
The Descent of Luna Rosé
Art of Love
Lite a Flame (The Animal Rights Song)
Louise's Church
Broken Rainbow
Walk the Dog & Light the Light (Song of the Road)
To a Child
I'm So Proud (*Curtis Mayfield*) / Dedicated to the One I Love (*Lowman Pauling/Ralph Bass*)

Production credits: Produced by Gary Katz and Laura Nyro; string arrangements, Nyro and Carlos Franzetti; horn and flute arrangements and additional production assistance, David Frank.

Musicians: Laura Nyro, lead voice, harmonies, and keyboard; Bernard Purdie, drums; Freddie Washington and Jerry Jemmott, bass; Elliott Randall, Michael Landau, and Ira Siegal, guitars; Bashiri Johnson and Eric McKain, percussion; Ellen Uryevick, harp; Lou Marini, Roger Rosenberg, Randy Brecker, Lawrence Feldman, and Michael Brecker, horns and wind instruments; Juliet Haffner, Sue Pray, Julie Green, Jeanne Le Blanc, Marilyn Wright, Belinda Whitney Barrat, Joyce Hammann, Beryl Diamond, Rani Vaz, Laura Seaton, Gene Orloff, Sanford Allen, and Mindy Jostyn, strings.

Posthumous Albums

2000
Live from Mountain Stage (Blue Plate Music BPM-403)

Oh Yeah Maybe Baby (The Heebie Jeebies) (*Spector/Hunter*)
My Innocence
To a Child
And When I Die
Let It Be Me (*Gilbert Becaud/Manny Kurtz*)/The Christmas Song (*Mel Torme/Robert Wells*)
Roll of the Ocean
Lite a Flame
Emmie
Japanese Restaurant
I'm So Proud (*Mayfield*) /Dedicated to the One I Love (*Pauling/Bass*)

2001
Angel in the Dark (Rounder 11661-3176-2)

Angel in the Dark
Triple Goddess Twilight
Will You Love Me Tomorrow (*Gerry Goffin/Carole King*)
You Were Too Good to Me (originally "He Was Too Good to Me")
(*Richard Rodgers/Lorenz Hart*)
Sweet Dream Fade

Serious Playground
Be Aware (Burt *Bacharach/Hal David*)
Let It Be Me (*Becaud/Kurtz*)
Gardenia Talk
Ooo Baby Baby (*William Robinson, Jr./Warren Moore*)
Embraceable You (*George Gershwin/Ira Gershwin*)
La-La Means I Love You (*Bell/Hart*)
Walk On By (Burt *Bacharach/Hal David*)
Animal Grace
Don't Hurt Child
Coda

Production credits: Recorded by Wayne Yurgelun, Dan Gellert, Peter Gallway, Steve Rosenthal. Executive producer Eileen Silver-Lillywhite, produced for release by Scott Billington and Lillywhite. Horn arrangements by John Tropea and Tommy Mitchell.

Musicians: Laura Nyro, lead vocal, harmonies, acoustic and electric pianos; John Tropea, electric guitars; Freddie Washington, bass; Bernard Purdie, drums; Bashiri Johnson, percussion; Randy Brecker, trumpet; Michael Brecker, tenor saxophone; Jeff Pevar, guitar; Will Lee, bass; Chris Parker, drums; Carol Steele, percussion.

Nyro Collections (Selected)

1980
Impressions (CBS, UK 31864)

SIDE ONE
Wedding Bell Blues
Stoney End
And When I Die
Stoned Soul Picnic
Sweet Blindness
Eli's Coming
Emmie
The Confession

SIDE TWO
Save the Country
Captain Saint Lucifer

Map to the Treasure
Beads of Sweat
Christmas in My Soul

1997

Stoned Soul Picnic: The Best of Laura Nyro (Columbia Legacy, C2K 48880)

DISC ONE

Wedding Bell Blues
Blowin' Away
Billy's Blues
Stoney End
And When I Die
Lu
Eli's Comin'
Stoned Soul Picnic
Timer
Emmie
The Confession
Captain St. Lucifer
Gibsom Street
New York Tendaberry
Save the Country (single version)
Blackpatch
Upstairs by a Chinese Lamp
Beads of Sweat
When I Was a Freeport and You Were the Main Drag

DISC TWO

I Met Him on a Sunday (*Owens/Coley/Harris/Lee*)
The Bells (*Bristol/Gaye/Gaye/Stover*)
Smile
Sweet Blindness (live version)
Money (live version)
Mr. Blue
A Wilderness
Mother's Spiritual
A Woman of the World
Louise's Church
Broken Rainbow (*Walk the Dog* version)

To a Child (*Walk the Dog* version)
Lite a Flame (the Animal Rights Song)
And When I Die (previously unreleased live version)
Save the Country (previously unreleased live version)

1998
Premium Best: *Laura Nyro* (Sony Japan, SRCS 8823)

Save the Country (single)
Eli's Comin'
Stoned Soul Picnic
New York Tendaberry
Upstairs by a Chinese Lamp
It's Gonna Take a Miracle (*Randazzo/Weinstein/Stallman*)
And When I Die
Blowin' Away
Stoney End
Smile
Sweet Blindness (live)
Mr. Blue
Mother's Spiritual
To a Child
A Woman of the World

2000
Time and Love: The Essential Masters (Columbia/Legacy CK 061567)

Sweet Blindness
Wedding Bell Blues
And When I Die
Blowin' Away
Eli's Comin'
Goodbye Joe
Stoney End
It's Gonna Take a Miracle
Stoned Soul Picnic
Lu
Save the Country
When I Was a Freeport and You Were the Main Drag
Blackpatch

Time and Love
Sexy Mama (*Ray/Goodman/Robinson*)
Up on the Roof (*Goffin/King*)

The Singles

September 1966   "Wedding Bell Blues" b/w "Stoney End" (original version) (Verve/Folkways KF-5024) **(No. 103/12 weeks)**

February 1967   "Goodbye Joe" b/w "Billy's Blues" (Verve/Folkways KF-5038)

April 1967   "Flim Flam Man" b/w "And When I Die" (Verve/Folkways KF-5051)

April 1968   "Eli's Comin' " (original ending shortened into a fadeout) b/w "Sweet Blindness" (Columbia 4-44531). Nyro's only picture sleeve.

June 1968   "Save the Country" (Bones Howe, arr.) b/w "Timer" (Columbia 4-44592)

October 1968   "Stoned Soul Picnic" b/w "Sweet Blindness," (Columbia JZSP139152)

November 1968   "Stoney End" b/w "Flim Flam Man" (Verve/Forecast KF-5095)

March 1969   "And When I Die" b/w "I Never Meant to Hurt You" (Verve/Forecast KF-5104)

June 1969   "Save the Country" (Bones Howe, arr.) b/w "Eli's Comin' " (edited) (Columbia Hall of Fame reissue 4-33159)

October 1969   "Time and Love" b/w "The Man Who Sends Me Home" (Columbia 4-45041)

October 1969   "Goodbye Joe" b/w "I Never Meant to Hurt You" (Verve/Forecast KF-5112)

January 1970   "Save the Country" (LP version, edited) b/w "New York Tendaberry" (Columbia 4-45089)

August 1970   "Up on the Roof" b/w "Captain St. Lucifer" (Columbia 4-45230) **(No. 92/2 weeks)**

January 1971   "When I Was a Freeport and You Were the Main Drag" b/w "Been on a Train" (Columbia 4-45298)

January 1972   "It's Gonna Take a Miracle" b/w "Desiree" (Columbia 4-45537) **(No. 103/3 weeks)**

February 1973   "Wedding Bell Blues" b/w "Flim Flam Man" (Columbia 4-45791)

December 1990   "Let It Be Me"/"The Christmas Song" b/w Shawn
Colvin, "Have Yourself a Merry Little Christmas"
(Columbia 38T73628)

Nyro Songs on Collections

1989
"Emmie" (from *Laura: Laura Nyro Live at the Bottom Line*)
  All-Ears Review, Volume 7 (ROM 21007)

1990
"Let It Be Me" (*Becaud/Kurtz*)/"The Christmas Song" (*Torme/Wells*)
  Acoustic Christmas (Columbia CK46880)

1992
"To a Child"
  'Til Their Eyes Shine: The Lullaby Album (Columbia CK 52412)

1999
"Stoned Soul Picnic"
  Respect: A Century of Women in Music (Rhino R2 75815)

Nyro on Others' Recordings

1975
Felix Cavaliere, "Love Came" (background vocal), *Destiny* (Bearsville
Records BR 6958)

1983
Kenny Rankin (written by Jan Nigro), "Polonaise" (unreleased duet)

1994
The Manhattan Transfer, "La-La Means I Love You" (co-lead vocal),
Tonin' (Atlantic 82661-2)

SELECTED COVERS

(peak Billboard chart position in boldface)

"And When I Die"
1966   Peter, Paul and Mary, *Album* (Warner 1648)

date unknown   Jr. Walker and the All Stars

1969   Blood, Sweat and Tears, *Blood, Sweat & Tears* (Columbia CS 9720; single Columbia 4-45008). Also on *In Concert Live* (1976, CBS 139/140). **(No. 2)**

1970(?)   Sammy Davis Jr., *Something for Everyone* (Motown 710)

1970   Chet Baker, *Blood, Chet & Tears* (Verve V6 8798)

1997   Kevin Burke's Open House, *Hoof and Mouth* (Green Linnet GLCD 1169)

1998   NRBQ, *Kick Me Hard* (Uni/Rounder); snippet of song sandwiched with "Spinning Wheel." Not on original 1989 release of the album.

"Billy's Blues"
1970   Susan Carter, *Wonderful Deeds and Adventures* (Epic BN 26510). Part of "Medley for Billie Holiday," which also included Holiday's "Lady Sings the Blues" and Nyro's "Lonely Women."
1998   Mary Foster Conklin, *Crazy Eyes* (Mock Turtle)

"Blackpatch"
1972   Fifth Dimension, *Individually & Collectively* (Bell 6073)

"Blowin' Away"

1969/1970   The Fifth Dimension, *Age of Aquarius* (Soul City 92006)
(No. 21)

"Buy and Sell"

1995   Claire Martin, *Offbeat: Live at Ronnie Scott's Club* (Linn 046)

1998   Nnenna Freelon, *Maiden Voyage* (Concord Jazz CCD-4794-2)

"California Shoeshine Boys"

1970   Karen Wyman, *Karen Wyman* (Decca DL 75211)

date unknown   Julie Budd (single on Bell Records B-886), produced by Herb Bernstein.

"Captain for Dark Mornings"

1998   Tuck and Patti, *Paradise Found* (Windham Hill)

"Captain Saint Lucifer"

1970   Melba Moore, *Living to Give* (Mercury SR 61255)

"Eli's Comin' "

1969   Three Dog Night (*Suitable for Framing*, Dunhill DS 50058; single: Dunhill 4215) **(No. 10)**

1969   Friends of Distinction, *Grazin'* (RCA LSP-4149)

1970 or 1972   Maynard Ferguson, MF Horn/MF Horn Two (TNK 33660)

1991   The Nylons, *Four on the Floor* (STB 75224)[On this live album, the a cappella group also does a version of "Up on the Roof" that echoes Nyro's arrangement from *Christmas and the Beads of Sweat*.]

"Emmie"

1969   Roy Ayers (vibraphonist), *Daddy's Back* (Atlantic SD-1538)

1970   Green Lyte Sunday (RCA Victor LSP-4327)

1970   Ronnie Dyson, *If You Let Me Make Love to You Then Why Can't I Touch You?* (Columbia 30223)

1970   Frankie Valli and the Four Seasons, *Half & Half* (titled "Emily")

"Goodbye Joe"

1970   Carmen McRae, *Just a Little Lovin'* (Atlantic SD1568)

date unknown   Glenn Yarbrough (called "Goodbye Girl"), *Let Me Choose Life* (Warner Brothers 1832)

"Hands off the Man (Flim Flam Man)"

1968   Peggy Lipton, *Peggy Lipton* (Ode Z12-44006)

1970   Robin Wilson, *Ain't That Something* (A&M SP 4299)

1971   Barbra Streisand, *Stoney End* (Columbia KC 30378)

"He's a Runner"

1970   Blood, Sweat and Tears, *Blood Sweat & Tears 3* (Columbia 30090)

1970   Mama Cass Elliott

1971   Fifth Dimension, *Love's Lines, Angles and Rhymes* (Bell 6060)

"I Never Meant to Hurt You"

1971   Barbra Streisand, *Barbra Joan Streisand* (Columbia PCQ-30792)

1986   Barbara Cook, *It's Better with a Band* (Live at Carnegie Hall, September 14, 1980) (Moss Music 104)

1994   Anita Kerr, *Favorites* (Bainbridge 2526)

"Lonely Women"

1970   Susan Carter, *Wonderful Deeds and Adventures* (Epic BN 26510). Part of "Medley for Billie Holiday," which also included Holiday's "Lady Sings the Blues" and Nyro's "Billy's Blues."

"Lu"

1970   Peggy Lipton (single on Ode Records 124) **(No. 102)**

"The Man Who Sends Me Home"

1969   George Duke (instrumental, retitled "The Woman Who Sends Me Home"), *Save the Country* (Pickwick Records SPC-3588, 1978 reissue).

"Save the Country"

1969   Julie Driscoll/Brian Auger and the Trinity, *Streetnoise* (Atco SD 2-701)

1969   George Duke, *Save the Country* (Pickwick Records SPC-3588, 1978 reissue)

1970   The Fifth Dimension, *Portrait* (Bell 6045) **(No. 27)**

1970   Karen Wyman, *Karen Wyman* (Decca DL 75211)

"Stoned Soul Picnic"

1968   The Fifth Dimension, *Stoned Soul Picnic* (Soul City 92002; single: Soul City 766) **(No. 3)**

1970   Supremes (lead singer Jean Terrell) and the Four Tops, *The Magnificent Seven* (Motown Records MS 717)

1968   Roy Ayers, *Stoned Soul Picnic* (Atlantic 1514) (instrumental)

1968   Chet Atkins, *Solid Gold 68* (RCA 4061) (instrumental)

date unknown   Staple Singers (on 2,000 *Volts of Stax*, Ace Records reissue)

1997   Swing Out Sister, *Shapes and Patterns* (Mercury)

2000   Laura Love, *Fourteen Days* (Zoë)

"Stoney End"

1967   The Blossoms (B-side of "Wonderful" single, Ode Records 101, reissued as the A-side and called "A Stoney End" in 1969)

1968   Peggy Lipton, *Peggy Lipton* (Ode Z12-44006) **(No. 121)**

1968   Linda Ronstadt, *Stone Poneys Vol. III* (Capitol ST 2863)

1971   Barbra Streisand, *Stoney End* (Columbia KC 30378) **(No. 6)**

1972   Barbra Streisand, *Live Concert at the Forum*

"Sweet Blindness"

1971   The Fifth Dimension, *Stoned Soul Picnic* (Soul City 92002; single: Soul City 768) **(No. 13)**

"Time and Love"

1970   Melba Moore, *Living to Give* (Mercury, SR 61255)

1969   Diana Ross, *Time and Love* (Motown 706—unreleased until *The Motown Anthology* in 2001; originally intended as Ross's first single as a solo artist, produced by Bones Howe)

1971   The Fifth Dimension, *Love's Lines, Angles and Rhymes* (Bell 6060)

1971   Supremes (w/Jean Terrell as lead singer), *Touch* (Motown) (uses Diana Ross's backing track)

1971   Labelle, *Labelle* (Warner Bros. WS 1943)

1971   Barbra Streisand, *Stoney End* (Columbia KC 30378). **(No. 51)**

1971   Petula Clark, *Warm and Tender* (Warner Bros. 1885) (produced by Arif Mardin)

1971   Liz Damon, *Liz Damon's Orient Express* (Anthem 5900)

1999   Kenny Rankin, *The Bottom Line Encore* (Velvel/Bottom Line)

"Wedding Bell Blues"

1969   Lesley Gore

1969   The Fifth Dimension, *Age of Aquarius* (Soul City 92006; single: Soul City 779) **(No. 1)**

1970   Bobbie Gentry, *Fancy* (Capitol 428)

date unknown   Bola Sete (Paramount Records, PAS 5011). (Acoustic guitar instrumental)

2000   Dan Barrett (Rebecca Kilgore, vocalist), *Blue Swing* (Arbors Records)

"Woman's Blues"

date unknown   Green Lyte Sunday

Miscellaneous

1970(?)   "Laura Nyro Suite: Woman's Blues/He's a Runner/Once It Was Alright Now (Farmer Joe)," United States Army Band

1970(?)   *The Music of Laura Nyro*, Ron Frangipane and His Orchestra

(Mainstream MRL-34). Includes "Blowin' Away," "And When I Die," "Eli's Comin'," "Stoned Soul Picnic," "Save the Country," "Sweet Blindness," "California Shoeshine Boys," "I Never Meant to Hurt You," "Farmer Joe," "Emmie"

1970(?)   *Ladies Choice*, Longines Symphonette Society. Includes "I Never Meant to Hurt You," "Eli's Comin'," "Wedding Bell Blues," "Save the Country"

1997   *Time and Love: The Music of Laura Nyro* (Astor Place TCD 4007, 1997; Peter Gallway, producer). Tracks: "Time and Love" (Phoebe Snow); "Stoned Soul Picnic" (Jill Sobule); "Buy and Sell" (Suzanne Vega); "Save the Country" (Rosanne Cash); "When I Think of Laura Nyro"—medley of "Stoned Soul Picnic," "Wedding Bell Blues," "Eli's Comin'," and "And When I Die" (Jane Siberry); "Stoney End" (Beth Nielsen Chapman); "Eli's Comin' " (Lisa Germano); "Wedding Bell Blues" (The Roches); "And When I Die" (Sweet Honey in the Rock); "Poverty Train" (Patty Larkin); "He's a Runner" (Jonatha Brooke); "Sweet Blindness" (Holly Cole); "Woman's Blues" (Dana Bryant)

2001   "Laura Nyro" by Glasgow-based Cosmic Rough Riders. On *The Pain Inside* (3-track single; Poptones M C5052SCX). Reached No. 36 on United Kingdom singles chart.

INDEX

"Mr. Blue (the song of communication),"
181
Mudd, Victoria, 210
Muldaur, Maria, 98
Munoz, Mason, 242
Murray, Deirdre, 270
Murray, Shaar, 165
Music of Laura Nyro (Frangipane album), 95
Music of Laura Nyro, The (songbook), 119–20
Musician, 200, 205, 206, 223
Musto, Michael, 91
"My Innocence," 181–82, 225

Nafshun, Lori, 224
Nash, Graham, 68
Nathan, David, 90
National Ballet of Canada, 127
National Women's Music Festival, 158
"Natural Woman," 124, 128
Negron, Chuck, 92–93
Nero, Peter, 23
"Nest, The," 183
Nested (Nyro album), 179–83
Nevelson, Louise, 240–41
New Musical Express, 156
New York Post, 155
New York Rock and Roll Ensemble, 20
"New York Tendaberry," 80, 88, 258
New York Tendaberry (Nyro album), 70–75, 75–
78, 78–81, 81–83, 98, 219–20
New York Times, 10, 55, 66, 70, 82, 89, 122,
185, 206, 221–22
Newley, Anthony, 22
Newman, Phyllis, 108
Newman, Randy, 128
Newmark, Andy, 170, 171, 179–80
Newsday, 90, 264
Newsweek, 97
"Nightingale," 123
Nigro, Dan (cousin), 8, 139, 221, 226, 231,
234, 246
Nigro, Esther Passov (grandmother), 2
Nigro, Gilda Mirsky (mother), 2–5, 5, 7, 20,
28, 39, 40, 49–50, 149, 161–62, 169,
191, 254
Nigro, Jan (brother), 3, 6, 7, 11, 12, 17–18,
22–23, 34, 40, 107–8, 144, 179, 187,
189, 196, 209, 250, 255, 261–62, 269
Nigro, Janice Reed (Jan's wife), 107–8, 154,
179, 186, 209, 261–62
Nigro, Jimmy (cousin), 116
Nigro, Joseph (grandfather), 2–3
Nigro, Laura. *See* Nyro, Laura
Nigro, Louis (father), 1, 2–3, 5, 6, 7, 23,
25, 39, 109, 121, 138, 161, 189, 198,
214, 255, 261, 273
Nigro, Michael (uncle), 2, 10–11
Nigro, Willette (cousin), 10
Nilsson, Harry, 85, 97, 128
Noga, Helen, 73
November, Linda, 31

"Nowhere to Run," 132
NPR (National Public Radio), 265–66
Nyro, Laura
appearance & personality, 10, 13, 16–18,
18–19, 35–36, 42, 55–56, 67, 81–82,
86–87, 113–14, 115–16, 125, 140–42,
229
attention deficit disorder, possibility of,
249–50
boyfriends and male relationships, 39, 68–
70, 115–16, 122–24, 158–59, 178,
179, 186, 189–90, 197
childhood and education, 5–7, 7–12, 18–
20
and Maria Desiderio, 196–98, 208–9, 217,
239, 246, 256, 261
drug and alcohol use, 16, 43, 44, 54, 55,
142, 143
family, 1–5, 5–7, 8
illness, death, funeral and memorials, 254–
57, 259, 261–62
lesbianism, 169, 196–98, 217, 230
lifestyle, 140–42, 142–45, 152–56, 212–
15, 232–33
marriage (David Bianchini), 120, 137–40,
143, 143–45, 152–56
motherhood (Gil Bianchini), 179, 183,
186–87, 187, 188–90, 192–93, 209–
10, 215, 225, 228, 229–30, 241
name change, 22–23
pets, 49, 81, 103, 181, 188
politics, feminism, vegetarianism, and
animal rights, 126, 143–44, 157–58,
188–89, 198, 202, 204–5, 206–7, 213–
15, 218, 232, 233–34, 236
religious views, 6, 110–11, 125–26, 186,
203
Nyro, Laura (career)
awards, tributes, and honors, 20, 233, 262–
63, 264–65,265–66, 266–67, 267–68,
269–70
Broken Rainbow (documentary film), 210–12
charts and lists, 36–37, 62–63, 64, 65–66,
82, 93, 96, 106, 113, 118–19, 126,
134, 156, 165, 176, 185, 205
Columbia Records, 49–50, 57, 72–73, 78,
81–82, 86, 117–18, 119, 176, 199,
205, 210, 243, 257–58
contracts, 96, 145–51, 223–24
covers, 91–96, 105, 126–27, 269–70
and electric keyboards, 216–17, 229
fans, 86–87, 89–91, 106, 114, 125, 142–
43, 156, 197, 214–15, 220, 222, 232,
234, 247
influence of, 91–100, 100–05, 105–6
influences on, 6, 7–8, 13–16, 28
press, reviews, interviews and public
relations, 6, 9, 29, 32, 36, 40, 41, 43,
44, 53–54, 61–63, 66–68, 71, 74, 75,
76, 82, 87, 88, 89, 90, 105–6, 118,
122, 123, 124–25, 128, 133–34, 136,